At the Violet Hour

Modernist Literature & Culture

Kevin J. H. Dettmar & Mark Wollaeger, Series Editors

At the Violet Hour

Modernism and Violence in England and Ireland

Sarah Cole

OXFORD
UNIVERSITY PRESS

OXFORD
UNIVERSITY PRESS

Oxford University Press is a department of the University of Oxford.
It furthers the University's objective of excellence in research, scholarship,
and education by publishing worldwide.

Oxford   New York
Auckland   Cape Town   Dar es Salaam   Hong Kong   Karachi
Kuala Lumpur   Madrid   Melbourne   Mexico City   Nairobi
New Delhi   Shanghai   Taipei   Toronto

With offices in
Argentina   Austria   Brazil   Chile   Czech Republic   France   Greece
Guatemala   Hungary   Italy   Japan   Poland   Portugal   Singapore
South Korea   Switzerland   Thailand   Turkey   Ukraine   Vietnam

Oxford is a registered trade mark of Oxford University Press
in the UK and certain other countries.

Published in the United States of America by
Oxford University Press
198 Madison Avenue, New York, NY 10016

© Oxford University Press 2012

First issued as an Oxford University Press paperback, 2014.

Library of Congress Cataloging-in-Publication Data
Cole, Sarah.
At the violet hour : Modernism and Violence in England and Ireland / Sarah Cole.
    p.   cm.—(Modernist literature & culture)
ISBN 978-0-19-538961-6 (hardcover); 978-0-19-938906-3 (paperback)
1. Violence in literature. 2. English literature—20th century—History and criticism.
3. English literature—Irish authors—History and criticism
4. Modernism (Literature)—Great Britain. I. Title.
PR478.V56C65   2003
820.9'3552—dc23   2012005223

9 8 7 6 5 4 3 2 1

Printed in the United States of America
on acid-free paper

For Martin

Contents

Series Editors' Foreword

It's one of the irreducible paradoxes of British literary modernism: a time of unprecedented violence on the world-historical stage resulted in a body of literature of unprecedented beauty. Violence issuing in beauty: a terrible beauty, indeed.

In one of Sarah Cole's early formulations in *At the Violet Hour: Modernism and Violence in England and Ireland*, modernist literary works "created intricate, often exquisite formal solutions to the challenges posed by violence." But, as she demonstrates powerfully in her reading of the "pandying" scene in *A Portrait of the Artist as a Young Man*, modernism largely refused to achieve its exquisite formulations by withdrawing to the kind of aesthetic distance that Maud Ellmann memorably dubbed the "poetics of impersonality." Cole's sensitive close reading of the intimate violence of that classroom scene is urgent and compelling, and puts the human experience back into a moment that can be written off as a parody of Stephen's pandy. That is to say, Cole rescues the scene from self-pity and restores to it the genuine pity that lies just beneath Joyce's vaunted "indifference." In so doing, Cole demonstrates one of the primary imperatives of *At the Violet Hour*: to find at the very core of the modernist canon propulsive moments of intimate violence, with consequences that ripple throughout a given text and an author's work, and throughout the period.

Cole's aim is to redirect our understanding of enchantment and disenchantment as fundamental, opposing principles of violence that oriented writing about violence in the twentieth century. That violence itself is of course unavoidable. In some hands it was promoted to a symbolic plane, the romantic notion of martyrs' blood nourishing the soil of nationalist revolt; think of the lines in Yeats's "Easter 1916," "our part /To murmur name upon name, /As a mother names her child /When sleep at last has come. . . ." In other hands, such mythologizing was explicitly rejected—as in the lines of Yeats's that follow: "No, no, not night but death; /Was it needless death after all?" As Cole writes, "Enchantment loves the metaphor of blood; disenchantment calls upon the hurt body, with its signal fluid, to look as real and frightful as it can."

As Cole demonstrates, "Easter 1916," Yeats's most enduringly popular poem, must then be read as "a dialogue of self and soul"—a debate over the legitimate uses of political violence, and the potential for disenchanted representations of that violence to be reenchanted. "Yeats recognizes," Cole suggests, "as he is writing the poem, that its language of enchantment is destined to become a convention (as, of course, it has) and hence to function less as a stimulus to thought than as an incantation of what one already believes"—that "murmuring name upon name." Indeed, as Cole points out, that murmuring of names is itself literally a form of en-chant-ment. And yet, Yeats and his contemporaries could never keep the generative cycle intact; its shadowy double, reprisal, stalks their works, providing a rhythm of its own and punctuating their delicate surfaces with disenchanting visions of endless killing.

As these examples from Ireland show, modernism's fitting attention to violence and the body in pain provokes a crisis in representation: how might literature attest to, without celebrating, the young century's violent predilections? How short-circuit the deeply entrenched tendency to enchant violence? Given modernism's commitment to "show, not tell," how can the engaged writer create a text that reliably produces a response in line with her own ethical commitments? The secret—not to give too much away here—is that, as Cole demonstrates early in her analysis of some representative poems of the First World War, even the project of disenchantment recognizes "the uses of enchantment," and occasionally stoops to its tactics. And taking a page from the writers she studies, Cole's writing itself is often enchanted and enchanting (in that other, less technical sense), even as it ruthlessly unmasks the politics of disenchantment.

There's so much here to admire, with tone-perfect readings of important texts from a wide range of modernist writers: Cole's work on *Portrait*, Conrad's *The Secret Agent*, Synge's drama, Yeats's violent poetics, Eliot's *The Waste Land*—all of which are read in the highly material contexts of terrorism, insurrection, and war, and which, she argues convincingly from this historical vantage point, conduct "experiments in miscegenating enchantment with disenchantment." One of the great strengths of the book is Cole's seamless theorizing across genres, as if blind to the "boundaries": fiction, drama, poetry, "creative nonfiction," the essay—even painting and photography. Indeed, at the risk of singling out just one (more) body of work that she reinvigorates, we need at least to gesture toward Cole's tour de force treatment of *Three Guineas* and the visual rhetoric of violence (as well as the recoil from photographic representations of such violence) that text manifests.

At the Violet Hour concludes with a chapter of great insight and great sympathy that reads much of Woolf's oeuvre; it sets her intensive, haunting, and far-reaching accounts of violence against a dark and brooding backdrop of 1930s reckoning with catastrophe, as violence comes to stand near the center of life itself, the very principle of incipience. As Cole brings her argument to a close, she manages to articulate one of her last texts back into one of her first, suggesting that "the violet hour" of *The Waste Land* can be productively remapped by the purple of *To the Lighthouse*, which "stands for the most disenchanted, visceral effects against the body, and also for the aesthetic work marshaled on the other side: the work of submerging and muting, but also of telling and making visible, ultimately of absorbing violence into a textual world where beauty and ugliness jostle for supremacy."

We're excited for the experience you're about to undergo, for the many brilliant insights—we Joyceans are tempted to call them "epiphanies"—that this book will deliver to you. It's been all we could do to keep most of the "spoilers" out of this foreword; having read *At the Violet Hour*, like us you will want to share its most exciting discoveries with those who care about this literature as we do.

—Kevin J. H. Dettmar & Mark Wollaeger

Acknowledgments

This book has been the product of many years of work, and was written almost entirely at Columbia University, an institution whose spirit of debate and dialogue has been a guiding ethos. My thinking has been enormously enriched by conversations with colleagues and students in the Department of English and Comparative Literature, and in many forums around the university. These groups include the Institute for Research on Women and Gender, the Heyman Center for the Humanities, the Institute for Religion, Culture, and Public Life, and the University Seminar on Cultural Memory. I am grateful to the Department of English and Comparative Literature, and to the University for leaves and valued support in all stages of researching and publishing.

It is difficult adequately to thank the many colleagues who have been the book's interlocutors. Marianne Hirsch is an inspiration, a tireless supporter, and the source for much of my thinking about violence and memory. Akeel Bilgrami has been an astute reader and all-round instigator of intellectual effort. Bruce Robbins offered probing insights that transformed my thinking at key moments. David Damrosch was there from the beginning, ready with his vast literary knowledge. Victoria Rosner has brought exceptional insights to bear on this work, drawn from an intimate, material understanding of the field. And Ramie Targoff, with her wisdom and depth, has been an invaluable advisor and advocate. Other colleagues have shared their ideas and example over the years, and are very much a part of this book. In particular, I am grateful to Rachel Adams, Jed Esty, Laura Frost, Michael Golston, David Kastan, Pericles Lewis, Michael Levenson, Sharon Marcus, Edward Mendelson, Liesl Olson, Cóilín Parsons, Paul Saint-Amour, Jim Shapiro, Paul Strohm, and Jay Winter. I also extend a special thanks to the two anonymous readers at Oxford University Press, whose challenging commentary helped to give the book its final shape.

Many students have contributed to this project. I have learned from them as much as I have taught them, and am particularly thankful for the hard work of students in recent graduate seminars, "Literature, Culture, and War in the Twentieth Century," "Virginia Woolf and Modernism," and "The Waste Land." I have been fortunate, too, in having received research help from several exceptional graduate students: Christine Leja, Lucia Martinez, Olivia Moy, Kate Trebuss, Emily Cersonsky, and, in the crucial final months, Bryan Lowrance and Max Uphaus.

It is an honor to be publishing this book with Oxford University Press as part of its Modernist Literature and Culture series. I am grateful to Brendan O'Neill for shepherding the manuscript through each stage with his habitual grace and humor, to my brilliant copy-editor Steve Dodson, and to the always-thoughtful series co-editor Mark Wollaeger. Above all, I wish to thank Kevin Dettmar, who has been a rigorous and inspiring reader of this book, as well as a model of scholarly generosity.

My deepest gratitude is to my family. With the passage of time, I am increasingly conscious of how much I owe to my parents and step-parents, Belle Cole, Robert Cole, Eleanor Swift and David Wilson, who have modeled for me what it means to be principled, intellectual, and entirely giving. Since I began writing this book, I have had two children, Freddie and Anna Vogelbaum. No words can describe the joy they have brought into my life, each and every day since they were born, or the sweetness and intelligence they radiate. My greatest debt is to my husband Martin Vogelbaum, who has provided the backdrop of love, security, laughter, and commitment that has sustained and enlivened me over this long project. I dedicate this book to him.

* * *

Several parts of this book have been previously published. A version of chapter one was published in *PMLA* as "Enchantment, Disenchantment, War, Literature" (Volume 124, no. 5 (October, 2009)): 1632–1647, and parts of chapter two appeared in *Modernism/Modernity* as "Dynamite Violence and Literary Culture" (Volume 16, No. 2 (April 2009): 301–328). I am grateful to the Modern Language Association and to the Johns Hopkins University Press for permission to republish these works.

At the Violet Hour

Introduction

Nothing is older than the story of violence. As anthropologists tell us, ancient cultures and religions drew their fuel from violence: acquiring its power, protecting against its ravages, rendering it divine or anthropomorphic, creating rituals and ceremonies to slake or reorient it, finding for it a language and an art. Violence is a beginning, not only because the first cultures saw it so, but because the pattern repeats, with modern nations often seeing in war or in other large-scale violent events their points of origin. The outcome need not be victorious; Easter 1916 is a glorious beginning, as is Masada, and in the ruins of Troy, Virgil conjures the seeds of Rome. In the *Aeneid*, it is a band of ragged survivors who eventually will found the empire, but first, they look like modern stateless people, huddling and afraid, traumatized refugees who have seen their families killed before their eyes, their glorious city burned to the ground. The outcome need not, moreover, be triumphant; the killing and uprooting of Native Americans, which can be named the founding violence of America, represents a blot on the nation's ideals, a form of engendering bloodshed that, shorn of its manifest destiny, compromises the culture's self-image. And the outcome is never complete: where there is a flood, there is also an ark. If violence is contemplated as an origin, it cannot entirely be so, the operations of transformation, carryover, and trace being as important as those of genesis and creation. Violence leaves its stains, and the long march of years, despite efforts at redemption or revisionism, will often fail to obscure them.

Literature, with its unique ability to embed long pasts into vibrant narratives of the present, and with its restless urge to rewrite inherited stories, has always offered an exemplary forum for making violence knowable, showing how it can be simultaneously the crucible for a culture's highest values (in war, especially) and a force radically to undermine those ideals. At the same time, the urgent, physical, primordial quality of violence can disturb the self-concept of literature, insofar as, in Matthew Arnold's once-commanding words, it seeks to yield "the best which has been thought and said in the world."[1] To linger on destruction and disgrace is a capitulation to barbarism, perhaps, a self-abnegation, when literature instead might be called upon to replace the raw and gruesome with the rare and comprehensible. Modernism, in particular, falls far along the historical spectrum from all those violent origins. Out to make it new, modernism aligned itself with innovation, snubbing the monuments and certainties of the past. Calling themselves "the moderns," writers of the period embraced their new century specifically as an era defined by novelty and found the reigning self-expression of their times, for better and for worse, in technology.[2] Yet modernism took a great interest in beginnings, and not only as part of an atavistic or conservative embrace of the past's coherence; it did so, rather, in the shadow of its own belatedness, espousing the role of reviver.[3] Modernist literature took up beginnings by resuscitating classical categories like myth and reimagining heroic wanderers on epic journeys, and also by thinking back through mothers or fathers into the tunnel of human history and consciousness. At times, too, it turned the historical lens on itself, creating an archive out of the local, domestic, and personal. What better moment, then, to look squarely and unflinchingly at violence, to consider both the productive and the shameful nature of its narrative? How could modernism, in fact, *not* be essentially and deeply concerned with violence, given its commitment to deconstructing great cultural institutions that are fundamentally sustained by violence, such as gender, social hierarchy, and empire, and to exploring the human psyche? It is astonishing, indeed, how thoroughly the problematic of violence as an organizing cultural and aesthetic fact underwrote the literature of the years between 1890 and 1940. The period fostered a literary culture that at times saw itself as terribly useless (Auden: "poetry makes nothing happen"), at other times reckoned its own power (Stephen Dedalus: "forge in the smithy of my soul the uncreated conscience of my race"), but always placed the literary work in gripping relationship with defining, destructive events in the world. The span and variety is enormous, with works as satiric about violence as Conrad's *The Secret Agent* seeming to construct an alternate moral and aesthetic universe from the eccentric symbolic absorptions of, say, Yeats's drama. Nevertheless, in detailing an intimate and intricate interleaving of violence into modernist works, this book will suggest some important consistencies. One of those is a restlessness determining the entire endeavor, as if the fact of arriving at a representational strategy adequate to the violence of life is itself a step toward accepting it. In engaging violence, modernist works often seem to say, success is failure; and, at the same time, the urgency surrounding literature's role in making sense of a violent world never wanes. W. G. Sebald puts it bracingly: "The ideal of truth . . . proves itself the only legitimate reason for continuing to produce literature in the face of total destruction. Conversely, the construction of aesthetic or pseudo-aesthetic effects from the ruins of an annihilated world is a process depriving literature of its right to exist" (ellipses added).[4]

In form as in theme, works of the modernist period were profoundly shaped by the call of violence: to answer its challenges, to seek out new representational strategies, to find a conceptual register cued to its brutalities. Scholars have, of course, noted the complex relationship between violence and language, and in particular the contradictory ways that violence can act both to diminish and to incubate literary language, either rendering people mute ("why speak not they . . .?" Wilfred Owen asks of those who "from existence' brink/Ventured but drave too swift to sink") or loquacious, compelled, like the Ancient Mariner, to share their torment.[5] In the wake of Elaine Scarry's work, critics have noted a great deal of silence around the body in pain ("grown silent," as Walter Benjamin had put it, "not richer, but poorer in communicable experience"), but have also uncovered a range of distinctive linguistic qualities that derive from pain, or emanate from war, or characterize trauma.[6] For all its sublimity, then, which at times seems to render it beyond comprehension or articulation, violence, like everything else, is subject to words and to the imagination. It has its language. The project of this book is to discover and elaborate one such language, with reference to English and Irish modernism. It is to reveal how literary works created intricate, often exquisite formal solutions to the challenges posed by violence, and to trace how violent events enhanced as well as deformed their structures and surfaces.

The formalization of violence stands as one of modernism's central endeavors, in a symbiosis that resists easy categorization. Form and violence are tightly bound, reverberating together, a yin and yang, often gorgeously so. Some of the period's most memorable expressions—"A terrible beauty is born," "April is the cruellest month," the brackets in "Time Passes"—are products of this intimacy. At other times, violence and form become too closely mapped, as the violent content collapses boundaries and shatters distinctions; allegory will then drop to symbol, or metaphor become incarnation. In all cases, one of the organizing motifs is excess; given the stark and hyperbolic conditions of violence, including physical pain and suffering, and the enormity of the twentieth century's orgies of violence, there will always be a quality of inexhaustibility about the subject. Robert Buch calls this "the pathos of the real," and sees in the most gruesome, literary embodiments of violence a number of reversing events: "the response to the real, violence and suffering brought up close," he writes, "is not limited to the sentiments of horror and awe," and instead includes such states as transcendence and revelation.[7] If enormity and excess are the condition, then the inevitable rectifying model, in the West, is of balance, this for that, economics as the last resort in meaning-making. "Was it for this . . .?" is the repeated question in the period—why have we bothered to create this civilization if its culmination is the senseless killing of whole generations in war?—reaching the endpoint of Enlightenment conviction. It is a formulation of agony, in part because it sees clearly how literature is a part of (not apart from) that which it is considering, the structures we use to understand and accommodate violence, in this case the model of exchange and balance. One thing that we will not find in this study, however, is the traditional view that modernism retreats from the fray; in all of the densely material settings I will be discussing, literary works are saturated, content and form, with the ample blood of their times.

Several large-scale events comprise the historical component of this study— terrorist violence in the late nineteenth century and into the twentieth, the aftermath of the First World War, the Irish insurrection of 1916 and the wars that followed, the Spanish Civil War and the 1930s aura of incipient conflict—to be considered in dynamic, dialectical relationship with individual writers and texts. I am especially drawn, in considering textual and visual materials initiated by these events, to the intellectual climate that arises before and after major eruptions of violence. These are the moments when literary strategies begin to congeal, as aesthetic order emerges in anticipation of and after violent chaos. In engaging major historical events like these, each of which produced its own full literature, one confronts a potentially limitless array of works and contexts, and I hope that my discussion will provide useful models for readers studying very different collections of texts. For this book, I am interested, first and foremost, in works or episodes that consider infliction, those moments when the body is attacked, violated, or killed—when, that is, we follow texts and characters as they witness a profound intimacy with violence.[8] This is not to say, however, that the intense expression of violence stays isolated or private, nor that such implosive topics remain the sole focus; on the contrary, modernist works share a distinctive leaning, with regard to their violent content, to create meaningful distances from the scene of infliction, to display wider figurations alongside the initial stress, telling stories about such large subjects as power and vulnerability. In fact, the scenario of represented violence, as I am unearthing it in this book, might be said to perform in itself one of the basic achievements of literature: to see in a single moment, episode, or narrative the intensity of subjective life, and also the inseparable interchange of that experience with the large forces of culture and history. Ultimately, the argument I want to make is as big—and as small—as the subject of violence itself: that the essential operations of literature are inexorably bound to the representation of bodily violation, so that if we excavate, pursue, and seek to understand literary violence, we will find ourselves looking at literature's very nerve center, the place where its most proud accomplishments and greatest limitations are engendered and defined. More, it is precisely this conflation of mastery with shame, in relation to violence, that modernist writing ultimately exhibits as one of its defining features, the site of astonishing and forceful presentations, but also the locus—and this we will find in each chapter—for recognizing where the literary text or writer is surpassed, as the present hurtles out of view.

In its strongest form, then, my argument aims to provide a new rubric for thinking about the self-concept of literature in the early twentieth century. But is this modernism per se? Given the historical orientation and cultural-studies approach of this book, the label "modernist" might seem inexact, calling instead for purely chronological descriptors, which might, in turn, help to deflect the label *ennui* that tends to grip this period's scholarship. The models I am establishing, moreover, ideally will prove resonant for literature from different historical periods, as well as for thinking about works from the twentieth century that do not fall under the modernism umbrella, hence loosening the power of the modernist designation. And yet, formal considerations ultimately stand at the heart of my argument, which consolidates around writers, especially Eliot, Conrad, Yeats, and Woolf, who have helped to define English-language modernism. The formal achievements of these and other writers, set in motion around violation and destruction, and coming often in emblematic scenes, lines, or textual maneuvers, in the end will be exported from their early twentieth-century contexts and carried forward, powerful aesthetic markers of one period's experiments in understanding violence. *At the Violet Hour* delineates a set of paradigms common to the modernist period, expressing some of its most powerful convictions and installing violence at the very center of its stylistic endeavors. Nevertheless, in each chapter, modernist writing engages reciprocally and productively with a variety of other texts and voices, and in some cases (especially in my consideration of Irish works in chapter 3) I am arguing for a discourse that cuts decisively through literary and cultural fields, so that to isolate one writer or formal sensibility (Yeats and modernism) would be to miss the large point about how the period's violence spread across and determined a host of imaginative efforts.[9]

The three sections below introduce some of the central paradigms that will inform my discussion of violence throughout the book. In the first section,

I discuss several of the most significant and moving formal approaches to violence that the period elaborated. Some of these have roots in the nineteenth century (and earlier); others are more specific to the modernist era. Following this discussion of literary rubrics, I turn to a number of key terms, including the concepts of political violence and force, to which I will return in different contexts throughout this study. The final section elongates the temporal scheme, establishing the most significant models for thinking about history and violence that tended to underwrite modernist literature. These last imaginative structures divide into two primary clusters, one of which emphasizes the extravagance and unavoidability of violence, while the other works to reveal its presence despite layers of burial and invisibility.

Violence and Form

Violence experienced subjectively—bruising, terrible, vibrant, productive—is, for modernist writers, where it all begins. As a template, then, for the dynamics of violence to unfold in the chapters that follow, I offer an intensely personal expression of victimization. An early sequence in James Joyce's *A Portrait of the Artist as a Young Man* (1916), it is a scene of searing and scalding consequentiality, and one that follows the novel's opening paragraphs in establishing the short textual block as repository for almost endless meaning-making:[10]

> Stephen closed his eyes and held out in the air his trembling hand with the palm upwards. He felt the prefect of studies touch it for a moment at the fingers to straighten it and then the swish of the sleeve of the soutane as the pandybat was lifted to strike. A hot burning stinging tingling blow like the loud crack of a broken stick made his trembling hand crumple together like a leaf in the fire: and at the sound and the pain scalding tears were driven into his eyes. His whole body was shaking with fright, his arm was shaking and his crumpled burning livid hand shook like a loose leaf in the air. A cry sprang to his lips, a prayer to be let off. But though the tears scalded his eyes and his limbs quivered with pain and fright he held back the hot tears and the cry that scalded his throat.
> —Other hand! shouted the prefect of studies.
> Stephen drew back his maimed and quivering right arm and held out his left hand. The soutane sleeve swished again as the pandybat was lifted and a loud crashing sound and a fierce maddening tingling burning pain made

his hand shrink together with the palms and fingers in a livid quivering mass. The scalding water burst forth from his eyes and, burning with shame and agony and fear, he drew back his shaking arm in terror and burst out into a whine of pain. His body shook with a palsy of fright and in shame and rage he felt the scalding cry come from his throat and the scalding tears falling out of his eyes and down his flaming cheeks.

—Kneel down! cried the prefect of studies.

Stephen knelt down quickly pressing his beaten hands to his sides. To think of them beaten and swollen with pain all in a moment made him feel so sorry for them as if they were not his own but someone else's that he felt sorry for. And as he knelt, calming the last sobs in his throat and feeling the burning tingling pain pressed in to his sides, he thought of the hands which he had held out in the air with the palms up and of the firm touch of the prefect of studies when he had steadied the shaking fingers and of the beaten swollen reddened mass of palm and fingers that shook helplessly in the air.[11]

The passage is conscious of its force in portraying injuring as elemental, intimate, and transformative, and it functions, in several respects, as an origin story. Language, first, finds a beginning here, with the agony of the beating registering initially as the most fundamental human noise, a cry, to be followed quickly by more social forms of language and behavior, such as prayer and repression. Stephen is fully in his body, a child experiencing the world largely through the physical intensity of the moment, before more intercultural possibilities are engendered. The word "burning" repeats this reflexive structure. First used to describe the initial attack ("a hot burning stinging tingling blow"), it is quickly transferred to the arm itself ("his crumpled burning livid hand") and then to the slightly more abstract entity, his pain ("fierce maddening tingling burning pain"); from attack to body to pain, we then reach the social construct of shame ("burning with shame and agony and fear"), in a development that pushes outside of the passage, pointing toward a later culmination in the lengthy and fervid imagining of hell that takes up a great deal of the novel's middle chapter. Empathy, too, seems born in the beating sequence. Stephen's tendency to distance himself from his own body, even at the moment of most intense bodily presence (suggested by his sorrow for his maimed hands, "as if they were not his own but someone else's that he felt sorry for"), may prefigure his later development of an aesthetic theory of detachment, but here provides something like an originating myth for the idea of pity. More, the process of figuration itself leaps forth in the passage, as suggested by Joyce's sudden and rather wild employment of lists of adjectives, many in gerund form ("maddening tingling burning"), and his usage, in the first descriptive paragraph, of back-to-back similes that suggest the most basic natural forces ("like the loud crack of a broken stick," "like a leaf in the fire"). The representation of injuring thus calls up the initiatory contortions that language makes, its generative propulsion.[12] If irony edges into this scene, with pity tilting toward self-pity or bodily suffering perhaps a hyperbole for nothing more than a slap on the wrist, it nevertheless stays near the margins, as the force of the beating in transforming both language and consciousness is credited with real efficacy. What the passage shows, in fact, is just how far the scene of explicit violence goes in redirecting narrative habits (such as the ironizing of childhood self-importance).

Crucial to the sense of elementary processing in the compressed passage is its handling of time. It is something of a truism that "pain stops time," that in the experience of pain, the body both crowds out and distorts the sense of time's passage. Indeed, time, space, and experience all become enfolded and massively intensified in the injuring scenario. In film, we get slow motion; in poetry, the vivid image; in narrative, subjective intensification (and all of these in the passage from *Portrait*). This sense that chronology is altered by violence is not solely a matter of pain, moreover, for the experiencing of violence can occur in time-stopping brilliance even when physical sensation has been numbed or delayed. Time stands still; the present enlarges; these basic features of violence and representation are supplemented, in many instances, by the compulsion to think back to the moment of infliction. The violent encounter in this sense conjures narrative, demanding that one return, at least imaginatively, to the event at the time of its inception and to the interior life of the person in contact with a destructive agent. In trauma, one of the psyche's mechanisms for accommodating violence at the breaking point, temporality is massively skewed, with the past disrupting the present—the past indeed manifesting *as* presence—or disappearing altogether, and hence therapeutically inviting a return to the violent incident itself. Whether from inside or outside of the violent situation, to be confronted with the body's radical suffering is to force the imagination back to the moment of injury, to read time empathetically. For Joyce, in the pandying passage, this imperative is resolutely met, for the beating is presented moment by moment, in a tightly packed narrative sequencing. We as readers are there, we register the sensations as they come, we are asked to feel alongside the young boy. Indeed, this reading of time as precise and affectively construed contrasts with other passages in the early portions of *Portrait*, which present themselves via disjointed impressions or in dreamlike ambiguity. As if to remind us that the sequence has a special temporal status, the beating is bracketed, near the beginning and end, by the phrases "for a moment" and "all in a moment." The beating sequence thus marks itself out specifically as a scene, something excerptable in time and space. And that, too, is representative of a broader pattern: the portrayal of violence lends itself to the model of tableau, the moment that stands apart, jolted out from the literary frame.

In addition to reflecting on violence as a site of origins, and as an experience in and of time, the passage offers a strong statement about the intertwining of intimacy and injuring. The disembodied prefect of studies stands as an image of almost pure power—a voice, a sleeve—and yet this disembodiment is not complete, for the single feature that most compels and confuses Stephen is the steady touch of the man's hand before each hit. That touch would seem to represent his humanity, a breaching of the distance between the two people, yet it also suggests the reverse, his ability to distance himself enough from Stephen to carry out the punishment without so much as a flinch. As with the emphasis on origins, the sensation here is one of discovery, as Stephen puzzles out in physical terms what might ultimately be generalized as a universal structure of power.[13] If the tactile exchange of hands has historically and mythologically been figured as a source of healing and creation, as in Genesis or the Christian Gospels, it is inevitable that within the religious frame, the proximation of touch with violence shocks and resonates in part because of its harsh contrast with these traditions of (re)generation via divine touch. In the pandying sequence, that history is certainly suggested, for the priest's touch, metonymically tied to Jesus's own, is distorted from healing to injuring. The feel of the prefect's hand is significant as a matter of political or theological ambiguity, and it also registers in its own right, part of the sensorium activated by the attack. People might touch one another across a spectrum from violence to caress, and if these forms of touch at times are clearly separated by motive and effect, at other times they overlap and intertwine.[14]

Equally salient to the personalized quality of the pandying episode is the way it reads as a parable of power.[15] On one hand, Joyce gives us a description of subjective, individual pain, in the form of Stephen's experience of victimization and physical hurt; on the other hand, it is all but impossible to read the sequence outside of a structure like allegory. The hierarchical configuration is decisive: priest and student, adult and child, punisher and victim, oppressor and oppressed, even colonizer and colonized, given Joyce's figuring, in *Portrait*, of the church as a colonizing power in Ireland, a predecessor and (perhaps counterintuitively) a companion to the domination by the British.[16] If the prefect makes himself known by shouts and blows, Stephen presents a picture of subjection, with his stammering, ineffectual whine, his physical acts of kneeling or raising hands, and his self-understanding in terms of almost pure feeling. The stress, moreover, on uniformity, in the form of the twice-appearing soutane sleeve, reinforces the idea that this performance can seem to move horizontally beyond the walls of Clongowes to Ireland more generally, and vertically back in time to the endless list of historical settings when power has been abused.

Here, then, is a critical point about literary representations of violence during the modernist period: they have a tendency to move in two opposing directions—toward the private, subjective, and personal, rooted in the body, with an emphasis on elemental experience and originary cultural constructions; and toward the representative, where larger, often political readings are invited. For all their divergence, these expressions are often engendered together, and, in fact, constitute in their mutuality one of modernism's primary insights about violence. Violence is, almost axiomatically, a site of excess; to experience violence in any register is to reckon with overflow—of pain, of bodily suffering, of helplessness, of sadism, of silence. In the literature of modernism, this quality of excess can be seen as a provocation, that which invites literary innovation, even if, in the end, there remains a strong sense that something—or everything?—has eluded capture. It is telling, in fact, how close these paradigms around violence are to modernism's generalized statements about its mission, whether Woolf denominating her cohort as those who chase down the elusive quantity she calls "life" ("Modern Fiction") or Eliot, in scripting the spatio-sensory dimensions of modernity, enjoining the contemporary writer to "force, to dislocate if necessary, language into his meaning" ("The Metaphysical Poets"). Such manifestos never mention violence—in "Mr. Bennett and Mrs. Brown," Woolf hammers the point home by setting the date when human character changed well before the war—yet they envision a literary endeavor that could be redescribed in terms of the encounter with violence: that most essential and urgent of all quantities, there in the world in an intensely affective and real sense, a subject calling forth experiment, something that will never be mastered.

Modernism was not unique in suturing the interior experience of violence to its larger social meanings, but it did so with a special vigor and urgency; and such constructions make sense within its output, for the late nineteenth and the early twentieth centuries mark a signal moment in the ascendance of formal representations of subjective vision, at the same time that this was an historical epoch marred by events of spectacular violence.[17] In other words, what made these years particularly ripe for a rich and significant exploration of violence was the conjunction of two phenomena. There was, first, the hallmark modernist imperative to take subjective experience seriously, comprised, for instance, of a developing vocabulary of unconscious processes and an expansion of interest in the individual's private vision. Alongside and contributing to these intellectual and aesthetic developments were the highly visible explosions of violence that virtually define the period, including the First World War and the lead-up to the next, as well as a spate of less expansive but no less savage conflicts across Europe and the colonized world. It is not that there was *more* violence in the early twentieth century than there had been before—the British nineteenth century is a time of "peace and prosperity" only if we overlook empire, industrialism, and sexual inequality—but that its heightened visibility conjoined with the direction intellectual currents were moving, in such a way as to produce especially layered and dynamic renderings of violence throughout its literary culture.

In nineteenth-century British writing, representations of violence tended toward an extensive mode, concerned with wide social forces and meanings. If Romanticism had created and elevated the subjective, interior focus that modernism would inherit (and at times link with bodily suffering), fiction writers later in the nineteenth-century looked to the violence spawned by industrialism as a necessary and appropriate topic for their works. The Victorian novel, with its recurrent ties to an agenda of industrial and urban reform, concerned itself with an array of violent configurations and situations, often making use of conventions of sentiment in concert with its visceral realism.[18] The Dickensian novel was brilliant at displaying the worker's hurt body—very selectively, to be sure—but especially at deploying that body into a wider story about the structures and spheres of modern social relations. For a host of important English industrial novelists, not only Charles Dickens, but also such varied figures as Benjamin Disraeli, Charles Kingsley, Mrs. Humphrey Ward, and Elizabeth Gaskell, the actual moment of violent infliction—registered in the mind and body—was less important than the wide, rippling ramifications of injuring as a part of the social and industrial context. It is, in other words, the representative qualities of bodily attack that were most avidly embraced as the nineteenth-century novel's particular arena, and readerly techniques, including the cultivation of such forces as "sympathy," became crucial features of the novel's project. To linger on violence was to linger above all on the social problems that created those ills and the appropriate responses that would help to alleviate them.

In the early twentieth century, literature took up violence more directly, as one of its central aesthetic problems, formalizing it in both new and old ways, employing radical innovations alongside ready conventions. One of the most resilient and recurrent figures to which modernist writers turned when considering violence was allegory. Along with less elaborate, related forms such as analogy or parable, allegory would seem an intuitive approach for writing about violence, since its principal utility is to tell a given story without having to engage it directly. The term, as commentators stress, incorporates the premise of breaks and disjunctions (*allo-* for "other," *agor-* for "speaking"); it is a pliant structure for jumping across gaps, for implying large narratives while telling more contained ones, or for constructing rich and surprising connections.[19] This may be why Walter Benjamin came to see allegory almost as constitutive of imaginative writing itself in the modern era. "In it," as Bainard Cowan writes of Benjamin's approach, "the world ceases to be purely physical and becomes an aggregation of signs."[20] My own usage is more narrow and normative than Benjamin's, and yet it is worth acknowledging from the outset that allegory has a real trenchancy in the modernist period, at least insofar as it is deployed around violence.[21] In this study, allegory emerges with special resonance in several guises, such as in the figure of the house or tree as representative of the nation, or of the woman's body as site of generativity. Nevertheless, allegory's premise of distinctiveness among its parallel modes, and of tending to extend these parallels beyond the momentary, are challenged by the very qualities of violence that make allegory attractive in the first place (its excess, its bodily severity, the way it forces private vision into wider narratives and back again). Though allegory has the capacity to suspend several strands of thought and imagination in elegant balance, we will also find that it is liable to collapse, in a burst or shudder or explosion.

Yeats's "Leda and the Swan" (1923), is especially illuminating in this context, providing a concentrated reflection on the overlapping of the intensive, physical experience of violence and the larger narratives or conclusions this might usher in. Like the pandying passage from *Portrait*, the poem crystallizes in its fourteen lines many recurrent dynamics common to modernist expressions of violence:

> A sudden blow: the great wings beating still
> Above the staggering girl, her thighs caressed
> By the dark webs, her nape caught in his bill,
> He holds her helpless breast upon his breast.
>
> How can those terrified vague fingers push
> The feathered glory from her loosening thighs?
> And how can body, laid in that white rush,
> But feel the strange heart beating where it lies?
>
> A shudder in the loins engenders there
> The broken wall, the burning roof and tower
> And Agamemnon dead.
>   Being so caught up,

So mastered by the brute blood of the air,
Did she put on his knowledge with his power
Before the indifferent beak could let her drop?[22]

The poem takes as its subject the precise moment when literary history and the history of violence become one. There is a specificity of temporality here: in that "sudden blow," the reverberating instant is isolated, asked to stand "still," in contrast to the unfurling of slow time out of its consequences ("And Agamemnon dead"). Yeats emphasizes fixity of place, too, with the middle of the poem focused on immobility (the "where" and "there" of lines 8 and 9 concentrating the rape forcefully in the woman's body). The fact that this reckoning takes shape in terms of relentless questioning—over 50 percent of the poem is bundled into question form, an exceptional situation even for Yeats, whose poems are filled with memorable questions—suggests that there is something inconclusive and open-ended about this collapsing of categories. And yet, one thing is clear from the start: in the sudden blow of the opening, an iconographic narrative of divine metamorphosis, detached from the world by its mythological setting, is envisioned as a real rape, the victim a helpless, staggering girl. At the same time, Yeats rejects a pure distinction between the masterful "brute blood of the air" and the disempowered rape victim. With grammatical uncertainties such as the identity of the "strange heart," an ambiguity about what the "shudder in the loins" implies about Leda's own sexual pleasure, and in the final question of whether and how she becomes empowered before being dropped, the poem suggests that power can be distributed in surprising, counterintuitive ways. The greater the import, perhaps, the less likely it will be that power will be meted out in strict dichotomizations.[23]

There is no "I" in "Leda and the Swan." Leda's subjectivity remains dispersed, her story drawn away from itself. To the extent that the poem is ambivalent about Leda's interiority, it invites allegorical interpretation. Indeed, in this poem, it is only insofar as the subjective vision disappears that there can be allegory. If we follow Edward Said and view Yeats not simply as an Irish national(ist) poet but as a voice of and for decolonization, the last lines in "Leda and the Swan" suggest an allegory of colonized and colonizer in which the nascent power of bloody revenge is embedded in the situation of colonization.[24] The poem envisions a structure of sedimented violence, in which abused power may be shifted, shared, and reapportioned, but never nullified. As time is condensed into the instant of rape, the poem suggests, so might history be viewed as a series of bursts of violence, which, in turn, produce a continuing narrative of brutality, grief, and vengeance, and also, importantly, a continuing sequence of literary and visual art. "Leda and the Swan" dramatizes the intertwining of an intensive imagining of a scene of violation—an initiatory moment of vibrant, clarifying violence—with an exceptionally extensive sequencing of future consequence.

"Leda and the Swan" differs in an important respect from the *Portrait* passage, in the sense that its reflection on violence is distanced from the events. It neither is nor wants to be a subjective, personalized account; its interest in the instant of erupting violence is seen through a telescope rather than a microscope. Yet in its positing of an almost ontological connection between violence (rape, war) and the generative literary act (the creation of poetry, the development of iconography and canons), it speaks a related language. In "Leda and the Swan," Yeats erects a shaky balance between an allegorical style, which submerges Leda's interiority, and an account of the "sudden blow," which promises to flood the poem with violent excess. Insofar as that blow inaugurates an idea that the vessels of culture and art are real violated bodies, the poem abandons its allegory and intimates instead a radical form of aesthetic incarnation. Such a mode has been adumbrated by Terrence Des Pres in his influential study on the structure of the Nazi death camps, *The Survivor*. Des Pres notes that at times of the most overwhelming horror, experience itself has the surprising tendency to lean toward the literary. Des Pres's claim about the overlap between symbolic language and the imperative to catalogue extreme violence is a powerful one:

> We might say, then, that in extremity symbolism *as symbolism* loses its autonomy. Or, what amounts to the same thing, that in this special case everything is felt to be inherently symbolic, intrinsically significant. Either way, meaning no longer exists above and beyond the world; it re-enters concrete experience, becomes immanent and invests each act and moment with urgent depth. . . . It is as if amid the smoke of burning bodies the great metaphors of world literature were being "acted out" in terrible fact—death and resurrection, damnation and salvation, the whole of spiritual pain and exultation in passage through the soul's dark night.[25]

Even if we scale back from the sublimity of horror that is Des Pres's subject, his argument is resonant: when the body is under tremendous assault or when the task of literature is, in part, to exfoliate an intimate experience of felt violence, representation moves inexorably toward such structures as archetype, which most closely seem to incarnate their content, and away from allegory, where categories must remain intact. It is what Paul Fussell, thinking about landscape and times of day in the battle zones, describes as "a metaphor caught in the act of turning literal."[26] The stakes for literature spike in this configuration, as if its very definition and sustaining concepts were at issue (as, in some of the writing we will consider, they are). Either literature is going to fall away, seeming trivial and insufficient, or, conversely, it is vigorously going to show its special uses. It is in this scenario of dire severity, faced with the worst, that texts remind us of why we read.

In part to evade such pressures, writers have often adopted indirect representational strategies. One of the most prominent and persistent, from the nineteenth century into the twentieth, substitutes a direct portrayal of violence against people with an analogy, violence against animals. A passage from an influential late-Victorian novel, Olive Schreiner's *The Story of an African Farm* (1883), provides an especially crisp example of how such a strategy works. *The Story of an African Farm* is set in present-day South Africa, and announces itself as centrally about that space and its multiform colonial configurations. The imperial conflicts among European planters are worked out in the novel in the muted language of domestic rivalries and ambitions, and the presence of black Africans is almost entirely erased. Yet there is one salient sequence, which bursts into the novel as if from nowhere, in which an ox is worked to the point of torture by a Dutch overseer, and which asks to be read as a parable of colonial violence:

> "He took out his clasp-knife, and ran it into the leg of the trembling ox three times, up to the hilt. Then he put the knife in his pocket, and they took their whips. The oxen's flanks quivered, and they foamed at the mouth. Straining, they moved the wagon a few feet forward, then stood with bent backs to keep it from sliding back. From the black ox's nostril foam and blood were streaming on to the ground. It turned its head in its anguish and looked at me with its great starting eyes. It was praying for help in its agony and weakness, and they took their whips again. The creature bellowed out aloud. If there is a God, it was calling to its Maker for help. Then a stream of clear blood burst from both nostrils; it fell on to the ground, and the waggon slipped back." (narrated in dialogue)[27]

In this sequence, black Africans are represented by the black ox, and the most brutal and unwarranted violence against them is exposed for the first and last time in the novel. The violently abused colonial body *does* need to figure into the story of Africa, Schreiner seems to be saying, but it can do so only through the figure of representative suffering. Here is one more use that animals provide: representationally, their bodies take the place of their human counterparts. It may have seemed untenable to ask her middle-class English audience to read about the routine violence to black human bodies that sustained the empire, but

Schreiner is counting on a reader who has the facility to segue into an allegorical mode, and who is, in effect, ready to "see" black Africans by suggestion, if not directly. The strategy is to project an extended and gruesome descriptiveness onto a being recognized as having no human subjectivity (hence both pain and responsibility are, in a sense, located in the reader). The awkwardness of having the ox call on God for help, however, indicates a problem for this stylistic, since it simultaneously requires that the animal seem human and, at the same time, remain obviously and significantly nonhuman. In the twentieth century, this symbolic or substitutive model became increasingly tenuous, especially in the colonial context, largely because the subjected people in question refused to stay silent and invisible, even in the most westernized accounts. We might think of *Heart of Darkness* (1902)—hardly a paragon of humanist empathy, yet in it black African slaves stare pointedly at Marlow; they are not given a voice, but neither can they be easily allegorized.

The decision, however, to consider human violence by way of animal suffering remains a potent literary strategy. It is employed regularly in the modernist period, and the tensions that surround it are emblematic of the equivocal place of animals in the ethical imagination of these years, but also, more centrally for this inquiry, of the uncertainty about the meaning, value, and consequences of displaying any kind of violence in literary works. The early twentieth century, like our own era, evinced an interest in animal suffering that at times (but only at times) was portrayed as urgent in its own right. Examples of such ambivalence abound, including in the ubiquitous images of horses screaming and writhing in the First World War, or in overdetermined hunting scenes writ as sexualized power spectacles, or in vivid images of food preparation.[28] In many of these, it remains unclear whether the text is ready to pose the kind of searching ethical questions that such contemporary writers as J. M. Coetzee explore, including a self-reflexivity about whether representing animals as stand-ins for humans is itself an ideologically problematic move, questions currently being pressed in the burgeoning movement of animal studies.[29] At the same time, modernist writers were intensely interested in the limits and edges of human subjectivity, in trying to derive and isolate what makes up our personhood, and in the way the body confronts the forces of modernity, all of which invite comparison to animals. The recurrent and always-mutating theme of cattle in *Ulysses* (1922) is suggestive of such questions, as the prospect of meat eating presses, at times uncomfortably, in multiple textual directions. Even more unsettling is the lengthy and ghastly depiction of a slaughterhouse that punches into the center of Alfred Döblin's novel *Berlin Alexanderplatz* (1929). Döblin's slaughterhouse—enormous, modern in method, and located uncomfortably adjacent to the novel's central action—seems itself to define the threshold between industrialization and deep subjectivity, and is notably analogous to the prison that stands in the background of the novel. It seems, in fact, to point simultaneously in two chronological directions—toward an ever more modernized future, which presages awful technologies of killing, and way back to ancient cultures, where killing animals represented a sacred act, central to culture. The animals in the slaughterhouse are systematically managed as if they were in an ordinary factory (or prison), yet their living-ness everywhere intervenes, not only with their streaming blood and insides, but also with their eyes, their trust, their complex behavior. To kill one of them should, the text almost wants to say, be sacramental, whereas instead their vitality sheers against an inhumane killing apparatus, a crossing that is symptomatic of the period, which continually came back to the deadly moment of contact between the mortal, vulnerable body and the forces of modernization.

It is not only the industrial qualities of the slaughterhouse, moreover, that make it an exemplary locus for considering violence; to see the animals killed there is to be forced to think about all forms of physical violation, in a novel that catalogues terrible physical calamities of violence and abuse. Clearly, Döblin wants us to reflect upon the connection between humans and animals. Thus the chapter subject headings say things like "For it happens alike with Man and Beast; as the Beast dies, so Man dies, too" (borrowing from Ecclesiastes), and the novel analogizes the slaughter of a calf with the murder of a young woman.[30] Just as clearly, the slaughterhouse sequence seems to evade that rubric, as comparison shrinks away and the sheer horror of the treatment of the animals becomes its own study. The spectacle, moreover, has an uncomfortable resilience throughout the novel, felt, for instance, in the presence of cattle dealers, in descriptions of meat eating, in continual tabulations of slaughterhouse inventory, and even in direct revisions of the novel's own statements of animal-human continuity, so that human loss is presented, finally, as more significant than the suffering of an animal. At the center of Döblin's novel, indeed, is the question: to what extent can the depiction of awful violence against animals be representative of anything other than itself, and, if we do press it to function allegorically, what kind of story can it tell? Such a basic question—which touches on the issue of how, exactly, one can represent violence of any sort without compromising the literary work—emphasizes the ethical discomfort lurking beneath all of these formal choices for figuring violence. If literature cannot avoid representing violence, if, in fact, it gains power and momentum from its intimacy with the violated body, it is also, in some essential way, haunted, stained, and defaced by that very reliance.

Power, Force, Political Violence

Violence is a broad and encompassing term, necessarily and importantly so. It involves two basic features, an agent of attack, precipitating the injury or violation; and a person or object on the receiving end of that attack, whose bodily surface is in some way overcome, hurt, trespassed, ruptured. Both parts of this equation warrant appreciation, as in the *OED*'s definition, which has, as its first sense, "the exercise of physical force so as to inflict injury on, or cause damage to, persons or property; action or conduct characterized by this; treatment or usage tending to cause bodily injury or forcibly interfering with personal freedom." The word carries with it suggestions of will and intention ("so as to inflict," "forcibly interfering"), as if to demand that one never lose sight of there being a driver, one person's will and body actively impinging on another's. In my readings, I will consider the agent's "exercise of physical force," but especially will emphasize the experience or imagining of finding the body (one's own or someone else's) in the force field of aggression. If the body is absolutely central in this arena of compulsion and contact, there is, nevertheless, a primary slide in the *OED* definition from bodily injury to the possible loss of "personal freedom," also subject to offense and disruption in the most basic sense, and this extension of the body to person is a constant presence in the imagination of violence. The concept of "violation" is thus fully allied with the primary term "violence," the two obviously linked at the etymological level.[31] What "violation" adds is a reminder that to have the body penetrated is to have the personal integrity also breached and defiled, so that the healing of an external wound in no way entails the healing of an internal one. Instead, these connections between external wounds and internal consequences call attention to the endlessly recursive nature of dualism; in the violent scenario, when the separation of body and mind seems most essential, it also becomes exceptionally fragile. The premise of the violence/violation interaction, that is, also suggests the underpinnings of psychological trauma. One of the effects of violence that most resonated for modernism, trauma, by definition, assumes a fluidity across seemingly divergent and exclusive spheres.[32]

Because the range, sweep, and import of violence vary enormously, one large question will always be to what extent violent incidents can or should be understood in political terms. The intensive focus often seems a private affair, isolating the sufferer in her body and resonating as a moment of origins. And yet, since at least the nineteenth century, violence has been understood and registered as an ineluctable aspect of industrial modernity. To seek the social and economic underpinnings of capitalist culture is to find endemic violence, and vice versa. Indeed, for contemporary theorists, violence is almost always political, and demands to be analyzed in terms of the unequal differentials of power it manifests. Thus a recent work by Judith Butler, to take just one very compelling meditation on violence, in a post-9/11 mood, begins with the evocative idea that the body's vulnerability to violence makes for a mimetic empathy among people, and an ethics of mutuality: "To be injured means that one has the chance to reflect upon injury . . . to find out who else suffers from permeable borders, unexpected violence, dispossession, and fear."[33] Butler is searching and sensitive to the interior aspects of violence, which she names "precarious life," and which she sees, in terms akin to those of Scarry, as revealing something irreducible about humanity. Nevertheless, for her, as for most political theorists, the overarching issue is always power. Whether considered by nation, class, race, wealth, gender, governing regime, or otherwise, the big question is how power is apportioned and wielded, what kinds of inequities it metes out, how violence is used or spared, by and against whom, in the name of what agent, ideology, or system of dominance. Beneath and in dialogue with these expansive questions of power are two slightly narrower rubrics, which will be important in the chapters that follow: political violence (named as such) and the concept of "force."

If all violence is political, then the hybrid "political violence" cannot be very meaningful, but there are, of course, forms of violence that are perpetrated explicitly and directly for political purposes, and these carry especially severe and polarizing connotations. The deploying of violence as an expressly political act transforms its character and valuation, pointing toward such contradictory possibilities as sanctification, atrocity, neutralization, and sensationalism. To attach violence to political philosophy is to heighten its status, prestige, and danger, at times to mitigate its illegality, or conversely to enhance its outrageousness and invite legal excess. For their part, radical political movements across the spectrum have always relied on the appeal of their ideological claims to transform the reception of violence from the criminal to the exalted, from the exclusionary act that ostracizes a person to glorifiable sacrifice that heroizes its protagonist.[34] And normative culture reacts in tandem, fearing and demonizing terrorism with special fervor. Political violence is notable, too, for its implications about language, since its defining feature is the idea that violence is a potent form of political expression. Violence, in that sense, becomes its own kind of language, and a host of terminology is called upon to describe this relationship: acts of terrorism can be seen as statements of belief or creed, threats of future violence as messages written in bodies and blood. Such metaphors were undoubtedly at the back of the composer Karlheinz Stockhausen's notorious comment, several weeks after 9/11, when he described the attack on the World Trade Center as representing "the greatest work of art that is possible in the whole cosmos."[35] As the response to Stockhausen's comments reminds us, the idea that there could be any relation between horrendous violence and aesthetics, or any kind of willed and serious meaning-making in such atrocities, is, for most people, entirely heinous and unthinkable. The issue is not solely about ethics; rather, as modernists repeatedly suggest, to set violence next to political meaning, in the hope of a clear alliance, is to invite a focus specifically on that impossible conjunction, on what, for most onlookers, will be a gap rather than a continuity. In other words, the expressive quality of political violence makes it compelling to literature largely for its failure to work coherently. Political violence becomes literary just when its meanings and uses cannot be aligned with its concrete, material effects. For Conrad and Yeats, in particular, when politics inflicts itself on the physical being, a reactive force is generated, as political meaning is thrust outward and rendered unreal. In considering political violence, then, modernists find an exemplification or hyperbolization of a more general phenomenon that drives their inquiry, the sense that literature has as one of its defining features the encounter with forces of extremity and incommensurability. Whatever approach a literary work might take in exploring, countering, or replicating the disproportions inherent in political violence, some disjunction will emerge between the principle of making meaning and the recognition of senselessness.

One term I will use in this study, to delineate an approach to violence and power that takes account of these contradictions and enables a flexible relation to political meaning, is "force."[36] I am borrowing my idea of force primarily from the pacifist philosopher Simone Weil, who defines force as a kind of superviolence, a sweeping and swirling phenomenon that belongs to no one group or person, and that touches those who wield power as well as those who are its victims.[37] In a celebrated essay on the *Iliad*, Weil thinks about how the violence of war consumes and transforms its universe.[38] When considered through the prism of Homer's epic, Weil argues, war is force and force is war:

> The true hero, the true subject matter, the center of the *Iliad* is force. The force that men wield, the force that subdues men, in the face of which human flesh shrinks back. The human soul seems ever conditioned by its ties with force, swept away, blinded by the force it believes it can control, bowed under the constraint of the force it submits to.[39]

The notion of force is itself sweeping, in a sense matching its content: it wraps together such differing experiences as the lust for combat, the sense of total helplessness in the hands of a merciless enemy, the awe-filled respect that soldiers feel for war's sheer magnitude, and the close ties that knit together such seeming antagonists as enemy and friend, past and present, combatant and civilian, sword and body. Weil's essay, written in the summer and fall of 1940, at the outset of the Nazi occupation of France,[40] offers a double perspective on the subject of war, as both a focus of literature—indeed, the very point of origin of the Western canon—and a dark and dominating reality for an ever-increasing swath of the world. For Weil, this doubled point of view amounts to a single insight, for "those wise enough to discern the force at the center of all human history, today as in the past, find in the *Iliad* the most beautiful and flawless of mirrors" (Weil, 45).

What that mirror shows, perhaps more than anything else, is that war turns all its participants, helpless victims as well as ruthless perpetrators, into "things." "Each, in contact with force, is subjected to its inexorable action, which is to render those it touches either mute or deaf," she writes, and further: "Such is the character of force. Its power to transform human beings into things is twofold and operates on two fronts; in equal but different ways, it petrifies the souls of those who undergo it and those who ply it" (Weil, 61). Weil's account of how perpetrator and victim are swept up together into a single phenomenon is deeply problematic as an ethical idea. She can, moreover, be an imperfect reader of Homer, sometimes schematizing or overlooking elements in the *Iliad*'s vision of the intersections among war, humanity, and culture. Nevertheless, she is persuasive in rendering a cycle of terror that promises to make death the ruler over life and in seeing in the vulnerability of humanity a basic feature of existence, connecting the contemporary world with the ancient, and the glamour of the hunt for glory with the drudgery of being a victim:

> The force that kills is summary and crude. How much more varied in operation, how much more stunning in effect is that other sort of force, that which does not kill, or rather does not kill just yet. It will kill for a certainty, or it will kill perhaps, or it may merely hang over the being it can kill at any instant; in all cases, it changes the human being into stone. From the power to change a human being into a thing by making him die there comes another power, in its way more momentous, that of making a still living human being into a thing. (Weil, 46)

It is the "other form of force" that most succinctly characterizes the savagery of the fascist regime: the potential for violence defines the state of terror, where the imminent threat of an always ready violence is seared into the consciousness of the populace (privy to previous scenes of terrible violence and understanding the logic of the regime).

Weil's notion of force approaches an edge, a place which the early-twentieth-century literary imagination loathed to reach, though often enough it touched that limit. Such possibilities as a person being reduced to a thing or the recognition of strange intimacies between oppressors and victims (like Stephen and the prefect) are invoked in the period, even before the 1930s, when they became much more widespread, as we will see more fully in the final chapter. It may indeed be that what the reckoning with violence does, and especially the consideration of such dispersed and devastating violence as that of world war, is to showcase and expose the moment when humanness and thing-ness come terribly close, in a proximity that has consequences for any literary work that hopes to encompass it. Force is an entity that corresponds less to any given act or individual than to a broad compulsion with the capacity to constrain, strike, or even annihilate. More generally, force, as I am imagining it, is almost a condition of existence, a way of considering the swell of power that surrounds and can demolish the individual, even as, in some cases, it provides a sense of that individual's purpose (to resist, to rebel)—or, as Holocaust survivors tell it, to resist or rebel by the bare fact of remaining human. It is, finally, a central insight of this period that, for all the contortions the literary text might make to adapt itself to the violent conditions of the world, raw force will always have the power to squelch and to silence. As 1984's villain O'Brien puts it, in one of English literature's grimmest statements, "If you want a picture of the future, imagine a boot stamping on a human face—forever."[41]

Confronting War, Imagining History

Weil's notion of force (like Orwell's dystopia) is a product of 1930s totalitarianism, but the mass violence that has always defined the era's literature emerged from the trenches of 1914–18. The First World War was endlessly written and rewritten, even from its outset, and scholars of the period have shown how profoundly the aesthetic culture of modernism was permeated and shaped by its violence. I will discuss some aspects of this relation in the next chapter, where I lay out the model of enchanted and disenchanted violence that I regard as an overarching principle throughout the period, especially keyed to conceptualizing war. Here, in order to clarify and distinguish my approach, I want briefly to mention—and also to qualify—several commonplaces about the period's aesthetics in relation to the First World War (and war in general). First, readers will readily note that many influential modernists on both sides of the Atlantic glamorized violence and aestheticized its effects. It is a truism that major writers of the period became infatuated with fascism and other forms of authoritarian politics in the 1920s and '30s (Pound, Eliot, Lewis, Yeats, and Lawrence come immediately to mind, to name only a few). Though debates persist over the precise importance of such politics for reading the literary canon, there is little question that an enthrallment with hierarchy, class stratification, and militarism had, already by the first decade of the twentieth century, come to pervade literary circles in England and elsewhere. In avant-garde milieus, from the pages of Wyndham Lewis's *BLAST* to the various Futurist manifestoes, bellicose in substance and style, writers eagerly celebrated a virile, often violent masculinism. These were short-lived trends—*BLAST* with only two numbers and Futurism giving way to and amalgamating with other movements—but they remain useful barometers of the period, illuminating at least one scheme for connecting violence to art: the one imitates and glorifies the other.[42] So Marinetti, in the first Futurist Manifesto, proclaimed war to be "the world's only hygiene—militarism, patriotism, the destructive gesture of freedom-bringers, beautiful ideas worth dying for, and scorn for woman."[43] And *BLAST*, Lewis's English answer to the "futurist moment," to use Marjorie Perloff's phrase, imagines an aesthetic movement geared to cheer on the artist troops.[44] The manifesto, which ran from 1914 to 1915 and comprised polemical pieces, fiction, poetry, and visual images, issued its own clarion call for a violent new aesthetics that would shake up and revitalize the arts. As Lewis wrote in his opening statement, "Blast sets out to be an avenue for all those vivid and violent ideas that could reach the Public in no other way."[45] Even *BLAST* 2, the so-called War Number, uncomfortably produced in 1915, continued to embrace violence, despite the elegy that tinges its pages (in part owing to the death at war of one of its primary contributors, Henri Gaudier-Brzeska). These statements, moreover, might be projected forward to the fascistic tide that partially engulfed high modernism in the later twenties and thirties, and backward to late-nineteenth-century figures like Nietzsche who had articulated an ethics and aesthetics of violence to be taken up in later years.[46]

There is nothing in this narrative per se that I want to challenge or correct, but in the chapters that follow, I hope that my consideration of violence will complicate the story. To give just one example, in the years after the war, and especially in the 1930s, the airplane helped to focalize the culture's contradictory self-understanding with respect to war, violence, and glamorization. If airplanes had seemed in the context of the First World War to line up with the adulatory scheme, its fliers inevitably rendered as the aristocrats of the military, later years would figure both technology and crew as menace. Meanwhile, the idea of flight can be seen as an example of how war ultimately yields to peace, destruction to commerce, the precision of killing to the triumph of human virtuosity. Flight is linked to the imagination, that which, in dark times, might seem to offer an alternative to the morass of competition and war. Ultimately, the airplane is best read as an emblem of the full enmeshment of violence and aesthetics, where all its signifiers of beauty, adventure, and dazzling elevation came equally to express violence, fear, and loss. In that sense, it exemplifies what I will be arguing more generally in this book, that violence in modernism is so deeply embedded as to function almost as the literary itself—like the wave in Woolf's writing or the swallow in *The Waste Land*, images of the accrual of meaning, inseparable from the violence they both represent and beautify.

In addition to the general dictum that modernists had a regrettable tendency to worship violence is another (contrasting) critical truism, also instructive as a point of departure: that the catastrophe of the First World War, with its shattering and disillusioning qualities, helped to create a modernism that stands, in part, as an aesthetic refutation of war. As with fascistic modernism, the varied elements that fall under this rubric are well known. They include questions of literary form— disjunctiveness, fragmentation, lapses, and breaks—and also of individual and cultural experience, reactions to violence like alienation and trauma, embitterment, loss of belief in the governing narratives of Western culture. As Paul Fussell summed it up in *The Great War and Modern Memory*, still the canonical statement of the war's role in shaping the modern imagination: "I am saying that there seems to be one dominating form of modern understanding; that it is essentially ironic; and that it originates largely in the application of mind and memory to the events of the Great War."[47] Fussell of course left off the "ist" in his title, and part of the power of his analysis comes from its eliding of distinctions between specifically literary responses to the war and a larger, more encompassing shift in sensibility that invites the term "modern." And certainly there is nothing automatic or truistic about the mutuality of artistic engagements with historical events and the shifts in consciousness that come to constitute an episteme. Thus Margot Norris opens a study of war and twentieth-century literature with an initial skepticism about such conjunctions: "Looking back at the twentieth century, we might at first be struck by the incommensurability of two of its hallmarks: modern mass warfare and innovative art."[48] Still, as Norris and many others have found, the intimate relationship of the war to the modernists who wrote in its wake remains an extremely compelling combination. It is, however, not a determining one, with the richest violence stories of this period only partially comprehended by the most familiar narratives linking the war and modernism. In this study, we will find overlaps and congruencies between the violence of war and other historical events of the period, and these relations might stimulate a critique of some general assumptions about whether and how the war set the terms for both modernism and modernity. Irish works of these years, for instance, fit only uneasily into the scheme, given that the war functioned for many Irish people not only as a spectacle of unimaginable violence but also as a wedge issue in the independence struggle. Irish writers were hard at work constructing a specific thematic of blood and power; the war intersected, intervened, contradicted, intruded. Or, to look in a different direction, if we assume that the devastating violence of explosion is primarily a matter of the First World War, how do we approach the many novels about radical bombers that pervaded the popular literary scene in the thirty years that preceded the war? It is undeniable that the literary output of these years was influenced by the war's cataclysm of violence, with its terrible legacy on bodies, landscapes, and the intellectual and spiritual life of the West, and yet it may also be that the war worked too well as an event from which myriad art forms could draw their defining strategies; its very extravagance of violence and destruction lent itself to schemes of aesthetic assimilation in such a manner as to virtually ensure canonization in such terms. The war provided a common language of literary violence, yet it need not be taken as a totalizing one.

The subject of shell shock illuminates how accepted narratives about war and modernity can be fruitful, but also incomplete. A term first coined in 1915 and quickly enshrined in both medical and lay vocabulary, shell shock represents the prototypical injury from the First World War and one of the most persistent symbols of psychic modernity. The image of contemporary consciousness suggested by shell shock is characterized by a severe rupturing in time, space, and personal memory, and the shell-shocked former soldier becomes a kind of tortured hero for modernism's particular theater. A threshold figure, he suggests many antinomies, such as protest and capitulation, silence and reconstituted language, destruction and tenuous rehabilitation. To name just a few of the many prominent literary examples, Woolf's Septimus Warren Smith in *Mrs. Dalloway* exemplifies the shell-shock victim, a "last relic straying on the edge of the world, this outcast, who gazed back at the inhabited regions, who lay, like a drowned sailor, on the shore of the world,"[49] as does Captain Herbertson in Lawrence's *Aaron's Rod*, a former officer whose obsessive, panicked urge to relive the war dominates and drives him, unleashing "a hot, blind, mesmerized voice, going on and on, mesmerized by a vision that the soul cannot bear."[50] Or, there is Chris Baldry, the protagonist of Rebecca West's 1918 novella *The Return of the Soldier*, whose war injury is an extreme amnesia. The war, whose slaughter appears in the brief imagined glimpses of its female narrator, comes home instead as a matter of psychic creativity and resistance, and Chris, in refusing his wife and with her the entire class structure, embodies a type of romantic hero. In addition to such canonical embodiments, shell shock entered countless other works, fictional, poetic, scientific, political, and journalistic. In all of these cases where the shell-shocked man becomes an embodiment and focal point of war, the structure is one of displacement—from the violence itself to its psychic residue or internalization. If one of the key aspects of violence in literary modernism will be its insistence that we be there, at the moment, shell shock represents an entirely different temporal schema, where the past constantly invades the present, distorting both, and where any access to the moment of violence is made tenuous.

The traumatic structure of shell shock lends itself to a particular temporal prism, and there are other leanings and occlusions that follow its dominance in the critical imagination. One involves physical injury, a whole landscape of wounded bodies that were every bit as problematic for the culture of postwar England, every bit as unhinging of expectations and comfortable commonplaces, as the troubled minds that are so often invoked and fetishized. In the years following the war, physical injury was an utterly ubiquitous phenomenon, as men with a huge array of often horrifying physical ailments, from blindness to amputation to tuberculosis, pervaded the civilian scene, often straying from such seemingly contained locations as hospitals and asylums, and unsettling basic categories such as old/young, masculine/feminine, and broken/whole. And yet, one might read many works of modernism, as well as the critical record since midcentury, without understanding the extent of postwar injury—how striking it is that Woolf, who rendered the war so richly throughout her work, includes no physically injured First World War combatants in her novels. In fact, it may be that the injured survivors of *all* modern wars create uniquely disturbing problems for their cultures, provoking issues from memorialization, to reparation, to civilian responsibility, to the nature of warfare itself.[51] One could press further, to argue that the emphasis on mental breakdown can be seen as part of a contest over who will, in effect, be in control of the enormous fund of cultural affect generated by the war's pain.[52] The transformation of the war's physical destructiveness to an event primarily of the mind shifts those imaginative artists whose special purview is the interior life to the forefront as the appropriate figures to narrate, conceptualize, and reconfigure the war for an ongoing civilian readership. The issue here is not that one form of representation (that which stresses the body's harm) is better or more truthful than another (that which refigures it), but rather to notice the dominance of any overarching story, in this case the shell-shock canonization. In this study, I would have us see shell shock in a kind of shadow game with other strategies for understanding, internalizing, and formalizing violence; its codification of one mode—personification—offers a special insight and visibility, abutting and at times concealing other representational principles.

Another example of how critical assumptions about the war both enable and inhibit an understanding of violence in the period's literary history relates to the war's technological innovations. The technologies that developed around the war for many years held a special place in the cultural imaginary. The Victorians had thoroughly exposed the industrialism of their era as a killing and injuring machine, but these were not willful forms of attack (an obvious point, perhaps: one might create or operate a machine with callous indifference to human life, but one designs a bomb in order to kill people).[53] It was the deliberate, scientific nature of war violence that most engaged the public imagination in the early decades of the twentieth century, when wars smashed back into the sphere of British consciousness after the relative quiet of half a century. If the ideal of scientific detachment could, by 1914, rest on very stable ground, the war brought to the fore an image of science gone catastrophically wrong. Foremost, of course, were the technologies of attack, whether in the form of mustard gas, machine guns, artillery, or the impressive hardware of tanks and airplanes, some of which would soon make their way into civilian life. The procedures of propaganda and organization for such a massive effort as the First World War were equally impressive, involving not only conscription but the creation of a busy arm of government dedicated to sending out clear messages and stimulating enthusiasm, as well as the legal means to repress dissent. If technology could seem to have turned monstrous, however, the technologies marshaled in the name of curing promised a return to humaneness, especially with the much-publicized development of prosthetics and other medical devices for the badly wounded. Finally, efforts to record war, especially photography and film, added to the range of innovations that surrounded the war from its beginnings to well past its end. Literary and cultural critics of the war have approached many of these topics, showing, to give a few heterogeneous examples, how an innovation like the tank was imagined, during the war years, as a symbol of both combatant and civilian participation,[54] how the reach of the state via its various legal and propagandistic arms entered and shaped public life, in some cases continuing on after the war had ended,[55] and how the resonance of photography came to influence the very grammar of many writers in the period, including those (like Eliot) who would not seem its most likely champions.[56]

At the same time, I would call attention to one feature I have discovered over the course of my readings: that in the face of violence, modern technology has a tendency to bind itself to the most primitive forms for hurting people. So in the war, it was as much the bayonet as chlorine gas that captured the public imagination as a symbol of the war's ferocity and barbarism. In fact, given how fundamentally disorienting and disillusioning the shift to modern, mass warfare was, for both combatants and civilians, it is especially notable and surprising that the atavistic image of one man bayoneting another became a gripping and defining image of brutality throughout the period.[57] Similarly, in the case of anarchist explosion, if the technology of the dynamite bomb seized the interest of radicals and conservatives alike, its effects tended to be juxtaposed, in many kinds of texts and reports, against the least advanced forms of technology, like the ditch or shovel. As Jean Rhys has it in *Wide Sargasso Sea*, catching the modernist moment with precision, the ultimate weapon can be nothing more sophisticated than thick walls and a heavy lock. In short, I am attempting, in thinking about violence and literature over the course of this study, to show that alongside the biggest stories that evolved from the war—an event that was unique for the extreme and blinding visibility of its destruction—there are other important patterns flourishing in darker cultural recesses. The violence of war was spectacular and unavoidable, and postwar culture in many ways came to define itself in and around its slaughter, taking itself to task. One key point I will be arguing about modernism, however, is that this spectacular quality is not so much a given in the period as the subject of literary effort. The extremity of visible violence is in many cases the generating fact behind modernism's portrayals of indeterminacy, and the reverse is also true: such violence embodies and makes spectacular a set of formal principles and modes of consciousness that were gaining steam in other contexts as well.

An equally important model of understanding violence in historical terms might be found under a rubric nearly oppositional to that of modernism and war: silence and dispersal. Rather than be confronted with the trenches that, in some grim way, culminated nineteenth-century culture in the West, this alternate paradigm reminds us of the many, many cases, in the present as in the past, where violence stays hidden. If we want to see it, we will have to know where to look. "The village was called Nyaunglebin," the narrator of George Orwell's *Burmese Days* (1934) says, "'the four peepul trees'; there were no peepul trees there now, probably they had been cut down and forgotten a century ago."[58] A passing reference, this language is significant for the way it strikes off into a different historical imagining from the narrative of visible violence that war and empire display, including the contemporary imperial situation Orwell's novel depicts—one thinks here of Rob Nixon's ecological concept of "slow violence".[59] The town's defining linguistic feature, the pipal trees have been removed, victims, perhaps, of the developing timber industry, that which drew the British to Burma in the first place and their engine of profit there at the time of the novel's publication.[60] Or perhaps they were cut down in order to build the village, the founding strike against the environment that defines human culture. Whatever the story—whether it is part of the universal narrative of human relations to their surroundings or an early passage in the depredation of the East by a greedy, violent West, which Orwell's novel ruthlessly exposes for the unvarnished hatred that drives it—all of that is long gone, and instead we have only an echo, a name that both holds and lets go of its history. And we might add: the word "pipal" (or the earlier "peepul") reads phonetically as "people," again raising the question of allegory—are these trees supposed to be telling a story about violence against people, here the Burmese?[61] (And Orwell's resonance goes further, though he may not have intended it, in that "pipal" is another name for the bo tree, under which the Buddha is said to have found enlightenment.) It is, of course, inherent in Western accounts of empire that it credits no history—or only distorted history—to the rest of the world, and, conversely, that it imagines the imperial domains as having access to a primordial past that the civilized West has long superseded. Orwell debunks all such logic in his novel, suggesting, rather, that the violence of empire corresponds and cooperates with other, indigenous forces. The British, too, leave names behind; perhaps we are to see these, from the perspective of some vague future (a century or so forward in time), as equivalent to the pipal trees as markers of a violent incursion that one day will be forgotten, to require translation and reimagination.

In *Burmese Days*, history is not really the focus, but other works of the modernist period dwell insistently and movingly on history and violence, and the model of an erased violent past, which nevertheless leaves its markers, held a central place in the imagination of these years.[62] We might generalize the motif, since it is a structure of understanding and naming with persistent application: in the past, a grove of trees grew here; I or my ancestors cut down those trees in order to build our house, create roads, or cultivate the land for agriculture; we named the street for those vanished trees, "Elm." The process is one that has been noted, particularly in the American context, where the culture constructs its present and future through acts of obliteration and forgetting, but also by preserving myths of the previous (comparatively pristine) condition.[63] Such preservation can be as minute as the embalmed trace of the street name, a small kernel or stunted narrative primed to resurrect a large history. Destruction, clearly, is at the core of the process. As Dominick LaCapra puts it, "The foundation of a polity as well as of a personality is often traced to some violent, traumatic, transgressive, often sacralized or 'sublimated,' event that is presumed to mark a turning point or rupture in history and the instauration of a new era."[64] With the clearing of land, this need not be understood as violent—through much of history, on the contrary, the transformation of the land for human use has been seen as a definitively humane act, often a sacred one.[65] Nevertheless, as the early twentieth century had begun to see, the first strike against the land often sets in motion an exploitative and expropriative process underpinned by violence and inequality. Most grotesquely, what can be at stake in all of this is the elimination of people, even populations. Philip Fisher calls these "hard facts," and sees in them a dynamic of visibility and invisibility at the heart of American literary culture.[66] In British works, where the configurations differ markedly, in part because national origins are not at issue in the same way, the pattern nevertheless has significant life, often (though not exclusively) in the colonial context. One paradigm that frequently emerges in British literature involves this emphasis on trace over narrative, with broken signals and symbols of a never quite vanished tale of violence taking the place of fuller narratives or visual representations. One thinks of Ian Baucom's spellbinding depiction of the horrendous violence of the late-eighteenth-century massacre of slaves on the slave ship *Zong* as inaugurating and emblematizing what Baucom argues is the political unconscious of the "long twentieth century."[67] Such partiality accords, too, with what Mary Favret has described as the attenuated, dispersed condition of "wartime," a quality of life and feeling in nineteenth-century Britain, where war is experienced as distance, something sensed but not known, a shadowy film never brought into distinct focus.[68]

Shedding light on and epitomizing the pattern in the twentieth century is a work written several decades after the modernist period yet very much in dialogue with it, *Wide Sargasso Sea* (1966).[69] Rhys's great novel has a complicated relationship of belatedness, critique, and overlap with the modernism that defined much of her career. There can be no circumventing of historical responsibility in *Wide Sargasso Sea*, which, like its characters, is obsessed with the erasures and distortions of history, where slave-owners who have raped untold black women can become church-sanctioned gentlemen, where individual and family pasts are continually invoked as secrets to be decoded (and hotly disputed), where ancestry is figured as determinism—some truth always lurking in the blood—and, above all, where slavery is the one institution the English do not want to acknowledge as a part of their own ugly past. In four short passages, Rhys gives the motif concrete form, creating a model for reading not only *Wide Sargasso Sea* but the literature of its recent past—modernism—which is one of the novel's primary alter egos and intertexts and about which Rhys is particularly astute:

> I looked at the sad leaning cocoanut palms, the fishing boats drawn up on the shingly beach, the uneven row of whitewashed huts, and asked the name of the village.
> "Massacre."
> "And who was massacred here? Slaves?"
> "Oh no." She sounded shocked. "Not slaves. Something must have happened a long time ago. Nobody remembers now." (*Rhys*, 65–66)

"If this is a sad story, don't tell it to me tonight."

"It is not sad," she said. "Only some things happen and are there for always even though you forget why or when. It was in that little bedroom." (*Rhys*, 82)

Next morning there would be very little sign of these showers. If some of the flowers were battered, the others smelt sweeter, the air was bluer and sparkling fresh. Only the clay path outside my window was muddy. Little shallow pools of water glinted in the hot sun, red earth does not dry quickly. (*Rhys*, 94–95)

I said, "There was a road here once, where did it lead to?"

"No road," he said.

"But I saw it. A *pavé* road like the French made in the islands."

"No road."

"Who lived in that house?"

"They say a priest. Père Lilièvre. He lived here a long time ago."

"A child passed," I said. "She seemed very frightened when she saw me. Is there something wrong about the place?" He shrugged his shoulders.

"Is there a ghost, a zombi there?" I persisted.

"Don't know nothing about all that foolishness."

"There was a road here sometime."

"No road," he repeated obstinately. (*Rhys*, 105–6)

Taken together, the passages offer a complete picture of the paradigm, where violent pasts are figured as severed, ambiguous narratives, and unseen forces invisibly direct and determine the traumas of the present. The violent deeds that define this novel's past (of which there are an almost infinite number) are erased and unavailable, even as they are compulsively reconjured. They exist somewhere between remembering and forgetting, like the zombie itself, which epitomizes many thresholds—living and dead, past and present, real and imagined, Africa and the Caribbean. What we know, what we remember, what we can imagine, what we deduce, what we infer: all these operations of mind confront and circle the gaps that violence creates and upholds. In the case of the Massacre sequence, Rhys offers a darker and more insidious version of what is found in Orwell: the foundational actions of the past have been obscured, but they have enough presence to unsettle the present, creating an aura of threat and incipience. To name a town "Massacre" is to make explicit what "Elm" (or "Nyaunglebin") evades, yet there is no shared, communal memory—much less official historical accounting—to give these landmarks the power to shame, or to revive, or to enforce. Such remnants might seem ready to tell buried stories, but they also call attention to the blunt reality that, in the 1840s when the novel is set, no one was accounting for the murder of slaves.[70] The issue of raw colonial power is even more at stake in the road/ no-road dialogue, a typically modernist sequence of echoing and redundancy, which also aligns with the novel's larger portrayal of miscommunication between people. The road and shrine signify control of the island, whether by French priests, local people (a heterogeneous group), or the English patriarchs who make it their business, first and foremost, to know what happened where. These are social facts, but the passages equally characterize the individual experience ("it was in that little bedroom"), and, moreover, seem agnostic as to speaker or narrative perspective; from the most noxious to the most sympathetic character, the historical pattern persists. And yet, if these broken narratives signal the continuity and reinvigoration of violence in the present, beauty also clings to them, at least in places. The pools and flowers are refreshed, sweet smelling, and all the passages have something lyrical about them, a refrain-like quality that reads almost as poetry.[71]

What makes *Wide Sargasso Sea* (a novel that was finally published in 1966) so resonant for the study of violence in the modernist period is that in the end, Rhys reveals modernism's own violence protocols as much as she does the Victorian era's, which, via her rewriting of Brontë, has always seemed the most prominent subject of literary critique. Modernism, in fact, might be said to function like those other severed narratives, its presence implicit as the trace of some brutal history. Unlike *Jane Eyre*, which becomes known through plot and character cues, modernism is there as form. Its signature technique—stream of consciousness—acts in the novel as another mode of imprisonment, aligned with all the other forces that Rhys has shown to lock women up: slavery, patriarchy, silencing. Or rather, modernist form functions paradoxically in *Wide Sargasso Sea*, as the only recourse left to the utterly exploited and isolated Antoinette, even as it lays the final nail in her psychic coffin. Rhys had been incubating this perception about modernism for decades, with her 1920s novels portraying their numbed and brutalized heroines as victims of a cosmopolitan aesthetic whose humanity has been fully leached. But it took another four decades, during which the nature of colonial violence became increasingly potent in her understanding, for the critique to become historicized.

In the wake of anti- and postcolonial consciousness, the paths of history come to seem rutted with shell holes; to think historically requires that a partially covered road, a single word, or even a sparkling flower petal be reinvested with its violent past. In the first decades of the twentieth century, writers were beginning to imagine the world in these terms, though the episodes are more partial, the indictment more ambivalent, and the element of beauty more pronounced. When set next to the dramatic aesthetic culture of the war, this structure of excavation and partial rediscovery looks especially lean and ambiguous, well cued to the modernist temperament. Or perhaps it is most useful to see the war's hyperbolic slaughter and the erased violence of the longer past as establishing two poles of historical imagining in this period, both of which provoked new and sophisticated systems for formalizing violence. Whether spectacular and undeniable or silent and resilient, violence demanded that a new language be forged to acknowledge, express, and embody it.

Chapters

At the Violet Hour is premised on the notion that very specific material conditions will always shape the literary work, and that such conditions are not only historical but generic; hence the chapters look at violent situations in the context of a panoply of written and visual materials, many with popular appeal, all of which, in turn, comprise the world of the modernist text. Despite heterogeneous historical contexts, these interactions produce some repeated patterns. In each chapter, I trace the generic surround (including popular novels, political polemics, and journalism); in each, there are moments when modernist works seem to hit their stride in the formalizing of violence; and each ends with the suggestion of an indefinite futurity, as the story of violence rampages onward into a future that is almost inevitably rendered in precarious terms. The four chapters are not entirely parallel in structure, however. The first develops a theoretical paradigm for the rest of the book, to be followed by three historical chapters, each of which presents a case study in the material history of violence, structured according to the particular logics of violence at hand. Thus with anarchism, the historical readings center on a set of preoccupations that emerged in late-Victorian culture, attentive to such phenomena as sensationalism and the appeal of melodrama, while the chapter on Ireland weaves through four distinctive modes for considering violence, following the events on the ground in the period around the Rising, and the final chapter builds an expansive political and cultural history into a reading of Woolf's novels. I conclude with a short coda pointing toward developments later in the century.

The first chapter sets up the dichotomizing paradigm of enchanted and disenchanted violence and represents the book's primary engagement with the First World War. I argue, here, that a major imaginative structure about violence—one way in which Western culture has understood violence in relation to itself, its values, and its aesthetic artifacts—can be schematized according to a model of generative violence, which I call enchantment, in tension with an insistence that all violence is unredeemable. In addition to elaborating this model, the chapter will make two further interventions. One is to consider war primarily through the enchantment/disenchantment structure, thus connecting its dominant imaginative configuration to other forms of violence in the period and to a structure of thought that has significant literary application. And secondly, I offer a reading of Eliot's *The Waste Land* (1922), a work that exemplifies the way enchanted and disenchanted violence can be developed and deconstructed, separated and interfused, and does so in especially complex, lyrical fashion. Given the poem's elevated status in modernism, to read it under the rubric of enchanted and disenchanted violence helps to demonstrate how thoroughly the paradigm underwrote the aesthetic achievements of the period.

The second chapter inaugurates the book's structure of historical inquiry. It is about dynamite violence, and also about anarchism, which stood behind an absorbing set of political events in the late nineteenth and early twentieth centuries and galvanized the public imagination. The gash or rent or, ultimately, the exploded body became the sign of a radically destabilizing politics, with provocative consequences for the literature that addressed it. That literature extends from popular dynamite novels, journalism, and anarchist writings into more canonical works of the turn of the century, most powerfully Conrad's *The Secret Agent*, all of which I consider in the chapter. Amidst a rich terrain of revolutionary personae, historical acts of sensational violence, perceived new threats, and fervent fantasies of destruction, I tease out two phenomena of special interest to modernism: the idea that dynamite violence epitomized meaninglessness, as it conjoined exceptional damage with a gaping absence of justification, and the gradual emergence, out of the late-Victorian and Edwardian frame, of the transhistorical figure of the terrorist. The chapter concludes with a reading of the suicide bomber as a resonant new type, an image of the future in which the key characteristic of violence becomes its potentiality: indefinite rather than spectacular, it casts a long shadow up to the present day.

In shifting to Ireland and the events surrounding the 1916 insurrection for the third chapter, I track a wholly different relation between violent actors and their publics. Anarchism's marginality is its abiding characteristic, while the rebels who ultimately forged the new Irish state could understand their violence as representing and embodying a national ideal. Yet the question of containment, as with dynamite violence, remains urgent in the Irish independence struggle as well. In the language that developed around the events of 1916, and especially during the years of war, we find a basic uncertainty about its exceptionalism, which would link it back to the kind of episodic violence embodied by dynamite, versus its permanence, where the notion of revenge points forward into infinity. Such cyclicality has a name, reprisal, and this becomes an absolutely pivotal idea in the period, its reciprocal formal structure offering a correlative in literary texts to its devastating effects in the material world. For Yeats, to work out the issue of reprisal was a poetic challenge linked with the broader cultural thematics of generative and cyclical violence that pervaded the nationalist scene, as articulated by such figures as Pádraig Pearse, Joseph Mary Plunkett, J. M. Synge, and Sean O'Casey, all of whom I consider in the chapter. More generally, I look at a span of imaginative constructs around violence in the period—"keening" (the language of ritual mourning in Ireland), generative violence, reprisal, and architectural allegory—and reveal a dialectical structure among these modes. Jostled between the promise of generative violence and the nightmare of reprisal, literary works looked to generate stability and beauty out of the archaic formalism of mourning or the capaciousness of the representative building.

In its culminating chapter, *At the Violet Hour* turns to one of the great formalists of violence in the twentieth century, Virginia Woolf, whose late works, especially, offer remarkably deep, moving, and idiosyncratic reflections on the darkening of the world around her, and on her contemporaries' dominant ideas about violence, war, and human nature. The chapter has its defining nexus in the 1930s, with special attention to the Spanish Civil War, which activated Woolf's social circle and took the life of her nephew Julian Bell, as well as more broadly consolidating the culture's understanding of what the next world war would mean. Fascism in the 1930s brought the specter of endemic violence perilously close and pressured the viability of pacifism in new terms, and it was in this political and intellectual climate that Woolf created her stunning and tortured late works, which fixate on the permeation of violence into culture and consciousness. These writings, composed in the key of incipient war—*The Years* (1937), *Three Guineas* (1938), and *Between the Acts* (1941)—blend a deep empathy for women's suffering and imaginative lives with a scorching critique of violent male power. They also build upon what Woolf's earlier novels, in particular *The Voyage Out* (1915), *Jacob's Room* (1922), *Mrs. Dalloway* (1925), and *To the Lighthouse* (1927), had begun to achieve, a distinct stylistics of violence, often revolving around the creation of abstract patterns. In keeping with the war photography that emerged from the Spanish war and Picasso's *Guernica*, its most famous artistic manifestation, Woolf and other antifascists were extremely conscious of the paradox in their endeavor: only as expressions of the deepest vulnerability might their works be able to claim historical significance. Uniquely, Woolf took the measure of that paradox as a guiding challenge, to be met by a language that would be bracingly honest, unflinching, and increasingly despairing, and which was ever working out the relation of its aesthetic principles to its humanity.

The precariousness of humanity, in the face of a bewildering array of powers—mass violence, totalitarianism, bureaucracy, technology, the onslaught of visuality—is one of the primary morals of the twentieth century. Modernity thus takes as one of its organizing conditions an imbalance between the individual (deconstructed and relativized as she may be) and enormously threatening forces, both visible and invisible; and this uneven configuration has motivated writers and artists since the industrial revolution, in new and enduring ways in the early twentieth century, where this study focuses, and on into the twenty-first century. The literary and cultural works of the modernist period were especially adept at creating aesthetic forms to contain and display both the excesses and the mundane realities of violence, according to the logics I will be pursuing in these pages: enchanted and disenchanted, intensively imagined and projected outward, asked to speak a political language and wrenched free of politics, governed by the terrible realities of force. Enfolded in these doubled, structurally ambivalent, contradictory forms, violence finds a voice. That such a voice is exceptionally conscious of its mutability and partiality, that it recognizes the power of giving narrative life to violence even as it often shrinks away to a mere whisper, that it forges some of the period's greatest expressions of humanity yet also despairs of that effort: all of this is to be expected, given the enormity of the subject and the tenuousness of any single literary expression. These efforts carry with them both the modesty and the accomplishment due their subject; they are, if nothing else, what Yeats delicately named "befitting emblems of adversity" (*Var*, 420).

1. Enchanted and Disenchanted Violence

There is magic in death. But there is also emptiness and finality in death. When death is violent, both its awesomeness and its meaninglessness increase. And if it is viewed as undeserved, it is asked to signify even more powerfully—or to admit its radical lack of significance. Thus, the ultimate story of magical transformation in Christian culture is the crucifixion/resurrection story, where unmerited, violent death yields nothing less than the promise of an afterlife and the salvation of mankind, while the ultimate expression of bleak emptiness comes in the extermination camp, where death is indiscriminate and the possibility of apotheosis foreclosed. These polarizing perceptions of violent death as either the fuel for generativity or the emblem of grotesque loss reach far and wide across Western culture, and they interfuse the literary field. I will call these modes "enchanted" and "disenchanted," and I offer them as central principles around which literary engagements with violence have tended to cluster.[1] Historically, it has been war that most powerfully calls forth these dichotomized understandings of violent death: as a sign and precipitator of sublimity (in a person, community, or nation) or, conversely, as a sign and precipitator of total degeneration and waste. This dichotomy carried special urgency in the first decades of the twentieth century, in part because of the power of the First World War in shaping the aesthetic consciousness, and writers of all political tendencies tended to filter expressions of violence through the enchanted-disenchanted lens.

Enchantment and disenchantment can be read as theories of violence that helped to structure the literary output of the modernist years, and as such they are the locus for a potent political imaginary, including feminist and antimilitarist stances, as well as nationalist ideals and a language of elevated militarism. Yet we need to be clear in demarcating politics from enchanted or disenchanted violence. These are overlapping but not coterminous categories; to create an artifice of enchanted violence is as basic to revolution as it is to conservative or fascist militancy and can contribute to radical left as well as to radical right programs. Moreover, much in the literary project of enchantment elaborates a very basic and important writerly function, which is not inherently politicized: to provide beauty and imaginative release where there is brutality and suffering. Healing, enriching, creating memorable visual forms to capture terrible realities—such operations have always helped to define the literary mission. Literature stands right in the center of the cultural history of violence; enchantment and disenchantment, as dominant binary categories that guide this important and complex relationship, are perhaps most compelling when least explicitly political.

I have two primary goals for this chapter. One is to set up a basic imaginative structure around violence, providing a vocabulary and usage to which I will return throughout the book; the other is to suggest that war incites this structure of thinking in especially polarizing terms, and that this has significant consequences for how the literary output of modernity (riven by wars) has been read. Of all the literary works that swivel on the axis of enchanted and disenchanted violence, none is more fully invested in these principles than T. S. Eliot's *The Waste Land*. A complex iteration of the paradigm, the poem showcases, too, how spectacularly war creates a fertile field for imagining art as a legacy of enchanted and disenchanted violence. *The Waste Land* reaches deeply into both traditions; indeed, its mixture and merger of the two modes demonstrates how subtly their aesthetic strategies can interpenetrate, even as they profess to stand, defiantly, as firm ideological antagonists. In fact, as *The Waste Land* indicates, the aesthetic slips easily across enemy lines—something like Isaac Rosenberg's queer sardonic rat—touching, as it were, both enchanted and disenchanted bodies.

Max Weber provides a touchstone for these concepts, with his compelling assertion that the modern world had, by the nineteenth century, become thoroughly disenchanted. The disenchantment of the world, a concept loosely borrowed from Friedrich Schiller and articulated in a variety of lectures and essays, refers to the large-scale diminishment of sacredness that, for Weber, was a product of industrial modernity.[2] As scientific rationalism and commodity materialism take the place of spiritual vibrancy, the organization of life across a range of institutions and practices squeezes out even the residue of any living spiritual presence. The rationalizations enacted by capitalism, the ascendancy of mass culture, bureaucracy, the rise of professionalism, and the scientific episteme—all contribute to this denuding of the magical, spiritual, and divine from modern existence. Ironically, the disenchantment of the world is in part a result of organized religion itself (Judeo-Christianity), which Weber sees as fundamentally aligned with a modernity it might seem to counter. Weber's idea, which has recently enjoyed a resurgence of interest and lively debate across scholarly disciplines, represents an early iteration of what has become, in the last fifty years, a more sustained attack on the Enlightenment, in this case on its consequences for spiritual fulfillment. Weber need not be right; as Akeel Bilgrami has recently shown, the Weberian notion that the Enlightenment at some necessary level involved a disanimation of the natural world might in fact represent a misreading of the history. Bilgrami argues that at the center of the Enlightenment itself, there was a dissenting empirical consensus that saw no need to prescribe an incompatibility between scientific principles and the presence of enchanting value in the natural world.[3] Nevertheless, the idea that for the last two hundred years an ongoing battle has raged between a world understood in terms of potential incarnation and one whose logic is imagined in purely rationalist terms, succinctly captured in Weber's language of disenchantment, has held abiding explanatory power.[4]

In this iteration of modernity, literary history has an important part to play. Since the end of the eighteenth century, literature has been tenaciously engaged with the whole question of what kind of intangible, inspiring potency inheres in the world, often filtering these questions through the aesthetic consciousness, and often setting up implicit or explicit binaries between spiritual richness and that which is bereft. It should be clear, however, that literature works both sides of the line; it can register and promulgate both enchanted and disenchanted visions of the modern world. Thus, a whole swath of literary forms might be said to perpetuate the secular individualism that Weber called disenchantment—in the form, for instance, of the novelistic realism critiqued by Lukács in his famous attack on the modern novel.[5] Equally clearly, the literary impulse would seem to stand against modernity's large-scale disenchantments, doing its part to reanimate the world through, for instance, the artist's special sensibility or the power imputed to the work of art to transcend the material world, figured as diminished, deadening and mechanical.[6] As Paul Fry proclaims, "the history of lyric and of defense of poetry is one long proclamation that poetry is verbal magic."[7] In this latter (Neoplatonic) narrative of art reaching beyond the ordinary world to a sphere radiating with the spark of the divine, there are two obvious high points in England: the Romanticism of the early nineteenth century ("Be thou, Spirit fierce/My spirit! Be thou me, impetuous one!" sings Shelley[8]) and the early twentieth century, when, under the sign of modernism, the "natural supernaturalism" of the English lake poets took residence among the cosmopolitan spirit-seekers of London, Paris, and other metropolises.[9]

Modernism, in particular, has seemed especially amenable to a narrative of (re)enchantment, well represented by such varied phenomena as Yeats's occultism; Eliot's celebration of Frazer, Weston, et al.; E. M. Forster's Eastern idealizations; D. H. Lawrence's theories of primal sexuality; and surrealism's investigation of the unconscious mind as source of creativity and transgression.[10] Historians have pointed, moreover, to the fact that the unorthodox fantasies of reanimation often associated with modernism were not limited to an eccentric and elite sphere of aesthetes and intellectuals but spread across a wide public spectrum. In her study of the occult at the turn of the century, Alex Owen claims that "the new 'spiritual movement' of which occultism was such a salient part was itself indicative of the continued relevance of spirituality for many thousands of people," and, even more forcefully, that "occultism was constitutive of modern culture at the fin de siècle."[11] In the case of the First World War period, when novel forms of spiritualism again became faddish, historians such as Jay Winter have persuasively argued that these attempts to make otherworldly connections with the dead, like the broader com-memorative activities developing in those years, represented a genuinely wide-spread desire, felt across the culture and in all the warring nations, to find new and satisfying religious practices to allay and assuage the grief of war.[12] Highbrow and mainstream, occultish and cultish, literary and popular: it seems that reenchant-ment was a burgeoning enterprise in the first decades of the century.

When we add violence to this story, the idea of enchantment becomes especially animating, productive, and surprising, but we need to change the meanings to a certain degree. In the ordinary dichotomy, disenchantment is an emblem of sec-ular modernization and is almost always presented as a negative, a signifier for loss. What "disenchantment" will mean, in my configuration, is not a passive recogni-tion of spiritual flatness, but the active stripping away of idealizing principles, an insistence that the violated body is not a magic site for the production of culture. "Enchantment" will refer, most succinctly, to the tendency to see in violence some kind of transformative power.[13] If we return momentarily to the pattern that emerged in the pandying episode in *A Portrait of the Artist as a Young Man*, we recall that the beating caused a dual action, a simultaneous contracting inward, revealing a dynamic of bodily pain and developing shame, and a movement out-wards to the extensive and abstract, revealing shapes of power. In the language of enchantment, a similar pattern can be discerned. On one hand, there is a strong impulse, in literary accounts of violence, to strip language down to its most bodily and elemental forms, to insist on the resonant presence of bodily experience: dis-enchantment. On the other hand, when the desire for spiritual plenitude meets the facts of historical violence, there is an equal and opposite tendency to enchant vio-lence, to see it as the germinating core of rich, symbolic structures. To enchant, in this sense, is to imbue the violent experience with symbolic and cultural potency; to disenchant is to refuse that structure, to insist on the bare, forked existence of the violated being, bereft of symbol, and expressing only a regretful beauty.[14] En-chantment, in this account, might sound like myth, but there are important differ-ences. Myth, even in its loosest usage, requires some kind of developed iteration; in order to find myth, one must have at least the suggestion of narrative structures that can be reproduced and developed. While enchanted violence often comes en-cased in mythic structures and stories, it is different in that it can be the product of a mere moment, of a fleeting impression or sense.

Enchantment would seem exuberantly aesthetic, disenchantment only unwill-ingly so, but as we look closely at them, we find, instead, that each draws on long literary traditions, and each demonstrates ambivalence about its own status in re-lation to violence. Enchanted violence relies primarily on metaphors of growth and germination; it steers as clear of the violated body as it can. And yet its attach-ment to the metaphor of blood—to give just one example—draws it back toward the warmth of physicality. Indeed, blood is perhaps the central metaphor for both enchanted and disenchanted modes; they come together via its associative magne-tism. Elaine Scarry has commented forcefully on the status of blood and the in-jured body in transforming violence into meaning. War, Scarry argues, relies for its power on:

> . . . the mining of the ultimate substance, the ultimate source of substantia-tion, the extraction of the physical basis of reality from its dark hiding place in the body out into the light of day, the making available of the precious ore of confirmation, the interior content of human bodies, lungs, arteries, blood, brains, the mother lode that will eventually be reconnected to the winning issue. . . .[15]

Whether or not one agrees with Scarry's claim that war gains its exceptional status from the mysterious properties of the body's displayed interior, her idea that the injured body represents "the precious ore of confirmation"—that which allows for deeply held beliefs to be developed and changed—resonates for both enchanted and disenchanted models of violence. If death, or killing, or even the gruesomely injured flesh does carry the radical power to confer meaning, neither enchant-ment nor disenchantment can be expected to forego it. Enchantment loves the metaphor of blood; disenchantment calls upon the hurt body, with its signal fluid, to remind us of its reality and frightfulness. Flesh, wounds, penetration: these provide the core figures for disenchantment, which resists the temptation to see transformation in death. Yet beauty it does find, and, as with blood, it is not always possible to separate a disenchanted state of awe at these terrors from an enchanted desire to make that awe culturally productive. In short, there are two proud positions, enchanted and disenchanted violence—both of which found exemplary articulations in the modernist period, both of which spoke to and for the culture in influential and significant terms—but there is an overlapping field of literary figures and cultural value, and the possibility of some arresting forms of miscegenation. Modernism, when put to the test, exemplifies this miscegenational idea, its very essence profoundly shaped by the mixing of the two systems of imagining violence.

In its most stark and direct guise, the notion of enchantment, understood as a form of generative violence, underlies nearly all forms of militarism. Weber himself seems to make an exception to his disenchantment theory when it comes to war:

> As the consummated threat of violence among modern polities, war creates a pathos and a sentiment of community. War thereby makes for an unconditionally devoted and sacrificial community among the combatants and releases an active mass compassion and love for those who are in need. And, as a mass phenomenon, these feelings break down all the naturally given barriers of association. In general, religions can show comparable achievements only in heroic communities professing an ethic of brotherliness.
>
> Moreover, war does something to the warrior which, in its concrete meaning, is unique: it makes him experience a consecrated meaning of death which is characteristic only of death in war . . . Death on the field of battle differs from this merely avoidable dying in that in war, and in this massiveness *only* in war, the individual can *believe* that he knows he is dying "for" something. The why and the wherefore of his facing death can, as a rule, be so indubitable for him that the problem of the "meaning" of death does not even occur to him. (Weber, 335, emphasis in original)

These lines are striking only insofar as they come from Weber. In other respects, they virtually codify the general premise of war enchantment: that in the peculiar conditions of war, violent death is transformed into something positive, communal, perhaps even sacred. Indeed, it has never been possible in the West to imagine war without some promise of transcendence developing out of bodily privation. Thus the task for war's supporters—given the pronounced fact of its gruesome attack on the body—cannot be to evade violence; it must be to find terms for revaluing it.

Instead of denying its often hideous bodily ramifications, champions of war in the twentieth century have often made the destroyed body itself the fulcrum for militarist and nationalist appeals. Rupert Brooke's "The Soldier" (1914), with its metaphorics of a germinative body both constituting and enlarging the national reach, offers a canonical, English case in point:

> If I should die, think only this of me:
> That there's some corner of a foreign field
> That is for ever England. There shall be
> In that rich earth a richer dust concealed . . .[16]

The poem could galvanize the national consciousness in part because it drew very poignantly on the generative ideal—the "rich" dust of France made "richer" by the inseminating English body—at a time when the country was perhaps looking not just for an icon (Brooke certainly filled that role) but also for a language that would frame the war's oncoming violence in terms of fruitfulness. Brooke's poem is complex and melancholy rather than simplistic and brutal (as it is sometimes misrepresented to be), yet it nevertheless manifests a wider pattern that sees the dead soldier as, in effect, the germination for a renewed nation. Victorian and Edwardian culture had always imagined war as a testing ground for masculinity and heroic character. During and after the war, the dead body became increasingly central to that story. In Germany, most notably, the construct took on new life in the 1920s, with the figure of the dead soldier providing a centerpiece in the iconography of sacrifice and revival that underwrote the fascist appeal.[17] More broadly, one central lesson from the years of both Nazi and Soviet rule is how skillfully the most violent regimes can manipulate and expand the cult of generative violence, as the creation of an aesthetics of mass violence is put into the service of ever more violence and control. The model of the dead body as fuel for regeneration has thus often been marshaled for destructive political and nationalist ends. At the same time, in the modernist period, it also overlapped with other, less aggressive theories of culture and violence, such as those emerging under the rubric of anthropology.

Both Sigmund Freud and James Frazer, to name two important figures, argued that to understand the beginnings of religion, social hierarchy, and (for Freud) psychic processes, one must return to scenes of violence, which function as the foundation stones for cultural development. For Freud, in such works as *Totem and Taboo* (1913) and *Moses and Monotheism* (1937), what is perhaps most surprising is the sense of immediacy he lends to these imagined origins. Thus he writes that "the Christian communion," which he depicts as a pantomimic reiteration of an initial patricide, "is essentially a fresh elimination of the father, a repetition of the guilty deed."[18] Past violence is both dead and alive, forgotten and relived, as Freud sees a strong affective connection between a violent past shrouded in centuries of myth and denial and a ritualized present that brings these buried deeds into flourishing presence. *Moses and Monotheism*, a quite outlandish text, makes its case for a reinterpretation of the Exodus narrative by imagining that the Moses of the Bible is really an amalgamation of two Moses figures, the first of whom was killed by the Jews. In their act of violent revolt, they threw off the Mosaic tyranny, but later, feeling remorse, they reinstated their former leader via the Exodus tradition. Even at the precise moment when communal, national, and religious identity is being solidified, Freud thus argues, what lies beneath these formations is an old murder. The fact that cultures deliberately erase their most shameful violent acts, even as they construct themselves out of the residue of such violence, forms a basic premise of Freud's argument about the dramatic creation of robust religious and cultural traditions.

Totem and Taboo has a similar, if more generalized, story line. Here Freud claims that the totem represents a developed iteration of an absolutely primal, formative act, the ceremonial meal in which the brothers eat the father whom they have banded together to kill. The primitive brothers rebel against the authority of the father, making the decision to murder and consume him in order to absorb and appropriate his power:

> The violent primal father had doubtless been the feared and envied model of each one of the company of brothers: and in the act of devouring him they accomplished their identification with him, and each one of them acquired a portion of his strength. The totem meal, which is perhaps mankind's earliest festival, would thus be a repetition and a commemoration of this memorable and criminal deed, which was the beginning of so many things—of social organization, of moral restrictions and of religion. (Freud, *TT*, 176)

Of course, such accrual of power cannot be achieved without a price; the murder and its ritualized aftermath become the fuel not only for a whole system of clan organization but also for guilt, and this guilt, in turn, yields a wealth of cultural consequences. In sum, "Society was now based on complicity in the common crime; religion was based on the sense of guilt and the remorse attaching to it;

while morality was based partly on the exigencies of this society and partly on the penance demanded by the sense of guilt" (*TT*, 181).

As if this were not enough by way of residue, Freud also argues that the originary murder and its ritual meal left artistic legacies. For Freud, no deep, important event of a traumatizing nature can occur without becoming buried in layers of transformative repression, and this process of embedding and sublimating becomes the fuel for multiple aesthetic outcomes. Most notable as an artistic retelling of the primal murder is Greek tragedy, especially its preclassical manifestations. Freud's account of the earliest Greek tragedies, and of the evolution of the form, leaves the primal murder as a dark burial ground on top of which the players operate, themselves enacting often terrible crimes which stand in for the original patricide. Even in archaic drama, that is, Freud sees a dynamic exchange between a sense of horrified guilt and a payoff in the form of aesthetic sublimity. For all the murderousness, guilt, pain, and urgent retelling involved in these transactions, that is, Freud argues that joy plays an equal part in the legacy of the primal horde. The ritual feast is a celebration as much as a memorial, a sign of death regretted but also of rejoicing in the tyrant's fall, and this quality of "ambivalence," to use Freud's term, marks the many examples he believes can be discovered in modern culture.

However eccentric Freud's fiction of the brothers killing and consuming the father is, not to mention his retelling of the Exodus saga, these notions nevertheless accord with those of more established cultural anthropologists, like Frazer, whom Freud and others of the modernist period treated as authorities.[19] For Frazer in *The Golden Bough* (1890), the resurrection becomes one example of what he argues is a worldwide and historically extensive phenomenon of spring rites that ingrain and ritualize narratives of past killing. When translated into human, cultural terms, such ceremonies tend to generate recognizable patterns, elaborate, often pantomimic practices that resemble one another, despite local particularities. These narratives—the crucifixion and resurrection story; the rituals Frazer associates with Adonis and other analogous god figures; the father and the horde—are tales not only of cyclical death and rebirth but, more concisely, of murder. Given the wealth of detail that Frazer accumulates in *The Golden Bough*, it is easy to overlook the rather startling fact that his study is an argument, at its core, for murder as the primary cultural deed. And in Jesse Weston's Frazerian work *From Ritual to Romance* (1920), famous today because of the noisy reference Eliot made to it in *The Waste Land*, she argues that the Grail legend derives from archaic practices of life-worship. Weston, like Frazer, emphasizes the bodily quality of the injured king, the blood from his wound leaking into the ground, and the way the structure of the Grail enacts and makes symbolic the often harsh, physical features of the ancient vegetative myths. Georges Bataille, too, contributes to the enchanting tradition in anthropology, in a career-long investigation of the interpenetration and mutuality of death and sexual desire. In his final work, *The Tears of Eros*, he returns (inevitably, even compulsively) to origins, finding in the strange wall drawings in the prehistoric Lascaux caves in France a story that, for him, will never really change over the millennia, that death and violence are the partners of sex and ecstasy, a conjunction that he sees unfurling, for instance, in a large swath of Christian painting and sculpture. These are all stories of a primal violence, very striking first for the physicality with which they are endlessly renarrated, and second for the vivid forms of compensatory ceremony that attend them. Whether in figurations of Jesus slowly dying as he hangs on the cross, a trenchant feature of Western iconography (to be supplemented by martyrs like Saint Sebastian); in songs and sculptures of Adonis's body pierced and bleeding; or in Freud's fiction of the father being ingested by his sons, these images emphasize a suspended bodily torture and/or a reabsorption of the murdered body into a new body politic.

If comparative anthropologists like Frazer, Weston, and Freud establish their world theories as a ground soaked in blood, many of the classical scholars of the period were equally interested in excavating a violent subtext to the familiar classical tradition. Greek drama, as even the most cursory familiarity will suggest, is utterly consumed with hyperbolically violent deeds and consequences, and it is not coincidental that a number of the most influential theorists of generative violence in the twentieth century (such as Bataille and René Girard) took Greek drama as its purest expressive form. From Homer to Euripides, the literary history of Greece manifestly tells a tale of the most brutal physical and psychic limits to which humans can be pressed. Thus it is surprising that in the nineteenth century, the Greeks were often imagined as cool and refined, representatives of the pinnacle of civilization—in aesthetics, emblems of symmetry and grace; in politics, of democracy and rationality; in philosophy, of idealism and the quest for perfection.[20] It was, in a sense, the goal of early-twentieth-century classicists to unsettle this benign image by bringing into focus a more confused, archaic picture of Greek religion and art as a legacy of far older, murkier traditions. Jane Harrison and her colleague Gilbert Murray at Cambridge, for instance, helped to reignite interest in Greek culture and history precisely because they offered up a picture of the Greeks as a product of Asiatic and Egyptian influences, matrilineal traditions, chthonic gods, and a certain strange otherness in conflict with the Olympian order that, in their view, would only belatedly (and tenuously) come to dominate the Greek consciousness.[21] Over the course of several volumes on Greek religion and art, Harrison in particular created an image of the Olympian pantheon as a messy amalgamation of earlier, often foreign influences, a kind of temporary hold on the sprawling, changing, and mysterious terrain of divine/human interaction. And we might note that Nietzsche, too, a very different kind of classicist, stressed the power of Dionysian excess over controlled aesthetic effects, of violence and brute reckonings over perfection and tranquility. In *The Birth of Tragedy* (1872), where he makes his case against the values that the nineteenth century had ascribed to Greek culture—the Apollonian virtues, as he dubs them—Nietzsche elevates instead the sheer terror of the human reckoning with violence and death. Nietzschean theory was, for all its eccentricity, of its moment, tending toward the revelation of violence as the critical ingredient in understanding and appreciating the aesthetic sublimity of the ancient world.

Occupying a rather different place in the cultural landscape from late-nineteenth-century classicists and anthropologists—but indebted to similar theoretical models of violence—are a host of revolutionary thinkers, from anarchists (see chapter 2) to Irish insurrectionists (see chapter 3) to syndicalists. Here, we might consider just one emblematic case. Georges Sorel wrote on a variety of political topics throughout his life, but particularly germane here is his book-length *Reflections on Violence* (1908, first English translation 1914), a work which has recently experienced a critical revival, in part for its newly appreciated influence on English modernism.[22] Mobilized, like many French socialists, during the Dreyfus Affair, Sorel was an activist in a range of causes, and one of the foremost voices for the syndicalist movement in France in the early years of the century. Above all, Sorel is remembered for promoting, as one intellectual biographer puts it, a "cult of violence."[23] Sorel believed in the power of myth in guiding and ennobling the violent overthrow of the oppressive state. Above all, in the first decade of the century, when *Reflections on Violence* was written, it was the general strike that Sorel most effusively championed. The strike held mythic connotations and powers for Sorel—indeed it was itself a form of myth, "a body of images capable of evoking instinctively all the sentiments which correspond to the different manifestations of the war undertaken by Socialism against modern society"—portending the first jolt that would inaugurate the destruction of the capitalist state.[24] As he puts it in his "Apology for Violence," a coda to *Reflections on Violence*, added in 1913:

> The conception of the general strike, engendered by the practice of violent strikes, admits the conception of an irrevocable overthrow. There is something terrifying in this which will appear more and more terrifying as violence takes a greater place in the mind of the proletariat. But, in undertaking a serious, formidable, and sublime work, Socialists raise themselves above

our frivolous society and make themselves worthy of pointing out new roads to the world. (Sorel, 298–99)

Sorel is especially revealing here for his use of terms like "sublime" and "make themselves worthy," notions that align him with the Enlightenment history against which his work would seem to stand, but, more to the point, suggest a spirit of enchanting. It is violence that will render the overthrow sublime, transforming its participants.

Yet all forms of violence are not equal in Sorel's estimation; specifically, Sorel defines a type of oppressive action that comes from the top, which he calls "force," and which he distinguishes from working-class violence. Sorelian force differs from Weil's, though both writers want to convey by it a sense of the enormous power the governing few can wield to terrify the citizenry. For Sorel, force belongs to the state—it is the pure power of modern governments, backed by the police, the military, the press, wealth—while violence belongs to those who rebel, the workers, the people, the strikers. "I think it would be better," he writes, "to adopt a terminology which would give rise to no ambiguity, and that the term *violence* should be employed only for acts of revolt; we should say, therefore, that the object of force is to impose a certain social order in which the minority governs, while violence tends to the destruction of that order" (Sorel 195, italics in original). Sorel's notion of a malign force emanating from the state stands uneasily next to his contemporary Max Weber's view, which is that the state is founded upon its entitlement to violence. As Weber wrote in 1915, "The state is an association that claims the monopoly of the *legitimate use of violence*, and cannot be defined in any other manner" (italics in original).[25] Sorel's dichotomizing of violence and force provides an interesting counterposition to this seemingly neutral, descriptive claim, insofar as it represents a contemporary theory for imbuing violence—in its very essence— with positive attributes, the resort of the disempowered in the face of power; it is necessarily defensible, even heroic. This is a generalized violence, an essential element in the revolutionary process. In this sense, Sorel downplays the role of the individual, concentrating on the broad scope of the general strike and the struggle between force and violence; this is the action of the galvanized masses. Even without the individually lauded or martyred figure, violence itself can be framed as heroic; it is not only a method but also a symbol for the empowerment of the oppressed and the seismic social and economic changes that radical movements of the period sought to manifest. We might think of Sorel's distinction between the force of the state and the violence of its rebels as a way of encoding, within the context of class struggle, a measure of enchantment into the very concept of violence.

At the same time, Sorel's eventual move in the direction of fascism, and the very easy absorption of his ideas into fascist rhetoric in the 1920s and '30s, demonstrates how smooth the move from left to right can be, without significantly altering the adherence to a generative violence defined in mystified terms.[26]

Even this brief overview should, I hope, give a sense of the varied nature of the modernist-era investment in the principle of generative violence, an appeal that has not been limited to the early twentieth century. If later scholars have tended to distance themselves from predecessors like Frazer and Freud (at least in his anthropological guise), and also from the rhetoric of figures like Sorel, we can nevertheless detect close convergences, in the conviction, especially, that cultures cannot do without violence.[27] For critics late and early in the century, what makes violence generative, rather than purely destructive or utilitarian, is the form in which it becomes symbolic. In *Violence and the Sacred* (1972), indeed, Girard argues that cultures depend on violence for their defining narratives and structures. Cultures do not banish violence so much as attempt to control it—to direct it away, via ritual, from their own inner workings and toward specified and containable targets. "The function of ritual," Girard writes, "is to 'purify' violence; that is, to 'trick' violence into spending itself on victims whose death will provoke no reprisals," or, in slightly different terms, "Ritual is nothing more than the regular exercise of 'good' violence" (Girard, 36, 37). The concept of reprisal is at the center of Girard's argument, since what for him defines a stable, living community is its ability to cut off reprisal, to stem the otherwise overwhelming flow of vengeance. Yet such redirecting of dangerous and potentially endless acts of violence is always precarious; "the sacrificial crisis," as Girard names the moment when the distinction between controlled and uncontrolled violence becomes blurred, is always proximate. In reprisal, then, the dichotomies dividing Sorelian enchanted violence from a nonenchantable idea of force disappear.

We might envision the situation Girard describes as a shaky balance between a culture on the brink of limitless bloodshed—as all ordering forces and principles break down, the flood of vicious reprisal unable to be stemmed—and a culture holding back these waves of destruction, creating bulwarks through narrative, ritual, and other ordering forms. So myth, for instance, is born: "Myths are the retrospective transfiguration of sacrificial crises, the reinterpretation of these crises in the light of the cultural order that has arisen from them" (Girard, 64). Tragedy, which mimes and dissects the sacrificial crisis, is another product, its formal structures of antagonism enfolding the back-and-forth nature of reciprocal violence, a dramatization in language of the overwhelming trouble of nondifferentiable violence. And especially, sacredness itself, as it accrues precisely to a violence that remains both hidden and, in redirected form, lavishly on view: "violence," Girard writes, "is the heart and secret soul of the sacred" (Girard, 31). Indeed, he goes so far as to assert the converse—"Any phenomenon associated with the acts of re- membering, commemorating, and perpetuating a unanimity that springs from the murder of a surrogate victim can be termed 'religious'" (Girard, 315)—arguing, in essence, that it is *only* in the connection to primal violence that we can find reli- gion's defining features. Girard frames his argument around premodern cultures, yet parallel claims with an overtly political cast would also be made by revolutionary theorists like Frantz Fanon. Fanon's account of colonial and anticolonial violence— though very much of its moment in the 1950s and early 1960s—nevertheless reflects on the power of enchanting violence more generally. It points backward as insightfully as it points forward.

In *The Wretched of the Earth* (1961), Fanon's most influential and celebrated work, violence is the catalyst for the imagined postcolonial order in many impor- tant respects—not only practically ("for the colonized, violence represents the ab- solute praxis"), but also imaginatively and psychologically.[28] As he writes at the outset of his polemic "On Violence," which opens *The Wretched of the Earth*, "decolonization is always a violent event," because colonization itself is a matter of absolute violence from its initial encounter, and is "continued at the point of the bayonet and under cannon fire" (note the bayonet again, here in one of most fre- quently quoted lines in *The Wretched of the Earth* [Fanon, 1, 2]). Violence spawns violence: this is the law of colonial history, and it is this symmetry of mimetic vio- lence that most consistently characterizes Fanon's analysis. The law of the colonial structure, built on the Manichean divide, is a logic of division and of usurpation; hence it engenders a similar mode in its counterforms, as the colonized draws close, in his aspirations and in his methods, to the colonizer. Fanon repeatedly addresses this Hegelian scheme of parallelism: "The violence of the colonial re- gime and the counterviolence of the colonized balance each other and respond to each other in an extraordinary reciprocal homogeneity" (Fanon, 46). Fanon cre- ates his own prose rhythm out of this oscillating and dialectical structure, in a sense encoding into its cadences the essence of reprisal (a stylistics also employed by Yeats, forty years earlier).

Of course, Fanon's emphasis on violence at the crux of revolution seems nearly tautological;[29] what I want to stress here is the way the theory of anticolonial vio- lence is linked with a more psychological, or even spiritual, image of generativity. Problematically embedded in a masculinist perspective, Fanon places anticolonial violence at the crux of colonial selfhood, or, more properly, colonial masculinity.[30] "[T]he dreams of the colonial subject are muscular dreams," he writes, "dreams of action, dreams of aggressive vitality" (Fanon, 15). Throughout his writings, Fanon was interested in desire, agony, and fantasy, indeed in all things that make one a fully realized person, formed in many cases by the distorting political conditions of empire.[31] Here, he moves quickly past dreaming, as the former victim of violence regains his autonomy and dignity through the infliction of violence against his oppressors: "The colonized man liberates himself in and through violence"; and, again, "At the individual level, violence is a cleansing force. It rids the colonized of their inferiority complex, of their passive and despairing attitude. It emboldens them, and restores their self-confidence" (Fanon, 44, 51). It is this claim about how violence restores and rejuvenates the humanity of the oppressed that represents one of Fanon's most exuberant convictions. Indeed, the infectious, celebratory quality of his rhetoric about the power of violence to remake history, culture, and the individual might be viewed as a signature not only for Fanon but for any theory of generative violence.[32] The fact that there is something deeply paradoxical in all of this—only violence allows for the undoing of the cycle of violence; one finds one's humanity in antihuman acts—is not actually all that surprising (though for Woolf in the 1930s, its logic is devastating). As Bataille renders it, back to the caves: ". . . in these closed depths a paradoxical accord is signed . . ."[33]

The move from Frazer to Fanon marks a broad sweep across the spectrum of enchanted violence, but the terms are elastic. War, especially, calls up the model of enchantment—though, as the above examples suggest, generative violence tends, perhaps inexorably, in universalizing directions. It is a sensibility whose strength and resilience comes from this ability to traverse discrepant events and circumstances. Can the same be said for disenchanted violence? Is there also a persistent idea or cultural crux around the attempt to strip away from the violated body all forms of symbolic valorization? I believe there is. The general principle is this: that violence—especially the rampaging violence of war—demands a style or technology of representation that pinpoints its experience and consequences without justifying or celebrating it. To oppose the mystification and mythologization of violence, texts with such a goal often focus on a moment of bodily injury (and the consequences that ensue from that violation), drawing the reader or viewer back to the moment of destruction, rejecting the thematics of metamorphosis and the idea of a purifying or cathartic violence. Instead, disenchantment looks in the direction of what we might, taking a cue from Hortense Spillers, call "the flesh." In an account of the slave woman's body, Spillers has this to say:

> But I would make a distinction in this case between "body" and "flesh" and impose that distinction as the central one between captive and liberated

subject-positions. In that sense, before the "body" there is the "flesh," that zero degree of social conceptualization that does not escape concealment under the brush of discourse or the reflexes of iconography. Even though the European hegemonies stole bodies—some of them female—out of West African communities in concert with the African "middleman," we regard this human and social irreparability as high crimes against the *flesh*, as the person of African females and males registered the wounding. If we think of the "flesh" as a primary narrative, then we mean its seared, divided, ripped-apartness, riveted to the ship's hole, fallen, or "escaped" overboard.[34] (italics in original).

Flesh, in these terms, effectively comes into narrative only when the body is ruthlessly travestied, as in slavery. Even in less extreme situations, however, the effort to demystify violence often conjures something like Spillers's zero-degree of flesh, which, in its terrible sadness and unmitigated materiality, blots out the rest of human civilization.

We might take as axiomatic, in establishing a thematics of disenchanted violence, a passage from Virginia Woolf's *Three Guineas*, a polemic written in the late 1930s against war and fascism, and also, of equal import for Woolf, against the deep-rooted practice in Western patriarchal culture of aestheticizing and valorizing many forms of cruelty and suppression:

Here then on the table before us are photographs. The Spanish Government sends them with patient pertinacity about twice a week. They are not pleasant photographs to look upon. They are photographs of dead bodies for the most part. This morning's collection contains the photograph of what might be a man's body, or a woman's; it is so mutilated that it might, on the other hand, be the body of a pig. But those certainly are dead children, and that undoubtedly is the section of a house. A bomb has torn open the side; there is still a bird-cage hanging in what was presumably the sitting-room, but the rest of the house looks like nothing so much as a bunch of spilikins suspended in mid-air.

Those photographs are not an argument; they are simply a crude statement of fact addressed to the eye . . . When we look at those photographs some fusion takes place within us; however different the education, the traditions behind us, our sensations are the same; and they are violent. You, Sir, call them "horror and disgust." We also call them horror and disgust. And the same words rise to our lips. War, you say, is an abomination; a barbarity; war must be stopped at whatever cost. And we echo your words.

War is an abomination; a barbarity; war must be stopped. For now at last we are looking at the same picture; we are seeing with you the same dead bodies, the same ruined houses.[35]

Woolf's (apparent) assumptions in this passage are manifold: that photography provides unmediated access to truth and reality ("a crude statement of fact addressed to the eye"); that war is a special category of horror against which photography might effectively be marshaled; that the effects generated by this kind of photograph in a viewer will always be consistent with those of Woolf herself (condemning war rather than, say, encouraging the thirst for revenge); and that there are no interesting aesthetics at issue in the photograph, in the viewing of it, or in its depiction in her own prose (but then why the emphasis on the birdcage, an object that seems to call attention to its own incongruity and symbolic value? And why the simile?).

The passage, in other words, invokes the core contradictions that virtually define the medium of photography: realism versus artifice, transparency versus manipulation, objectivity versus ideology.[36] Woolf may want, at one level, to treat the photographs as direct transfusions of violent reality, free of form (as of politics), yet even in the case of photographs like these, which fall at the far end of the aesthetic spectrum, she cannot avoid calling up a welter of questions about photography and truth that have stalked the photographic image from its inception in the mid-nineteenth century. One thinks, for instance, of the controversy surrounding James Fenton's shifting of the cannonballs in the "valley of death" that gave his famous Crimean War photographs their name.[37] Are they merely props, subject to manipulation to suit the needs of the photograph? Or is the haunting reality of war, which gives the pictures their power, belied by such artistic maneuvers? These are serious provocations, especially when the subject is photographs of war and other human crises. Susan Sontag raised them throughout her writing, as in her final work, the ruminative and partially self-corrective *Regarding the Pain of Others* (2003), which comes back over and over to the notion that it is deeply suspect to imagine photography as a direct and value-free conduit to the truth of war and suffering.[38] For Sontag, there are always two fundamental problems in thinking that photography can provide the Western, liberal viewer unmediated and benign access to the horrors saturating much of the world: the inevitable subjectivity of the photographic process (including not only its creation and development, but the settings and forms through which it is viewed) and the equally problematic situation of the person looking (including the voyeuristic satisfactions that might inhere in the desire to witness other people's painful experiences). Sontag is impatient, for instance, with the idea that there could or should be a form of war photography that eschews aesthetics.

But is there really an insuperable contradiction between recognizing beauty and being privy to the display of other people's suffering? In the passage from *Three Guineas*, Woolf seems to be aware of an aesthetic sensibility even in these pictures. The parallels she suggests between human bodies and houses (both with sides ripped off) suggest as much, as does her focus on the birdcage; and if we move deeper into *Three Guineas*, we find quite a complex and knowing treatment of photography. What distinguishes the Spanish photographs in *Three Guineas* is not that they are free of aesthetics but that their form of realist, shock-inducing representation elicits a distinct response: "our sensations are the same, and they are violent." Awful violence (war) creates desirable violence (outrage), a process that begins with two people—not necessarily known to one another—"looking at the same picture," or, we might add, reading the same account. Disenchantment relies on an aesthetic that forces violence into a certain kind of view. Its claim on horror and also on form is neither contradictory nor expendable.

For Woolf, photography does what other kinds of representation can perhaps only dimly emulate: it gives violence its due. Pictures like this one, in Woolf's view, encourage a response appropriate to the destruction they depict. Their power is in direct proportion to their attempted transparency—we might call it their "realism," or their identity as "reportage," considering the new resonance of photojournalism in the Spanish Civil War. Such faith in the realist enterprise has of course been fundamentally challenged, all the more in our own era of endless digital manipulation, yet for Woolf, in the desperate situation of the mid-1930s, they are the best available resource for bringing disenchanted war into people's consciousness. At this moment of crisis, photography is given a special role to play in denouncing and resisting war, as its seeming transparency of medium thrusts the sheer visuality of violence in front of the viewer, who is instantly pressed to respond. To describe these in prose, moreover, is to partake of that power. Ripped and mutilated bodies, in this account, have a presence and authority that belie any efforts to make them culturally regenerative, mythic, or symbolically extensive. And yet, the more Woolf stresses that precious ore of injured bodily presence—which, if we believe Scarry, confers powerful meaning—the more she invites the camel of enchantment under the tent of disenchantment, since, after all, her own sense of those bodies is itself transformative (it makes for political activism). Even more centrally, Woolf's depiction of the photographs' genuine and perhaps irreproducible power raises the beguiling question of why she did not reproduce them herself in *Three Guineas*. In the original edition, she included a raft of other photographs, so we can assume that the idea must have crossed her mind. Part of the concern, surely, is authorial control; in presenting them solely as verbal descriptions Woolf remains in charge of their power—leaving uncertain, for instance, the exact nature of their aesthetics, as well as ensuring that her readers will share her response to them. We are guided by Woolf to feel the outrage of war in her terms, to see the pictures, almost literally, through her eyes. They become literary, rather than visual, testaments, and hence their form of disenchantment can be marshaled in the direction Woolf's polemic demands. At the moment of the text's publication, indeed, such visual statements might actually have raised a feeling of fury (rallying the English to help in the fight against the fascists), which, of course, is what the Spanish government hoped to encourage. Given what Woolf believes to be the disenchanting power of the photographs, to include them risks turning the text's argument over to them. This risk becomes more acute if we consider Woolf's own formal eccentricity in *Three Guineas*, which is anything but realist. *Three Guineas* can claim to form part of the campaign to expose and condemn the violence of war, but it does not belong to the documentary mode of the Spanish photographs, and hence, in a certain way, competes against them. In the end, the question may be one of medium; Woolf attributes an insistently disenchanting style to the photographs, which can then be contained within her own, more unevenly patterned text.

Woolf takes the Spanish photographs as her springboard, but photography had been marshaled in the antiwar cause well before Franco began bombing civilians and had formed part, in earlier contexts too, of a larger political and representational project. In considering the wholesale effort to disenchant violence, for instance, we might consider the figure of Ernst Friedrich, who deployed the power of the photographed flesh in the interwar period toward a complete condemnation of war. Born to a working-class family in 1894, Friedrich became radicalized largely in response to the war, which sickened and horrified him, and in which he refused to serve. A sometime socialist, communist, and anarchist, in trouble with the authorities from his early years and eventually a refugee from the Nazis, Friedrich was politically engaged in diverse radical causes over several decades. The principle he upheld most consistently throughout his political life was an adamant opposition to war and militarism, a position displayed in the most notable artifact of his career, his 1924 book *War against War!*. The monograph, published simultaneously in four languages (German, English, and French, with a fourth language in accordance with place of publication), at a time in Germany of remilitarization and a rising tide of nationalist revisionism about the war, makes its pacifist case via shocking documentary photographs from the war. Juxtaposed against such images as sketches of children's toys, propagandist slogans, and photos of various public figures on holiday, and counterpoised by ironic captions, come the startling photographs: horribly mutilated bodies on the battlefield, mass graves, ruined architecture, the skeletons of starved Armenian children, all in grisly focus. But most shocking are the culminating photos, close-ups of the mutilated faces of former soldiers. These extreme disfigurements seem as far from the aesthetic on the representational spectrum as one can go: nearly unviewable, they are effective in part because they insistently remind us not only of the ghastliness of extreme injury to the flesh, but also of the injured person's humanity.

Friedrich, like Woolf, believed in the sheer power of such visual confrontations, and he felt that to strip away (the metaphor is his) all layers of false ideology from the truth of bodily violation and mutilation would have real consequences. From our own vantage point, it seems clear that Friedrich's pacifist agenda strongly marks how a viewer approaches his photographic archive—his strategies for staging and ironizing the photographs, as well as his choice of these particular images (many of them apparently obtained from medical facilities for maimed soldiers and hence offering a seemingly scientific objectivity) are effective, but they are not neutral. In presenting the photographs, however, he adeptly evokes an *ideal* of transparency, admitting no sense of aesthetic structuring on his part, and calling on the images' powerful directness to combat all forms of celebrating, heroizing, and sanctifying war.[39] "The pictures in this book," he declares, in his brief, manifesto-style introduction, "show records obtained by the inexorable, incorruptible, photographic lens . . . And not one single man of any country whatsoever can arise and bear witness against these photographs, that they are untrue and that they do not correspond to realities."[40] In both Woolf's and Friedrich's accounts, photographs of horrendous injury make special claims on their viewers, but the first claim is that we look, something not always easy to do. Interestingly, Bataille concludes his *Tears of Eros*, a work dedicated to a version of enchanted violence, with an archive of photographs that are nearly impossible to bear, from a 1905 torture, in which the prisoner is eviscerated while still alive. Bataille is enthralled by the photographs, one of which he owned, in part because of the man's transfigured expression ("This photograph had a decisive role in my life," he writes; "I have never stopped being obsessed by this image of pain, at once ecstatic (?) (*sic*) and intolerable" (*Tears*, 206)). In these pictures, Bataille reaches the culmination of his life's work on eroticism and death (here unimaginably violent death), "the instant where the contraries seem visibly conjoined, where the religious horror disclosed in sacrifice becomes linked to the abyss of eroticism, to the last shuddering tears that eroticism alone can illuminate" (*Tears*, 207). And yet, despite these claims, there is something irreducibly disenchanting about these utterly horrendous photographs (the fact, acknowledged by Bataille, that the man had been given opium also raises doubts about his transfiguration thesis). Its placement in a kind of afterword seems appropriate; we may have to close the book.

The torture photos occupy a troubling spot as the final statement on sexual desire and death, but for Friedrich, no such ambiguity stands; he positions his photographs of the dead and maimed as pure witnesses, and this emphasis on testimony—often juxtaposed against artfulness or fiction—was a major feature of postwar culture, insofar as it attempted to look at war directly and unflinchingly, to see its corpses and rubble without its heroics and sacrifice. Perhaps most radical in this regard was the French literary critic Jean Norton Cru, an illuminating figure in the debates about how to remember and canonize the First World War. A combatant in the war, Cru spent the better part of the postwar decade reading every word that had been written about it, and compiling a massive report on these works, which he titled *Témoins* (1929), and which he shortened and self-translated into English as *War Books: A Study in Historical Criticism* (1931).[41] Cru was immediately controversial, in part for his willingness to critique high-profile literary works like Henri Barbusse's *Au Feu* and Remarque's *All Quiet on the Western Front* for what he called their dishonesty and distortion: they relished death and killing, their horrors outpaced even the actual grisliness of combat, they represented yet another myth of war. Cru has a number of criteria on which he bases his evaluation, all of which circulate around the integrity of the witness. We will recognize the accurate accounts, says Cru, because they all tell the same story, unvarnished and direct. There are true stories of war (a very few) and there are false ones (many), and their relative consequences are grave and long-lasting. "These testimonies," he promises, "will teach the sociologists, the psychologists and the moralists that man comes to the point of making war only by a miracle of persuasion and deception practiced on the future combatants, in peace time, by false literature, false history, and false war psychology" (Cru, 19).

Cru's antiwar agenda in some ways aligns him with writers like Woolf, who hoped that a combination of will, activism, and stylistics might help to effect a genuine disenchantment of war, yet his argument represents an extreme edge to the discourse. For Cru, whose dream would be to replace fiction with a pure model of testimony, is fundamentally suspicious of imaginative writing. Accordingly, novels are judged not for their expressive power but for their factual correctness and their utility in furthering an epistemological goal (to know the facts of war). So he writes, "The usefulness of the novels of Barbusse and of Dorgelès, the usefulness of the novel of Remarque—this book is a much more significant case in point—is scarcely more real than the usefulness of a fictitious medical study," and, even more stringently:

Professional writers, gifted with the mob sense, and aware of the unhealthful attraction exerted by the gesture that kills, the bloody knife, and the mutilated corpse, they have played on these things unconscionably while reshaping them artistically, and have served the sheep-like crowd what it has been reading for centuries but colored now after the fashion of the hour. (Cru, 48, 49)

Cru's strategy is to hold up good science (testimony) against bad (Remarque), or, more pointedly, to contrast science (a good medical study) with artifice (a bad one). And it is artifice, ultimately, that is his real antagonist. The issue is not one's stance for or against war; any kind of aestheticizing is dangerous. In this rendition, then, the disenchantment of violence is tantamount to a full rejection of the literary.

For all the hyperbole and strangeness of Cru's view, the tension he registers about what the relation should be between the imperative to disenchant violence (here war) and the medium of expressive writing about it swept wide across postwar culture. *The Waste Land* becomes perhaps the greatest exemplification of such a balancing act, but in other works Eliot holds firmly to the disenchanting position. Most salient as a skeptical riff on war is "Gerontion," a prelude, in some respects, to *The Waste Land* (and Eliot had considered attaching it as a prologue to the longer poem, a scheme rebuffed by Pound), composed between 1917 and 1919 and establishing itself as a commentary on war from the locus of one likely to have a polarized perspective—either to enchant through the haze of nostalgia, or to mock youthful self-indulgence. The old man, as it happens, defines himself first and foremost as one who stayed out of war, a noncombatant. A series of not/nor lines in the opening stanza establishes his credentials in such terms, a listener more than an actor, yet with a richly physical sense of what war is[42]:

> Here I am, an old man in a dry month,
> Being read to by a boy, waiting for rain.
> I was neither at the hot gates
> Nor fought in the warm rain
> Nor knee deep in the salt marsh, heaving a cutlass,
> Bitten by flies, fought.[43]

Critics have long noted the combined resonance of the First World War, only just ended—its gates still hot—and ancient precursors, most explicitly the Thermopylae or literal "hot gates" of the Greek wars against the Persians. If the speaker denotes himself by dearth and dryness, the description of war drips with humidity, the warm, repeated vowel sounds (fought, warm, salt, marsh), themselves bounded by the doubly used "fought," suggesting something lush and tropical in the salty scene. Lush but arduous; war is hard work, as evocative of Greek slaves as of the famous warriors. Moreover, if the Spartans' heroism at Thermopylae represents a high point in the mythologization of sacrifice, comradeship, stoicism, and intra-Greek harmony, to be praised and emulated for centuries, Eliot embeds in Geron-tion's monologue another Greek reference, less noted by critics and much less celebratory of war, Aeschylus's *Agamemnon*.[44] It is the herald, just returned from Troy, announcing the imminent arrival of the king. He describes no great feats:

> Were I to tell you of the hard work done, the nights
> exposed, the cramped sea-quarters, the foul beds—what part
> of day's disposal did we not cry out loud?
> Ashore, the horror stayed with us and grew. We lay
> against the ramparts of our enemies, and from
> the sky, and from the ground, the meadow dews came out
> to soak our clothes and fill our hair with lice. And if
> I were to tell of winter time, when all birds died,
> the snows of Ida past endurance she sent down
> or summer heat, when in the lazy noon the sea
> full level and asleep under a windless sky—
> but why live such grief over again?[45]

In Aeschylus's fifth-century Athens, the disenchantment of war—not just any war, the definitive Homeric one—comes as a shock, yet the play holds its course. More than ferocious battles, brilliant stratagems, tragic adventures, or magical journeys, the war is denoted, here in the herald's statement, by its physical hardships and its elemental struggle (needless to say, there are no lice in the *Iliad*!); by the signal Greek malfeasance, repeatedly mentioned in the play, of desecrated altars; by con-cubinage and revenge; and above all by the needless slaughter of the young, whether the beautiful Iphigenia, killed by her father's own hands to make it all possible, or the countless young men of Argos, who had left their towns in proud ships, but "now, in place of the young men,/urns and ashes are carried home/to the houses of the fighters" (*Aeschylus*, 48).

In channeling Aeschylus's dark and cynical reflections on his culture's great war, Eliot sows disenchantment deep into the roots. The old man's mind, acting as a collective or ancestral memory of war and other historical crises ("in the juves-cence of the year/Came Christ the tiger"), carries with it an old story of pointless war, whose consequences are as far-reaching as Western history itself, in many senses the overarching subject of the poem.[46] Indeed, like *Agamemnon*, the poem is fundamentally concerned with aftereffects—all those "issues" whose genealogy is lost in the labyrinthine welter of the past's unpredictable designs, as it is in Gerontion's winding thoughts. In the case of war, those issues seem entirely resistant to any kind of self-satisfaction or Enlightenment rationalizing. The old man's canonical, rhetorical question is an apt one—"After such knowledge, what forgiveness?"—for the possibility of any kind of generative telos emerging from the mess of the recent war (or, perhaps, from any war) seems dim. Even with Christ making a double appearance in the poem, there is no vista of salvation, resurrection, or rebirth; the devouring tiger shares the field with other predators in the pagan tradition ("the shuddering bear"), while the governing natural force in the poem is not of growth or blooming, but of chaos and destruction: wind.[47] The closest the poem comes to the afterlife, indeed, is an infernal reference to some of the most memorably (and perhaps undeservedly) punished of Dante's sinners, the prophets whose heads are twisted backwards, their tears left to drip down their buttocks ("wrath-bearing tree" indeed). What violence and war birth into the world, in other words, is more likely to be wrath and predation than honey of generation.

Eliot's disenchantments of war in "Gerontion" follow complex routes, in keeping with the instability built into the dramatic monologue form, and thematically, the poem is thickly knotted (war being only one of its many subjects of reflection, refracted in the wilderness of mirrors), but others from the First World War generation made it their business, first and foremost, to expose the crude realities of war. Most familiar, for English readers, are soldier-poets like Siegfried Sassoon and Wilfred Owen, who attempted in their lyrics to force war's brutal reality into the purview of wartime and postwar Europe, which continued to sanitize war, and into the genre of poetry, which had for centuries served to glorify it. In the well-known story, these writers attempted to rescript the narrative of the war from one of glorious and heroic self-sacrifice to one of useless and demeaning slaughter. Their poems were created in a spirit of urgency, designed to make a major intervention into the culture's self-understanding; it is a political poetry, which faces off against its readers, demanding that we see war in all its degraded ugliness. Critics, moreover, have focused not only on this reconceptualization of the war from heroic to disgraceful, but also on how that shift actually took place—over more than a decade and in the context of severe postwar convulsions, and with important consequences for other, alternative stories that were marginalized in its wake. The fetishization of war experience (what James Campbell has called "combat gnosticism"), in particular, has laid the ground for a mode of thinking about war that gives primacy to soldiers—as its victims and its narrators—hence often obscuring the experience of the enormous number of war victims whose suffering takes different forms (targeted civilians, refugees, prostitutes, children).[48] These have been important and corrective discussions, yet there remains something irreducible and compelling about the war writers' endeavor to pit the unimaginable violence of war against its enchantments.

Indeed, in the canonical literature of the First World War, the disenchanting of violence becomes in many ways the primary work of the writer.[49] Sassoon, perhaps more than any of the other famous soldier-poets, consistently hammers away, in poem after poem, on the troubling consequences of enchanting violence. His poetry works feverishly to expose and ironize the conventional discourses that glorify and romanticize war. So "Glory of Women," one of the most canonically angry of his works, pits a naively enchanting set of conventions (the "worship" of decorations, "chivalry," the "thrill" of war narratives, martyrdom, maternal pride) against the disenchanting facts of "war's disgrace," soldiers being "killed," fear and panic, and, most centrally, corpses and blood: "You can't believe that British troops 'retire,'" the poet scornfully accuses his female addressees, "When hell's last horror breaks them, and they run, /Trampling the terrible corpses—blind with blood."[50] That women are held partially responsible for perpetuating the fatal and callous deceptions that turn men's bodies into corpses increases the demystifying agenda of the poem; even gender itself—perhaps the ultimate, underlying institution sustaining the romance of war—is repudiated as just another violently consequential fiction. The poem offers a jagged critique of enchanted violence as both a creator and consequence of gender conventions, even without letting go of its own misogyny. Sassoon's war poetry, by and large, keeps disenchantment front and center, though we might note that his memoir—the more famous and widely read of his works in his lifetime and for decades thereafter—is more equivocal. Its portrait of upper-class, stoic, military masculinity strains, to some degree, against his own war poetry.

All of the other well-known First World War poets, and especially Wilfred Owen, structure their works around a visceral disenchantment; at the same time, they incorporate elements of enchantment into their verse. A poem like Owen's "Dulce et Decorum Est," to take perhaps the most widely read of the English war poems, exemplifies the pattern.[51] The poem generates its force from a division of war language into two opposing styles: the generative mode of the Horatian ode, in which war is glorified and made symbolic, and the ruthlessly disenchanted mode of the contemporary poet, in which war is figured through its pitiful soldier victims. When the poet turns angrily on the reader in its final stanza, having depicted a gas attack that choked and strangled a soldier amidst a group of bedraggled, retreating comrades, leaving its narrator shell-shocked and aghast, he gives a name to the ideal of generative violence against which his poem stands: "the old Lie."

"Dulce et Decorum Est," along with many other poems in the same family, exposes the betrayal enacted in all such old lies, making the dichotomy between sacralized violence and the ugly reality of war its central object.

Owen mocks and condemns a classical tradition of glorifying and aestheticizing war, but his poem makes its own use of some powerfully enchanting images. We might note several arresting phrases along these lines: "Drunk with fatigue," "An ecstasy of fumbling," "vile, incurable sores on innocent tongues," even the accusatory Latin line, which includes the lovely word "dulce." At these moments— and throughout the poem—Owen absorbs and reconstitutes many figures often associated with the old lie: states of exaltation engendered by war, traditional notions of innocence and purity, soothing rhythms concealing harsh realities. Indeed, the more searing the visual tableau, the more thickly his metaphors are pasted, as for instance when the choking man is depicted as "flound'ring like a man in fire or lime" and "As under a green sea." Visually compelling, these images do not represent a direct or simple transcription of a body in agony; they require real imaginative reach. Perhaps most significant is Owen's repeated use of drowning imagery. Throughout the poem's ABAB rhyme scheme, there are no repeated words except for the final rhymed pair in the middle stanza:

> Dim, through the misty panes and thick green light,
> As under a green sea, I saw him drowning.
>
> In all my dreams, before my helpless sight,
> He plunges at me, guttering, choking, drowning.

For all its terrors, drowning adds something muted and consoling in these lines. By comparison, say, with "flound'ring," "guttering," or "choking," drowning suggests a kind of peace, and is redolent of many literary conventions. I do not think we could say that Owen enchants violence, but his poem exults in its ability to make the language of enchantment do the seemingly contradictory work of exposing and rejecting violence.

One thing recurs repeatedly in poems with a disenchanting agenda: the deployment of carefully chosen images of bodily rupture and pain. From the rolling eyes and "guttering, choking, drowning" face of the gas victim in "Dulce," to the "legless" veteran, "sewn short at elbow," in Owen's "Disabled," to the "muscled bodies charred" in his "Miners," to the German soldier in "Glory of Women" whose "face is trodden deeper in the mud," to Isaac Rosenberg's "We heard his weak scream/We heard his very last sound,/And our wheels grazed his dead face" in "Dead Man's Dump," the appearance of a body in a state of acute and terrible mutilation is a critical feature of these lyrics.[52] Clearly, images of bodily injury and decomposition are meant to shock and activate the reader, along the lines of Woolf's reaction to the photographs sent by the Spanish government. Just as clearly, they work symbolically—Owen's gas victim has a hanging face, "like a devil's sick of sin," and Rosenberg begins "Dead Man's Dump" by invoking "many crowns of thorns"— even as they are presented as an argument against symbol (Owen, 117; Rosenberg, 81). Too, critics have recently voiced a wariness about the impulse to become the spectator of such violent injurings, even among well-meaning readers ready to be skeptical of war.[53] The point, then, is not that the famous antiwar poems transcribe violence with pure transparency (we know that is never possible) or that they eschew figurative language (they are poems, after all) or even that the impulse to read them is unqualified by a certain voyeurism (how could one ever prove that?), but rather that they remain committed to the idea that poetry must expose rather than elevate the violence of war. Violence is meant to linger in the imagination and from there to compel change, but it is not the germ of culture, the force for national uplift, or the sign of sublimity. In *All Quiet on the Western Front*, in the interwar years posed as a German prose companion to the developing canon of English war lyrics, Remarque offers his version of this commitment. As the novel progresses in its steady course of death, loss, and imaginative diminishment, the earth—site of nurture and fertility early in the novel—comes to represent a scene of extinctive degeneration:

> The rifles are caked, the uniforms caked, everything is fluid and dissolved, the earth one dripping, soaked, oily mass in which lie yellow pools with red spiral streams of blood into which the dead, wounded, and survivors slowly sink.
>
> . . . Our hands are earth, our bodies are clay and our eyes are pools of rain. We do not know whether we still live.[54]

We might take that muddy, swallowing swamp as disenchantment's answer to the fecundity of enchantment's growth motif. Its signal mode is devolution, and blood—the magic ore—here becomes just one more garish bodily liquid.

The Waste Land

Both the enchanted and the disenchanted modes of imagining violence pivot on war, the most extravagant and devastating expression of violence that most cultures undergo. Perhaps more than any other field of experience, that is, war tends to invite the thematics that surround generativity, and to do so in dichotomizing terms. In Homer's *Iliad*, we find an originary language of war as generator of aesthetic productivity:

> He dropped then to the ground in the dust, like some black poplar,
> which in the land low-lying about a great marsh grows
> smooth trimmed yet with branches growing at the uttermost tree-top:
> one whom a man, a maker of chariots, fells with the shining
> iron, to bend it into a wheel for a fine-wrought chariot,
> and the tree lies hardening by the banks of a river.[55]

As with the general Homeric dictum that wars are fought to give singers their subjects, the relation here between art and death in war is intimate. The warrior's body is likened to the tree which in turn becomes part of the chariot, a "fine-wrought" work of art, and, in circular fashion, an important war tool. So organic is the enchantment of violence here as to be almost invisible (though we might note that violence will appear in visibly disenchanting form later in the epic, when Achilles descends, with wild brutality, on the battlefield). In the early twentieth century, as we have seen, a robust discourse of disenchantment attempted to propel its readership in the opposite direction from what the poplar/chariot simile suggests, to take apart what Homer so exquisitely aligns (war, bodies, art, productivity). Yet we have also seen how interconnected and mutually dependent enchanted and disenchanted violence really are, aligned, especially, when they come close to the magic ore of blood, or when they consider concepts like drowning, which touch both on unredeemable nastiness and on the urge toward creation.

Exemplary and iconic, Eliot's *The Waste Land* comes to express all of these motifs. The poem contemplates both the ideal and the drawbacks of enchanting violence; it is simultaneously a reflection on violence in general and a primary work in the literary and cultural history I have been presenting. Critics have read *The Waste Land* as many things, including, of course, as an aesthetic reckoning with the war. The thematics and imagery of the war underlie the poem at many levels, beginning with its memorial opening and encompassing its burning cities, soldier songs, shell-shocked London citizenry, ubiquitous dead, burial phobias, even the rats.[56] The poem has been personalized, historicized, and deconstructed, as it asks to be. But it has never been understood as providing a robust theory of violence and art, encompassing but not limited to the war, a deeply considered and sensitive engagement with those dominant cultural approaches to imagining violence I am calling enchantment and disenchantment.[57] The enchantment of violence is both the product and the subject of *The Waste Land*, and yet the poem, with its famously contradictory style, cannot easily glory in the tradition of Western literary culture it elicits, for it also recoils from the brutality that sustains that edifice.[58]

The Waste Land disperses and disseminates a complex language of aestheticized violence, but the configuration is quietly condensed in one interlude, "Death by Water":

> Phlebas the Phoenician, a fortnight dead,
> Forgot the cry of gulls, and the deep sea swell
> And the profit and loss.
>
>   A current under sea
> Picked his bones in whispers. As he rose and fell
> He passed the stages of his age and youth
> Entering the whirlpool.
>
>   Gentile or Jew
> O you who turn the wheel and look to windward,
> Consider Phlebas, who was once handsome and tall as you.[59]

In accordance with its truncated status among the poem's five acts, "Death by Water" has unique features.[60] Its powerful, unbroken brevity seems to set it off from the rest of the poem (Eliot appended no notes to this section), creating a sense of completeness that the image of the whirlpool also highlights, a drawing inward, as an antidote to the wild outward spiraling that characterizes so much in the poem's diffuse atmosphere.[61] It is the most meditative section in the poem, a rumination on death, something like a reflective, later stage in the mourning process set in motion by the poem's opening, "The Burial of the Dead." Moreover, death by water, prophesied and promised by the poem's ironized seer, Madame Sosostris, functions as an aestheticized and dreamlike contrast with other forms of bodily degradation in the poem. Even if Phlebas enters a deep forgetfulness—metaphor for death, of course—the water and whirlpool have the effect of reconstituting and recalling, as many of the poem's reiterated motifs return here in a softened manner, their edges blunted. The purifying power of the waters, one of the poem's continuous symbolic strands that trace back, in part, to Weston, here takes the form of a gentle dematerializing. The whirlpool acts *in* the poem the way it acts *on* Phlebas, generating a very specific kind of transformation.

In "Death by Water," this ideal of an enchanting transformation of violence and bodily harm to wonder and beauty suggests, in its calm and gestural way, a paradigm for poetic consolation. The body is now a corpse, Phlebas's life is gone, mortality asserts itself, yet the whirlpool, with its whispering tones, offers some kind of satisfying compensation, with the material life of the body, attached as it is to profit and loss, dissolving and passing. More generally, enchantment in *The Waste Land* is at once a magical spell (as the term suggests), a way of figuring the artist's touch, and also, in the case of the Shakespearean motif of enchantment that appears throughout *The Waste Land*, a kind of trickery. The poem is particularly attached to Ariel's song from *The Tempest*. "Those are pearls that were his eyes": the refrain, repeatedly conjured in the poem, gives a succinct language for the large process of moving from the horror of death (here drowning) into the creation of beauty. From a corpse to a pearl, each item of the otherwise bloated and gruesome body is mutated into "something rich and strange," Ariel's arresting phrase for the outcome of water's aestheticizing powers. Or at least its fake powers: what Ariel describes never in fact happens; his song not only analogizes fiction, it is fiction. Like such musical charms, the whirlpool at the swirling center of "Death by Water" presents a force for imagining the process of change as a process of enchantment, and this both correlates and contrasts with the larger discourse of death and rebirth in the poem. On one hand, the materiality of rotting corpses permeates the poem, as readers can hardly fail to notice; on the other hand, to enchant is to imagine the body not in its physical agonies or material decomposition but as an agent of the imagination, for the churning of images into aesthetic wonders.

And yet, we should perhaps pause to note the oddity of this aestheticizing of drowning, a form of death that might be seen as uniquely horrific. In the late poem *Four Quartets*, when Eliot returns to the seas and waters, depicted in rich, ruminative language as agents of both history and the imagination, he is highly aware of the awful human cargo that the oceans have swallowed. "We cannot think," he writes "of a time that is oceanless/Or of an ocean not littered with wastage," and the river, too, "with its cargo of dead negroes," is adrift in the old, terrible crimes of the past.[62] On those occasions when it does reemerge from its watery grave, the drowned body is a grim spectacle, bloated and disgusting, inevitably encrusted with the sea's detritus. In Homer, to return to origins, drowning presented a distinctly dishonorable form of death, and warriors at risk of drowning typically berate the gods for not having given them death on the fields of Troy, where they might have received proper burial and mourning, rather than be lost at sea. Drowning, for Homer's superlative men, is tantamount to invisibility, almost not to have existed in the first place. Or drowning can be reckoned as all too material. In

Eliot's manuscript notes, he had drafted a "Dirge" in which the character Bleistein, known to readers from "Burbank with a Baedeker, Bleistein with a Cigar," makes an appearance as a cadaver under water, and this fragment, in which crabs and lobsters consume Bleistein's flesh and his gold teeth shine ironically from the sea floor, comes much closer to indexing the ghastliness of drowning than the published text.[63] "Dirge" has a comic tone; yet the unpleasant corporeality and indignity of Bleistein's situation bring Eliot's anti-Semitism to the fore (and hence seem a welcome omission from the published *Waste Land*), at the same time that these features suggest Eliot's own recognition (aided perhaps by his editor Pound) that the drowned body is in fact a quite *in*apt figure for aesthetic power. Or perhaps it is the reverse: by offering the drowned body as site of literary wonder, he points to the virtuosity of this medium, its flex and magic, and to his own conjuring powers. If "Gerontion" manifestly kept within the consciousness of its aging protagonist, with the whirlpool Eliot displays his most magisterial authorial presence. Drowning, it seems, offers up two contrastive possibilities: the disappearance of the body, which Homer deplored, but which allows for the kind of elegiac transformation that Eliot develops in *The Waste Land*, or the reappearance of the corpse, in a scenario that calls up gruesome visions of the body's materiality. Literary history, in its long tradition of figuring drowning, has tended both ways, with elegies that celebrate drowned young men alongside more realist works sickened by the sight of a reemerged corpse. Stephen Dedalus, meditating on Sandymount Strand, gives the two possibilities raw and vibrant life:

> Bag of corpsegas sopping in foul brine. A quiver of minnows, fat of a spongy titbit, flash through the slits of his buttoned trouserfly. God becomes man becomes fish becomes barnacle goose becomes featherbed mountain. Dead breaths I living breathe, tread dead dust, devour a urinous offal from all dead. Hauled stark over the gunwale he breathes upward the stench of his green grave, his leprous nosehole snoring to the sun.
>
> A seachange this, brown eyes saltblue. Seadeath, mildest of all deaths known to man.[64]

Stephen, like Eliot, sees in drowning the essence of transformation (all those "becomes"), balancing in his mind the fleshly, grim prospect of the drowned body with its more lyrical literary complement.[65] For *The Waste Land*, the latter of these must serve; Eliot's omission of Bleistein's corpse indicates the direction the poem will go. The unsightliness of drowning is occluded, in a poetic that abstracts from the body, emphasizing the transformative magic and generative power that, in the whirlpool/poem, the flesh leaves in its wake.

In this poem of sailors and seafarers, the sea holds many associations.[66] Not only is it a site of death and longing and a metaphor for purifying change, but it also represents a set of commercial routes and passages, as suggested by one of its representatives in the poem, the Smyrna merchant.[67] Mr. Eugenides, with his pocket full of currants, functions as a double for Phlebas, also at the mercy of currents, and the sexual suggestion of a weekend at the Metropole has led critics to connect both of these men, along with the hyacinth girl/boy, in a web of homosexual fantasy.[68] Moreover (and perhaps relatedly), Smyrna, the ancient trading city, calls up an image of Asiatic antiquity, pointing backward, that is, to other eras of global trade, colonization, prosperity, and warfare. Smyrna is a place of commerce, both in its ancient and modern renderings. In the period when Eliot was composing *The Waste Land*, it was also a place of intense internal violence. As anyone reading the papers from 1919 until the time of the poem's publication would have known, the fierce fighting between Greeks and Turks, which enveloped what would become the modern nation of Turkey after the dismantling of the Ottoman Empire, reached a peak in the city of Smyrna. Not only was there a Greek occupation and combat in the streets, but Smyrna also became a locus for the policy of forced migration of Greeks and Turks into their respective nations. If the enmity of Greece and Turkey had been ferociously alive for a century, Smyrna represented one of its most virulent contemporary embodiments. Eliot himself took a keen interest in these events, writing a letter to the *Daily Mail* in 1923 in which he praised the paper's coverage of the war in Turkey.[69] Here, then, was a location that dramatized the chaos and spiraling violence still being unleashed by the First World War as the old imperial order disintegrated.

And one more thing: Smyrna is a reputed birthplace of Homer, as Eliot certainly knew.[70] For Homer—the presiding genius of Western literature in general, and of the poetry of war and the seas in particular—to be associated with the fraught city of Smyrna is a hint at what *The Waste Land* perhaps always wants to promise, that aesthetic potency will develop directly out of real-world agony. In the years immediately following the war, Homer's connection to Smyrna and to Troy must have provided a powerful and poignant association, for the notion (widely held among classicists) that the real "first world war" was the Trojan War suggested an almost infinite historicity in the cycle of violence, in which war was increasingly intertwined with global commerce, but also, for Eliot, with artistic payoff. If some of Eliot's most powerful influences and closest friends— most notably Pound—had become virtually obsessed with the sinister intertwining of war and trade, emphasizing in particular the diabolical persona of the Jewish financier, cast as the villain of the world's recent catastrophes, the

Smyrna merchant sets those intersections in a different light. Certainly, there is something off-color about him, with his casual attitude and demotic language. And yet the Smyrna merchant holds in his person the explosive and terrible history of modern nations; he simultaneously brings the complex legacy of modern war into view and obscures the picture, as the poem ultimately pursues its own goal of erecting new monuments on the site of still-smoldering ruins. Viewed in this way, the Smyrna merchant's mutation into Phlebas in the following section, himself soon to be metamorphosed via watery transformation into something rich and strange, seems a kind of willful relief, an aesthetic forgetting of modern calamity, or perhaps a signal that even such intransigent conflicts as the legacies of hatred left by the Ottoman Empire can be amalgamated into the imaginative project of enchantment. In this fantasy, neither capitalism, which now rules the waves (supplanting and supplementing the British navy), nor internecine war, in which geography is breached by violence, is immune to the power of death by water.

The whirlpool may create an inward spiral, a vast embrace and ingathering vortex, but *The Waste Land* opens with burial in the ground, and it is the problem of the corpse, both buried and distressingly present, that in many ways requires Eliot to invoke the sea as a contrastive death fantasy. In the poem's celebrated opening, Eliot sets the stage for a rumination on the land and the dead. The communal mourning of a people emerging from war is aligned with universal motifs that reframe the pain of immediate loss and individual grief, with an anthropological and generative cast. The lines (so different in spirit from the drunken brothel scene that had inaugurated the draft version) convey multiple valences on the way death and land conjure one another, including the vegetative structure of resurrection and life-worship alluded to in Eliot's opening note to the poem, in which he references Frazer and Weston. The lines invoke the parched earth which nevertheless will breed, the land impregnated by dead bodies (no-man's-land made general), and the cruel discomfort and pain of bringing blossoms out of such a soil. In all of this, the sadness associated with loss, death, burial, and the recent war is hitched to the inevitable cycling of the seasons, poignant precisely because it cannot be avoided or altered. Of course, it will not be long before the metaphor of death leading to new flowers takes comic shape in the blooming corpse:

> There I saw one I knew, and stopped him, crying, "Stetson!
> "You who were with me in the ships at Mylae!
> "That corpse you planted last year in your garden,
> "Has it begun to sprout? Will it bloom this year? (*TWL*, 69–72)

The absurdist tone here differs from the mournful concerns that make up the April lines, but in other ways the passage marks a continuity. Ever since Fussell discussed the trope of the blooming corpse in 1975, it has seemed axiomatic that the red poppies of Flanders' bloody fields lie at the base of Eliot's imagery, a mordant ironizing of the truism that the violence of war can be germinative.[71] Other wars are present too, the cumulative, ongoing sense of war enfolding and accruing individual conflicts, as suggested by the fleeting appearance in the poem of the battered Coriolanus from Shakespeare's play, who carries the scars of old wars on his back. In *The Waste Land*, moreover, we have the Great War's bones and rats, and if these bones do not sing or chirp as loudly as they will in a later poem like "Ash Wednesday," still "the grass is singing/Over the tumbled graves" (*TWL*, 386–87). The graves and corpses are abundant here, yet as critics have forcefully noted, they were missing from the local parishes in the years after the war, the bodies of the dead soldiers remaining an absence.[72] Nevertheless, their music in *The Waste Land* remains in keeping with the poem's overall idea that dead bodies must produce song, as Phlebas's body is slowly transformed in "Death by Water," and as the whole achievement of the poem is cast in terms of the transforming of old wrecks into new wonders.

Standing on the cusp of the contrasts between sea and land, transformative creation and terrible disintegration, is Jean Verdenal, and, behind him, another iteration of the First World War's narrative of violent death. Verdenal's status in *The Waste Land* has been much discussed by critics, beginning with John Peter's argument in 1952, immediately suppressed by Eliot's estate, that *The Waste Land* represents a homoerotic love song and tribute to Eliot's friend Verdenal, "mort aux Dardanelles," to whom Eliot dedicated *Prufrock and Other Observations*. As with later queer-theoretical iterations, this argument makes the case that Verdenal's death functioned as a traumatic catalyst for Eliot, inaugurating his mental breakdowns, partially unleashing a crisis of sexual ambivalence, and requiring articulation in oblique and redirected language. Whatever one may think about Verdenal's role in Eliot's psychosexual development, the image of a young man, full of promise, whose life is cut off by the war was a powerful and ubiquitous trope in the period of *The Waste Land*.[73] Eliot's decision in 1925 to append the phrase "Mort aux Dardanelles" to his *Prufrock* dedication, for instance, suggests a perceptiveness about such associations, as Eliot puts his own stamp on the familiar signifier of the tragically dead young men. Often associated metaphorically with flowers, not only the poppies of Flanders, but also such overdetermined Greek species as narcissus and hyacinth, these men were inevitably described as the "flower of manhood" (also as "lads"), their deaths often mourned within the framework of the pastoral. The war period marked a moment when the Romantic propensity to conjoin the English countryside with an ethos of masculinity seemed reborn in the person of the male flower, the lost youth, the tragically self-sacrificing soldier, emblem of the Lost Generation.[74] At some level, that is, Verdenal's death in the disastrous Gallipoli campaign provokes one of the central issues in *The Waste Land*: the romantic allure of death being fruitful, perhaps even death by water—anything rather than mud.

In *The Waste Land*, there is a real dread of the soil as the ultimate (or premature) home for the body, and, indeed, this rendering taps into a common war fixation. Notwithstanding the poem's repeated warning to "fear death by water," what the majority of soldiers in the First World War feared was death in the ground, or, worse, death via the ground. In surveying writing from the trenches, one finds a powerful, widespread, shared anxiety about being buried alive, and, more generally, the image of the dismembered corpse filling in the land is ubiquitous in the war's many representations. Again, Eliot's poem seems divided, on one hand suggesting a poetic enactment of burial and regrowth, where the possibility of recovering and blooming after the war is painful but possible (recalling Brooke's "The Soldier"), and on the other hand offering an alternative fantasy of consigning the body not to the ground but to the sea, where the whirlpool, in its whispering ways, will dematerialize the body, making art out of organs, pearls out of eyes. In fact, these two forms, drowning and burial, each reach out toward the possibility of enchantment, which is suggested not only by the whirlpool, but also by several other images. Most central is color, a riveting site of intensity. There are many colors in the poem—white, brown, ivory, gold, green, orange, black, and red (this last particularly pronounced)—and these form part of the dense sensorium that characterizes *The Waste Land* at every stage.

But there is something special and unique about one color, and that is violet. It is entirely adjectival, for one: the word is used four times in the poem, twice in quick succession, and each time to modify a certain kind of ethereal noun and to describe something in the atmosphere:

> At the violet hour, when the eyes and back
> Turn upward from the desk, when the human engine waits
> Like a taxi throbbing waiting . . . (*TWL*, 215–17)

> At the violet hour, the evening hour that strives
> Homeward, and brings the sailor home from sea,
> The typist home at teatime . . . (*TWL*, 220–22)

> What is the city over the mountains
> Cracks and reforms and bursts in the violet air . . . (*TWL*, 370–71)

> And bats with baby faces in the violet light
> Whistled, and beat their wings . . . (*TWL*, 379–80).

The hour, air, and light: each iteration attempts to capture something both precise and uncertain in the nature of the moment. In the first two examples, the violet hour is twilight, a time of transitions and transformations, literally, as day turns to night, and figuratively, as a moment of hovering between one mode of existence and the next, a thick and tense anticipatory pause, as indicated by the image of the human engine throbbing—a vast being comprising the whole working city.[75]

Indeed, the violet hour is a time of enchantment, in the sense I have been developing. The hour in question is not going to bring the valiant sailor home to his beloved and long-suffering wife, but the young man carbuncular to the cramped accommodation of the typist, heralding a scene famous for its depiction of depleted, degraded, modern sexuality, a bored encounter which resembles a rape, in which the victim is barely involved, sensorially or psychically, in her own "folly" (*TWL*, 253). Yet the word "violet" does add luster and shine to the sordid occasion, if only momentarily. Its use is partly mock-heroic and ironic, but it is also real; its beauty and resonance transform the lines, enhancing the sense of both anticipation and tragedy in the scene. When air and light and the hour are violet—the color of sorcery in *The Odyssey*, of Mary's poignant humility in Christian iconography, of both mourning and royalty in the modern world, and of brilliant flowers prevalent in springtime throughout the northern hemisphere—they seem piercing, aesthetic, saturated, deepened.[76]

Perhaps most importantly, the word "violet" is so close to "violent" as nearly to become it, and certainly to suggest it. This metonymic affinity is further tightened when we consider that each time "violet" is used, it is at an instant in the poem when violence impends. As with the general concept of enchantment, that is, violetness crops up precisely at those times when some kind of violent reality is ready to be transformed into—and via—the aesthetic experience. The violet air tolls with the apocalyptic sound of bells and the explosions of warfare; the violet light is the light of terror, after and before such reverberations, the place of burning cities, and also of bats and hysteric strains; the violet hour is a time of compressed urban rage, the human energy beastlike in its containment, and also of impending sexual assault. "A sudden blow," Yeats proclaimed for the moment of rape and knowledge and loss, but here the moment comes more slowly, as part of an ongoing process of transformation, a time of flickering transition and pause, yet it holds its own piercing and intense qualities. For *The Waste Land*, the nature of violet is to usher in violence, to herald or represent it; but it is also to soften and beautify it. Indeed, violetness is perhaps the ideal emblem for enchantment at its most enriching; its transforming energy is all in the direction of the aesthetic, forging an exceptionally sensitive kind of perception.

Other moments of sexual violation, however, seem depleted of this violet vibrancy; one thinks, for instance, of Lil, whose narrative of decay and reproductive trauma appears in its own flickering light, amidst the closing rituals of pub life. On one hand, the scene in the pub where Lil is featured has its lyrical aspects, especially in the goodnight sequence, a kind of Joycean melody. The "hot gammon," perhaps alluding to the aborted child, adds a gothic element to the scene, and this, along with the bartender's reiterated call and the catty female rivalry, makes for a chaotic and partly comic tone. And yet, Lil's body is the subject of suffering and horrible manipulation, as "them pills I took, to bring it off" have left her aged and sickened, and this, we learn, came only after other devastating reproductive experiences: "(She's had five already, and nearly died of young George.)" (*TWL*, 159, 160). Eliot, with his own personal and marital history of psychological treatment, gives a vague suggestion of near-criminal neglect and indifference on the part of the medical industry, represented here by the chemist, and, more generally, presents Lil as a woman whose physical and sexual life remains entirely at the mercy of men, her soldier husband Albert first among them.[77] Indeed, in Lil's body, many vectors of contemporary life converge—domestic inequality and abuse; the war's paradoxical empowerment and disempowerment of men; the limited medical possibilities for working-class women; the tight social arrangements that lead to neighborly surveillance as much as to community support; the position of the pub as a social meeting ground—and this amounts, in the end, to a kind of confused pain for the hapless Lil. Lil's stretched and exhausted body thus becomes a metaphor for the deeply physical realities of modern life (another lilac from the dead land). In a brilliant analysis, moreover, Paul Morrison has made the case that Lil represents a modern incarnation of the poem's other terrifically unhappy woman, Philomela.[78] The phonetic miming of their names is only the most ocular sign of their affinity. Lil's face, expressive of sadness and weak defiance; her muted protests; her deteriorated mouth; her tortured reproductive system—all of this indicates not only an individual but a whole cultural history of rape and sexual abuse. She forms part of the landscape of harsh, physical reality that underwrites the poem, and seems as much in need of enchantment or aesthetic transformation as the drowned Phlebas or the rotting bodies of the war's dead.

If Lil's is a modern case of a battered and beleaguered body, her ancient predecessor, the mutilated Philomela, represents an even more deeply troubling prototype, a figure associated with the swallow, and whose story haunts the poem.[79] It enters first in "A Game of Chess," where it forms the subject for art, a painting to adorn the lady's room:

> Above the antique mantel was displayed
> As though a window gave upon the sylvan scene
> The change of Philomel, by the barbarous king
> So rudely forced; yet there the nightingale
> Filled all the desert with inviolable voice
> And still she cried, and still the world pursues,
> "Jug Jug" to dirty ears.
> And other withered stumps of time
> Were told upon the walls; staring forms
> Leaned out, leaning, hushing the room enclosed. (*TWL*, 97–106)

Philomela's is a terrible tale: dragged to the woods by her sister Procne's husband, King Tereus, she is isolated, raped, and then silenced by having her tongue cut out (a precursor to a later raped girl with a similar fate, the atrociously mangled Lavinia in Shakespeare's *Titus Andronicus*). That she is ultimately able to communicate her tale via clever ruse, spinning her story into a loom, and that she and her sister, having taken grisly revenge on the king, are transformed, along with Tereus, into birds—such artistic outcomes seem only mildly reparative after the extremity of her violation and suffering. Indeed, in Ovid's canonical telling of the myth in *Metamorphoses*, there is no sense of recompense (no "yet") in the "inviolable voice" of the nightingale. It is Eliot's proclivity to stress the compensatory nature of song, "the change of Philomel." Or, if one prefers the alternate reading of "yet," meaning "continuing," so that the lines suggest that Philomela will persevere in singing ("And still she cried"), in an endless refrain to remind the world of her suffering, again, this represents an Eliotic, as distinct from Ovidian, emphasis (the "still" also, anticipating "Leda and the Swan").

Interestingly, when Eliot refers to Philomela again in the last stanza of the poem, via the Latin line "*Quando fiam uti chelidon*," ("when shall I be as the swallow?") he refers not to Ovid, but to a later version of the story, as it appears in the anonymous *Pervigilium Veneris* (*TWL*, 429). By the end of the poem, the narrative has become increasingly impacted in the sediment of literary history. Already in the fifth century or so, a process of transformation is underway: the girls, turned into birds, provide songs, which are then imagined as a shared, or shareable, expression of longing and sorrow.[80] For the writer of *Pervigilium Veneris*, the sting attached to Philomela's narrative is especially raw, since her futile cries follow a poem that extols fruitful love and blossoming sexuality. Eliot's poetic voice calls up this welter of associations, so that his "swallow swallow" alone is enough to become an aching dirge and many-purposed lament. What is both lost and never quite lost in this movement is the rape and mutilation of Philomela—the victimized female body, the visuality of the horrible scene, the sense of outrage that the story of Tereus's "barbarity" invokes.

Perhaps most ironic and complex in this cycle is the substance of the poet's lament; what the narrator of *Pervigilium Veneris* is actually regretting is not so much the horror of Philomela's treatment but the failure of her voice, her muteness. If the birdsong represents an abstraction—an image of communication rather than actual communicability—still it symbolizes voice over silence, a voice for which Philomela longs with all her energy. These short bursts—twit twit, jug jug, swallow swallow—represent, for the truly desperate, a badly needed form of utterance, cathartic if bleak, a saving language. And there is power in those repetitions, as there is in the poem's final benediction, the thrice-repeated Shantih. On one hand, such instances represent language pushed to the breaking point, on the verge of becoming extralinguistic. On the other hand, the narratives bound to those repeated words are dense, elaborate, and terrible, and hence what they offer is, in their own way, thick with history and experience. To cry for the swallow is to wish for a voice that simultaneously does and does not communicate; it is to lament one's current silence, and also the silence entailed even when one does speak.

Throughout *The Waste Land*, questions of voice have been paramount; here, in the swallow's call, language oscillates between a dreaded silence and a burst of sound that expresses all too much. In Swinburne's poem "Itylus" (1866), to which Eliot makes reference (though without citing it) in his "O swallow swallow," the question of silence and song is further complicated by the issue of memory, of keeping alive the most hellish of stories.[81] Swinburne's lush, swooning lyric, with its reiterated onomatopoetic "s" sounds, itself performs a kind of enchantment, coating the narrative in softness and luxury and suggesting a lethe-like, drugged quality that recalls Keats's "Ode to a Nightingale":

Swallow, my sister, O sister swallow . . .

O swallow, sister, O fair swift swallow,
Why wilt thou fly after spring to the south,
The soft south whither thine heart is set? . . .

Sister, my sister, O fleet sweet swallow . . .[82]

It is Philomela's voice that we hear, and she is not so much fixated on the atrocities committed against her as on the murder she and her sister exacted on the little boy, Procne's son, whom the sisters killed and served as a meal to Tereus. The great imperative of her song is to plead insistently for the bloody tale not to be lost, never to be forgotten:

> O sister, sister, thy first-begotten!
> The hands that cling and the feet that follow,
> The voice of the child's blood crying yet
> *Who hath remembered me? who hath forgotten?*
> Thou hast forgotten, O summer swallow,
> But the world shall end when I forget. (Swinburne, 189, italics in original)

Eliot, as it happens, has his own version of how the world ends ("not with a bang..."). More to the point, Swinburne links the unending commemoration of crimes to the very survival of civilization, a provocative notion for a poem like *The Waste Land*, where the issue is not so much willful forgetting of the past as the inescapable traces that the past leaves on everything that succeeds it. Swinburne's birds ask for poetry to ward off the silence of moral compromise; in Eliot's poem, neither silence nor the extremities of language can escape the wrongs that comprise the world's— and literature's—history.

The image of the swallow, it is becoming clear, is one of those overdetermined *Waste Land* constellations, suggesting not only a whole thicket of themes involving the Philomela narrative and its later artistic instantiations, but also the idea of swallowing. For a poem with an insatiable appetite, the act of swallowing reflects the poem's own processes, the impulse to contain the whole of Western culture (with a large dollop of the East), and to recombine them, so to speak, via aesthetic digestion. Like his contemporary Joyce, Eliot in *The Waste Land* has often been described as having an omnivorous relation to the cultural past, and it is perhaps not coincidental that the figure of Conrad's Kurtz—symbolized so memorably in *Heart of Darkness* by his dramatic open mouth—should be one of the contemporary fictional characters who most resonated for Eliot (and Kurtz's "The horror! the horror!"—those last words, uttered in a "supreme moment of knowledge," had provided the epigraph of the original draft [Eliot, *Fasc*, 3]). The swallow takes us in the direction of both silencing and ingesting, and the story of Philomela acts as the thread uniting these operations, and tying them, in turn, to the poem's insistent theme of transformation. It is, after all, the "change of Philomel" that is recorded in the sylvan scene, and, more specifically, the poem emphasizes the way music or art or poetry becomes a resonating, lingering record, a sensory trace, for the violence that cannot be spoken directly—as Philomela cannot herself speak her own story and must create a form of pictorial writing to convey the events.

Nevertheless, despite Eliot's emphasis on the way the rape and mutilation are, in effect, enchanted into art, the poem is not complacent about such an outcome. For one, the transliteration of "jug jug"—even before we get to the "dirty ears"—is an ugly sound, very far from the lyrical beauty, the "ecstatic sound" or "full throated ease," of Keats's or Hardy's nightingales.[83] And, too, "other withered stumps of time/Were told upon the walls": these "stumps" suggest Shakespeare's Lavinia, who not only had her tongue chopped off but also her hands (to prevent her from taking Philomela's route of writing her way to explication and revenge), and, more generally, the phrase suggests a weariness with the subject matter of art in its most time-weathered manifestations. Those staring forms seem less exalted than traumatized, an ancient, painted version of contemporary shell shock.

The stumps can also be read more literally: they evoke amputated arms, bringing the visual spectacle of the war's injuries into view. If much in contemporary culture seemed to avert its collective glance from the war's lasting attack on the flesh, here the disenchanting imperative to see those amputated limbs is enfolded into Eliot's larger plotline. The stumps have withered; they have begun to heal; they indicate a long future, past the immediate blast of injuring. Art, it seems, continually tells stories of brutality. Its narratives cannot erase, perhaps cannot even fully beautify, the horrors that humans inflict on one another. On one hand, then, the poem relies heavily on the chain of powerful associations that the history of literature has bequeathed, including the history of ghastly violence; it makes its music from these. The poem here is like Philomela herself, who wove the letters in her loom in the one color we might have intuited, purple. She is a creature of the violet hour; indeed, hers is perhaps the underlying, haunting narrative of violetness. Moreover, in the lines following the "withered stumps of time," Eliot gives yet another case of an art form produced out of desperation and pain, with the image of a fiery, savage music created by the lady's hair, a kind of eccentric, female artistry that seems to epitomize both the pity and the vitality of a culture. On the other hand, the poem hates these "stumps," and their reiterated appearances within the poem have the effect, almost, of a sputter, an involuntary cough, irruptions that simply cannot be avoided.

The withered stumps of Philomela's rape return on several occasions, always in disruptive, broken phrases, suggesting the kind of abrasive and uncomfortable role within the poem that actual stumps played in postwar civilian culture. These passages (there are only a few in the poem) read like chunks of linguistic jetsam, torn or broken bits that have floated off from their original masses to reappear in the midst of the poem's larger sea:

> Twit twit twit
> Jug jug jug jug jug jug
> So rudely forc'd
> Tereu (*TWL*, 202–06).[84]

Eliot's repetition of these bird cries is highly evocative, for they embody what the poem depicts in so many forms, that the most horrendous species of violent attack becomes part of the language of culture, and these cries, in turn, cannot be excluded from Eliot's larger poetic project. These strange sounds have their own special character, acting as signs or traces of a larger, terrible set of stories, simultaneously exposing and not exposing. The phrases hold in their tight, nearly nonrepresentational packages a sense of what the world does not want to be its oldest stories; they are withered stumps of time, but they are also resonant little bits of song in their own right, an interesting and important complement to such melodies as the nymphs' chorus ("Weialala leia/Wallala leialala"), the Augustinian chant ("Burning burning burning burning"), the cry of the desert ("Drip drop drip drop drop drop drop"), which Eliot thought one of the most beautiful parts of *The Waste Land*, even the poem's final three shantihs (*TWL*, 277–78, 309, 357).[85] At the same time, these bursts of language could also be read in almost the opposite way, as broken echoes of disenchantment, or perhaps as symptoms of an antiaesthetic spirit that emerges, side by side with enchantment, from the violent events at the base of the poem.

In *The Waste Land*'s final burst of stuttered lines, Philomela's story returns once again in the image of the swallow, solidifying its place at the endpoint of the poem's violent trajectory and returning us to the poem's other primary locus for aestheticizing violence, the whirlpool. Indeed, the swallow and the whirlpool come together in several ways, abutting one another, presenting alternative visions of poetic enchantment. The swallow represents the way art filters and keeps alive the most detestable of crimes, through an ambiguous process: its language is of tortured remembering, forcing a withered history into the present, and yet it also represents that burst of song that rises even from the pits of human experience. The whirlpool, too, with its transformative, magical properties, makes art out of destruction. If the swallow combats silence, the whirlpool creates it, its whispering currents a kind of speaking silence. In both cases—indeed, more generally in *The Waste Land*—the central idea is to utilize imagery of change, rebirth, resurrection, and metamorphosis as part of a reflection on the troubling relationship between art, with its core commitment to beautiful forms, and the violence that has wrecked human life throughout history.

The Waste Land can come to no conclusion about such a basic contradiction. To recognize that art neither flees violence, nor transcends it, nor merely represents it, but rather trades on its power, at times appropriating its force and creating something especially brilliant, at other times succumbing to the sheer ruin that violence leaves in its wake: such an insight represents, in poetic form, one of the signal achievements of Eliot's poem. *The Waste Land* offers a way to understand literature as a self-conscious artifact produced out of and within a history of violence, recognizing its origins in a frightful set of half-forgotten tales. One need only look at the many layers of embedded destructiveness in the poem's penultimate lines to see how fundamentally it views literary history as a history of violence. This willingness to offer a poetic of enchantment that at the same time ruthlessly disenchants its own origins sets Eliot's work off from many other engagements with violence in the period, especially those that grew out of the war, with is dichotomizing energy. Perhaps, counterintuitively, it was the immediate context of the war that actually enabled *The Waste Land*'s balancing act, since the war created an exceptional urgency to conceive violence in relation to a wider cultural legacy. The more massively devastating an event, it seems, the more it calls forth the forces of generativity; ugliness demands beauty, destruction invites transformation, old wrecks become wonders. Ultimately, *The Waste Land*, founded on these paradoxes, works almost too well. It spawned generations of imitators, but when it comes to seeing violence and culture in a relation of mutual creativity, no other works of the period could join in its combined aura of celebration and devastation. It is one of the poem's unique accomplishments, indeed, that it can see in violence the genesis of beauty and form, and can also make vivid the human tragedies that are swept into that old, innocuous phrase, "the waste of war."

2. Dynamite Violence
From Melodrama to Menace

There are sell out magistrates,
There are big-bellied financiers,
There are cops,
But for all these scoundrels
There's dynamite . . .
Long live the sound
Of the explosion!
—Attributed to Ravachol, *French anarchist*[1]

The explosion of bombs is an inescapable feature of the contemporary world. Marked by suicide attacks around the globe, and in the aftermath of a century that turned the bombing of civilians into the norm for warfare, our era seems unthinkable without such destruction. In the nineteenth century, by contrast, dynamite explosion represented an entirely new form of violence, as Alfred Nobel's invention of 1866 helped to sweep the world into its modern shape. From the moment of its inception, dynamite violence became an immediate and ever-escalating sensation, with its stunning ability not only to kill and maim, but within seconds to level an entire landscape.[2] The violence of dynamite reverberated across the sensory spectrum as something novel (hence sensational in that way, too), from its chemical smell, to its shattering sound, to its extreme tactile effects, and it held pronounced political associations, quickly becoming associated with terrorism. It shattered, exploded, ripped, and tore; it created its own palpable and recognizable form of wreckage; and its employment for radical causes suggested a future with unknowable and potentially frightful contours. In sum, dynamite violence added a potent new element to the modern imaginary.[3]

Dynamite's violence might be wide and indiscriminate, but its users were very particular: revolutionaries, and in particular anarchists, who were figured incessantly and in near-caricature as bomb-wielding maniacs.[4] "In late-nineteenth-century America," as the historian Margaret Marsh explains, "the mention of the word 'anarchist' brought to the minds of most people a particular image: an unkempt, bushy-bearded man, swarthy and dirty, lurking in a dark alley with a bomb hidden under his coat."[5] The bomb and the anarchist were partners; to understand the significance of one is to penetrate the world of the other. The story of the anarchist— his development as type, his association with explosive violence, his place in the literary imagination—holds rich critical potential. To resurrect the cultural and literary history of anarchism in England in this period is to draw a variety of conclusions about how the imagining of political violence and literary form did and did not cooperate. Moreover, one of the critical trajectories we will follow in this chapter is from the particular phenomenon of the anarchist to the more general one of the terrorist, a movement that is both historical (anarchist violence faded as a world phenomenon; terrorist violence did not) and theoretical (at any given moment, the prospect of a given political actor shifting into a generalized destroyer is always live and pressing). In addition to conjuring a typology of violent actors with lasting resonance, the presence of dynamite next to anarchism made for complex, often flamboyant, plots and styles, and its effects on the body created exceptional challenges that literary works both met and dodged, engaged and elided. For modernists, it is precisely the gaps and imbalances in the story of dynamite violence—the excesses of harm in relation to the imagined payoff; the combination of cynicism with idealism in the person of the bomber; the tremendously awful effects of dynamite on bodies and buildings; the powerful attachment to an idea often presented as without substance—that make the topic intriguing. In this sense of incongruity and imbalance, the content of the dynamite narrative overlaps almost entirely with the formal proclivities of the modernist tale about it.

For anarchists themselves, dynamite held highly idealized associations; it offered new vistas of power, not solely for its potential to wreak destruction, but also for its ability to terrify a wide public. The connotations of dynamite for radical politics are hard to overstate, for it brought together, with fearsome efficacy, the capacity to destroy with ease of procurement and deployment. It was the ultimate weapon of the one against the many, of any individual with only a smattering of training, or connection to other revolutionists, and a will to kill. (Nietzsche: "I am no man. I am dynamite."[6]) The dynamite bomb seemed tiny in proportion to its capacity to do harm; it could fit easily into a small bag, or even a pocket. Above all, as the historian Paul Avrich argues, dynamite had virulent class connotations, and this is why its association with anarchism and with other kinds of radical threat was so profound:

> Dynamite, in the eyes of the anarchists, had become a panacea for the ills of society. They saw it as a great equalizing force, enabling ordinary workmen to stand up against armies, militias, and police, to say nothing of the hired gunmen of the employers. Cheap in price, easy to carry, not hard to obtain, it was the poor man's natural weapon, a power provided by science against tyranny and oppression. . . . Just as gunpowder had broken the back of feudalism and made way for the rule of the bourgeoisie, so dynamite would bring down capitalism and usher in the reign of the proletariat.[7]

If anarchists hailed dynamite for its equalizing properties, the broader culture was similarly infatuated. The figure of the anarchist bomber (the "dynamitard," in contemporary parlance), his violent acts (referred to as "outrages" or "*attentats*"), his favored technology (especially dynamite), and his uncertain aims (total destruction, according to popular accounts) together presented the British public with a nexus of enthralling ideas and images to be explored for three decades in journalism and in fiction.[8] Not surprisingly, popular novels that invoked the specter of anarchist violence flourished in this period, in a subgenre—the dynamite novel—that freely employed elements common to such nineteenth-century conventions as the detective novel, the industrial novel, (proto)science fiction, fantasy novels of invasion or world war, and melodrama.[9] These texts—with such titles as *A Modern Dedalus* (1885), *Dynamiter* (1885), *For Maimie's Sake: A Tale of Love and Dynamite* (1886), *Hartmann the Anarchist* (1893), and *The Angel of the Revolution* (1895)—helped to configure the anarchist as type, and also focused on the idea of dynamite, with villains inevitably designated as chemists, the residue of dynamite often coloring their hands and clothing, and the smoke of detonated bombs a feature of the threatened landscape. More lavish dynamite novels, in which imagery of revolutionary violence reaches feverish proportions, might feature hyperbolic uses of the substance, such as anarchists raining fire on London by dropping dynamite bombs out of fantastical airships.[10] The power to destroy, in these works, offered the guiding principle in figuring political and social change. Indeed, the most salient and consistent characteristic of dynamite, as it was imagined and represented in fiction and elsewhere, was the hyperbole and excess it generated. The fact of excess, as we have already begun to see in this study, gives violence a particular representational charge in modernism, forcing the literary text into a pointedly self-conscious position, and generating elaborate formal gymnastics. In the case of dynamite violence, this constellation of effects is, in a sense, already in place by virtue of the subject matter alone, which affiliates throughout the century with two related phenomena, the emergence of sensationalism as a bold new feature of Victorian media culture, and the presence, across many genres, of melodrama.

In particular, dynamite violence and melodrama continually overlap and express one another. A remarkably pliant construct throughout this period, melodrama began as a style of stage play in England and France in the middle of the nineteenth century, but more widely expressed a sensibility that could be fitted to many types of writing and performance, so long as these were geared to emotional extremes, ethical absolutes, and exaggerated situations. Peter Brooks has dubbed this emotional and gestural framework "the melodramatic imagination" and Elaine Hadley "the melodramatic mode,"[11] and though there are particulars that denote and ground the term "melodrama" in the period, these critics demarcate a swath of literary and popular culture whose conventions are as recognizable today as they were in the Victorian period. Brooke terms these "the indulgence of strong emotionalism; moral polarization and schematization; extreme states of being, situations, actions; overt villainy, persecution of the good, and final reward for virtue; inflated and extravagant expression; dark plottings, suspense, breathtaking peripety" (Brooks, 11–12), and Hadley: "familial narratives of dispersal and reunion . . . emphatically visual renderings of bodily torture and criminal conduct . . . atmospheric menace and providential plotting . . . expressions of highly charged emotion, and [a] tendency to personify absolutes like good and evil" (Hadley, 3). As these lists indicate, the elements that comprise melodrama are neither fixed nor static; it is a moving field, and one whose malleability has always been mined by an exceptionally diverse array of writers. Melodrama can, for instance, be highly political in purpose—an enormously influential case being *Uncle Tom's Cabin* (1852)— with a politics that necessarily conforms to its own language conventions, sustaining and perpetuating its logic of good/virtue versus evil/vice. It can, too, rehearse in secular, consumable form many Christian themes. Once derided as middlebrow and feminine, melodrama has emerged as a significant category in cultural studies, and for good reasons: first, because a great variety of texts can be (re)considered according to its tenets; second, because persistent structures of thought and action like the melodramatic frequently produce generic mixtures and shifts; and because there are certain topics that are invariably figured in melodramatic terms. Dynamite violence is melodramatic in this last sense. The moral polarities, affective excess, invitation to delve into secret zones, and literal explosiveness generated by radicals with their bombs were enthralling in ways perfectly suited to melodrama. By the end of the nineteenth century, in other words, melodrama and anarchist violence had both become bywords for sensational events, overwrought emotion, and schematic plots, and thus their yoking has about it an inescapable logic. At the same time, in modernism, any such conjunction is subject to deconstruction; the mutuality of dynamite and melodrama occasions literary representation in mimetic terms, to be sure, but also generates powerful examples of conflict between these two partners, as instability and uncertainty replace the fixity that melodrama generally seeks to encode.

The most canonical rendering of anarchist violence in English modernism comes in Conrad's *The Secret Agent* (1907), and a reading of that novel forms the crux of my discussion. But Conrad's work points outward toward a variety of intimately related issues, including the popularization of the dynamite theme in varying literary media, the intractable question of sensationalism in relation to violent radicalism, and the thicket of contradictions surrounding the figure of the anarchist himself. All of these topics embed *The Secret Agent* in its late-Victorian context, but the novel also generates the conditions for an entirely new kind of danger, which will come to dominate the violent imaginary of the later twentieth century, the terrorist. At the pivot is the bomb-making Professor, who slips out of the melodramatic frame altogether to incorporate and instantiate this new phenomenon of terrorist as urban threat. Terrorism and anarchism were not synonymous in this period, though they were often closely allied in the public imagination, with the idea of terrorist, especially, abhorrent to the vast majority, but for a very few, a great honor. Anarchism is engaging as a topic in part for its historicity, but terrorism emerges from this welter as an exportable abstraction, that which can (and of course does) move from place to place, era to era, cause to cause. And if anarchism operates within an active field of Victorian imaginative constructs, of which the terrorist forms an emerging part, his presence in *The Secret Agent* has a catapulting and transformative effect. For Conrad, as for many others, dynamite became a marker for a threat of violence that was virtually defined by its ability to disappear, and *The Secret Agent*, which delves deeply into the nature of secrecy, propounds a logic of increasing invisibility with respect to violence. The novel registers a triple move: from reckoning with the attacked flesh as enacted violence, into a melodramatic rendering of violence as theatricality, and ultimately toward an image of modern violence as pure, endlessly suspended potential. Violence, we might say, goes underground in *The Secret Agent*, much as anarchists themselves were forced to do by the beginning of the twentieth century; or, better, Conrad traces a wider phenomenon of the period that spans from the events of the novel (1894) to its composition and publication thirteen years later, whereby the *spectacle* of theatrical violence mutates into the threatening yet obscure *possibility* of attack. That this latter condition tracks both Foucault's definition of modern cultures (as discipline internalized) and the general condition of a terrorist threat up to the present time (recognizing the possibility of explosion at any moment) suggests that for all its satire and excess— and despite its generally conservative politics—the novel has something exceptionally astute to say about the intertwining of violence and modernity.

Imagining Revolutionaries and their Acts

The last two decades of the nineteenth century might well be called the era of anarchism. The period was marked by a string of sensational acts of violence against individual leaders and representative targets, which riveted the public and were heavily reported by the press in England, America, and across Europe. To give just a few of the most notable examples: in 1883, the German anarchist Friedrich Reinsdorf, along with several accomplices, attempted to kill the German emperor by blowing up his carriage; in Chicago in 1886, a bomb was thrown at the police as they broke up a labor gathering—the infamous Haymarket case—for which five anarchists were wrongly executed (the actual bomb-thrower was never identified); the anarchist Alexander Berkman shot the steel magnate Henry Clay Frick at close range in 1892, injuring but not killing Frick; in 1894, the anarchist Émile Henry threw a bomb into the Café Terminus in Paris, wounding twenty people, killing one, and generating a frenzy of press attention; in the late 1890s, major public figures in France, Spain, and Austria were all killed by revolutionaries with anarchist affiliations; and in 1901, President McKinley of the United States was shot and killed by a Polish man with loose anarchist ties. In England, no lethal bombing of a public place or prominent leader was ever carried out, the only person to be killed by an anarchist attack in England being Martial Bourdin, the bomber whose accidental self-immolation at the Greenwich Observatory forms the basis of *The Secret Agent*. Yet a slew of attacks and attempted attacks received intensive coverage in the press, including attempts to blow up London Bridge (1884), Westminster Abbey and the Houses of Parliament (1885), and Greenwich Observatory (1894); multiple plots to assassinate Queen Victoria; the arrest and sentencing of a group of anarchists in the city of Walsall for bomb manufacture (1892); as well as international anarchist incidents and trials, such as those listed above.[12]

Indeed, in the public eye, anarchism has always spelled violence, "a bloody and smoking chaos, a heap of ruins of all existing things, a complete loosening and severance of all ties that have hitherto bound men together: marriage, the family, the Church, the State, unbridled men and women no longer held in order by any authority, and mutually devouring each other," in the words of one fictional commentator of the period.[13] In keeping with the hyperbole of such terms, the sense that the political movement of anarch*ism* signaled the unleashing of anarch*y* became a persistent misconception in the period, one that has never fully abated.[14] In fact, when anarchism embraced violence, it was as a means to an end that was supposed to be peaceful and orderly: a utopian future in which the state and its oppressive mechanisms would have melted away, replaced by a harmonious world order. Nevertheless, the anarchist ideal of the destruction of the state, when yoked in the public mind with high-profile assassinations and bombings, invited a fervent, dystopic response. "To destroy everything" is the avowed aim of the movement, according to an anarchist character in Émile Zola's *Germinal* (1885): "Set fire to the four corners of the town, mow down the people, level everything, and when there is nothing more of this rotten world left standing, perhaps a better one will grow up in its place."[15] The idea of leveling is especially noteworthy, conjoining an image of social equalization with physical devastation. Or, in the words of one revolutionary from the forgotten novel *Hartmann the Anarchist*, "'Violent diseases often demand violent remedies . . . Regard us anarchists as excising the foul ulcers of Humanity and as forced to perform that duty with no anæsthetics to aid us.'"[16]

What was anarchism?[17] The word "anarchy" means "no authority," and it is the opposition to all forms by which one person can hold power over another that most succinctly characterizes the philosophy. Anarchism comprises different branches and emphases, but in every case it opposes the defining institutions of formal power and authority: the government, the church, and the legal system. It stands absolutely against the state—any kind of state, worker or bourgeois, post-revolutionary or capitalist—which it believes inevitably institutes inequality and injustice.[18] From its beginnings in the political theory of William Godwin at the end of the eighteenth century, anarchism developed in the early 1860s, largely out of the writings of the French philosopher Pierre-Joseph Proudhon and the activities of the Russian Mikhail Bakunin, whose life in exile involved the creation of several notorious secret societies. It entered what we might call its heyday from the early 1880s until the end of the century, when anarchist movements flourished across England, America, and the Continent, and when public fascination was at its apogee. In the twentieth century, anarchism had sporadic life in many parts of the world, significantly in Spain, where anarchist groups were central actors in the

Civil War, fighting against Franco's fascist army (1936–39), and in the United States, where public fear of the phenomenon was reawakened by a series of sensational bombings in 1919. In England, however, the anarchist movement began its decline around the turn of the century, as aggressive tactics of police suppression, including the shuttering of anarchist journals and the tightening of immigration and deportation laws, eventually mitigated any serious presence. Up to then, England's relatively lenient laws had provided refuge for anarchists exiled from more repressive parts of the world. Historically, anarchism emerged side by side with other radical political movements of the mid-nineteenth century, a response to the egregious injustices of the industrial revolution. Proudhon famously claimed that "property is theft," yet anarchism was not, for all its attack on private property, specifically a workers' movement. It took its membership from all classes, and it had high-profile embodiment in the persons of Bakunin and Peter Kropotkin, both Russian aristocrats.

The principle of cooperation, writ small and large, functions for anarchists as the driver of their desired social apparatus, including quite complex functions, such as the creation of central banks and the organization of agriculture and industry. As Kropotkin, the most respected anarchist of the late nineteenth century, wrote in his 1905 *Encyclopædia Britannica* entry:

> Anarchism . . . [is] the name given to a principle or theory of life and conduct under which society is conceived without government—harmony in such a society being obtained, not by submission to law, or by obedience to any authority, but by free agreements concluded between the various groups, territorial and professional, freely constituted for the sake of production and consumption, as also for the satisfaction of the infinite variety of needs and aspirations of a civilized being.[19]

Kropotkin believed in mutualism as the essential principle not only of anarchism, but of any thriving form of human community. In his most famous book, *Mutual Aid* (1902), he makes the argument that the pseudo-Darwinian emphasis on survival of the fittest as a description of biological and social development is dead wrong, with cooperation and mutualism in fact marking and determining the success of a given species. "Sociability," he writes, "is as much a law of nature as mutual struggle."[20]

Kropotkin has been called "the ethical anarchist," but other brands of anarchism tended to place more emphasis on the individual; sometimes calling themselves "egoists," these theorists believed in the ascendant individual as the only meaningful social entity.[21] Rejecting any form of external constraint, many drew inspiration from Max Stirner's fearsome, proto-Nietzschean *The Ego and His Own* (1844, sometimes translated as *The Ego and Its Own*), which propounded an individualism that elevated the sovereign self to a position of near impunity. Kropotkin's cooperative ideal seems entirely at odds with the egoistic philosophy of Stirner, and, in fact, there was always a tension in anarchist thought between the stress on cooperation and the sanctioning of isolated, individual action. Nevertheless, the various camps did hold in common some basic precepts. Most broadly, they were distinguished from other radicals of the nineteenth century by their firm attachment to the principle of a future without government, and hence, almost by default, the demand for a massive leveling had to be part of the program.

Perhaps the best moniker for depicting how anarchists and their bombs were imagined in their own time comes in the term anarchists coined to rationalize and explain their mode of violence: propaganda by deed.[22] Propaganda by deed became canonized as allowable violence, and, as such, it partially underwrote the movement. Moreover, its effective transposition into terrorist ideology makes it one of the critical links between this late-Victorian chapter in history and the long era of terrorism that has not yet ended. Clearly, there is something seductive for revolutionaries in the act of violence, and anarchists often invoked a rhetoric of purity and fertility in destruction. Bakunin wrote, "Revolution requires extensive and widespread destruction, a fecund and renovating destruction, since in this way and only in this way are new worlds born,"[23] or, in the words of the Italian anarchist Errico Malatesta, "the insurrectional act which is intended to affirm socialist principles by deeds, is the most effective means of propaganda and the only one which, without deceiving and corrupting the masses, can penetrate down to the deepest levels of society."[24] Thus anarchists might call for "a clean sweep" of the social order as a necessary preface for a revived, better world.[25] As Zola's anarchist in *Germinal* has it, this desired new world can only be brought about "By fire, by poison, by the dagger. The brigand is the true hero, the popular avenger, the revolutionary in action, with no phrases drawn out of books. We need a series of tremendous outrages to frighten the powerful and to arouse the people" (Zola, 254). As early as 1881, when an international anarchist conference was held in London, the advocacy of propaganda by deed had become manifest among anarchists, and the conference welcomed it as such, with speeches celebrating individual acts of destruction.[26] The delegates took special note that anarchists needed to pay attention to scientific and technological developments that could aid them in perpetuating offensive tactics—to wit, training in explosives. The science of bomb making would remain a central feature in anarchist literature, the most notorious instance being Johann Most's *Revolutionary War Science* (1885) a bomb-making tract that circulated widely and clandestinely throughout Europe and America for decades, and made the German-born Most one of the most feared and famous anarchists in the world.

A Girl Among the Anarchists (1903), a semiautobiographical novel by Helen and Olivia Rossetti (nieces of Dante Gabriel Rossetti and cousins of Ford Madox Ford, writing under the pseudonym Isabel Meredith), offers a canny rendering of propaganda by deed from the perspective of an English, middle-class woman, taking a quietly rational approach to the inflammatory subject.[27] The novel traces the involvement and eventual disillusionment of its first-person narrator, whose commitment to the amelioration of social injustices has led her to a group of anarchists. Like the Rossettis, who edited an anarchist journal (*The Torch*) in the basement of their family home, the fictional Isabel becomes the editor of *The Tocsin*, and hence is situated at the center of anarchist activity in London. From such a vantage point, she explains the place of violence within the movement:

> Very diverse in nature were the motives which prompted the committal of these acts of violence—these assassinations and dynamite explosions—in different men. With some it was an act of personal revolt, the outcome of personal sufferings and wrongs endured by the rebel himself, by his family or his class. In others violence was rather the offspring of ideas, the logical result of speculation upon the social evil and the causes thereof. These Anarchists referred to their actions as Propaganda by Deed.[28]

The narrator's tone is always moderate and explanatory, and the anarchists are sympathetically imagined as motivated by the drive for social equality and justice. Indeed, in the only case where one of the novel's characters commits an outrage, the bomb-thrower has been deteriorating into paranoia and mental breakdown; his crime represents the final movement of his descent into insanity. The Rossettis' novel posits a certain marginality in the idea of propaganda by deed, and hence stands against the conception of the general public, for whom it was the defining (and perhaps the only interesting) feature of anarchism.

It is not only the theory of propaganda by deed that caught people's attention but the term itself, which was used ubiquitously. At the literal level, the term stresses the revolutionary message ("propaganda," a word whose negative connotations postdate this period) over the violent "deed." Despite the quaintness of the term to contemporary ears, the stress on violent action as message links historical anarchists with terrorist practices over a longer historical span. Theorists of terrorism in our contemporary context have argued that terrorism is best understood as a form of communication, however distorted and monomaniacal such an idea of communication might be. Without minimizing the often horrendous facts of terrorist violence, this approach emphasizes that terrorist violence is meant to encode meaning into action, to utilize highly spectacular and news-garnering violence as a form of language—what Émile Henry, the Café Terminus bomber, called "the voice of dynamite."[29] Or, as Vladimir declares of anarchists in *The Secret Agent*, "bombs are your means of expression."[30] Or again, in the words of an "anarchic poet" in Chesterton's novel *The Man Who was Thursday* (1908), "the man who throws a bomb is an artist."[31] As suggested in the introduction, it is this notion of terrorist violence as language that Karlheinz Stockhausen seemed to have been reflecting upon when he praised the 9/11 attacks as a tremendous work of art, yet in the present, as in the previous two centuries, such thinking always conjures its antithetical idea, that there can never be an alignment of violence and legitimate meaning. Propaganda by deed is a principle of action that assumes interpretation, under the premise that those reacting from the outside will see a clear and causal relationship between the destruction at hand and a political intention. It is, in this sense, a theory that demands an unlikely cohesion between perpetrators and public.

The idea that violence might act (or be imagined to act) as a form of language is a startling claim, though one that has become so familiar in its contemporary terrorist context as perhaps to pass without notice (or, again, to become shockingly noticed when articulated in terms that seem laudatory). I have already described in the introduction, and critical discourse since the publication of Elaine Scarry's *The Body in Pain* has often assumed, a deep and abiding silence surrounding the felt experience of violence. At the same time, in the pandying episode from *A Portrait of the Artist as a Young Man*, Joyce offered an image of violence bringing forth language, in a sequence that had the force of an origin story. Indeed, one of this study's central objectives is to see how violence and at least one large swath of language—literary form—intersect and produce one another, and so to find in the notion of propaganda by deed a formulation that insists on a ready interchange between explosive violence and the realm of language and interpretation is to confront a significant conceptual moment in the modern history of violence. In the assumptions behind propaganda by deed is embedded a powerful understanding about the nature of violence—that it transpires in dense and crowded significatory settings. In the particular case of "the voice of dynamite," violence speaks in tones that are meant to be loud and clear, the message blunt, even if the political theory itself is complex, at times incoherent. The concept of propaganda by deed figures violence acting upon the world in the form of hyperbolic and wrenching drama, one that seems simultaneously to expand a political meaning and to nullify its value.

This theatricality is also captured in the word "deed," which has a formal cadence, suggesting something elevated and serious, even a bit archaic.[32] The image—and this was typically highlighted by anarchists in their own self-representations—was of a lone actor, motivated by rage and passion, taking the message of the revolution into his own hands, in an act of violence that was also self-sacrifice. Such an image differs in important ways from another central formula for radical violence in the period, the general strike ("direct action"), in which the individual actor is submerged by the group, and the power of sheer numbers replaces the individual bomb-thrower as instigator of change. Or perhaps it is best to see these two distinct modes as contributing together to a broad conceptualization of radical violence in the period, where direct action conjures the vast organized (or perhaps dangerously disorganized) masses, while propaganda by deed suggests the supremely motivated individual. With the theatricality of propaganda by deed, the central actor is figured in grand, gestural terms, as one who understands himself to be engaged in performance, and the whole enterprise radiates with an exuberantly aesthetic quality.

A hybrid of revolutionary self-representation and equally vivid reactionary portrayal, the person of the anarchist bomber was typically figured in stylized terms—a repository, we might say, for a certain literary zeal. For instance, the question of what kind of person would or could become an anarchist and how to amalgamate such people into an understandable frame of reference came wreathed in intriguing contradiction. As the narrator of Conrad's "The Informer" remarks, "anarchists in general were simply inconceivable to me mentally, morally, logically, sentimentally, and even physically."[33] On the one hand, it was unsurprisingly the case, as Haia Shpayer-Makov argues, that the anarchist "was greeted [in the press] with the stock rhetoric and imagery commonly applied to the Irish, the socialists, and other 'deviant' groups. . . . The anarchist was associated with revolutionism and violence, and as such stood in opposition to the self-image of British society as an orderly and law-abiding community."[34] Yet, for all the invective and anxiety directed toward anarchists and other "degenerates," there was an appealing mystery about this figure. In popular dynamite novels, anarchists were often surprisingly likable, their motives laudable, even as they tapped into (and helped to refill) a reservoir of anxiety about revolutionary madness.

An amalgam of historical personae and fictional characters, the anarchist as rendered across the culture embodied a number of often clashing traits. The very question of how anarchists operated at all opened up a plethora of issues surrounding their identity and individuation. In some cases, the anarchist was understood to be so embroiled in layers of secrecy, and in organizations beneath organizations, as to have virtually no individual reality. Historically, it was probably Bakunin who did most to foster a sense of obsessive secrecy as a signal trait among anarchists, as a founder of several secret organizations. In the fiction of the period, writers imagined elaborate plots involving secret societies with Masonic-styled initiations and codes. Perhaps most revealing are those works—the most elaborate case, but not the only one, being Dostoevsky's *The Devils* (1871)—that imagine a single actor, ruthless and clever, convincing others of the breadth and power of a movement that, in reality, does not exist at all. Secrecy, in other words, was imagined as enabling vast networks of subversives to be joined together in an expansive network, and it was also seen as a chimera allowing a single fanatic wildly to extend his reach.

The idea that anarchism is more of a phantasm than a reality, the unfurling of a single individual's radical will-to-destroy rather than a real movement, reaches its fullest exemplification in Chesterton's *The Man Who was Thursday*, a strange fable that is simultaneously a story about worldwide anarchist plotters and about the complete unreality of that threat. The principal conceit of the novel is of a group of powerful anarchists—the leaders of the European anarchist movement—who have been infiltrated by the novel's protagonist, the policeman Gabriel Syme. What transpires, however, is not a tale of violence unmasked, but rather of the identifying of the anarchist leaders as, to a man, agents of the police, leading to the infamous, terrifying Sunday. Despite an initial scene in which Syme witnesses a room full of sinister modern weapons, the giant, international anarchist threat—like the novel itself, subtitled "A Nightmare"—is a fantasy. In this Foucauldian world, there are no powerful violent anarchists plotting assassinations; there are only policemen performing the role of anarchists, creating the characters they fear and imagine, keeping up the chase (quite literally, with the novel staging a whole series of outlandish chases). Critics have noted that Chesterton, like Conrad in *The Secret Agent*, is attending to anarchism at a moment, in England, of its relative belatedness, and suggest that the extravagantly allegorical nature of his conception of anarchism depends upon this condition of muted threat. This seems accurate to a degree, yet the novel's extreme denuding of political content from anarchism, alongside a paranoid exaggeration of its importance among police and government functionaries, was not uncommon, even in anarchism's prime.[35] Chesterton's parable sees anarchism as a form of political violence that prolifically generates fantasy, defined by the gulf separating political content (anarchist theory) and method (terrorist violence). This breach is represented in the novel, or so it seems at first blush, by a strange riddle, with the anarchists named for the days of the week, and the mysterious Sunday seeming to stand for some exceptional concept (an eccentric version of God himself, indeed). And yet, when the political narrative falls away, the whole rationale for the allegory also disappears. In this case, the allegorical structure collapses not because the violent content is too real to be governable by its form of discrete categories (as in "Leda and the Swan"), but because there is no violent content calling for the allegory in the first place. All these names and guises are simply tricks. What is at stake for Chesterton, in developing and undermining his strange formal apparatus, is the way anarchism is imagined to conjoin terror with political vacuity. That which hinges propaganda to deed evaporates, and the result, in *The Man Who was Thursday*, is a wild literary exercise that has puzzled readers since its publication.

In most cases, however, the anarchist was imagined not as hallucination, but as real and thriving. First and foremost, he was a destroyer, unconstrained by ordinary ethical norms, single-mindedly driving the revolution via the commission of "outrages." The historical names attached to this image are full of flair: Sergei Nechaev (sometimes spelled "Nechayev") set the tone, authoring a chilling tract entitled "Catechism of the Revolution," which spelled out the image of the terrorist in cool, calculated detail.[36] Johann Most, the maker of bombs, offered an image of science gone horribly wrong, as he willingly dispersed the technology of killing, seemingly indifferent to human life.[37] The exuberantly self-righteous and famous Ravachol was a French anarchist who became something of a folk legend, after being guillotined in 1892 for a series of dynamite attacks; his song, "La Ravachole" (a revamping of the Revolutionary anthem "La Carmagnole" and the epigraph for this chapter) remained as an echo of his fiery views, with lines like "Let's blow up all the bourgeois/We'll blow them up!," and its refrain, "Long live the sound/Of the explosion!"[38] Then there was Émile Henry, who declared to the judges at his trial for the Café Terminus bombing, in which he was sentenced to death, that "those who have suffered are tired at last of their sufferings," and that anarchism "will end by killing you."[39] Alexander Berkman, as unapologetic at his trial for shooting Frick as Henry was at his, depicted the attempted assassination, in a widely read prison memoir (1912), in riveting, moment-by-moment narration. The list goes on, but what seems most notable in each case is the sense of drama, sensation, and narrative possibility around each of these (in)famous figures. Even in the nonfictional language surrounding anarchists—and central to their self-presentation— the characteristics are exhibited that motivated dynamite novelists, and that writers like Conrad would present in terms of thick, modernist conundrums.

Nechaev's landmark "Catechism," written in 1869 as a statement of revolutionary methods and creeds, and garnering long-lasting status as underground doctrine, provided an image of the terrorist that was in every sense literary: it both derived from and inspired fictional characters, it very self-consciously imagined the terrorist as a persona, and it carried a strong sense of aura or mood. The excess that always surrounds dynamite violence is here personified. The first line, "The revolutionary is a doomed man," establishes its ethics of insurrectionary violence primarily as a matter of the commitment, courage, and ultimate selflessness of the terrorist himself:

> For him there exists only one contentment, one consolation, one reward and one satisfaction—the success of the revolution. Day and night he must have only one thought, one goal—ruthless destruction. Striving coolly and tirelessly toward this goal, he must be ready to perish himself and to destroy with his own hands everything that hinders the realization of his goal. . . .[40]

The rebel of the "Catechism" feels an intimacy with death: he not only kills, but does so with his bare body, his "own hands." A complete loner, the anarchist-as-terrorist is enjoined to foreswear all ties of personal affiliation, indeed to relinquish his very humanity in the name of the cause: "All tender softening sentiments of kinship, friendship, love, gratitude and even honor itself must be suppressed in him by a single cold passion for the revolutionary cause." This ideal of a revolutionary with an absolute and dominating purpose reached far and wide within radical circles. John Henry Mackay, in a semiautobiographical novel about London anarchism in the 1880s, sums up the influence in creating one of his characters as a disciple of Nechaev: "At the age of twenty-four he is a terrorist. He has learned them by heart, those mad eleven principles 'concerning the duties of the revolutionist to himself and to his fellow-revolutionists' . . . He journeys from city to city. Everywhere he tries to undermine the existing order of things . . . He trusts only in the revolution henceforth."[41] Restless and itinerant (another hallmark of historical anarchists), the anarchist of the "Catechism" seems to be everywhere and nowhere, a subversive agent of the modern world, relentlessly working to carry out his mission of destruction.

In constructing an image of the revolutionary as ascetic, devoted body and soul to the cause, Nechaev calls to mind a fictional character who, beginning in the early 1860s, became something of a celebrity on the revolutionary circuit, Rakhmetov, from a novel by the Russian N. G. Chernyshevsky, *What Is to Be Done?* (1863). Chernyshevsky's novel, which was famous in its own day even before Lenin's pamphlet adopted its title, deals primarily with questions of how the "new generation" of progressive young Russians approach such matters as sexuality, gender, social interactions, family ties, and the proper economic relations among the classes. Rakhmetov, a shadowy figure whose terrorist activities are alluded to only vaguely, is brought into the novel, according to the author's own claims, to show what an extraordinary person looks like, someone above and beyond even the novel's very admirable protagonists. An aristocrat who renounces his wealth, Rakhmetov leads a life of self-denial, swearing off such luxuries as alcohol and sex ("He said to himself, 'I shall not drink one drop of wine. I shall not touch any women'"), eating only in such a way as to strengthen his already considerable physique—but never for enjoyment—and, in times of "trial" for an unspecified upcoming hardship, sleeping on a bed of nails.[42] *What Is to Be Done?* was translated and serialized in anarchist journals, and the character of Rakhmetov (or "Rakhmetoff," in its nineteenth-century transliteration) became shorthand for the idealized terrorist; the name was used as an alias by Berkman, for example, in the lead-up to his attempted assassination of Frick.

For all the asceticism and grim determination in these portrayals, we also find in many works a streak of joy and pleasure in the act of destruction, viewed as revenge-taking against deserving exploiters—the *jouissance* of the deed. Berkman, for one, saw in reprisal killing the germination of his own manhood: "Could anything be nobler than to die for a grand, a sublime Cause? . . . And what could be higher in life than to be a true revolutionist? It is to be a *man*, a complete MAN. A being who has neither personal interests nor desires above the necessities of the Cause; one who has emancipated himself from being merely human . . ." (emphasis in original).[43] One notes, here, the conjunction between Nechaev's ascetic ideal and a Fanonian model of generative violence, which, as we have seen, imagines a virile masculinity emerging from the fight against European oppressors. Both of these radical positions, in turn, gain momentum from a conventional Christian rhetoric of martyrdom and self-sacrifice, as the revolutionary investment in the body aligns itself with other mystical and masculinist traditions. In Berkman's language, two different sacrificial bodies are suggested: that of Frick, who stands in for all exploiters, and that of the incarcerated or executed revolutionary, whose expendable body is subsumed by the cause.[44] The dualist underpinnings of Western sacrificial logic, the apotheosis accorded to the person who gives his body in the name of some larger commitment, the Christian promise of a glory that disdains bodily pleasure and rewards privation—such conventions are perpetuated in radical conceptions of the revolutionary hero.[45]

Indeed, a central component in many representations was an almost religious fervor defining the anarchist. Zola's Souvarine, in *Germinal*, is one such figure. The novel details a mining strike whose ultimate effect is the near-complete decimation of both company and workers. Though the novel's leading figures (including the protagonist Étienne) hope to avoid violence, the miseries attending the conditions in the mine, along with the strike's escalation, beget an ever-widening circle of horrific violence, which culminates in Souvarine's destruction of the mine by sabotage. Though Souvarine's affect in general is one of ironized detachment in relation to the strike (nothing more than "foolery," as he repeatedly terms it), he becomes powerfully animated when he describes his vision of the destruction of the world: "As he talked, Souvarine grew terrible. An ecstasy raised him on his chair, a mystic flame darted from his pale eyes, and his delicate hands gripped the edge of the table almost to breaking" (Zola, 254). Such mystic transformation is as powerful as it looks, moreover, for Souvarine's ultimate act of terrorism overshadows the many local, grisly, often frightful scenes of violence the novel catalogues. The anarchist's form of destruction, mirroring his feverish power, is on an entirely different order from even the most feared forms of revolutionary rampaging. "He had vitality enough in him to bring the dead to life, passion enough for a hundred men," is how one sympathetic novelist depicted the leader of the Haymarket anarchists.[46]

Insofar as anarchists were imbued with mystical zeal and power, they begin to metamorphose into one of their avatars, the terrorist. Thus, in another dramatic rendering of the mystic revolutionary, in his *Underground Russia: Revolutionary Profiles and Sketches from Life* (1883), the anarchist Stepniak paints a vibrant portrait of his own version of "The Terrorist." (Stepniak, pseudonym for Sergei Stepniak-Kravchinsky, was a Russian residing in England, garnering a following among well-to-do English leftists; in that sense, he was like Kropotkin after him, though Stepniak, unlike Kropotkin, had credentials for violence, having himself assassinated the chief of the Russian secret police in 1878.) Of the terrorist, he writes: "He is noble, terrible, irresistibly fascinating, for he combines in himself the two sublimities of human grandeur: the martyr and the hero." The terrorist, moreover,

> . . . is the type of individual force, intolerant of every yoke. . . . He bends his haughty head before no idol. He has devoted his sturdy arms to the cause of the people. But he no longer deifies them. And if the people, ill-counselled, say to him, 'Be a slave,' he will exclaim, 'No;' and he will march onward, defying their imprecations and their fury, certain that justice will be rendered to him in his tomb. . . . Such is the Terrorist.[47]

In Stepniak's rendering, the revolutionary is a person powerfully motivated to change the world. It is on the future, and perhaps on the past, that he fixes his dreamy gaze; the present will always be the object of destruction, and contemporaries will be the least likely to embrace the terrorist himself. And, in fact, the terrorist's relationship to the future is one of his hallmarks; he is always pressing (or thrusting, rushing) the present into the future, the temporal realm of his vivid imaginary. There is something intensely compelling about this willed and contorted relation to temporality, which dispenses with time as it is actually lived, in the present, a feature of terrorist rhetoric and belief that continues to hold sway in the present period. Yet figures like Stepniak's fighter, with his dreamy qualities and exaggerated characteristics, also lends himself to parody, or to a charge of inefficacy and fantasizing. The icon of the lone terrorist out to change the world with his bombs was always ripe to become a ludicrous image of narcissistic self-delusion.

Even such an ironist as Oscar Wilde took an interest in the figure of the feverishly devoted, revolutionary assassin. It may come as a surprise to find Wilde creating this kind of protagonist, but *Vera, or the Nihilists,* his first play, takes up the topic of political assassination with all the relish of a dynamite novel and offers an idiosyncratic generic response to terrorism's appeal. The play presents a roster of idealized Russian insurrectionists, who are motivated to become assassins by a combination of ardent social vision and personal grievance against the czarist regime.[48] Composed in 1880 and originally slated for production in London the following year, the play was withdrawn because of the sensitivity of the political topic—the czar, a target of revolutionaries for years, was assassinated in 1881. The play combines what will become the Wildean hallmarks of arch, decadent, urbane dialogue with a focus on the heated doings of a group of radicals, committed to harassing and, if possible, killing off Russia's rulers. The eponymous Vera, along with her brother, enters the secret comradeship to avenge their other brother, who had been imprisoned and killed by the regime. As the effective leader of the organization, Vera meets and falls passionately in love with one Alexis, who turns out to be an infiltrator, and none other than the czar's son, whom Vera is required to kill. Unwilling to do so, she kills herself with a poisoned dagger, and, despite his wish to die by her side, she saves him, in a hyperbolic gesture, by throwing the dagger out of the window. As a protagonist, Vera is not a character we might ordinarily associate with Wilde; she is strong, passionate, humorless, devoted, and ultimately tragic.[49] And the play as a whole is an uncomfortable arrangement. It consists of two divergent groups of characters, the revolutionaries, who are quite free from irony (they are earnestness embodied) and the members of the czar's ruling council, especially the witty Prince Paul Maraloffski, who belong fully to the world of Wildean reversal and urbanity. Though the dialogue among the council can be amusing, there remains something incompatible in the play's two worlds, epitomized less by their differences in class than by a stark tonal discrepancy. It juxtaposes, rather than melds, two generic tendencies: the melodrama characterizing the revolutionaries and the canny, wry commentary that provides a disjunctive surround for this central narrative.[50] The play offers a glimpse of

Wilde's developing style, emerging disharmoniously from the welter of the period's generic indices for political violence. For Wilde, typical of his time, political violence finds expression in melodramatic gestures, well suited to portray its excesses; yet such extravagance cannot be squared with his more pervasive idea, to be pursued throughout his career, that social violence is a much more dispersed, buried, and fragmented construction.[51]

From Vera to Souvarine, from Rakhmetov to the generalized terrorist, where does all this enthusiasm originate? What is the source of the passion? One persistent idea is that the terrorist might be personally motivated, his outrage against the government deriving from some specific injustice against himself or his family. Wilde's Vera fits this mold, as do the central figures in George Griffith's *The Angel of the Revolution: A Tale of the Coming Terror* (1895), who nurture extreme personal grievances against the Russian government. Griffith's popular dynamite novel imagines a small band of self-described "terrorists" who make war on Europe and America, overthrowing all existing governments and replacing them with a socialist paradise where war has been eradicated. To say that the revolutionaries hold grudges against the czar does not capture the novel's flair for establishing deep political conviction: their wounds are literal, marked onto their bodies. In the case of Natas, the founder of the terrorist Brotherhood and leader of the revolution, his crippled legs bear witness to his treatment years ago in the Russian mines, though his even greater bitterness involves the fate of his wife, who had been captured, raped, and kept by a Russian soldier, before she died in misery. Natas's familial tale is highly sensational, and the novel's Victorian values, when it comes to gender, are not particularly revolutionary; this history of female violation is enough to justify nothing less than world war. Equally spectacularly, two other key members of the terrorist organization bear witness, on their permanently scarred backs, to imperial Russia's viciousness against political dissidents. With Radna Michaelis, we only "see" her torture in facsimile: a painting of a half-stripped woman, being whipped by Russian soldiers, adorns the walls of the Brotherhood's headquarters, a reminder of her horrifying ordeal and a motivation for action. But for Alexis Mazanoff, who suffered a similar fate, we readers are privy to his scarred flesh:

> As he said these last words, [Mazanoff/Colston] let go Arnold's [the protagonist's] shoulders, flung off his coat and waistcoat, slipped his braces off his shoulders, and pulled his shirt up to his neck. Then he turned his bare back to his guest, and said—
> "That is the sign-manual of Russian tyranny—the mark of the knout!"

Arnold shrank back with a cry of horror at the sight. From waist to neck, Colston's back was a mass of hideous scars and wheals, crossing each other and rising up in to purple lumps, with livid blue and grey spaces between them. As he stood, there was not an inch of naturally-coloured skin to be seen. It was like the back of a man who had been flayed alive, and then flogged with a cat-o'-nine tails.[52]

The baring of flogged flesh is an always intriguing narrative formula, one that continues to serve, into the twenty-first century, as the sign of torture in war.[53] We might recall Bataille's obsessive attraction to the torture photograph, which for him expresses the culmination and full embodiment of the eros/death continuum. Here, the wounded flesh returns us, ineluctably, to the scene of the attack itself, another staging of the sudden blow, or violent origin, that spins forth narrative and also continually recalls the reader or viewer back to itself. More generally, the dramatic unveiling of the scarred body ratchets up the pitch: both dramatically (a striptease, a sudden transformation in our estimation and understanding of the character) and thematically (introducing the decimated flesh as both cause and consequence of revolutionary activity), the passage serves to sensationalize the saga, but also in a sense to humanize it. With these wounds marking their bodies, the revolutionaries seem bound to turn the war against flesh in another direction. As they enact their revenge, they hope to shift the narrative written on their bodies from one of victimization to one of ultimate victory.

These never-quite-healed wounds, in other words, call forth the dynamic of reprisal: flesh calls for flesh, blood for blood. I will discuss this motif in some detail in the next chapter, since it provided the underlying logic for much Irish writing in the aftermath of the Rising. Here I want to note, just briefly, the prevalence of such imagery across the spectrum of radical literature in the nineteenth and twentieth centuries. The same assertion can be heard over and over: the body is the ground that nourishes modern civilizations, and it will also be the ground for revolution. In accounts of exploited labor, exhortations for systemic change, or panegyrics to heroic self-sacrifice, radical writers offered the spectacle of the body as the force—unacknowledged, yet justifying glorification—beneath all forms of cultural growth.[54] The violated and exploited body was, in this sense, enchanted, holding generative potential. We find this formulation at the opening of Mackay's *The Anarchists*:

. . . how many human lives might lie crushed beneath these white granite quarries [of the Embankment], piled one upon the other so solid and unconquerable? And he thought again of that silent, unrewarded, forgotten toil that had created all the magnificence round about him.

> Sweat and blood are washed away, and the individual man, on the corpses
> of millions of unnamed, forgotten ones, rises living and admired . . .
> (Mackay, 5, ellipsis in original)

For his part, Kropotkin writes, in his tract *The Conquest of Bread* (1892; first English translation 1906), "Every rood of soil we cultivate in Europe has been watered by the sweat of several races of men. Every acre has its story of enforced labour, of intolerable toil, of the people's sufferings. Every mile of railway, every yard of tunnel, has received its share of human blood."[55] And Berkman declares: "The steel-workers were not the aggressors. Resignedly they had toiled and suffered. Out of their flesh and bone grew the great steel industry; on their blood fattened the powerful Carnegie Company."[56] In all of these cases, and indeed very broadly, what is perhaps most notable is the intermingling of enchantment with disenchantment; the body's unique power to cultivate vibrant growth is cut across by a desire to expose the real suffering and misery of starved, ruined, exploited bodies, whose situation should never, in the eyes of the reformers, be sanctified or justified. A sense of ruination is inevitably attached to disenchantment, yet for all the effort to focus on that decimation, radical writers also sought a vista of enchantment to redirect their narrative toward enrichment and change. In this sense, they mirror the war writers discussed in the last chapter, who freely deployed enchanted language within their generally disenchanting frameworks.

In *The Secret Agent*, the "old terrorist" Karl Yundt employs a heated version of the metaphor of exploited flesh: "Do you know what I would call the nature of the present economic conditions?" he asks, "I would call it cannibalistic. That's what it is! They are nourishing their greed on the quivering flesh and the warm blood of the people—nothing else" (*SA*, 44)[57] And he is even more grotesquely explicit in characterizing the legal system: "And what about the law . . . the pretty branding instrument invented by the overfed to protect themselves against the hungry? Red-hot applications on their vile skins—hey? Can't you smell and hear from here the thick hide of the people burn and sizzle?" (*SA*, 41). Conrad may have been thinking here of a notorious essay with the suggestive title "An Anarchist Feast at the Opera," which was found in the belongings of several anarchists arrested in 1892 for bomb making (the Walsall Anarchists). The essay ghoulishly and gleefully imagines the probable effects of a bomb being exploded in the London opera house, scene, of course, of materialist self-indulgence, including reflections on the smell of bourgeois flesh burning ("Would not a single one among us feel his heart beat with an immense joy in hearing the shriveling of the grease of the rich and the howlings of that mass of flesh swarming in the midst of that immense vessel all in a blaze?" and so on[58]).

The essay was read aloud at the trial of David Nicoll, the editor of the primary English radical newspaper *Commonweal*, who was sentenced to two years in jail for inciting violence. The "Feast," summarized in news accounts during the trial, offered a grisly version of the more familiar rhetoric of reprisal against the powerful for abusing the bodies of the workers, and seemed to suggest that anarchists had taken the metaphor of flesh demanding flesh with a shocking literality. The truth is that the essay's authorship and intent are dubious, but the public sensation of its rhetoric was unchecked by such scruples.[59]

Flesh-consuming or messianic, anarchists in the British imagination were always understood as foreign. There is some legitimacy to this stereotype, for anarchism was fundamentally international in spirit. Its roots ran deepest in Russia, though foundational thinkers came from all over the continent, including England; there was a great deal of itinerancy among anarchists, so that a typical anarchist meeting in London might include Russian, French, German, American, and other Eastern European participants; and Jews made up a robust complement of the movement, especially in London and in large American cities like New York, Philadelphia, and Chicago, where Yiddish-language journals flourished alongside those in English, French, German, Italian, and Russian.[60] The anarchist's canonical foreignness cut in a variety of directions. The question, for instance, of what might attract an English person to the cause became the subject for speculation. Dynamite novels often figured an English protagonist who finds himself immersed, for one reason or another, in an anarchist organization created and dominated by foreigners. In *The Angel of the Revolution*, discussed above in relation to the scarring of several of its Russian characters, the protagonist is something of a regular English type—a public-schoolboy bachelor, an unlikely candidate for anarchism—who eventually becomes a leader in the movement. Robert Louis and Fanny Stevenson, coauthors of a strange little pastiche of a novel, *Dynamiter*, portray a series of English male dupes seduced by beautiful revolutionary women. And for its part, the Rossettis' *A Girl Among the Anarchists* gives us a detailed genealogy of its protagonist's attraction to and eventual break from the movement, in an attempt, perhaps, to address the question they know will be on everyone's mind: "Why would an English girl . . .?" Indeed, the scandal of the young narrator spending late nights editing her radical journal as Italian anarchist refugees (men, of course) sleep on the floor around her was not likely to pass without notice among the novel's middle-class readers.

Conrad, too, took up the thread, considering in some detail the national, class, and gender affiliations of anarchist violence. "The Informer," a story composed just before *The Secret Agent*, offers a variety of familiar anarchist types, including its internal narrator, Mr. X, a French aristocrat who is "the greatest rebel (*révolté*) of modern times" and who repeatedly jolts the primary narrator with statements like "There's no amendment to be got out of mankind except by terror and violence."[61] A variety of other recognizable figures also populate the scene, ranging from the inevitable chemist who spends his days concocting bombs in the attic of the anarchists' meeting house to the police informer who gives the story its title. And though the narrator professes himself speechless at the conundrum of Mr. X—"He was alive and European; he had the manner of good society, wore a coat and hat like mine, and had pretty near the same taste in cooking. It was too frightful to think of" (*CS*, 312)—it is primarily a young, middle-class woman, who is largely bankrolling the story's anarchists and who looks suspiciously like the Rossettis, that most flusters both narrators. Quite simply, they cannot fathom a British, middle-class, woman anarchist, their responses to her betraying a residual sexism: "She had acquired all the appropriate gestures of revolutionary convictions—the gestures of pity, of anger, of indignation against the anti-humanitarian vices of the social class to which she belonged herself," says Mr. X.; "All this sat on her striking personality as well as her slightly original costumes," and so on (*CS*, 315). For the male narrators of the story, whose radicalism quite notably steers clear of gender, the conundrum of "why" is never really raised; a middle-class English girl could never be an anarchist, she can only acquire his gestures.[62]

More complexly and subtly than perhaps any other writer on this subject, Henry James considered the appeal and repulsion of anarchist violence in national and gender terms. *The Princess Casamassima* (1886) concerns a young, impressionable English protagonist, Hyacinth Robinson, who commits himself by oath to a shadowy anarchist organization, promising to carry out unspecified acts of violence at the will of the group's leader. Though Hyacinth comes to anarchism through his English friend Paul Muniment, the anarchist society in *The Princess Casamassima* is resolutely international, as one would expect—its leader Hoffendahl is a notorious German terrorist, and its members are drawn from all over Europe. Yet what interests James, above all, is Hyacinth: his attraction to the movement, his slow disengagement with it, and his stance with respect to what he has contracted to do. James described the novel originating out of his own history of London street-walking, and it is out of this biographical narrative that he conjures his protagonist, a creature of refined, aesthetic sensibility and low social status, following his author's path:

> I arrived so at the history of little Hyacinth Robinson—he sprang up for me out of the London pavement. To find his possible adventure interesting I had only to conceive his watching the same public show, the same innumerable

appearances, I had watched myself, and of his watching very much as I had watched; save indeed for one little difference. This difference would be that so far as all the swarming facts should speak of freedom and ease, knowledge and power, money, opportunity, and satiety, he should be able to revolve round them but at the most respectful of distances and with every door of approach shut in his face.[63]

The image of Hyacinth springing from the London pavement suggests a form of radical national affiliation—"a product of the London streets and the London air," as he puts it in the novel (James, 104–5)—an idea of citizenship that is more local than ethnic, more physical than metaphysical, and, in this sense, more like the French ideal of *citoyen* than the English one of national character. At the same time, Hyacinth, who is half French, is no more a prototype of Englishness than his creator James. Moreover, as we are told here, his poverty shuts off many outlets for him, while his aesthetic sensibility distances him from the radicals of his circle, leaving him in a strangely empty zone of class, a nonidentity for which his anarchist connections do not compensate.

Instead, in James's portrait of Hyacinth, we see the image of someone who is drawn toward anarchist violence magnetically more than culturally, if we might put it that way. The language of watching in the above passage suggests magnetism, and, more generally, Hyacinth is consistently figured as a spectator. A number of crucial scenes in the novel take place at the theater, and Hyacinth takes spectatorial pleasure watching the parade of Parisian life from the perch of an outdoor café or meandering endlessly through London, his habitual and favored occupation. He even describes his most profound experience, the oath-taking itself, in ocular terms: "I was hanging about outside, on the steps of the temple, among the loafers and gossips," he says of his time before meeting Hoffendahl, "but now I have been in the innermost sanctuary—I have seen the holy of holies" (James, 330). Hyacinth is drawn toward anarchism, he looks into its "depths" (to use James's repeated term), but he does not and cannot become a terrorist of the sort British culture typically envisioned. Hyacinth perhaps marks a limit, an outer edge of that persona. He reacts to, rather than instantiating, the violent threat and appeal of radical politics. Or we might say that Hyacinth is distanced from the explosive side of anarchism, its destructive hunger, only taking up its violence when he turns it onto his own person in a final act of suicide.

The Princess Casamassima is dense with reflections on the dilemma into which Hyacinth falls, and these touch on a variety of familiar motifs surrounding the portrayal of anarchist violence in the period. James hews quite closely, for instance, to conventions that characterized the dynamite novel, including the inevitable chemist among the characters (Paul), the stress on secrecy and shadowy worlds-beneath-worlds, the crediting of a genuine social vision to the revolutionaries, and the emphasis on the oath as the signal act-that-generates-acts. This last is especially important for James, as it was for other dynamite novelists, who often imagined a thicket of Masonic rites and elaborate oath-taking protocols, proclivities shared by Wilde's nihilists. In all these cases, the speech act of dedication to a revolutionary cause became as riveting (psychologically and personally) as the sensational acts of violence that might follow. For James, especially, the apparatus of loyalty entirely supersedes the political content in whose name it is supposed to function, and it is in this gap—between the evacuated meaning and the exaggerated performance, or, if one prefers, between the disappearing signified and the flamboyant signifier—that the drama of the novel is generated.[64] So Hyacinth, after experiencing an initial burst of fervor for the revolutionists and for Hoffendahl, soon becomes disillusioned both with the anarchists' precept of destroying the existing social order and with the anarchists themselves. It is really his love for the Princess Casamassima—a dyed-in-the-wool radical—that keeps him at all focused on the movement. With little enthusiasm for the cause, he yet remains fixed in and by the oath he has sworn, to be ready at any moment to take up *any* act, as specified by Hoffendahl. In the end, when the summons comes, Hyacinth is unwilling either to betray his oath or to fulfill it. Suicide being the natural finale of tragedy (and often, too, of melodrama), Hyacinth's choice to kill himself marks the culmination of his dilemma, as well as a generic endpoint for the text. Hyacinth's political bind within the novel thus takes its course at the level of form: there is no outlet for him that will not partake of emotional heightening and tragic formulae.

When Hyacinth turns his gun on himself, he thus completes a process that the novel had been evolving all along: the occlusion of political violence by melodrama.[65] James's narrative operates on the line between an introspective cultural commentary, in which the forces of history work in complex fashion to mold the characters and plots, and the sentimental mode, in which high-pitched emotion and symbolic gesture drive the narrative. Hyacinth himself comes to anarchism (and stays with it) largely because of his infatuation with the beautiful princess, flirting more with the fairy tale than with the grim destructive realities that Hoffendahl represents. More generally, Hyacinth's story, beginning with his mother, carries all the hallmarks of Victorian melodrama, from his lowly origins as the son of a wronged woman who dies in prison (sentenced for the murder of her lover) to his idealistic and futile love for the Princess. Other characters—the saintly Lady Aurora; the indigent, disabled, ever-cheerful, and aptly named Rosy Muniment (younger sister of Paul); Miss Pynsent, who selflessly raises Hyacinth amidst her pinched and cramped quarters, dreaming of the aristocracy—are even more permeated by pathos. James may have pictured Hyacinth as a facsimile of himself, wandering the streets as a new arrival in London, but he places him in a setting with quite different literary attachments. What this means is that the representation of political violence finds itself lodged within a sentimental plot structure that has its own prerogatives. Indeed, *The Princess Casamassima* ultimately shows just how inexorably anarchist violence merges into the melodramatic, and this is not surprising, given the prominent role of sentiment in the reform novels of the period, James's literary context for the novel. The hyperbolic understanding of anarchist violence, as it developed throughout the late nineteenth century, makes powerful generic demands, which are not easily brushed aside. Dynamite might give the subgenre its name, but in James's rendition, the shattering violence of explosion, like the politics that engender it, fades away, the theatricality of explosion rewritten as the psychological combustion of melodrama.

Explosion and Melodrama: *The Secret Agent*

James suggests, in the end, that his English-born protagonist has no real affinity with anarchist destruction, but in *The Secret Agent*, Conrad proposes that we press the question in a different way, as it was also urgently posed by the historical bombings on English soil: what does it mean for dynamite violence to lodge right here, at home? Though its darkly comic tone and hyperbolic parody debunk the anarchist movement and its personae—leading some commentators to see it primarily as a reactionary fable—*The Secret Agent* offers a rich and deeply considered reflection on political violence.[66] Like *The Princess Casamassima* and other works of the three preceding decades, Conrad's novel enters the world of revolutionaries and their bombs, and does so both with comic zeal and with pointed introspection. Indeed, what makes *The Secret Agent* especially rewarding as a reflection on the culture of political violence at the turn of the century is that it plunges headlong into the material realities of dynamite violence, even as it capaciously incorporates nearly all the tropes and strategies for representing terrorism that circulated in the contemporary culture. Along the way, Conrad considers the nature of dynamite's sensation: how dynamite violence registers ethically as a subject for fiction, what its shock value means for characters and plots. In *The Secret Agent*, we find all the key terms brought vividly together—dynamite, anarchism, terrorism, sensation, melodrama—and out of this jostling group of historical and literary phenomena emerges a new and eerie image of the future. The literary flamboyance of sensationalism and the popular consolations of melodrama are given moments of triumph in *The Secret Agent*, before they are eroded by an insinuation of ongoing and infectious dread. Ultimately, *The Secret Agent* charts an evolution from the anarchist moment, in all its Victorian detail (which the novel relishes), toward the full-fledged terrorist mode, a more generalized condition of existence extending into the future. It is not a straightforward journey, finding accommodating generic structures for its violent content along the way—only to abandon each. In fact, it is the creed of the novel to refute the possibility that literature can manage the excesses of political violence, for the novel is built around the idea that such acts are the epitome of senselessness.

Indeed, the distinguishing features of Conrad's tone with respect to his subject matter are his insistence on the meaninglessness surrounding the Greenwich bombing and his stress on the contrast between motive (obscure and cynical) and outcome (gruesome and extreme). In an author's note appended to the 1920 edition of *The Secret Agent*, Conrad describes the Greenwich explosion in terms of its unfathomability. The Greenwich affair was, he declares,

> . . . a blood-stained inanity of so fatuous a kind that it was impossible to fathom its origin by any reasonable or even unreasonable process of thought. For perverse unreason has its own logical processes. But that outrage could not be laid hold of mentally in any sort of way, so that one remained faced by the fact of a man blown to bits for nothing even most remotely resembling an idea, anarchistic or other. (*SA*, 5)

If the underlying precept of propaganda by deed is interpretive—that there is, in fact, an idea at the basis of every terrorist act—Conrad dismisses this premise, substituting his own ethical and literary standards for the anarchist theory of political violence. The expression of violence and the expression of motive are thoroughly disengaged, and it is in this gap that he finds the literary challenge. Dynamite explosion thus brings to the fore such Conradian features as ambiguity and unknowability—a disjunction between horrendous realities in the world and obscure signifying practices—or, as he repeatedly figures it in *The Secret Agent*, the specter of insanity. "Madness alone is truly terrifying," says Vladimir; Heat insists to Verloc, "you must have been crazy"; Winnie's suicide becomes inscribed as a question of "madness or despair"; and the novel ends with a vision of the professor sowing his own insanity in unknowable new directions (*SA*, 31, 160). These evasive and yet figuratively rich possibilities—the gulf of meaning surrounding extraordinary violence, its madness—makes dynamite explosion particularly resonant for Conrad, drawing him to consider its cultural and bodily expressions.

It should not surprise us to find Conrad intrigued by dynamite outrages, since a broad inquiry into the shapes and consequences of violence forms an essential part of his literary legacy. In addition to his career-long exploration into the endemic violence of imperialism, Conrad turned with special interest to nineteenth-century revolutionaries, and to anarchists in particular. In a cluster of works of the first decade of the century (*Nostromo*, 1904; "An Informer" and "An Anarchist," 1906, later in *A Set of Six*; *The Secret Agent*, 1907; *Under Western Eyes*, 1911), he probed the question of what political violence is, how it works, what it accomplishes, what its protagonists look like, and what the fiction writer's role might be in addressing this complex equation. In all of these works, and especially in *The Secret Agent*, Conrad goes well beyond simply representing revolutionary violence: he considers its metaphysical, historical, material, and personal ramifications; he creates characters (such as Chief Inspector Heat in *The Secret Agent*) who want to understand violence in its essential forms; and he returns over and over to the moment of violent action and to the nature of bodily catastrophe.[67] These texts, like the bulk of Conrad's work, are marked by relentless irony, and he heaps contempt on revolutionaries of all sorts. But such tonal issues ought not to blind us to the seriousness with which Conrad took on the problem of political violence, or to the complexity of outcomes that his works on the subject develop. The novel thus recalls the pandying passage from *A Portrait of the Artist as a Young Man*, where the central depiction of violence as originary and transformative was left intact even by Joyce's habitual ironizing.

Certainly, Conrad knew a great deal about anarchism, notwithstanding his protestations to the contrary. In both personal letters and in his author's note to *The Secret Agent*, he declared himself to be uninformed about the workings of anarchists in general, which he brushed off as only of vague interest, and about the Greenwich bombing of February 1894 in particular, which he claimed not to have followed in the papers at the time or to have researched in any detail when composing the novel. But critics have refuted these statements and shown quite conclusively that Conrad was highly educated on the topic of anarchist violence.[68] He had access, through Ford, to the London anarchist scene (such as that portrayed in *A Girl Among the Anarchists*) and to insider accounts of what may have actually transpired in the Greenwich case; there is every reason to believe he had, in fact, followed the reportage of the Greenwich explosion at the time and read further about it in later years; and his personal and familial history gave him a special interest in the workings of European revolutionaries.

In fact, even without scholars chasing him down, Conrad gives himself away. In the author's note, written over a decade after the novel, Conrad's prose is still inundated by the journalistic language of anarchism (he uses terms like "outrage" in double and triple senses, repeatedly employs "anarchism" as both a philosophy and a form of meaningless destruction, and is still consumed with the sensationalism of dynamite explosion). The novel itself, composed, it should be stressed, well after the period it depicts, is so replete with characters and plots out of that earlier period as to read like a handbook of late-Victorian conventions for construing the anarchist scene. So, for instance, the idea that anarchism and violence are inescapable partners is writ into the saga as a premise; the presence of dynamite is the linchpin of the text; the anarchists in *The Secret Agent* fall into typologies as they so often did in the literature of the period, each portraying some aspect of the terrorist; semifictionalized events like the Rome conference to which Vladimir refers have historical counterparts[69]; and the novel returns incessantly to a number of themes that dominated the late-Victorian rendition of anarchism, such as the emphasis on bombs as the inevitable tool of anarchists, the freighted relation between words and deeds, and the international quality of the movement. Moreover, Conrad mirrored in his novel the coverage of the Greenwich bombing in many particulars. That reportage was elaborate and detailed. Over many weeks, it followed the progress of the investigation; analyzed the bomber Bourdin's personal and political history, as well as anarchist activity more generally; drew comparisons and connections to the Café Terminus bombing in Paris (which had only just occurred); and reported on Bourdin's funeral, a large event whose public and celebratory nature outraged many in the general public. The newspaper coverage was also gruesome, as, for instance, in *The Times'* initial report of the scene: "The first [park keeper] to arrive found a man half crouching on the ground. His legs were shattered, one arm was blown away, and the stomach and abdomen were torn open. [new paragraph] As the keeper came up to him the man faintly besought help and then fell forward on his face, unconscious, in a great pool of his own blood."[70] Such reportage would have been hard to miss, even for someone without Conrad's particular interests and connections. The sensational newsworthiness of anarchism provided its essential, guiding principle, yet this was a quality that also made Conrad want to distance his novel from the historical setting.

Conrad's ambivalent position about writing what we might call "historical fiction" suggests a central orientation of his novel: an oscillation between an attention to the materiality of both history and the body and a recourse to generic forms like caricature and melodrama that reduce the pointedness of such effects. We might look, for instance, to the novel's first page, to see how this dynamic gets established:

The window contained photographs of more or less undressed dancing girls; nondescript packages in wrappers like patent medicines; closed yellow paper envelopes, very flimsy, and marked two and six in heavy black figures; a few numbers of ancient French comic publications hung across a string as if to dry; a dingy blue china bowl, a casket of black wood, bottles of marking ink, and rubber stamps; a few books, with titles hinting at impropriety; a few apparently old copies of obscure newspapers, badly printed, with titles like *The Torch*, *The Gong*—rousing titles. And the two gas-jets inside the panes were always turned low, either for economy's sake or for the sake of the customers. (*SA*, 9)

Conrad's realism here is oblique, since it gives a detailed and evocative sense of setting precisely through a language of evasion ("more or less," "nondescript," "like," "as if," "hinting at," "apparently," "obscure," "either . . . or"). When we do get a concrete detail, in the names of the two anarchist journals, Conrad's method shows its elusive qualities even more pointedly: one of these, the *Torch*, was an actual journal (edited by the Rossetti children), while the other *The Gong*, is fictional, a takeoff on such real "rousing" periodicals as *The Alarm*. Why mix the historical detail with the parodic? The answer, I think, is that the novel wants to have it both ways with respect to history. It wants simultaneously to offer a harrowing account of violence and to evade that materiality via the ruses of literary conventions like melodrama geared to such excesses and predicated on some distance from factual history. Conrad thus develops an accordion-like movement in and out of history, which in turn also implies a movement closer to and further from the body. In this novel, the body, in a certain sense, is history; to come close to one is also to approach the other. Conrad makes these counterpointing moves—in the direction toward and away from an embodied sense of history—from the novel's first paragraphs through to the author's note of the next decade, but it is in the text's crisis event that this structure takes most powerful form.

I have said that dynamite explosion in this period signified ungovernable excess. Nowhere is such an explosion more vividly imagined than in the destruction of Stevie in *The Secret Agent*:

Another waterproof sheet was spread over that table in the manner of a table cloth with the corners turned up over a sort of mound—a heap of rags, scorched and blood stained, half concealing what might have been an accumulation of raw material for a cannibal feast. It required considerable firmness of mind not to recoil before that sight . . .

... The Chief Inspector's eyes searched the gruesome detail of that heap of mixed things, which seemed to have been collected in shambles and rag shops.

'You used a shovel,' he remarked, observing a sprinkling of small gravel, tiny brown bits of bark, and particles of splintered wood as fine as needles.

'Had to in one place,' said the stolid constable. 'I sent a keeper to fetch a spade. When he heard me scraping the ground with it he leaned his forehead against a tree, and was as sick as a dog.' (SA, 70–71)

Weil's "thing" produced by force comes to mind here, along with its inexorable conjuring of the humanity lost to its power. And Stevie's story embodies real pathos, from his beginnings as the victim of paternal brutality, to a life marked by scant affection and by frustrated attempts to imagine and promote social justice, to his hideously violent demise. Chief Inspector Heat perhaps speaks for all of us when he surmises about the effect of the bomb's "ruthless cruelty" at the moment of Stevie's death: "The man, whoever he was, had died instantaneously; and yet it seemed impossible to believe that a human body could have reached that state of disintegration without passing through the pangs of inconceivable agony" (SA, 71). It is crucially important for the novel's reflection on violence, as well as its meditation on time, that Conrad jumps over the bombing itself, giving us only its remnants, yet insisting that to contemplate these remains is to step imaginatively back in time to the moment of their horrific creation. It may simply be impossible, in *The Secret Agent*, to bracket the moment of explosive violence, hence the Professor's feverish labor to create the perfect detonator—one that will, however, never be able to eliminate the fateful twenty seconds between detonation and explosion.[71] As we shall see, the issue of what kind of imaginative acts evolve to account for the gap in time that mark Stevie's death—and for those unforgettable remains— is a highly potent question for the direction the novel will take.

Stevie's empathy for suffering brings him closer than anyone else in the novel to the social vision of the period's revolutionaries. If the novel's four anarchists— Yundt, Michaelis, Ossipon, and the Professor—are eviscerated of any real humanity and represent something like an amalgamated and distorted portrait of actual and imagined terrorists, Stevie-as-representative lurches in the opposite direction, embodying a generalized empathy for suffering of the sort that animated historical anarchists to an important degree.[72] Or we might put it this way: Conrad very self-consciously sets out to caricature the anarchists at the same time that he gives us a version of anarchism's message in the person of Stevie, who functions as a whirling vortex of impressions stamped by the sadistic world around him. Stevie's sense that life is marked by pain and cruelty, and his status as the whipping boy for the world's brutality, make him especially responsive and susceptible—literally, as he is destroyed by violence, and figuratively, as he reacts to the suffering he envisages around him. Dogged by a "morbid horror and dread of physical pain," Stevie visualizes physical suffering in others, as, for instance, when he responds to Yundt's vivid depiction of the ruling classes as cannibalistic torturers: "Stevie knew very well that hot iron applied to one's skin hurt very much . . . it would hurt terribly" (*SA*, 42). Where Yundt's language dwells with evident relish on the misery of exploited flesh ("Can't you smell and hear from here the thick hide of the people burn and sizzle?"), Stevie's response is visceral, personal, and direct—in a word, humane (*SA*, 41). We are told, moreover, that the fourteen-year-old Stevie, riled to fury at the mistreatment of fellow workers, had set off fireworks in the office where he was employed as an errand boy, in the hopes, apparently, of destroying the place. Such an event quite clearly refers to a type of anarchist "outrage," in marked contrast to the novel's Greenwich bombing, whose social and political meaning is entirely contrived by cynical operatives, working in the interest of their own power.[73]

Stevie the anarchist even has a slogan of his own, developed in his sputtering way, in response to his interaction with a one-armed cabman and his decrepit horse: "bad world for poor people" (*SA*, 132). "Bad world for poor people" is certainly an accurate description of the state of poverty in urban London, and it also mirrors the kinds of messages about social injustice that anarchists and other revolutionaries worked to disseminate. The scene in which this lesson is learned, however, is a tour de force of comic writing (a simultaneous satire and enactment of the classic industrial novel, and a blistering riff on Raskolnikov's dream in *Crime and Punishment* [1866]), and it would be very difficult to take Stevie's moral encapsulation of the social drama witnessed there as the novel's own unironic credo.[74] As a spokesman for social justice, the well-meaning Stevie is nevertheless a caricature, just as the image of him as modern artist is equally parodic: "the innocent Stevie, sitting very good and quiet at a deal table, drawing circles, circles, circles; innumerable circles, concentric, eccentric; a coruscating whirl of circles that by their tangled multitude of repeated curves, uniformity of form, and confusion of intersecting lines suggested a rendering of cosmic chaos, the symbolism of a mad art attempting the inconceivable" (*SA*, 40).

If Stevie's status as artist and anarchist is at once constructed and denied, his physical being remains shockingly visible. More generally in *The Secret Agent*, the flesh of humanity has an inescapable and ubiquitous presence. Conrad seems unusually repulsed in this novel by the body, which appears outsized, a stifling physical cage to match the claustrophobia of the urban scene. And these are not incidental suggestions of disgust; James English, for one, has located the crux of Conrad's political intervention in his creation of such figures as the fat anarchist, an irony that encapsulates a variety of contradictions in the political imaginary of the period. For the anarchist to be fat is to represent precisely that which he is supposed to destroy (the fattened bourgeoisie being a stock image for the hated status quo, as in my epigraph from Ravachol) and to embody a whole series of ironies about their (in)efficacy and belatedness.[75] All of this attention to the flesh reaches its apex in the person of Stevie, whose quivering body reacts to the felt reality and to the mere prospect of pain. When Stevie is blown up, his dripping, shattered remains seem like a confrontation to any form of conceptual or literary accommodation. Stevie is now all flesh; his anarch*ism* reduced to the anarchy of cells and bones and organs and muscles, his chaotic artistry the abstraction of a body whose contours have been entirely fragmented and erased. In this scenario, his body's radical fleshiness loses its status as satire and becomes, instead, an unbearable burden.

This notion of burden is literalized in the object that comes to symbolize Stevie's decimated state: the shovel. The shovel that they use to scrape up his scattered body parts—the shovel that is a part of every reference to his death—becomes the metonymical trace of a physical situation almost too gruesome to contemplate. The novel pulls back from Stevie's death—the thought of what kind of agony he might have suffered in the instant of explosion left as a haunting question—but it repeatedly returns to the shovel. A rustic and primitive implement, a distinctly humble object, the shovel is associated not so much with the cityscape of London as with the ground in general, the site of agriculture and also of burial. It is strikingly an object; with its simple form and universal recognizability, it is completely visually available. When pain becomes unimaginable, it seems, the imagination turns to what it knows, the world of objects. In the passage where Stevie's remains are initially described, this crystallizing of affect into the shovel takes two forms: first, it is the sound of the shovel (rather than the sight of Stevie's exploded body) that induces the keeper's vomiting, and second, the invocation of the shovel immediately follows two metaphors ("what might have been an accumulation of raw material for a cannibal feast" and "which seemed to have been collected in shambles and rag shops"), both of which are jarringly incongruous, and which, in a sense, are replaced by this much more vivid image. The shovel works metonymically; more than any metaphoric solution (cannibal feasts, rag shops), by holding and touching the body's remains, it stands imaginatively for their terrible reality. Metonymy nudges out metaphor, bringing us closer to the body, but that metonymy immediately works too well, generating a vivid return to the body (in the form of the keeper's reaction).

The fragmented body of Stevie creates a powerful challenge, which will call up a variety of responses. But the first is to linger on the shovel. Winnie, for one, returns instinctively to it:

> That's where the boy was killed. A park—smashed branches, torn leaves, gravel, bits of brotherly flesh and bone, all spouting up together in the manner of a firework. She remembered now what she had heard, and she remembered it pictorially. They had to gather him up with the shovel. Trembling all over with irrepressible shudders, she saw before her the very implement with its ghastly load scraped up from the ground. (*SA*, 195–96)

Though Winnie's structures of thought may not be exactly normative—her susceptibility to journalistic phraseology, for instance, approaches the pathological—her response to Stevie's body in ruins does function paradigmatically. An excess of violence, here, pushes the imagination not toward any given political meaning—as the principle of propaganda by deed would suggest—but toward an imagism that exists at the opposite end of the intelligible spectrum. There is no "idea" to associate with the shovel; its work seems to belie the very notion of interpretability.

Such spare imagism, a reaction to the exploded body, must nevertheless confront dynamite's other central attribute, its sensationalism. Dynamite violence was sensational almost by definition, incorporating its key components of graphic violence, the threat of escalation, social transgression, and mystery. Sensationalism, one of modernity's favorite self-fulfilling vices, represented a pivot point in late-Victorian conceptions of modern crime. Over and over, the culture asked itself whether and how the media (newspapers, penny dreadfuls, novels) influenced criminal behavior, thus indicting its own most basic impulses, such as the dissemination of information and the abhorring of violence. The never-solved Ripper murders in London's East End (1888), to take the most notorious case, spawned their own textual industry, in a lavish display of interest, fascination, anxiety, and seemingly endless hand-wringing with respect to responsibility.[76] The mutuality linking horrific crime with the ever-broadening news media thus represents a rich topic in Victorian cultural history; the history of anarchism and the theatricality of dynamite violence in particular were always thoroughly intertwined with sensationalism. The notion of propaganda by deed, for one, depended on a sensationalist-minded press, which would spread word of anarchist outrages far and wide and help to stir public fear and interest. More generally, what makes a crime "terrorist" in structure is its determination to send a message, and for this journalism was the central form of communication.

The Secret Agent, which makes the proximity between the novel and the newspaper visible at every turn, indirectly confronts its own relation to news in general and to sensationalism in particular. As with the shovel and the body, Conrad presents the language of the press in a relation of adjacency to the reader's consciousness (rather than as lodging within the mind, encased by it). So, for instance:

> It was a raw, gloomy day of the early spring; and the grimy sky, the mud of the street, the rags of the dirty men harmonised excellently with the eruption of the damp, rubbishy sheets of paper soiled with printers' ink. The posters, maculated with filth, garnished like tapestry the sweep of the kerbstone. The trade in afternoon papers was brisk, yet, in comparison with the swift, constant march of foot traffic, the effect was of indifference, of a disregarded distribution. (*SA*, 65)

Layers upon layers of proximity: the ink rubs against the papers (an interesting form of writing), the city's grime against people and advertisements, the papers against the passing multitudes. Every element in the city soils every other element, but the printers' ink seems the most transferable, leaving its traces on a population that is all the more receptive for its obliviousness and indifference.

"Rubbing off" seems the appropriate figure for the uneasy relation of the news media to political violence, both within *The Secret Agent* and in the contemporary understanding more broadly. The question of what effect journalism had on the escalation of anarchist attacks was always a thorny one. If journals of all sorts made much of the specter of anarchist violence, there was also an uneasiness as to whether their coverage might contribute to the celebrity, and hence, in a certain way, the success, of the revolutionaries. The anarchist Stepniak, to take a surprising example, lays heavy blame on journalism for fomenting high-profile anarchist violence, which he felt hurt the broader cause. In addressing "The Dynamite Scare and Anarchy," he writes:

> . . . it is the sensational journalism which deserves the palm for its efforts in spreading and protracting the dynamite epidemics. It is the noise made about these outrages, the shocking rush after every personal detail of the lives of their authors when detected, interviewing them, hunting up their genealogy, recording their words, which gives them the proud sensation of having shaken with one blow the foundations of society, and which may turn the heads of outsiders as well. Against this influence of journalism we are powerless.[77]

Not surprisingly, Conrad offers a variety of viewpoints on the question of sensational journalism.[78] On one hand, in *The Secret Agent*, he suggests that the grimy printers' ink has rubbed off on the populace to such a degree that they can only think in terms of journalistic formulations. So Winnie is driven mad by the phrase "the drop given was fourteen feet"; her mantra-like repetition of these words, whose precise meaning is as vague to her as her children's book vision of the gallows, transforms her from an independent, "free" woman (as she conceives herself in the moments after her mental break from Verloc) into a cringing mess, clinging desperately to her rescuer Tom Ossipon. And Ossipon, in turn, for all his self-serving callousness, is also haunted by the language of the newspapers, in this case the melodramatic account he reads of Winnie's death: "*An impenetrable mystery seems destined to hang for ever over this act of madness or despair*" (*SA*, 228, italics in original). The suggestion here is twofold: that people learn how to read their own interior lives by what they read in the papers (a familiar postmodern insight), and that the nature of this particular "simple tale," as Conrad subtitled the novel, is so entwined with the kinds of events covered in newspapers and journals as to make it almost emanate from the press. It is highly appropriate, then, that when Winnie learns about her brother's death, her first response is to rip a newspaper down the middle. In a sense, her shredding of the paper functions as her first act of revenge (the second being Verloc's murder), a lashing out against the textual matter that Winnie, at some level, understands to be partially responsible for her brother's death.

Yet if the novel critiques the insidious power of the press to construct human interiority, it also succumbs to the general infatuation with anarchist violence, as understood and imagined by journalists at the time of the Greenwich bombing. Though the shovel appears to have been Conrad's innovation, and though Bourdin was actually alive when first discovered (quite unlike Stevie), the novel remains true to contemporary newspaper accounts, which returned ineluctably to the bomber's exploded body. The degree to which Bourdin was mangled, the image of his torn body in what appeared to be a kneeling position, the speculation about where and how the explosion occurred and what the effects must have been on his person—all of this formed part of the news coverage. Conrad insisted that Bourdin's death was meaningless, but the tendency within the press was to attempt to make the Greenwich bombing comprehensible in human and political terms, and something like this, too, is a major endeavor of *The Secret Agent*. Conrad's decision to write a novel about the Greenwich bombing at all testifies to his attraction to sensational news, since no "outrage" generated more coverage in England than this one. As Vladimir—Conrad's alter ego in the novel, who plots its course and explicates its mysteries even before they exist—muses, "Every newspaper has ready-made phrases to explain such manifestations [as political assassination] away," but an outrage like the Greenwich bombing would be sure to "raise a howl of execration" (*SA*, 30, 32).

More generally, Conrad was concerned both with how the press reports violent events and with the way such reportage correlates to the imaginative capacities of the citizenry. In "Autocracy and War" (1905), an essay he wrote as he was composing *The Secret Agent*, he makes a strong case against the way violence is and can be reported.[79] The essay focuses on the Russo-Japanese War, then underway, which Conrad believed forecast the ultimate demise of the Russian empire. Conrad lodges a heavy critique of the coverage of the war—odd, in some senses, given that, as Frederic Sharf writes, "No war in prior history had ever been observed as closely, or recorded in so many formats," with foreign journalists stationed in Russia and Japan, and as "written and pictorial accounts of the war were brought together and distributed on an unprecedented scale and speed" all over the world.[80] Nevertheless (or perhaps in response to this relative onslaught), in Conrad's view, such reportage cannot approach the real suffering that war entails:

> . . . the war in the Far East has been made known to us, so far, in a grey reflection of its terrible and monotonous phases of pain, death, sickness; a reflection seen in the perspective of thousands of miles, in the dim atmosphere of official reticence, through the veil of inadequate words. Inadequate, I say, because what had to be reproduced is beyond the common experience of war, and our imagination, luckily for our peace of mind, has remained a slumbering faculty, notwithstanding the din of humanitarian talk and the real progress of humanitarian ideas. Direct vision of the fact, or the stimulus of a great art, can alone make it turn and open its eyes heavy with blessed sleep . . .[81]

The first part of this passage, with its language about the dim veil through which we view war and its condemnation of inadequate language, seems to promise an attack on the press for its insufficient reporting of a severe human catastrophe. And the self-serving last line seems to point to a happy solution, great art. Yet what is striking is that Conrad does not, in fact, single out the newspaper for its failures; instead, he suggests that the problem lies in the ordinary human faculties for apprehending and imagining violence in its full, embodied reality.

As for statistics and numbers, these are even less effective in stimulating the empathetic mind:

> An over-worked horse falling in front of our windows, a man writhing under a cart-wheel in the street, awaken more genuine emotion, more horror, pity,

and indignation than the stream of reports, appalling in their monotony, of tens of thousands of decaying bodies tainting the air of the Manchurian plains, of other tens of thousands of maimed bodies groaning in ditches, crawling on the frozen ground, filling the field hospitals; of the hundreds of thousands of survivors no less pathetic and even more tragic in being left alive by fate to the wretched exhaustion of their pitiful toil. (NLL, 112–13)

Conrad is troubled by the fact that a person in England might react with apathy to the horrendous suffering of victims in a distant war, but with sympathy to a dying horse and an injured man in the street. Such a comparison suggests ignorance, surely, but, more pointedly, it raises the possibility that there is something inauthentic and suspect in one's feeling "horror" and "pity" at the spectacles of London. Most centrally, by contrasting sympathy for the suffering of the poor at home with the indifference to those out of reach, Conrad establishes and attacks a particular structure of feeling. The problem may not derive from bad faith (suggested in the phrase "official reticence" or in the general condemnation of the press) so much as from a narrowness in the imaginative range of the reading public.

What differentiates the horrendous situation of the victims of a modern war from the sad state of the overworked horse and man—to Conrad's late-Victorian imagination—is that the former is infused with politics and the latter with melodrama. Conrad's own descriptions of soldiers' suffering certainly stress the human, physical, one might say universal, elements of the war's devastating effects, and hence, as Elaine Scarry reminds us, those elements that are external to politics, but his larger insistence in "Autocracy and War" is that this war represents a major turning point in world politics ("the ghost of Russia's might is laid" [NLL, 120]).[82] In a certain sense, the suffering of those injured, writhing bodies on the Manchurian plains is attached to the long history of imperial Russia, and thus is infused with political significance. But journalism can do justice neither to the richness of history nor to the magnitude of a human crisis: "there must be something subtly noxious to the human brain in the composition of newspaper ink," Conrad reflects, "or else it is that the large page, the columns of words, the leaded headings, exalt the mind into a state of feverish credulity. The printed page of the Press makes a sort of still uproar, taking from men both the power to reflect and the faculty of genuine feeling; leaving them only the artificially created need of having something exciting to talk about" (NLL, 121). As in The Secret Agent, where the newspaper is figured in terms of its materiality, here, too, the physical paper—its ink, style, format—determines its effects. That format, in Conrad's view, transforms a story of both physical and historical magnitude into a catalyst for inauthentic feeling.

The desire for "something exciting to talk about" replaces any serious engagement with the significance of the war; heightened emotion of a comfortably familiar variety elbows out the more difficult reckoning with political violence on the large scale of war.

And this is exactly what happens in *The Secret Agent*: it turns from the unendurable reality of Stevie's body and the shovel to the melodramatic story of Winnie's revenge and suicide. In doing so, it moves from a form of violence whose contours are unfixable, as the body itself becomes fragmented beyond recognition, and whose connections to political violence carry over all the incommensurabilities inherent in dynamite violence, to a kind of violence that can be understood because it can be attached to familiar literary traditions (familiar and also adaptable). Or, we might say that it shifts from political violence to domestic violence, and in this shift, it taps into available narrative conventions.[83] When the Assistant Commissioner notes that "from a certain point of view, we are here in the presence of a domestic drama" (*SA*, 168), he articulates a truth about the novel in several senses. At one level, the distinction is between what is English and what is foreign, a divide that interests Conrad precisely for its instability. If the conventional representation of anarchists as a foreign infection had become canonical by the time Conrad wrote *The Secret Agent*, and if Conrad gives his anarchists the requisite international credentials, he nevertheless deconstructs these conventions. The sequence in which the Assistant Commissioner wanders through Soho, dining at an Italian restaurant, is particularly rich for its evocation of a new hybridity that casts suspicion on the idea of authentic national markings or characteristics. The Assistant Commissioner is himself identified as "foreign-looking," while the actual foreigners in this scene are as much a simulacrum, a product of the new commercial phenomenon called the restaurant, as they are representatives of anything "foreign" in the usual sense. (This sequence perhaps also recalls Conrad himself, the Polish-born British citizen, who always spoke English with a heavy accent, and who, following James in the preface to *The Princess Casamassima*, refers in the author's note to a vivid memory of "solitary and nocturnal walks all over London in my early days" [*SA*, 7]).[84]

But the characterization of the tale as a "domestic drama" also applies more specifically to the novel's propulsion as it turns its focus to Winnie, and refers to the domesticity of the home—a home that, in this case, is anything but protective.[85] For Winnie's story, like her brother's, is a story of spiraling and shifting violence. Winnie's childhood in a brutal home, where, cowering herself, she had attempted to shelter Stevie from the attacks of their father, comes back in the form of memories of those half-successful attempts to nurture and protect:

She remembered brushing the boy's hair and tying his pinafores—herself in a pinafore still; the consolations administered to a small and badly scared creature by another creature nearly as small but not quite so badly scared; she had the vision of the blows intercepted (often with her own head), of a door held desperately shut against a man's rage (not for very long); of a poker flung once (not very far), which stilled that particular storm into the dumb and awful silence which follows a thunder-clap. (*SA*, 183)

All of this has been internalized by the adult Winnie, whose placid exterior belies a reckoning of the world as defined by violence. Hers is the interiority of "the potential violence of tragic passions"; she feels her brother's death as "a white-hot iron drawn across her eyes." Like Stevie, she has a visceral empathy for victimization, born of her own terrified childhood (*SA*, 160, 182). Conrad treats Winnie's family background allusively, by suggestion more than detailed narration, but his representation of the traces of domestic violence in the persons of Winnie and Stevie nevertheless suggests something important about how violence operates. Conrad, like the nineteenth-century industrial novelists who preceded him in considering an endemic social violence, presents this brutal background as a matter of exposing the violence that attends the lives of the working classes ("bad world for poor people," to recall Stevie's formulation), but also as a kind of metaphor or originating point for the ensuing violence that sweeps through the novel.

In this sense, he demonstrates the doubled nature of intensive (subjective, private, originary) and extensive (outward, public, allegorical) modes for representing violence, as initially encountered in the passage from *A Portrait of the Artist as a Young Man*. Winnie's powerfully interiorized, if half-remembered, experiences of victimization, like Stevie's reactive body and psyche, bring to the fore the most intimate reckoning with violence, while their stories sweep outward in the direction of a broader social critique. In this sense, her story tracks with a common literary tendency in the period, as the concerted effort to express a sense of primacy in the instant of experienced violence meets an equally motivated social drama. The moment of internality and the impulse to widen the narrative are melded in such reckonings, suggesting continuities and parallels, and illuminating the very thorough permeation of violence into both private and public spheres. In *The Secret Agent*, the shift from political violence to domestic violence suggests that violence never abates or disappears. Stevie's death is a culmination of his life, just as Winnie's revenge against Verloc culminates her own story of frustrated, ineffective efforts at protection.

And yet, the domesticating of violence in *The Secret Agent* also makes it conceivable; with Winnie's murder of her husband, violence can find its conventions.

The first killing in the novel—the destruction of Stevie—was one that, as we have seen, Conrad claimed "could not be laid hold of mentally in any sort of way." The second murder, by contrast, bears the hallmarks of a kind of sensationalism that can be considered amenable to a reading public, indeed to those very readers of grimy newspapers with bold headlines of whom Conrad had despaired in "Autocracy and War." Though both bodies inspire their discoverer to vomit (the keeper in the case of Stevie, Ossipon for Verloc), the spectacle of Verloc's body is quite different from the "sort of mound" that marked Stevie's lumped remains:

> It was the handle of the domestic carving knife with nothing strange about it but its position at right angles to Mr Verloc's waistcoat and the fact that something dripped from it. Dark drops fell on the floor-cloth one after another, with a sound of ticking growing fast and furious like the pulse of an insane clock. At its highest speed this ticking changed into a continuous sound of trickling. Mrs Verloc watched that transformation with shadows of anxiety coming and going on her face. It was a trickle, dark, swift, thin . . . Blood! (*SA*, 199)

What a striking contrast divides the defining object that touches Verloc's body—the carving knife—from the shovel that bore Stevie's remains. If the latter suggested a challenge to metaphor, along with an imaginative return to rusticity and the fundamental mortality of the body, the carving knife brings us back to the realm of fiction, and particularly to sensational crime fiction. As a talisman, the carving knife promotes itself as the signifier for a popular literature that stands in the same relation to Conrad's ironized tales of political intrigue as the "sea life of light literature" read by a young Lord Jim stands to Conrad's fractured imperial tales.[86] *Lord Jim* may at first promise to give us that popular literature of empire only by way of nostalgia, but in the Patusan sequence, Conrad unfurls his own florid, romantic tapestry, an interlude seeped in orientalism and exuberant as a generic getaway. Likewise, *The Secret Agent* eventually presents the dripping blood of a thriller; it becomes, at least for a while, a suspense story. Or perhaps it would be more accurate to say that both implements, the knife and the shovel, signal the promise and the problem of sensationalism in their own forms: the shovel by way of self-critique, pointing to the novel's concern with its own adjacency to journalism and to the illegibility of the brutal, modern city, the knife by way of inaugurating a style within a style. Conrad himself described *The Secret Agent* as "a sustained effort in ironical treatment of a melodramatic subject," but it might be more accurate to say that irony gives way to melodrama in the novel, as the language depicting the novel's later crimes, with its attachment to popular forms, overtakes the murky nonconventions that obstruct the approach to Stevie's obliterated body, the user and victim of dynamite.[87]

If we return to Winnie's "pictorial" response to her brother's death, we will find the movement from inconceivable explosion to literary accommodation encoded in her structure of thought. I have quoted this passage in my discussion of the first reaction to Stevie's body, the turn toward the shovel ("Trembling all over with irrepressible shudders, she saw before her the very implement with its ghastly load scraped up from the ground"). What follows is a departure from that implement into a more frenzied pictorial panorama:

> Mrs Verloc closed her eyes desperately, throwing upon that vision the night of her eyelids, where after a rainlike fall of mangled limbs the decapitated head of Stevie lingered suspended alone, and fading out slowly like the last star of a pyrotechnic display. Mrs Verloc opened her eyes. (*SA*, 196)

The garishness of Winnie's vision of her brother's head floating in the sky suggests an entirely different imaginative system from the grounded realism of the shovel. In fact, that realist moment fell in the middle of this sequence, momentarily freezing the working of her fervent vision, making her shudder (like Stevie himself), but she circles back, as her eyes close, to the fireworks where she began, which recall Stevie in a double sense, since his exploding of fireworks was the early sign of his anarchist tendencies.

As Winnie's imagination indicates, explosive violence ultimately calls for figurative hyperbole, not imagism but imagistic overload—indeed the supplanting of the unimaginable body by the concrete object makes the first move in that direction. At one level, the simple shovel with its material load would seem to offer the kind of image that literature especially rewards, in comparison with the bizarre fireworks that surround it. But, in fact, when the night of Winnie's eyelids descends, what emerges is the flamboyant image, the extreme metaphor, the flaunting of figuration. The horribly mangled body, with its telltale implement, stops the imaginative process short; it returns Winnie to her own body, as she shudders irrepressibly; it functions as an impasse. When her vision of fireworks resumes, the exuberance of the figurative capacity reasserts itself. This showcasing of an extreme literary flair, I am suggesting, mirrors, encodes and propels the novel's wider transformation from ironized political drama, where the reality of dynamite violence ferociously cuts through the text, to a melodrama which continues the thematics of violence—and sharing the sense of an originary field of violent, determining events—but within a more theatrical, derealized mode. It is a mode that makes room for open-endedness ("*an impenetrable mystery seems to hang for ever over this act of madness or despair . . .*"), and where the sensation of an invisible suicide has all the pathos missing from the awful remains of an unknown—and, for Conrad, ontologically unknowable—anarchist. The unfathomable nature of exploded bodies and political crime thus gives way to another kind of mystery, one kind of madness to another.

Dynamite and the Future

When dynamite explodes, it can leave behind total fragmentation; but it also can create gashes and tears in the landscape, and these imprinted patterns lead us on a brief side tour, to the novel Conrad wrote immediately before *The Secret Agent*, *Nostromo*, which has more in common with the later work than might immediately be evident:

> Charles Gould was not present at the anxious and patriotic send-off. It was not his part to see the soldiers embark. It was neither his part, nor his inclination, nor his policy. His part, his inclination, and his policy were united in one endeavour to keep unchecked the flow of treasure he had started single-handed from the re-opened scar in the flank of the mountain.[88]

In this passage, and in *Nostromo* more broadly, Conrad gives an elaborate and quite precise view of one kind of gash in the landscape: the San Tomé mine. Overdetermined and foundational, the mine is inescapably envisioned as both a wound on the landscape and a site of unending consequentiality. If for Zola the coal mine continually demanded more and more blood in an endless cycle of destructive revenge, Conrad's depiction of the reopened scar in the mountain's flank deflects both politics and violence—yet not exactly. The novel, that is, offers much by way of analysis of more properly political violence (civil war; the grisly hanging of a political prisoner), but what the mine-as-rip adds is a form of productivity that simultaneously avoids and emanates from those eruptions. The gash of the mine, site for the endless production of silver and engendering point for the buried treasure that is such an overdetermined motif in the novel, functions implicitly alongside the many explicit forms of violence in the text. The mine never technically incites political violence; on the contrary, it is repeatedly imagined as the source for political stability and peace, and yet, of course, its telltale gash calls up the explosiveness that stood in the late nineteenth century for dynamite violence, and its hidden wealth drives the political economy of the region.[89] It is simultaneously a zone cordoned off from war, just as Charles Gould recuses himself from overt political and patriotic activities, and the ultimate image of how the colonized land-scape, penetrated by force, yields its wealth, in both material and cultural terms. The mine, with its magnetism and power, is able to exude what the act of political violence never can: success. Its gash, unlike the ripped flesh and exploded sites that became the familiar marks of a highly questionable political violence in the period, lies at the very center of cultural development.

But there is more: ever canny, and perhaps echoing his author's sense of the ironic structures of power, Charles Gould ensures continued ownership of the mine (and thus, in his view, the mine's protection) by threatening its complete de-struction: "I have enough dynamite stored up at the mountain to send it down crashing into the valley," he explains, "to send half Sulaco into the air if I liked" (*Nostromo*, 170). Or again, "He was prepared, if need be, to blow up the whole San Tomé mountain sky-high out of the territory of the republic" (294). Charles Gould's use of dynamite as prophylactic against political upheaval represents a brilliant reimagining of the contemporary infatuation with dynamite as the material par excellence of anarchism and revolution. By surrounding the mine, dynamite cre-ates a safety wall around it; by promising to explode the mountain completely, it leaves the partial explosion (the gash) intact, thus continuing to yield its many treasures, material and cultural—the creation, in fact, of an entirely new republic—in the interest of the English and their allies.

Gould's trick is spectacularly successful. It also spawns a surprising imitator, the Professor in *The Secret Agent*, who safeguards himself from arrest by carrying a bomb on his person at all times, ready to explode himself (and his potential arresting officer) at a moment's provocation. As he explains it, "'they [the police] know very well I take care never to part with the last handful of my wares. I've it always by me.' He touched the breast of his coat lightly. 'In a thick glass flask'" (*SA*, 55). In *Nostromo*, the dynamite is kept at a slight remove from the mountain, just as the gash remains only analogous to the body. But in *The Secret Agent*, the bomb is nestled on the body, and the hand remains vigilantly on the India rubber ball. The masturbatory image of the Professor grasping the ball in his pocket is no doubt comic (incongruously recalling Pip at the opening of *Great Expectations*), but it is also menacing, crude, and precise.[90] By lodging the device on his body, the Professor indissolubly links protection with annihilation, the prophylactic of *Nostromo* combined with the immense destructive (and self-destructive) force of popular accounts of anarchism, the ultimate mechanism of survival with an extreme vision of destruction—"a dreadful black hole belching horrible fumes choked with ghastly rubbish of smashed brickwork and mutilated corpses" is how Ossipon expresses his disenchanting vision of the likely effects of the Professor exploding (*SA*, 56). It is as if, in the figure of the Professor, Conrad has distilled the dispersed political imaginary surrounding anarchist violence into the tightest of spaces, the "frail" little being of this destructive agent (one of only a few characters in the novel who is not fleshy and obese), folding into itself a generalized image of violence that, in the case of the mine, was instead *exfoliated*—political violence as culturally productive because always held at bay. In closing the gap between weapon and the object of destruction, the Professor enacts what we will see elsewhere in this study at the linguistic level, a drop from allegory into incarnation, or from metaphor into literalness. When that distance is eliminated, moreover, one is left in the profoundly claustrophobic space of an urban sphere that, like the aquarium to which Conrad repeatedly compares London in *The Secret Agent*, seems confined in and by its own vulnerability.

The Professor is, of course, a suicide bomber, or at least he holds out that possibility as his final card to play; in this role, he assumes a new kind of power in the text, what he calls "force."[91] It is the power of the weapon become the person, a complete intertwining of the man himself with an explosive device. In an early discussion with Ossipon, the Professor credits his effectiveness ("I am deadly") to what he calls "force of personality," a sheer will to destruction, which matches his desire for "a clean sweep and a clear start for a new conception of life," language that echoes actual and fictional anarchists from the period (*SA*, 57, 56, 61). Monomaniacal in his search for a perfect detonator, indifferent to any form of human attachment, ascetic in his habits, the Professor has much in common with Nechaev's terrorist from the "Catechism of the Revolution," and, as in Nechaev's treatise, this combination suggests an image of disproportionate power. The Professor is no man of the people—indeed his detestation and horror of the masses represent his most notable weakness—a preacher less of revolution than of simple destruction. In his opening colloquy with Verloc, Vladimir had fantasized about the perfect dynamite attack as one lodged *into* "pure mathematics," but we can also see such a logic extended to the person of the Professor, who represents something like the potential for an attack *of* pure mathematics (*SA*, 31). Conrad seems to agree with the Professor's own arrogant sense of his destructive reach, yielding the novel's final paragraph to him and, perhaps surprisingly, given what many critics take to be an attitude of contempt for all the anarchists in the text, partially echoing his self-assessment:

And the incorruptible Professor walked too, averting his eyes from the odious multitude of mankind. He had no future. He disdained it. He was a force. His thoughts caressed the images of ruin and destruction. He walked

> frail, insignificant, shabby, miserable—and terrible in the simplicity of his
> idea calling madness and despair to the regeneration of the world. Nobody
> looked at him. He passed on unsuspected and deadly, like a pest in the
> street full of men. (*SA*, 231)

For all Conrad's diminishment of the Professor here ("a pest"), the bomb on his body nevertheless transforms London's citizens into his potential victims, a condition that virtually defines the state of terrorism. "He was a force": the repeated term recalls what we have already learned about the idea of "force," what distinguishes it from other forms of violence—its overpowering and sweeping qualities. Here force, in a reversal of Weil's later usage in relation to war, is invisible, and it is that quality which gives it its charge, its "terrible . . . simplicity." Indeed, *The Secret Agent* is a "simple tale" not only for its focus on the bare dynamics of familial revenge, but because it culminates in the "simplicity" of a violence that is pure in its propulsion of a politics-free lust to destroy.

The Professor may himself have "no future," but he offers, quite precisely, an image of the future for the rest of modernity's citizens. It is a future defined by the bomb's hidden presence, by the invisible threat of a single individual, a mere speck amidst "the multitude of mankind," with an excess of violent will. "He was going over there, to the unknown. He was going tranquilly to extermination, wherever there might be dynamite to blow up towns and men. He will be there, without doubt, when the middle class in agony shall hear the pavement of the streets bursting up beneath their feet": not the Professor this time, but Zola's Souvarine; these agents of future destruction were imagined, in a sense, as survivors of their own era, hurtling forth into a dystopian futurity (Zola, 504–5). If the general melting of anarchism into melodrama seems to suggest an eclipsing of its threat into a literary-historical comfort zone, the preserving of the terrorist bespeaks quite a different reckoning with violence in the future. In the end, the structure of dynamite violence seems to come down to two poles: the exploded body (Stevie's physical obliteration) and the menace of the Professor (endlessly seeking a form of extreme destruction). What differentiates them, of course, is agency: the body whose destruction represents an insane crash of force from nowhere and for no purpose, and the body whose self-construction as bomb represents the potential blast of force from a single point and in a surfeit of pure purpose. Once again, it is a structure of everything and nothing, excessive consequence confronting denuded value.

In the end, the afterlife of anarchist violence turns out, tautologically, to be the idea of afterlife. In conceptualizing the body-as-weapon as sheer potentiality, Conrad figures dynamite as an insistent and ineradicable possibility. It would be a technology whose users might change, but whose link with a radical desire to destroy the social structure—or just to destroy human bodies and their landscapes—would remain a constant. There has been no "end of history," as was projected in the late 1980s, but there are points of no return; the violent prospect associated with an individual bomb-thrower, or a man with a bomb in his pocket in the crowded city, is one such point.[92] A bomb explodes in a meeting hall in Australia, killing and injuring. All we really know—all the author feels we need to know—is that "the bomb thrower was an unknown anarchist, probably a new immigrant from Europe."[93] This is D. H. Lawrence's 1923 novel *Kangaroo*, where the anarchist and his bomb make only a cameo appearance in the novel, to serve as deus ex machina and to provide a culminating image for the violence that has been gathering force.[94] But for Lawrence, the bomb also has the effect of releasing the text from its agonistic structure. In the midst, that is, of competing political factions whose rival visions have reached the point of out-and-out clash, Lawrence inserts the anarchist, a figure whose very epithet seems to connote random killing. By the nineteen-twenties, anarchist violence in England could be evacuated of any real meaning—any significance beyond its destructive capacities—but its imaginative utility had broadened and elasticized. Whether in London or Canberra, Lawrence reminds us, our modernity is defined, in part, by its forms of violence. One of these, now and forever, is the explosion—it will be detonated by an unknown actor, "probably a new immigrant from . . ."

3. Cyclical Violence
The Irish Insurrection and the Limits of Enchantment

... the more costly the life-generating processes are, the more squander the production of organisms has required, the more satisfactory the operation is ... The movement of human life even tends toward anguish, as the sign of expenditures that are finally excessive, that go beyond what we can bear. Everything within us demands that death lay waste to us[.]

—Georges Bataille, *The Accursed Share*[1]

Revolutions are incubators of symbolic language. They incite dreams and demand hyperbole; they fictionalize beginnings and project futures; above all, they wrench from violence an abundant cultural value. The Irish Rising of 1916, perhaps more than any other event of the modernist period, conjoined violent political conditions with prolific literary imagining.[2] The language that surrounded it was steeped in imagery of blood sacrifice, and its combined aura of tragedy and triumph invited symbolic interpretation in its own day and for subsequent generations, within just a few years generating a story of national beginnings that was seared into the public consciousness. Indeed, the insurrection was understood and presented, at every level, in a metaphoric language, which stressed apotheosis, resurrection, and transformation. Decades of romantic, nationalist writing preceded and prepared for it to be read in such terms, its leaders deliberately chose Easter Monday as the starting point, the young poets who helped to lead the insurrection presciently invited their own transformation into martyrs, and even its moniker, "the Rising," suggested its symbolic essence. It is thus not surprising that the canonical literary work of the Rising, Yeats's poem "Easter 1916," scrutinizes the process of making revolutionary violence into the aesthetic. With the repeated phrase "All changed, changed utterly:/A terrible beauty is born," Yeats created an especially deft and gorgeous framing for a nearly ubiquitous idea in the period, that in the cauldron of the insurgency, historical violence had forged something arresting and important, in both cultural and aesthetic terms. (As Maude Gonne described the rebels, "they have raised the Irish cause again to a position of tragic dignity."[3]) With the marginalized rebellion of anarchism, literary form expressed a divergence between insurrectionist actors and their publics; in the Ireland of the Rising, by contrast, literary form found an almost exquisite match between its own processes and a readership in sympathy with its metaphors.

Nowhere, it would seem, was the enchantment of violence more available as an imaginative model than in Irish writing of these years. With the fever of self-sacrificial violence running high, and in a culture where the Christian comparison provided easy resonance, the enchantment motif was almost inevitable. Again, "Easter 1916," which was written in the several months that followed Easter week, projects its mood with precision: "Hearts with one purpose alone/Through summer and winter seem/Enchanted to a stone/To trouble the living stream," Yeats wrote.[4] The "trouble" for Yeats is not only about hearts—not only that "too long a sacrifice/Can make a stone of the heart," a vexing concern as he interacted with some feverishly devoted nationalists—but about enchantment. What are *its* consequences, as a cultural formula, as a convention for representing violence, as, in these months after the Rising, near doctrine for nationalists? In the last stanza of the poem, Yeats refutes the relentless tendency to metaphorize and sacralize violent death, answering the enchanting question "What is it but nightfall?" with the disenchanting, "No, no, not night but death." Perhaps it was this refusal, alongside his ambivalent treatment of the insurrectionists (such as John McBride), that irked Gonne, ever the enchanter of violence; she bluntly declared in a letter, "No I don't like your poem, it isn't worthy of you & above all it isn't worthy of the subject."[5]

Enchantment provides the gravitational pull for much Irish literature of these years; it seems to define the aura of the period. As we have seen, however, at the level of aesthetic form and content, enchantment and disenchantment almost always find a way to stain one another. Moreover, the aesthetics of the revolution developed from a broader constellation of effects than the dis/enchantment model alone suggests. Critics of Irish literature have overwhelmingly focused on the generative violence theme when discussing the literary culture of the Rising period, and, in the case of Yeats, have tended to view his presentation of violence through the lens of his politics (construed and valued in highly dichotomous terms, as I will discuss later in this chapter). One central intervention I want to make in considering the language of violence in the Irish revolutionary moment, in contrast, is to argue that generative violence was only one among a series of powerful, often interlocking, and in some cases deeply contradictory paradigms for imagining violence. To read Yeats and his contemporaries as expressing a developing series of imaginative constructs around violence—in concert with the changing political situation and introducing energizing formal consequences—is to eliminate the cumbersome questions of for or against, pro or anti, radical or conservative (in relation to the developing nation, Britain, the Protestant Ascendancy, the middle classes) that have occupied scholarship in this area. Ripping right through the center of the imaginative life of this period were a host of shattering events, and to read the literature of this period in dialectical and active relationship to those realities helps to show how fully violence can lodge as the crux and pivot of the literary work, or the author's career, or the aesthetic unconscious of a period. There is, in this situation, no final resting point or culmination, as there is, really, no beginning; instead, at each stage, literary works recognize their own temporal tentativeness, as well as their own limitations (a sense of obsolescence, the fear of contributing to the cycle of violence, a beauty that lulls where it should provoke), as they nevertheless push restlessly forward into an uncertain future.

In addition to enchantment, the three other dominant paradigms by which violence was conceived and formalized are these: "keening," the Irish term for ritual forms of mourning, traditionally (though not exclusively) the province of women; reprisal, the dark doppelgänger of generative violence, a model of endless, unredeemable violence that became intensely pertinent in the period of the Anglo-Irish and civil wars that followed the Rising; and lastly, a turn to architectural allegory, where the image of destroyed houses and landscapes is asked to take the burden, as sign and symbol of violence, from the beleaguered body. As we have seen elsewhere in this study, the motivation to employ allegory as a container for violent histories or events is betrayed by its content, which corrodes the differentiating walls on which the form relies. Its usage in this period in Ireland is often partial, as well as collapsible, yet the slow movement in the direction of representative buildings does promise a way out of the reprisal vortex, with its feverishly disenchanted understanding of violence. We might, schematizing slightly, describe the progression this way: the core problems surrounding violence throughout the independence period were understood and filtered through the opposing possibilities of generative versus reprisal violence. In the years of war, the generative ideal was all but swallowed into the reprisal cycle, and facing this crisis, writers often envisioned one of two imaginative releases, the healing rituals of keening or the focus on representative buildings, which are asked to carry heavy metaphoric burdens. The burdens are, indeed, enormous; the incarnational destiny of this material in the end will overtake whatever balanced literary resolution it might have invited.

In part, what I trace in these modes—various in style and not exactly parallel as categories—is a development, changing through time and partially conforming to the shifting revolutionary situations of the period. My discussion of keening is set primarily in the pre-1916 years, as the culture adapted itself, as it had for a century, to its tragic past and looked ahead to the potential cataclysm of violence that a war of independence against England might portend. Keening is not itself a structure of representing violence but a cluster of traditions for articulating a response to its ravages. Generative violence was the mode of the Rising itself: the moment in April 1916 when a small band of nationalists, leading their modestly numbered citizen militias, rose against the British and occupied Dublin, to be defeated at the end of the week, its sixteen leaders executed shortly thereafter. Technically a defeat, the Rising represented (and still represents) the symbolic origin for modern Ireland. As for reprisal, not surprisingly, its thematics drive the literary output of the years that followed the Rising when, the First World War now over, Ireland fought its more concerted independence struggle against England, followed by the Civil War of 1922–23. In both of these conflicts, targeted reprisal killings became the norm. My concluding section on landscape and architectural allegory begins in the Civil War period and pushes forward into the indefinite future of the young nation. In that sense, the discussion here lines up with the culmination of the dynamite story in the previous chapter, where the forecasting of terrorist potential into the future recalibrated the assumptions about what such explosion might mean, how it can be imagined. The representative building becomes a holder for a variety of harsh partisan and sectarian positions, yet it also projects out from the moment of bodily harm into a wider and longer panorama.

I will discuss a range of voices over the course of this analysis. Organized thematically and historically rather than by author, the chapter invites voices to return and recur in different contexts and gives a sense, I hope, that what is at stake is less any specific writer's stance than a set of patterns and changes in the conception of literary violence across the culture. Yeats is central to the whole discussion, his extensive corpus of works on violence providing an ever-mutating body of imagery and expression over a nearly forty-year period. Pádraig Pearse, the dominant writer of the Rising, also plays a critical role, especially in defining the terms for the ideal of generative violence. Over the course of the chapter, I will also discuss other influential figures from earlier in the nineteenth century, such as John Mitchel; leaders of the Easter rebellion (next to Pearse) like Thomas

MacDonagh and Joseph Mary Plunkett; and literary figures like J. M. Synge and Sean O'Casey, who, along with Yeats, helped to create a lasting aesthetics for a foundational era in Irish literary consciousness.[6] It is a very masculine corpus, despite the significant presence of such figures as Augusta Gregory, and this is not incidental; much in the violent language of the time reverberated in terms of a resurgent anticolonial power, and this often took a marked gender turn.

This material, moreover, shares with other major engagements with violence in the modernist period an essential reckoning with the idea of excess; here, the notable structure is one we might call an "economy of excess." In this scheme, it is giving, rather than accumulating, that represents wealth, and richness is demonstrated through neglect. The model is Dionysian rather than Apollonian; it welcomes lavishness and waste rather than frugality. Highly evocative for much of the language surrounding the insurrection, such an emphasis might also be couched in the terms enunciated by Bataille in his eclectic study of culture *The Accursed Share* (1967), from which I have taken my epigraph. What characterizes the "play of energy on the surface of the globe," according to Bataille, is not equivalence or balance, but the need to spend "gloriously or catastrophically," an expenditure and display that represents cultural accomplishment (Bataille, v.1, 21). In "September 1913" and elsewhere (*Where There is Nothing, The Unicorn from the Stars,* "Poetry and Tradition"[7]) Yeats made some of these motifs canonical:

> Yet they were of a different kind,
> The names that stilled your childish play,
> They have gone about the world like wind,
> But little time had they to pray
> For whom the hangman's rope was spun,
> And what, God help us, could they save?
> Romantic Ireland's dead and gone,
> It's with O'Leary in the grave. (*Var*, 289)

For Yeats in "September 1913," the profligate giving of one's very essence in the suspended Irish cause—"all that delirium of the brave"—emblematized a romantic nationalism that had become all the more valuable for its being "dead and gone."[8] Contrasting the givers of the past, who had little time to pray, with a mean and niggardly modern "you," who "fumble in a greasy till" and add "prayer to shivering prayer," he establishes a decisive image of value as waste: "They weighed so lightly what they gave." For Yeats, such selflessness is associated with the aristocracy, with the Fenian journalist John O'Leary who was his political mentor, and later with Lady Gregory's son Robert, killed in the First World War. In these associations, he was idiosyncratic, but he stands on conventional ground when he evokes Edward Fitzgerald, Wolfe Tone, and Robert Emmet, those earlier heroes who "stilled your childish play" (*Var*, 289–90).

"September 1913," indeed, articulates a notion of reckless giving that had been gathering force in Ireland for over a century (though in England only more recently). Tone himself, not one for extended figures of speech, characterized that majority of English people who opposed the French Revolution as being like "merchants," calculating loss and benefit, while the Irish had an abundance of sympathy that could make them recklessly loyal. Their alliance with the revolution was natural, in Tone's view; being "oppressed, insulted, and plundered," they could, in a sense, only give.[9] John Mitchel, one of the most radical of the nineteenth-century nationalists, carried on this tradition, deriding England (the oppressor) for being mercantile, while rebellious France (Ireland's friend) "recognises a higher national life . . . than mere trading. France mints the circulating medium of thoughts and noble passions."[10] And for Pearse, it was "excess of love"—his ideal of national affect, and a phrase Yeats borrowed in "Easter 1916"—that best conveys this sense of abundance: "A love and a service so excessive as to annihilate all thought of self, a recognition that one must give all, must be willing always to make the ultimate sacrifice."[11] "Giving, giving, giving, she had died," thinks Lily Briscoe of Mrs. Ramsay in Woolf's *To the Lighthouse* (1927) and it is really only the tone—bitter rather than ebullient—that separates her assessment of domestic, female selflessness from a masculine heroics that had permeated the Irish imagination for decades.[12] This male economy of excess held exalting connotations of flight and martyrdom, but also, to return to Bataille, invoked the inexorable and contrasting demand that "death lay waste to us."

The Long Past: Keening

What would war or revolution be without its language of mourning? As cultural historians have shown, the literary forms that surround mourning (elegy, ode, recitation, even epic) represent active ways for individuals and communities to engage with histories of violence, whether recent or long past. Like all major poetic forms, elegy and its counterparts have traditionally been the province of men, and yet Western culture for millennia has afforded to women the more general role of mourners.[13] *The Iliad* may lavishly describe Achilles's grief at Patroclus's death, but the epic ends with three women's laments, evoking a tradition that, classicists tell us, predated Homer by centuries.[14] Mothers, above all, have the prerogative in mourning. As Nicole Loraux explains, rooting these traditions in the ancient prototypes, "from epic on, the mother is the one whose grief, suddenly expressed, gives the signal of social mourning."[15] In the twentieth century, images of mourning women and mothers have had tremendous cultural life, often extending from the prime mourner, the mother, into the broader family circle, as with the globally ubiquitous images of mothers holding up photographs of dead sons for the world's cameras. These are pietàs for a secular culture; they image the grief of the mother in religious but also in generalizing terms, a lament, in the final instance, for all humanity. As Jay Winter writes of the sculptor Käthe Kollwitz's memorial to her son, killed at the front in 1914, "At Roggevelde [Belgium, where the memorial is situated], on their knees, Käthe and Karl Kollwitz suggest a family which includes us all; and that may be precisely what she had in mind. The most intimate here is also the most universal."[16] At points of national combustion especially, such as war or revolution, representations of lamenting women and families carry extra weight. The stoic female mourner, proud of her dead son and continuing to believe in the cause for which he was killed, can function as a bridge from personal loss to national gain. Or the reverse: angry, embittered, and all but destroyed by grief, she threatens the status quo, becoming a lightning rod for protest.[17]

In Ireland, there is a rich and lovely term for the rituals of lamentation: the keen.[18] Keening may not offer a form for representing violence, but it does register a performative language that responds vigorously and lushly to death. Keening was figured as a deeply rooted part of the Irish emotional and ritual being, a response to a tragic national history whose most poignant losses included the victims of famine in the nineteenth century, the martyrs (Tone, Emmet, and others), and, more generally, the nation's own life, in need of symbolic mourning after centuries of occupation and economic hardship. With its ties to the national history, keening gestures toward a probably violent future; ritualizing violence in the past, it prepares for more trials to come. For J. M. Synge, the most powerful and moving exponent of ritual mourning in this period, keening performs a grief that emanates from the deepest place in the national consciousness. Thus he locates its essential presence in the far west of Ireland, especially on the Aran Islands, where Synge believed there resided a raw, primal Irish spirit. Synge took several visits to the Aran Islands, residing with a local family; he chronicled his time there in book form, and from it he derived the material for several of his most famous plays, including *The Shadow of the Glen* (1903), *Riders to the Sea* (1903), and some aspects of *The Playboy of the Western World* (1907).[19] At the end of the nineteenth century, there was little visible sense of the British presence in places like the Aran Islands— the omnipresence of the Gaelic language being the most overt manifestation of this cultural impregnability—and representations of the Islanders tended to stress not only their primitivism but their de facto freedom from the colonial condition and British influence.[20]

Synge's romanticism about the Aran Islands is especially lavish in his description of the islands' keening women. He observes a funeral procession:

> While the grave was being opened the women sat down among the flat tombstones, bordered with a pale fringe of early bracken, and began the wild keen, or crying for the dead. Each old woman, as she took her turn in the leading recitative, seemed possessed for the moment with a profound ecstasy of grief, swaying to and fro, and bending her forehead to the stone before her, while she called out to the dead with a perpetually recurring chant of sobs.
>
> . . . This grief of the keen is no personal complaint for the death of one woman over eighty years, but seems to contain the whole passionate rage that lurks somewhere in every native of the island. In this cry of pain the inner consciousness of the people seems to lay itself bare for an instant, and to reveal the mood of beings who feel their isolation in the face of a universe that wars on them with winds and seas. They are usually silent, but in the presence of death all outward show of indifference or patience is forgotten, and they shriek with pitiable despair before the horror of the fate to which they are all doomed.[21]

When Synge takes up the ethnographer's position, his tendency is to see in the Aran Islanders a place-bound consciousness; they are molded by their geography of island isolation—"winds and seas." His interest in their rituals also bends him the other way, however, so that they come to incarnate something universally ancient. The women "possessed . . . with a profound ecstasy of grief" recall the priestesses of Delphi, or medieval women mystics; they harbor a kind of old European memory—perhaps Eliot would find in them "tradition"—of the deepest pain. Like Kollwitz's sculptures, these women are at once very local representatives and vivid symbols of women's passionate grieving across time and space. Their grief is both bruisingly local and expansively extensive. Synge notes, too, that such attributes can be accommodated, even updated, as exigencies demand, so that, for instance, at a second funeral he attends, this one of a young man, "the keen lost part of its formal nature, and was recited as the expression of intense personal grief by the young men and women of the man's own family" (*AI*, 134).

For Synge, grieving seems to define the inhabitants of the west of Ireland, and this quality of ongoing lamentation has consequences; in *Riders to the Sea*, also set in the Aran Islands, whole generations are lost, and it is the mother who is left to keen them. In the final lines of the play, the mother Maurya offers, in Christian terms, a version of universal keening:

> They're all together this time, and the end is come. May the Almighty God have mercy on Bartley's soul, and on Michael's soul, and on the souls of Sheamus and Patch, and Stephen and Shawn [*bending her head*] . . . and may He have mercy on my soul, Nora, and on the soul of everyone is left living in the world. [*She pauses, and the keen rises a little more loudly from the women, then sinks away. Continuing*] Michael has a clean burial in the far north, by the grace of the Almighty God. Bartley will have a fine coffin out of the white boards, and a deep grave surely . . . What more can we want than that? . . . No man at all can be living for ever, and we must be satisfied.[22]

There is a substantial distinction to be made between the wild ritual keening of the women in *The Aran Islands* and this figuration of Christian resignation. Maurya is a figure for submission and futility; she bends her head and is satisfied.

Not everyone wanted to keep up the keen. Yeats's *Cathleen ni Houlihan* (1902), the most famous of the early-twentieth-century Irish plays (then and now) to represent the drama of rebellion in pointedly allegorical terms, takes an oppositional attitude toward mourning and fighting. Yeats's political allegory in *Cathleen ni Houlihan* is direct and continuous throughout the play, with Cathleen wandering the roads asking for young men to join in her defense, expel the usurpers from her lands, fight for her, and give up their lives and families for the cause. For Yeats, moreover, the feminization of Ireland in the person of Cathleen, now aged but once goddesslike in her loveliness (and played by Gonne in the initial Abbey production), invokes a different gender association from Synge's portrayal of the national mother. Over and over, in the nationalist literature of the period, the call is for manliness—defined in part in terms of self-denying profligacy or "delirium of the brave"—and one form such masculinity takes is the refusal of mourning. Earlier in the nineteenth century, the Young Ireland movement (in many ways a precursor of twentieth-century nationalism), with its strong cultural-nationalist program, had begun to distance its revolutionary spirit from the keening mode that characterized many traditional songs and ballads. Thomas Davis, the leader of Young Ireland, championed the development of a new ballad tradition that would move away from the "despairing" tone of the past, injecting a more robustly masculine tone into the national poetry.[23] Yeats's Cathleen, in calling for young men to join in her defense and leave behind their wives and families, keeps to the Davis line, and makes a staunch case against keening:

> Do not make a great keening
> When the graves have been dug to-morrow.
> Do not call the white-scarfed riders
> To the burying that shall be to-morrow.
> Do not spread food to call strangers
> To the wakes that shall be to-morrow;
> Do not give money for prayers
> For the dead that shall die to-morrow . . .

> They will have no need of prayers, they will have no need of prayers.[24] (ellipses in original)

The premise of these lines is clear: in times of war and rebellion, the performance of women's mourning is expected, with all its rituals and formalities, yet it must be resisted. Cathleen calls for a break with the past, and for substituting one kind of national spirit (defiant, self-sacrificial) for another (the ancient prototype of Irish mournfulness).

For Pearse, by contrast, keening is an important part of the revolutionary moment (indeed, he has a story entitled "The Keening Woman").[25] It is only natural, he will repeatedly suggest, that Ireland's mothers be encouraged in their ancient role as keeners, even as they are exhorted to send their young men out to die.[26] Most histrionic as an account of the nationalist potential of keening is *The Singer*, a play written in 1915 (never performed in Pearse's lifetime, but published soon after, in a 1917 Dublin collection of his works) that anticipates the martyrology of the Rising in precise terms. The protagonist MacDara is a virtual incarnation of the singer persona romanticized by the ballad movement of the nineteenth century. What is more, by the end of the play he has become nothing less than a figure for Christ. "One man can free a people as one Man redeemed the world," he declares as he heads out to fight the British single-handedly, "I will take no pike, I will go into the battle with bare hands. I will stand up before the Gall [foreigner] as Christ hung naked before men on the tree!"[27] MacDara is an outsized male hero, who is joined in the play's martyrology by his equally brave and reckless young brother, who also goes out unaided to die at the hands of the English.

But it is the women who in some sense most acutely mark *The Singer*. They are keeners with a cause; their role is simultaneously to encourage and to mourn. "I am proud . . . to think of so many young men," says the reverential Sighle, MacDara's beloved, who knows she will be a widow even before they have been wed, "young men with straight, strong limbs, and smooth, white flesh, going out into great peril because a voice has called to them to right the wrong of the people" (*PSP*, 10). Flesh, I have suggested, makes its presence uncomfortably felt at moments of enchanted violence; Sighle's language here, though offered as a statement of awed support for those adored limbs, is perhaps too embodied, too full of desire. The life of those bodies is real and appealing, and it cannot be fully sated by the consolations of martyrdom. But Maire, MacDara's mother, inhabits her position to perfection, calling on her fellow women to embrace their role as incipient mourners: "Weave your winding-sheets, women," she exhorts, "for there will be many a noble corpse to be waked before the new moon!" (*PSP*, 42). If Yeats's Cathleen had dismissed mourning as counter to the cause, Pearse jubilantly celebrates it. Maire, like many mothers in his works, glories in her sorrow. To weave the winding sheets, for her, is one of the women's primary contributions to the national cause and an act of bravery. That these woven sheets also suggest written pages is unsurprising; language, ritual, and voice are conjoined in these active mourning performances.

Keening as nationalist courage, or as resignation, or as an age-old expression of Irishness—all of these are important functions, especially in the anticipatory moment, and there is yet one more possibility, that keening offers a language for shared suffering that cuts across political lines and intimates the possibility of change. Not surprisingly, this alternative construct arises in a war-weary later stage of the national history. Here the most explicit enunciation comes from Sean O'Casey, who wrote his blistering dramas primarily during the years of the Anglo-Irish and Civil wars. His denunciation of all ideological certitudes and his suspicion of writers like Pearse, who breathed the air of nationalism and embodied its principles with romantic effusiveness, was as central to his work as was his focus on the crowded, working-class neighborhoods of Dublin. Perhaps it is this skepticism about the guiding psychic mechanisms underpinning political belief, alongside a sturdy refusal to treat either the rural Irish or mythological themes, that has made O'Casey unpopular among critics.[28] In his most canonical work, *Juno and the Paycock* (written in 1924 and set in 1922), a scathing and ironical drama about a family's implosion, keening cuts through the play like a knife. Where all other conventions around death and nationalism are ruthlessly pinioned, women's lamentation offers something admirable and potent. The play presents a chronicle of tragedy and sheer bad luck for the Boyle family, residents of Dublin's tenements and representatives, in a sense, for a people embroiled in and undone by the continuing struggle. Boyle, the Falstaffian patriarch (a loafer and malingerer who might be a total good-for-nothing if it weren't for his irresistibly poetic dialect and his tremendous resilience), believes he has inherited a fortune, only to squander most of it before learning that it was all a mistake; his daughter Mary, pretty, clever, and something of a new woman (she reads Ibsen and is a labor activist), falls in love with the slick, middle-class Free-Stater Bentham (a theosophist and prig, and perhaps just a bit of a parody of Yeats), who impregnates and abandons her; Johnny, crippled and desperate after the fighting of 1916, is ultimately taken out and shot by the Republicans for treachery; and finally, Juno, mother of mothers, keeps the family's bodies and souls together with her homespun spirit, and meanwhile exerts a surprisingly powerful feminist energy. At the end of the play, having learned of her son's brutal killing, she chooses to leave Boyle for good and to spend her future with Mary and the illegitimate baby; responding to Mary's lament "My poor little child that'll have no father," she counters, "It'll have what's far betther—it'll have two mothers."[29]

Mothers have many burdens in the world of *Juno and the Paycock*; but perhaps most saliently, they are called upon to mourn. Juno will not be the first. Her lament for Johnny at the end of the play follows that of another resident, Mrs. Tancred, whose son's bullet-ridden corpse had been found in a creek the night before and is now the subject of graphic newspaper accounts and much tenement conversation. The funeral procession falls exactly in the center of the play, punctuating one family's drama with another's. Juno is the only Boyle family member moved by the neighbor's plight, and, as we later learn, she internalizes Mrs. Tancred's lament, which she repeats verbatim when it is her turn to grieve, in a choral structure that comes as a surprise in O'Casey's realist playbook:

> Me home is gone now; he was me only child, an' to think that he was lyin' for a whole night stretched out on the side of a lonely counthry lane, with his head, his darlin' head, that I often kissed an' fondled, half hidden in the wather of a runnin' brook. An' I'm told he was the leadher of the ambush where me nex' door neighbor, Mrs. Mannin', lost her Free State soldier son. An' now here's the two of us oul' women, standin' one on each side of a scales o' sorra, balanced be the bodies of our two dead darlin' sons. . . . Mother o' God, Mother o' God, have pity on the pair of us! . . . O Blessed Virgin, where were you when me darlin' son was riddled with bullets, when me darlin' son was riddled with bullets! . . . Sacred Heart of the Crucified Jesus, take away our hearts o' stone . . . an' give us hearts o' flesh! . . . Take away this murdherin' hate . . . an' give us Thine own eternal love!" (*CPI*, 54–55, first ellipses added).

This is the essence of civil war: two mothers, longtime neighbors, whose sons have effectively killed one another, staring at each other over a gaping chasm of strife which is also recognized as a mere illusion of distance. The structure is ironic, tragic, and formally arresting.[30] In shifting to a prayer to the Virgin (another mother of a killed son) in the second half of the passage, Mrs. Tancred looks to stanch the flow of blood unleashed by vengeance and civil war by turning to the structure of Christian love and forgiveness. Mrs. Tancred's keen is capacious, including references to the past, prayers for the future, and a language of empathy that might be unexpected at such a moment of personal sorrow and despair. We might note, moreover, her use of the word "flesh," whose mention inevitably and instantly destabilizes the operative model of violence. To recognize the facts of flesh—to return from an exalted, enchanted state of political commitment back to a state of embodied reality—is the fervent (the only?) hope in this situation of seemingly endless killing.

The Rising: Generative Violence

In the hands of nationalists like Pearse, even such prototypically memorial forms as keening can be generative. This is the symbolic imperative of the insurrection: death must become fruitful, blood must be seen as a nourishing source, lilacs must grow from the dead land. It is not at all surprising, then, that Pearse made especially good use of the graveside as a potent locale for arousing a spirit of inspired and inspiring violence. Most notably, the burial in August 1915 of Jeremiah O'Donovan Rossa, exiled Fenian and exemplar of what historians call the "physical force tradition," offered Pearse a prime location for a speech steeped in the metaphorics of blood sacrifice and enchantment.[31] Pearse took his performative cues in the Rossa commemoration from works like the Gettysburg Address; in both speeches, the hallowed ground of dead soldiers becomes the mystical source for continued dedication. "I propose to you," he enjoined his listeners, "that, here by the grave of this unrepentant Fenian, we renew our baptismal vows." The oration is shot through with such imagery, as indeed is all of his writing: "We stand at Rossa's grave not in sadness but rather in exaltation of spirit," he declares, and:

> Our foes are strong and wise and wary; but, strong and wise and wary as they are, they cannot undo the miracles of God who ripens in the hearts of young men the seeds sown by the young men of a former generation. And the seeds sown by the young men of '65 and '67 are coming to their

miraculous ripening to-day. Rulers and Defenders of Realms had need to be wary if they would guard against such processes. Life springs from death; and from the graves of patriot men and women spring living nations. (*PWS*, 134, 135, 136–37)

Ripening, seeds and growth, violence as a potent vitalizing force: these are the reiterated terms. Such generative symbols, in turn, are amalgamated to a continuous history of rebellion, made up of the various moments of insurrection (here 1865 and 1867, often including 1798 and 1803). Each failed uprising engenders its heroes and plays a part in developing the national story-in-waiting, bearing out the promise of violence as a productive agent in history and culture.

No one was more deliberate in his usage of such symbolism than Pearse, and no one was more influential in his conviction that nations spring from the graves of great men. Through the school he founded, St. Enda's at Rathfarnham, his lectures, his published writings, his leadership in the insurrection, and of course through his death, Pearse came virtually to incarnate the ideal of generative violence. So, for instance, in a precursor to his famous Rossa oration, he spoke in 1913 at Tone's grave, where he called for all assembled to breathe in the spirit of that soil, and to join him as "we set our faces towards the path that lies before us, bringing with us fresh life from this place of death, a new resurrection of patriotic grace in our souls!" (*PWS*, 57). Later that year, in laying out his hope for "The Coming Revolution," Pearse wrote that "bloodshed is a cleansing and a sanctifying thing, and the nation which regards it as the final horror has lost its manhood" (*PWS*, 99). Finally, and most controversially—given the deep antagonism toward the First World War felt by many of his peers—Pearse wrote in December 1915 that "[w]ar is a terrible thing, but war is not an evil thing"; rather, "[i]t is good for the world that such things should be done. The old heart of the earth needed to be warmed with the red wine of the battlefields" (*PWS*, 217, 216).[32] It is thus entirely appropriate that Yeats would have Pearse say, in "The Rose Tree"—the most tonally ambiguous among the insurgency poems published in *Michael Robartes and the Dancer* (1922)—"O plain as plain can be/ There's nothing but our own red blood/Can make a right Rose Tree" (*Var*, 396). There might, in the end, be quite a bit to muddy and complicate this "plain" connotation, but in the Pearsian mode of these years, the story of blood and fecundity was one of certainties.

It is not difficult to find instances of this mode across the period—they are endemic. Here, two slim volumes of poetry can stand as exemplary. Both published in 1916, both in a sense memorials of the Rising and epitaphs for their subjects,

Poems of the Irish Revolutionary Brotherhood and *The Poems of Joseph Mary Plunkett* share with Pearse's work a sense of distilling and perfecting the ideal of enchantment as a statement of nationalist sentiment. At twenty-eight, Joseph Mary Plunkett was the youngest of the executed insurrectionists. A poet and disciple of Pearse, he was always in poor health (he had tuberculosis), yet his short life was dominated by radical nationalist activity, including a trip to Germany in 1915 aimed at securing German aid for the insurrection and a prominent role at the Post Office during Easter week despite his compromised health. In short, Plunkett embodied the Rising's romantic spirit. In the 1916 volume, edited and lovingly introduced by his sister, there is a great deal of blood, suffering, sacrifice, and enchantment, as one would expect, but it is largely apolitical, revolving around the address to an unnamed beloved and around Plunkett's strong Christian aesthetic—ecstatic about Christ's blood and stressing themes of crucifixion and resurrection.[33] Yet several carefully placed national lyrics burst into the volume midcourse and in a sense recast the entire work as a paean to the Rising. Like the resurrection, which shadows the volume, the insurgency is prefigured as a silent and defining event of paradoxical violence—glorious as failure and eternal through its mortality.

One poem, "The Little Black Rose Shall Be Red at Last," is especially revealing as a statement of enchanted violence. Dedicated to Cathleen ni Houlihan, "The Little Black Rose Shall Be Red at Last" follows immediately after the three most directly political poems in the volume (several of which were also included in *Poems of the IRB*) and it links their familiar lexicon—martyrs, swords, ancient heritage, defiance, mourning for lost leaders—with a Christian-leaning eroticism that characterizes the volume more generally. In addition to the connection between the rose and Ireland,[34] the poem's title has at least two clear reference points, both in the national tradition: a poem entitled "The Little Black Rose" (first line "The little black rose shall be red at last") by Aubrey de Vere (1814–1902) a prominent nationalist poet in the Celtic tradition, and "The Dark Rose," a political ballad from the sixteenth century (translated periodically in later centuries, including an influential version by James Clarence Mangan and another by Pearse), in which the title rose again turns red. In De Vere's poem, each item in a pastoral landscape points toward political allegory. The little black rose "shall redden the hills when June is nigh"; the cow (another old national symbol) may be "mild," but "she shall feed full fast"; and the pine tree, "long bleeding, it shall not die!" "This song is secret," the poet declares, but the secret seems a relatively open one.[35] As for the traditional "Little Dark Rose," the final stanza offers an apocalypse of fruitful blood: "The Erne shall rise in rude torrents, hills shall be rent/The sea shall roll in red waves, and blood be poured out,/Every mountain glen in Ireland, and the bogs shall quake/Some day ere shall perish my Little Dark Rose!"[36] Very clearly, Plunkett's title calls up the enchanting tradition from within an Irish/Celtic canon.

His poem, like the countryside of the earlier poem, is full to overflowing. It begins with a conventional invocation to the beloved, a strangely personalized, sexualized opening for a song devoted to the nation (via Cathleen). The blood of two bodies, erotically overcharged, is soon merged with national iconography:

> And when my heart is pillowed on your heart
> And ebb and flowing of their passionate flood
> Shall beat in concord love through every part
> Of brain and body—when at last the blood
> O'er leaps the final barrier to find
> Only one source wherein to spend its strength
> And we two lovers, long but one in mind
> And soul, are made one only flesh at length;
> Praise God if this my blood fulfils the doom
> When you, dark rose, shall redden into bloom.[37]

One thinks of Blake's "The Sick Rose," an unsurprising presence, given Blake's heroic stature (along with Shelley) among this generation of Irish poets.[38] But the sexual mutual destruction of Blake is here redirected toward the coming rebellion, and the darkness of Blake's poem is reimagined as generativity, "redden[ing] into bloom." In short, Plunkett finds in the reddening rose a fruitful confluence: a revolutionary Irish poetic heritage, Romantically themed erotic destructiveness, Christian allegory, and a muted prophecy of the personal sacrifices soon to be made.

If the overall spirit of Plunkett's volume grows from just a kernel of generative violence (but isn't that the idea?), *Poems of the IRB* more directly positions itself as a poetic statement of the Rising, containing poems by four of the executed rebels (Pearse, MacDonagh, Plunkett, and Roger Casement) and beginning with a biographical introduction that helps to establish the hagiography of these figures. Interestingly, it includes only two poems by poets not directly affiliated with the Rising, an introductory lyric "The Ways of War" by Lionel Johnson and, as the final note, Yeats's "Red Hanrahan's Song about Ireland" (1894), an early poem in which Yeats comes as close as he ever will to a Pearse-like embrace of generative violence.[39] The poem is grounded in an image of stoic resilience:

> The old brown thorn-trees break in two high over Cummen Strand,
> Under a bitter black wind that blows from the left hand;
> Our courage breaks like an old tree in a black wind and dies,

> But we have hidden in our hearts the flame out of the eyes
> Of Cathleen, the daughter of Houlihan. (*Var*, 206–7)

The poem sets up the struggle as smoldering rather than active, befitting its composition date in the 1890s. Once included in the nationalist volume, however, its spirit of embodied, quiet defiance seems strategic. It is no wonder, indeed, that the IRB (the major underground nationalist group of the pre-Rising period, often also referred to as the Fenians), of which Yeats was a sometime member, would want this poem in its post-Rising compilation, since its inclusion lent Yeats's considerable authority to an event about which he was, in fact, ambivalent. And the poem does make a strong statement about courage in the face of oppression. The subjugation of the Irish is likened in the poem to natural powers—"bitter black wind that blows from the left hand" and "wet winds . . . blowing out of the clinging air"—embodying the idea of force. Force is power; it swirls through the world fiercely and indiscriminately. Resistance, in turn, requires a paradoxical submission, for the ways of violence, in opposing force, are always those of the guerrilla. Generative violence here is not so much a statement of the present, then, as a promise for the future, figured by the smoldering flame ("we have hidden in our hearts the flame out of the eyes/Of Cathleen, the daughter of Houlihan").

The IRB volume is largely melancholy and reflective rather than triumphant or resurrectory, exuding a brooding mortality, and yet its romantic spirit takes the form of enchanted violence, as one would expect.[40] All four of the poets partake. MacDonagh, in "O Star of Death," returns to the rose as symbol of regenerative violence:

> O star of death! I follow, till thou take
> My days to cast them from thee flake on flake,
> My rose of life to scatter bloom on bloom,
> Yet hold its essence in the phial rare
> Of life that lives with fire and air,—
> With air that knows no dark, with fire not to consume. (*Poems of the IRB*, 22)

Enchantment in this poem does not take its metaphors from the body; there is no heavy blood, as there is in Yeats's poem, no precious ore. Instead, the images are ethereal—"life that lives with fire and air"—and this, too, is not an uncommon approach to envisioning generative violence. Ireland, the rose, and the poet's soul are bound together, and though their sign is the "star of death," their unity promises futurity, even immortality. In both of these 1916 volumes, then, we find a poetic of generative violence that is linked to its moment. Enchantment in these works stresses a paradoxical permanence: it is fleeting, temporal, and tied to mortality, in poems pulled magnetically toward death and melancholy, even as its effects are figured as carrying an ongoing cultural power.

With this in mind, let us return to "Easter 1916," which expresses the promise, as well as the limits, of enchanted violence in exceptionally memorable terms. "Easter 1916" represents a breaking point in the discourse of enchantment, fully working out (and rendering canonical) the period's generative metaphorics, and also taking stock of the troubling implications of these dynamics being fulfilled in verse. Critics have long noted Yeats's ambivalence in the poem: the insurrectionists simultaneously heroized and treated with condescension; the poet's role elevated as the final voice of and for the rebellion and, at the same time, marginalized and feminized; the status of transformation uncertain.[41] This last I have suggested can be understood in terms of enchantment, in the sense that the poem creates an arresting aesthetic of generative violence (the shift from "casual comedy" to tragedy—"a terrible beauty is born") and also questions the value of that commitment: "what if excess of love/Bewildered them till they died?" Perhaps more than any other issue, the poem is divided about what kind of literary strategy is appropriate and possible in relation to the Rising. Clearly, there is nothing of the disenchantment paradigm here: unlike other works by Yeats, which I will discuss in the next section, "Easter 1916" avoids any reference to actual episodes of violence. There is no evocation of the fierce week of fighting in Dublin, or of the execution of the sixteen leaders. It skips over the whole turbulent sequence, shifting from a set of pre-Rising portraits to a reflection on the status of these seemingly unremarkable people once they have been transformed by death.[42] The poem is less interested in providing an account of violence, in other words, than in reflecting on its power.

It is in the final lines of the poem that these crucial questions about the status of enchanted violence are worked out. Having created flashlike memories and epithets for the leaders and considered the value of the events in both personal and political terms, the poem turns, in the end, to incantation, intoning a soft, rhythmic repetition of the insurrectionists' names:

> I write it out in a verse—
> MacDonagh and MacBride
> And Connolly and Pearse
> Now and in time to be,
> Wherever green is worn,
> Are changed, changed utterly:
> A terrible beauty is born. (*Var*, 394)

The passage calls special attention to itself, with its metatextual and somewhat re-dundant self-description: "I write it out in a verse." And the lines do make a sur-prising formal gesture. As Declan Kiberd has noted, the phrase "wherever green is worn" has about it the ring of conventionality ("jaded formulae"), suggesting, as the poem moves to its close, a reversion to a language of national culture that is, in these years of the escalating independence struggle, becoming well-worn.[43] Even the word "verse," as distinct from "poem," could—if we follow the logic Meredith Martin has laid out in *The Rise and Fall of Meter*—seem to tag Yeats's own line as drifting into the popular realm, verse written for consumption, as opposed to po-etry written to disrupt.[44] Moreover, we might even say that the poem's own refrain is heading in the same direction, in the sense that it has started to feel like a con-firmatory tag: beautiful, lulling, and familiar, it confirms where much else in the poem questions. It seems, in other words, that Yeats recognizes, as he is writing the poem, that its language of enchantment is destined to become a convention (as, of course, it has) and hence to function less as a stimulus to thought than as an incan-tation of what one already believes: that violence in the name of the nation is trans-formative, that it creates a special kind of beauty.

The one stanza that does not end with "terrible beauty" offers a quite different account of change, mutation, and continuity. By far the most challenging part of the poem, the third stanza imagines a Heraclitean scene of movement and flux, with images ranging from the splashing of water to the shifting shadows of birds and clouds. It is a stanza about the impossibility of fixing any moment in time, yet it is bracketed by the poem's clearest image of stasis, the stone: "Hearts with one purpose alone/Through summer and winter seem/Enchanted to a stone/To trouble the living stream" inaugurates the stanza, and "The stone's in the midst of all" completes it (*Var*, 393). Critics have noted a web of connection in this poem and elsewhere in Yeats's works between women and stones, or, more precisely, between Maude Gonne (whom Yeats loved fiercely and often frustratedly for much of his adult life) and an image of a hardened, fierce nationalism that Yeats abhorred in part because it marginalized him in her world. The stone of course also characterizes men like Pearse, who indeed haunts the poem; thus even without the personal (and gendered) angle, the third stanza sets the terms for critiquing the underlying logic of the rest of the poem. Contrasting the most immobile with the excessively fluid, the stanza suggests that the temporality of the poem, based as it is on the ideal of transformative violence and allying with a calcifying nationalist politics, might misconstrue the way change works in the actual, nonideal world. The stanza thus acts, in part, as a bulwark against the rest of the poem, instigating a radically different model of transformation from the generative violence ideal.

Yet the final stanza recovers, and from the wild changefulness of the stream, figured in a way as life itself ("Minute by minute they live"), it returns to a more restful atmosphere—indeed, to death.

The whole final stanza suggests death. The idea of falling asleep permeates its metaphors and phrases ("when sleep at last has come," "What is it but nightfall?" "We know their dream; enough/To know they dreamed and are dead"), and its tone is dominated by a sense of hopelessness ("O when may it suffice?" "Was it needless death after all?"). Even more centrally, Yeats suggests in the poem's final section that he sees his own work implicated in a process of transformation that has troubling (or deadening) consequences. In what Elizabeth Cullingford has called "the most famous question in Irish literary history," Yeats would ask much later (1938), "Did that play of mine send out/Certain men the English shot?" (*Var*, 632), referring to *Cathleen ni Houlihan*. Yet "Easter 1916" is already wondering whether its poetic is contributing to the process whereby violent events become "enchanted to a stone."[45] Moreover, the listing of names, like the "wherever green is worn" phraseology, is conventional—a lullaby, a casualty list, a verse memorial— and has its own logic (so we get only four of the sixteen, and they must be names that scan and rhyme). It also enchants, quite literally, as if one were actually chant- ing the names. In other words, "Easter 1916" simultaneously enacts the ideal of generative violence—erasing the body and occluding the moment of violence, re- placing these with a statement of lovely transformation—and sees that process as threatening to obliterate the kind of thought-inducing, propulsive language that Yeats always sought to create in his poetry. In "Easter 1916," poetry is eclipsed by violence in two ways: straightforwardly, because the violent actors-cum-victims shift from ordinary people to heroes, offering up a "terrible beauty" that poetry can only echo; and, paradoxically, because the literary process of enchanting vio- lence is so successful that it ends up diminishing its own cultural function—to intervene in the formulizing of language, to make it urgent and disruptive, to force it out of sleep.

Critics have, of course, amply discussed the poem's relationship to violence and politics, and, more generally, have considered the large questions of how to read Yeats's approach, throughout his long career, to a thicket of questions sur- rounding violence, often culminating in the question of his authoritarian and fas- cistic leanings.[46] Most succinctly, the debate revolves around the question of whether to understand Yeats as primarily a nationalist who sought, in his literary output no less than in his work for the theater and for Irish literary culture in general, to help establish a powerful new language for the independent nation or, conversely, as primarily an ascendancy champion, whose loathing of the middle classes and idealization of the aristocracy melded with his (English) Romanticism and late fascism in a poetic that may proclaim itself national but is in fact sectarian, elitist, and, in the worst case, violently divisive. The lightning rod for this latter view was a 1965 essay by Conor Cruise O'Brien, which makes the case that Yeats's fascism was always endemic to his politics (rather than the flirtation of an old, embittered man); that he was "cunning" and reactionary throughout his career, even with regard to such seemingly leftist expressions as his support for the Dublin workers during the 1913 strike; in short, that the national reverence for him is misguided.[47] On the other side, Cullingford's persuasive appraisal of Yeats as "first and foremost an Irish nationalist," and in no interesting sense a fascist, stands as the most influential rebuttal. Cullingford sees Yeats's romanticism as an element of his Irish commitments, and stresses his connection with many left-leaning nationalist figures, from O'Leary to Pearse (Cullingford, vii). As Jonathan Allison summarizes the debate, in a volume meant to elaborate and adjudicate the division, the key question centers on "a revaluation of the work of the Irish Literary Revival in general and Yeats in particular, whose work is sometimes seen, especially in Ireland, as an expression of an antimodernist, reactionary sensibility that has ultimately been insidious to Ireland's self-image and that has inadvertently prolonged a quasicolonial mentality."[48]

And yet, a focus on enchantment shows that the elitist/nationalist polarization does not explain all that much about the complex and mutating state of violence in his works. It is clear, for instance, that the enchantment of violence can be linked to fascism and ideals of aristocratic power, and just as clearly can sustain a revolutionary politics. As Michael Tratner has argued, Yeats was inspired by the promise of generative violence to create "a new species of man . . . from terror," specifically as part of a desire to merge with the masses and to find inspiration in a broad Irish history and imaginary. For Tratner, "the problem that generated [Yeats's] poetry" is "how to generate the myth that would make violence revolutionary and passionate, not merely chaotic," or—Girard's terms are helpful here—to make it sacred rather than purely destructive.[49] For our purposes, the question of Yeats's political attitudes is less central than is Tratner's question of how, precisely, violence spurred, informed, troubled and/or anchored Yeats's work. In fact, to seek a consistent stance over the course of Yeats's career runs counter to my aims in this discussion, since I am arguing for a mutating, unstable relationship between literature and violence in the period, whereby each of the major forms (keening, generative violence, reprisal, architectural allegory) implicates the others and where political attitude per se is not definitive of literary outcomes. To consider the range of Yeats's works that are oriented around generative violence is to note, first, a diversity of political positions and interests, and second, some crucial tension points around the very idea (and ideal) of generativity.

In addition to "Easter 1916," and to a lesser degree "Red Hanrahan's Song about Ireland," the poem that offers perhaps Yeats's most resounding and concise engagement with enchanted violence is the commemorative lyric "An Irish Airman Foresees His Death." The poem is one of several Yeats wrote to honor Lady Gregory's son, Robert, who had enlisted in the Royal Flying Corps and was killed in action in February of 1918. It would be difficult to overstate the confusion and devastation Robert's death presented to his mother's community, not only for the normal human reasons (the loss of one's only son to war, the terrible grief surrounding smashed promise) but for more delicate political ones as well. Robert's enlistment as an officer in the war certainly testified to the aristocratic legacy in which he had been raised, but for the son of a nationalist like Lady Gregory to fight in England's war, and to be killed in it, created an extra level of torment and tension. The subject of Ireland's participation in the war was always fraught and divisive, and cannot be schematized entirely as northern allegiance versus southern resistance. In August 1914, the leader of the Irish parliamentarians, John Redmond, enjoined Irish citizens of all classes to enlist, under the view that this would further Home Rule goals, yet the nationalist position, overall, was to repudiate participation, with the insurrectionists famously seeking Germany as a potential ally in the lead-up to the 1916 rebellion.[50] And yet, loss is loss; employing an enchantment from the skies, Yeats took up these conflicts in "An Irish Airman Foresees His Death" in a sense by distancing himself—and, within the poem Gregory—from the political structure of the war. Indeed, by making his metaphorics out of distance itself, Yeats was able to effect a political distancing that might be impossible to articulate directly.

Spoken in Gregory's voice, the poem imagines death in the sky as a rarefied expression of will rather than as part of war's slaughter or Ireland's colonial dilemma. The poem reads:

> I know that I shall meet my fate
> Somewhere among the clouds above;
> Those that I fight I do not hate
> Those that I guard I do not love;
> My country is Kiltartan Cross,
> My countrymen Kiltartan's poor,
> No likely end could bring them loss
> Or leave them happier than before.
> Nor law, nor duty bade me fight,

> Nor public men, nor cheering crowds,
> A lonely impulse of delight
> Drove to this tumult in the clouds;
> I balanced all, brought all to mind,
> The years to come seemed waste of breath,
> A waste of breath the years behind
> In balance with this life, this death. (*Var*, 328)

Waving away all the ordinary incitements to enlist—adherence to the cause, a feeling of enmity against the enemy, a sense of historical responsibility, anticipating conscription—Yeats instead presents Gregory as joining the RFC almost as a metaphysical incitement. He is given a robust "I" voice, very much in control of his "fate." Even his consciousness is saturated with power. With regard to the title, for instance, we might note the effect of "foresees" as against other verbs Yeats might have selected, such as "contemplates" or "imagines." A prophet of sorts, Gregory's immensely capacious mind in the poem is able to contain all the antinomies and oppositions suggested by the war, which the poem's own dichotomizing logic does much to emphasize.

More generally, the poem reads as a meditation on death as desire, life as waste, and employs a classical language of fate that is very far from the Christian, resurrectionary thematics that underpinned so many of the enchanting Rising texts. Though death is chosen, it is not for the rewards of afterlife or martyrdom. Death represents, instead, the essence of a solitary ethos, valued in and of itself, "a lonely impulse of delight." In many of Yeats's works, such solitariness can be connected with a form of social ostracism, invited if rued, which is connected to Yeats's Protestant identity, to his sense of the artist's position, and to his general reverence for an imagined aristocratic distance from the concerns of the world. Here, this infrastructure is suggested obliquely, via Gregory's status ("My country . . . My countrymen"), and his solitary impulse is figured in rarified, personalized terms. The airman is simply drawn—magnetically—to death.

Despite the elevated feel of the poem, aloof from the world as its subject is aloft in the "clouds," it is not without its economics, as with so many modernist efforts to find a structural antidote to the extremity of violence. In this case, Yeats conjures the kind of economy of excess I have called a guiding principle among many works in the Irish canon of these years, as in "September 1913." Life is easily expended— "The years to come seem waste of breath,/A waste of breath the years behind/In balance with this life, this death." What matters, instead of life, is "balance," to use the poem's term, or what we might call "the aesthetic." The word "balance" is used twice in the poem ("I balanced all, brought all to mind," "In balance with this life, this death"), and, more generally, "An Irish Airman Foresees His Death" is itself a beautifully balanced, controlled poem, with several "Second Coming"–like repetitions from line to line ("My country is Kiltartan Cross,/My countrymen Kiltartan's poor"), a variety of "nor" phrases that set up crisply weighted oppositions, and a rhyme scheme that emphasizes an interesting series of oppositions that also collapse into one another: fate/hate, Cross/loss, fight/delight, crowds/clouds, and especially breath/death. To choose death in this poem is not "delirium," it is not a call for martyrdom, and it is not about blood; it is, instead, the choice of form, an extension in the human and metaphysical sphere of the poem's own creed of elegant equilibrium. The poem thus accomplishes something rare in this period, enchantment as form, an idiom that works its violent overload into aesthetic harmony.

"Red Hanrahan's Song about Ireland," "Easter 1916," and "An Irish Airman Foresees His Death" are among a small handful of Yeats's poems that explore forms of enchanted or generative violence without suggesting an undertow of vengeance and reprisal; among his plays, a whole cluster of works falls under that rubric, including *Cathleen ni Houlihan*, the Cuchulain cycle, and several of his most stylized late works, composed for private viewings in a salon setting. These last share a central component: they generate their core energy from sexual violence. Like "Leda and the Swan," discussed in the introduction as an instance of the relation between intimacy in violence and the unfurling of outwardly directed consequences, these plays envision a form of generative violence inaugurated by sexual violation and trauma. *The Herne's Egg* (1938) offers a Leda-like figure in the person of the priestess Attracta, whose prime motivation in the play and in her life is an eagerness to assume her role of "bride" (i.e. object of sexual predation) of the great bird-god, the herne, a rhapsodic enthrallment with sexual violation that remains unchanged even after Attracta has been raped by seven soldiers. *A Full Moon in March* (1935) and *The King of the Great Clock Tower* (1935) are similar to one another in theme and structure, both featuring the bizarre scenario of an intoxicated, ecstatic queen who dances around the severed head of her would-be lover.[51] In all of these plays, troubling fantasies of female subservience to male power contribute to a broader image of violence as the catalyst for strange, highly formalized aesthetic patterns. These plays, abstract and figural, suggest history only in attenuated terms—but it is there. In both *A Full Moon in March* and *The King of the Great Clock Tower*, when the queen comes to dance before the singing severed head, her trance-like ecstasy calls to mind the ancient Bacchae, but also makes a gesture to the spirit of the Rising period, twenty years in the past, when an intoxication with death and martyrdom often took gendered forms (as in Pearse) and generally enraptured a wide public.

The further Yeats moves from historical representation of violence and politics, the more he can abstract and schematize the enchantment of violence he felt to be a defining feature of revolutionary Ireland. Politics, history, even the standard mythic history that often sustained Yeats's drama have all been depleted in these plays, replaced by a gestural language that, in the *Collected Plays* edition (actively edited by Yeats) takes on a life of its own. Referencing backward and forward in his stage directions and using the same props over and over, Yeats created an idiosyncratic repertoire for staging and aestheticizing violence. In this sequence of late plays, then, the treatment of violence as a symbolic center around which figures literally circulate creates an almost anthropological mood of enchanted violence. The narratives tend to revolve around old, obscure myths of bloody deeds and sexual taboos. "There is a story in my country," says the swineherd in *A Full Moon in March*, "of a woman/That stood all bathed in blood—a drop of blood/Entered her womb and there begat a child," to which the queen responds, "She took it in her hands;/She stood all bathed in blood; the blood begat" (*CP*, 393). Both the swineherd, soon to be decapitated, and the queen, soon to be seen dancing in a mimicry of "climax" around the bloody head, cooperate in bringing this ancient story to fulfillment (*CP*, 396). In this play, to occupy positions of mutual violation, such that one is killed and the other entranced by his blood, represents a kind of charm or spell—enchantment in that sense, too. In *The King of the Great Clock Tower*, similarly, the intoxicated queen will sing "He longs to kill/My body, until/That sudden shudder/And limbs lie still" (*CP*, 401). Her language of course recalls Leda, suggesting a double overlapping in the "sudden shudder": the queen and the imagined lover, Leda and the swan. Rape and perverse forms of impregnation underpin all of these works, providing their guiding motifs and principles of aesthetic pleasure. Attracta makes the case most forcefully:

> When I take the beast to my joyful breast,
> Though beak and claw I must endure,
> *Sang the bride of the Herne, and the Great Herne's Bride,*
> No lesser life, man, bird or beast,
> Can make unblessed what a beast made blessed,
> Can make impure what a beast made pure. (*CP*, 419)

It may be difficult, as a feminist reader, to take much of this very seriously. Yeats himself seems a bit entranced, working his way out of the revolutionary history of violence by envisioning a sexually dubious enchantment. The idea that war and rape are the fuel for beauty and generation has been treated, in *The Waste Land*

and "Leda and the Swan," with intricacy and depth, but here the paradigm is reduced, like the plays' settings, to a more schematic outline.[52]

And yet, with his last play, *The Death of Cuchulain*, where Yeats returns both to mythic and actual history, and, not coincidentally, to a rendering of female desire that wrenches free of the trope of victimized pleasure, the generative violence frame changes—indeed, is broken altogether. Cuchulain's death, it should be noted, is overdetermined; a reader not entirely versed in the mythic stories might well have thought it already accomplished when he appears to drown at the end of *On Baile's Strand* (1904), and within *The Death of Cuchulain* he is wounded sequentially, his body absorbing the vengeance of many foes, before his head is cut off by a blind man who is eager for the proffered reward of twelve pennies. Like the vagrants in *A Full Moon in March* and *The King of the Great Clock Tower*, Cuchulain is ultimately reduced to a severed head, yet there is no frenzied, erotic circling of that icon. The image of a generative bloodletting issuing in rhythmic movement is itself severed, for Cuchulain's death, unlike the various singers who precede him in the sequence of dramas, is layered into the twentieth-century history that remains very much in the background of these works.

When Cuchulain is finally gone, the stage darkens, and the final lines are spoken by a singer, in a summation that inevitably reaches out beyond the play itself. Like "The Circus Animals' Desertion," the close of *The Death of Cuchulain* has the ring of self-scrutiny, a culminating statement of poetic and political work and thought. In the voice of a harlot, the singer asks some famous questions:

> Are those things that men adore and loathe
> Their sole reality?
> What stood in the Post Office
> With Pearse and Connolly?
> What comes out of the mountain
> Where men first shed their blood?
> Who thought Cuchulain till it seemed
> He stood where they had stood? (*CP*, 445–46)

From the point of view of enchanted violence, this passage is highly provocative and also highly inconclusive. What comes out of the mountain where men shed blood, it turns out, is Cuchulain—which is to say, the mythic history of violence as envisioned, especially, by Pearse (who always elevated Cuchulain as one of the great Irish figures to emulate) and by Yeats himself. Is the poet inserting himself—as one important maker of cultural nationalism—into the Rising, at the very site of its violent, transformative being? In part, yes. And yet in the final question, "Who thought Cuchulain," he supplies no agent; "till it seemed" is entirely vague as to when and in whose view the intertwining of the insurrection with the (Yeatsian) mythic past became the accepted story. On one hand, to create an image of Cuchulain standing ghostlike in the Post Office, ready to be recognized as the spirit of the Rising, is to suggest that the enchantment of that event is really about the power of literature rather than the power of historical violence, hence a reversal of "Easter 1916." On the other hand, there is a sense of inevitability in all of this. Eventually, the spirit of one era's mythic violence, epitomized by Cuchulain, is reborn in another era's generative violence, epitomized by Pearse and Connolly, in a sequence of historical resurrections and re-formations. In a strange way, then, violence is not so much generative as simply part of the cyclical story of nations and their icons: era after era brings forth its heroes, who are then understood as reanimating and superseding their predecessors.

In concert with this tonal change about generative violence, the image of female desire in the play's last lines also marks a shift from the "sudden shudder" works, if we might schematize them thus. The harlot who concludes *The Death of Cuchulain*, like Crazy Jane, is full of her own desire, real and embodied; she is no delirious recipient of male sexual predation. "I adore those clever eyes," she says of the mythic male heroes, now long dead, "Those muscular bodies, but can get/No grip upon their thighs" (*CP*, 445). Living bodies are more troubling, naturally:

> That there are still some living
> That do my limbs unclothe,
> But that the flesh my flesh has gripped
> I both adore and loathe. (*CP*, 445)

There is something wonderful about these lines, with the female speaker owning her promiscuity and her sexual ambivalence. Sex here is not a route to any form of enchanted futurity, freighted with consequence and taking its toll on the victimized body. We might say, by contrast, that it is disenchanted, belonging to limbs and "flesh"—always the keyword designating that the material body has begun to act as a counterweight to the ideal of transformation and productivity. Leda and her followers were sites and catalysts of male potency, generating culture; the harlot is all flesh, and with that change comes a wholly different relation to violence. Sex need not be violent, in this scenario, and it need not be fruitful. It is disengaged from the entire construct, just as the questions that immediately follow are new and surprising—stunningly so—in relation to the rather repetitive, weary cycle of plays that precedes *The Death of Cuchulain* in *The Collected Plays* and also to the poems of generative violence we have discussed. "What stood in the Post

Office/With Pearse and Connolly" is an unanswered and unanswerable question, a stimulus to think about culture and violence according to a range of possibilities, while "a terrible beauty is born" has finality built into its beautiful phrasing, suggesting an endpoint—as "sleep at last has come/On limbs that had run wild."

Yeats's late plays were inspired in part by Japanese Noh drama and go far in the direction of nonrepresentational, gestural abstraction, and this allows them to think about violence as itself almost figural: a shape (the parallelogram of the severed head), or a color (red), or a style of movement (Bacchic, entranced).[53] Generativity—the signal mode of the Rising—mutates, sheds its skin, moves in the direction of a highly conceptual expressivity. Overall, Yeats's generative violence canon contains a range of political positions, from "Red Hanrahan's" early song of inceptive nationalism to Cuchulain's resurgence late in Yeats's life; it is expressed in a variety of formal registers, from the incantatory and partially lulling "Easter 1916" to the wild sexual energy of his late plays; and, above all, it proposes a number of aesthetically mixed outcomes. For all this seeming expressive freedom, the stakes were always high when it came to representing violent national themes of any sort. As Yeats himself found with his two Cathleen plays, in the loaded period leading up to rebellion, a writer is asked to stand either for or against the national agenda, and violence is read, in polarizing terms, as uselessly disenchanting (*Countess Cathleen*) or as inspiringly enchanting (*Cathleen ni Houlihan*). In the public world, it seems, the experiments in miscegenating enchantment with disenchantment that we have found to engender exquisite effects meet with little favor, as the most controversial work of these decades revealed with such clamor, Synge's *The Playboy of the Western World* (1907).[54]

In concluding this discussion of generative violence, I want to consider Synge's enigmatic and compelling play, since it demonstrates especially clearly the relationship between generative violence and that which so often succeeds it, reprisal. *The Playboy of the Western World* thus functions as a segue in this analysis, as we will turn, in the next section, from the relative promise of generativity to the vortex of vengeance, and will find that these seemingly separable forms are in fact entangled. The trajectory in *The Playboy of the Western World* from an atmosphere of generative violence to the cycle of reprisal is so operational as to be registered at the level of plot and structure. The play is set in a small community in County Mayo, in an unspecified time that appears to match the play's composition, and concerns the fallout when a young man, Christy Mahon (the "playboy") wanders in from the roads, seeking rest and protection. Having, he declares, killed his father with a blow to the head, he is on the run. The community is ravished by this patricide and welcomes Christy. With women swooning over him (especially the female protagonist Pegeen Mike, who had been engaged to another man at the start of the play), while the men are either terrified or admiring, Christy becomes a local hero, winning a host of sports contests and generally stealing the hearts of the community—until, that is, his unkilled father returns and upsets the narrative. Christy is soon expelled, cursed most viciously by those who had adored him with the greatest passion. In terms of the violence narrative, we might schematize *The Playboy of the Western World* as follows: Christy happens in on a community that, unbeknownst to itself, reveres violence; he is welcomed as a celebrity for his imagined ferocity (and for trespassing a great taboo) and is offered the best that the community can give, in the form of protection and his choice of wives (he chooses Pegeen); it does not take long, however, before a counterviolence begins to develop (as, for instance, when Pegeen's father Michael rebuffs him, worrying about the consequences of having a parricide in the family); with the arrival of Christy's father, a storm of violence is unleashed on the playboy, taking its most disturbing form in Pegeen's burning of her lover's leg with a torch. Succinctly, the play figures the Mayo villagers as a community coming to terms with its internal violence. In Girard's language, what we find in *The Playboy* is an instance of redirected violence, whereby the possibility of internal fracture within a group is warded off by the localizing of violent energy in the person of an outsider. Kiberd, in a compelling reading of the play that focuses on its imbrication of poetry with violence, employs Girard's model: "Such a people desperately need a hero who can bring their instincts to violence into a single clear focus: a hero, moreover, whom they can then convert into a scapegoat onto whom may be visited any troublesomely violent tendencies that are still unfulfilled" (Kiberd, 166).[55] Yet, as Kiberd argues, and as a Girardian reading would predict, the outcome of such an instance of "sacrificial crisis" can be radical and surprising. For Kiberd, what emerges from Synge's reflection on a culture drunk with a violence that it cannot fully control is ultimately an image of a hero—Christy—who epitomizes the nation. In this reading, Christy in effect escapes from the Girardian cycle, instead embodying a Fanonian one: he displays, first, a colonial mentality (taking his self-measure from the community around him), then a national one (beginning to utilize a nationally inflected, self-created language), and, at the close of the play, arrives at Fanon's third and final stage of independence (commanding his father in the final sequence and spurning the villagers' attacks on him).

And yet the national allegory is not the only endpoint for Synge's withering interrogation of the direction violence takes in the community. The play draws an exceptionally individual portrait of a community expressing a powerful push and pull with respect to violence. That relationship is founded on several overarching premises: that, in this culture, violence is a crucial marker of masculinity (so Christy as murderer becomes an object of female desire, while the cowardly and conventional Shawn Keogh, the man to whom Pegeen had been betrothed, is viewed with universal contempt[56]); that there is a hierarchy of forms for desirable violence (with patricide at the top, but the Widow Quinn's slow and ambiguous killing of her husband a less admired affair); and that the line dividing glamorous from sordid violence depends largely on its remaining out of view (the villagers are awed by Christy's description of the murder, but jeer when he later attacks his father in front of them). But what is most striking is to see how fully the community is drawn out of itself by the idea of violence. The envisioning of a terrible act awakens the villagers, who, at the opening of the play, are surrounded by death and enervation—a wake is in progress down the hill from the shebeen where the action transpires, and the imminent marriage between Pegeen and Shawn is entirely sapped of vitality. With the evocation of Christy's killing of his father—such a blunt transgression of basic taboos, carrying an overload of political and Freudian significance—it is as if their blood is stirred, and they move from deathliness to a newly vibrant mood.

From a scene dominated by mortality and convention, then, comes the prospect of enchanted violence. Crucially, this sense of a powerful, generative violence is not the product of visitation from outside (Christy does not import it), but rather arises via the villagers' own imaginative processes. One of the most arresting sequences in the play, for instance, comes in Act I, when the villagers slowly extract from Christy the story of his deed, pulling closer and closer to him and to it as they gradually tease the story from him. The sequence has Dantean qualities, as the villagers move through a list of more and more dangerous crimes, into deeper and deeper rungs of the criminal imaginary, and seem infatuated not only with Christy but with their own verbal process for eliciting the murder. There is something catechistic, or perhaps legalistic, about the way they question Christy, beginning with the suggestion of theft and running through forms of anticolonial and political violence ("Was it bailiffs? . . . Agents? . . . Landlords? . . . Maybe he went fighting for the Boers . . .?"). The trail ends with Christy's claim, "I killed my poor father, Tuesday was a week," a stunning statement that brings the community together in awe and admiration.[57] The catechism immediately restarts after this, with the question of the weapon ("And you shot him dead? . . . It was with a hilted knife maybe? . . . You never hanged him . . .?") and continues until the whole story has been revealed, as if the villagers cannot quite let off from expressing their unifying urge to draw near an act of ferocious violence (*Playboy*, 106). There is something magnetic in these sequences, which comes not so much from Christy's language as from the villagers' responses to him. Violence is not exactly enchanting here—it is not transformative, purifying, or ennobling—but it allows the villagers to feel qualities of elation and exultation that partake of enchantment, and given the symbolic overdetermination of the crime, permeates their world with a sense of significance and power.

Once the intoxication with Christy's act of violence has spread across the community, two critical developments can then unfold: first is the creation of a robust and beautiful poetic out of Christy's voice, which is focused primarily on his wooing of Pegeen and which borrows from an Irish idiom (he cribs from Douglas Hyde's *Love Songs of Connacht*, as Kiberd has shown, and, more generally, represents a tour de force when it comes to imbuing the English language with a Gaelic intonation, one of Synge's greatest accomplishments); and second is the unfurling of that enthrallment with violence into a generalized brutality that sweeps through the community and lands, eventually, back on Christy, who had elicited it in the first place. Not only is vengeance unleashed in the latter parts of the play—inaugurating a cycle of reprisal—but the community is generally diminished, so that, for instance, Michael, who was once a champion of defiance, now becomes a resigned spokesman for convention. Early in Act III he had said:

> It's the will of God, I'm thinking, that all should win an easy or a cruel end, and it's the will of God that all should rear up lengthy families for the nurture of the earth . . . A daring fellow is the jewel of the world, and a man did split his father's middle with a single clout should have the bravery of ten, so may God and Mary and St. Patrick bless you, and increase you from this mortal day. (*Playboy*, 140)

Michael's nearly blasphemous language here is provocative, full of images of sparkle and life ("the nurture of the earth," "the jewel of the world"). By the final lines of the play, in contrast, he is reduced to: "It is the will of God that all should guard their little cabins from the treachery of law" (*Playboy*, 146).

It is Pegeen, however, who is given the final words; significantly, they come not from the tradition of generative violence, nor from the spiraling world of reprisal, but from the lexicon of keening: "*Putting her shawl over her head and breaking out into wild lamentations,*" as the stage directions say, Pegeen cries, "Oh my grief, I've lost him surely. I've lost the only playboy of the western world" (*Playboy*, 146). One gets the sense, in much of the literature of this period, of a finite set of imaginative resources when it comes to violence. It is understood, most emphatically, as generative, more darkly as retributive, and, failing these, one returns to the ancient convention of keening. That overarching expression of national sorrow, embodied by women, offers solace, for it connects the person who expresses it back in time to the shared past, and outward in space to all of Ireland.[58] At the same time, the turn to keening reflects a form of linguistic enclosure, in the sense that the language is ritualized and prescribed; as we saw in the case of *Juno and the Paycock*, part of its strength derives from the fact that it can easily be lifted and substituted from person to person. The language of keening at the close of the play does not produce the kind of defeated idiom of, say, Michael's cramped utterance, and yet there is something diminished about it. Insofar as the keen steers away from the act or expression of violence itself, it misses the spark and energy that inhere in that vibrant, originary moment. For Kiberd, the end of the play reads in bracing, postcolonial terms, as Christy stalks off the stage, embodying a masculine, independent Ireland, but he is less concerned with Pegeen, left echoing an old lament. The language of keening is, in a sense, what remains—onstage, in the domestic settings of women's experience, in history itself—when the violent actors have walked off the stage. In the push toward a futurity of violence which, one hopes, will yield ultimate and long-lasting peacefulness, there is always an echoing language.

The Years of War: Reprisal

"A bunch of martyrs (1916) were the bomb and we are living in the explosion": so wrote Yeats in a 1922 letter to his friend Olivia Shakespear, in a formulation that startlingly clashes with his canonical expression of the Rising's enchanting outcome, "a terrible beauty is born."[59] This image of wreckage and explosive consequence has its own resonance, for it suggests a different consciousness about violence, one that found increasingly wide expression in the years following the Rising, but which in fact has roots much further back in the nationalist struggle. If Yeats's "bunch of martyrs" formulation reminds us of the language of dynamite explosion, moreover, such a confluence is not coincidental; much in the violent imaginary of Ireland from the middle to the end of the nineteenth century coincided with the worldwide enthrallment with dynamite violence. Moreover, there were historical congruencies between anarchists and Fenians. Partly a matter of technology and strategy (dynamite, prison breaks, sensational acts of violence against carefully chosen targets), this linking of Fenian violence and anarchism in the English and American public understanding also held cultural and racist connotations, since, in the English and American view, the "foreignness" of the anarchist could easily be allied with denigration of the Irish. We should thus be especially clear in our own demarcations:

not only did some Fenians (such as Yeats and O'Leary) share with many Irish people an objection to the "physical force tradition," but the aims, political histories, and literary output of the two movements have little in common. Still, at the level of the theorizing of violence, there are overlaps. What the anarchism example helps to clarify, above all, is how extensively a tradition of reprisal violence had been written into the European imaginary of this period, with political connotations that were inevitably revolutionary and with dynamite as one symbol of its technological reach. For the Ireland of the modernist era, three elements converge in this imaginary: a general tone of nihilistic resentment, sharing some of its language with the anarchist movement; a cycle of vengeance that superseded the ideal of generativity, especially potent in the post-Rising and post–First World War years; and, perhaps most simply, the possibility of being motivated by hatred.

The gospel of hate, as everyone for a half century seemed to agree, had been spread by John Mitchel. Relatively obscure among American readers today, Mitchel was one of the most important voices for Irish revolutionary nationalism in the nineteenth century, standing as an ideological rival to Daniel O'Connor, in many ways the most renowned figure in the nationalist movement before Parnell. While O'Connor worked toward separatism from England via organizational and parliamentary means, Mitchel viewed such tactics as insufficient and fruitless. A leader of Young Ireland and founder, along with Gavan Duffy, of the primary nationalist paper of the 1840s, *The Nation*, Mitchel was arrested for sedition in 1848 and deported, spending fourteen years as a convict in Van Diemen's Land (Tasmania). His *Jail Journal*, published in 1876, became something of a sensation. He influenced all of the figures we have discussed so far, including Yeats, who evoked him in the late poem "Under Ben Bulben" (1939), and Pearse, who included him in his elite pantheon of founding voices of Irish nationalism. For both Yeats and Pearse, Mitchel is distinguished by his injunction to hate. Pearse, for instance, wrote that Mitchel's language "flames with apocalyptic wrath, such wrath as there is nowhere else in literature" (*CWS*, 365). Mitchel calls for violence, but not of a generative or enchanted kind; his belongs to a different category altogether, and this leads even Pearse into a defensive posture. If, by the first decade of the twentieth century, it had become quite easy to laud generative violence, it was still problematic to call for the violence of hatred or of euphoric destruction.

For his part, Yeats adopted varying stances, over the course of his career, on what Mitchel represented and, by extension, on what kind of motivating violence is most productive. Writing in 1907, as he looked back on his own political arc up to that point, he indicated, along the lines of Pearse, that Mitchel stood rather simply for hate: "New from the influence . . . of William Morris," he recalls,

"I dreamed of enlarging Irish hate, till we had come to hate with a passion of patriotism what Morris and Ruskin hated. Mitchel had already all but poured some of that hate drawn from Carlyle, who had it of an earlier, and, as I think, cruder sort, into the blood of Ireland" (*EI*, 248). To emulate Mitchel, in this formulation, was to tap into a nationalist well of resentment and anger, but one— importantly for Yeats—with close ties to the English intellectual and political tradition represented by Carlyle, Ruskin, and Morris. Twenty years later, in "Under Ben Bulben," Mitchel looks somewhat different, carrying with his hate a glimmer of enchantment:

> You that Mitchel's prayer have heard,
> "Send war in our time, O Lord!"
> Know that when all words are said
> And a man is fighting mad,
> Something drops from eyes long blind,
> He completes his partial mind,
> For an instant stands at ease,
> Laughs aloud, his heart at peace.
> Even the wisest man grows tense
> With some sort of violence
> Before he can accomplish fate,
> Know his work or choose his mate. (*Var*, 638)

One might read this stanza alongside "Leda and the Swan" and the other "sudden shudder" works, since, like them, it imagines productive violence in the vivid moment, a flash of personalized intensity that becomes a form of powerful subjective enhancement. Yet for all that, this is not a moment of generativity in the "Leda and the Swan" mode. The taking apart of the word "violence" into its syllabic parts— vi-o-lence—as required by the scan, indicates what the poem also demands of its readers, that we understand violence in its component parts, that we break it up and render it strange. In the next stanza, Yeats will invoke the Sistine ceiling, a work of art that shares something with the moment of contracting violence (generating a heating of the "bowels" for its "globe-trotting" viewers, which recalibrates the "grows tense" of the earlier stanza), but Michelangelo's work, unlike Mitchel's— which is only momentary and limited in effect—gives "Proof that there's a purpose set/Before the secret working mind:/Profane perfection of mankind" (*Var*, 638–39). No perfection follows from Mitchel's program of violence as the outcome of hate, even if Yeats and others found this state of consciousness genuinely absorbing and powerful, and not unprincipled.

In Mitchel's own words, the injunction to violence carried suggestions of over-whelming destructiveness. Notwithstanding his privileged, Trinity-educated status, Mitchel was a real revolutionary, in many ways more complex a theorist of violence than either Pearse or Yeats admits. On the one hand, his *Jail Journal* is surprisingly erudite in style. It takes long excursions to consider the likes of Aristotle, is sprin-kled with Latin and Greek quotations, and is limited in its political expressions. On the other hand, when he does make political commentary, it is vigorously violent. "[T]here is," he writes of the Irish situation, "but one and all-sufficient remedy, *the edge of the sword*" (*JJ*, 24, italics in original). (We might note, again, the ubiquity of the sword/bayonet, anachronistic symbols for modern ferocity.) Mitchel does indeed call for "war in our time," as Yeats puts it, fantasizing about a European cataclysm, to be set off by the French revolutionists of midcentury, which would "cut down and overthrow, root and branch, the whole government and social ar-rangement of England" (*JJ*, 91). War, says Mitchel, is much preferable to the slow starvation of colonized life; "to pour out your full soul in all its pride and might with a hot torrent of red raging blood" is far better than to "perish in a nation by tame beggarly famine" (*JJ*, 94). Given Mitchel's reputation for bellicosity, one is not sur-prised by these hot torrents of blood. What is interesting and unexpected, however, is to find the language of revolution, indeed almost of anarchism. Creative destruc-tion, an idea we have seen to be associated, for instance, with Bakunin, becomes the endpoint of Mitchel's discourse on violence, which moves quickly from an encomium on war to the praising of destruction more broadly. Invoking the Book of Revelations, Mitchel likens the most terrible violence to the painful but ultimately cleansing powers of tornadoes, wildfires, and other natural catastrophes (treated as visitations from God). "Ah!" he thinks, "the atmosphere of the world needs to be cleared by a wholesome tornado," and continues in this vein:

> In all nature, spiritual and physical, do you not see that some powers and agents have it for their function to abolish and demolish and derange— other some to construct and set in order? But is not the destruction, then, as natural, as needful, as the construction?—Rather tell me, I pray you, which is construction—which destruction? This destruction *is* creation: death is birth and
>
> "The quick spring like weeds out of the dead."
>
> Go to:—the revolutionary leveller is your only architect. (*JJ*, 96, 98, italics in original)

To be sure, the passage evokes generative violence ("death is birth"), but Mitchel's primary leaning here is in the direction of a different mode of destruction, one that overlaps with images of the mystic terrorist discussed in the last chapter. The term "leveler," for instance, was a favorite of anarchists, since it brings together the idea of social equalization with an image of total destruction—social classes erased, the human world razed.[60] Mitchel here is thinking less about generative, symbolic moments of violence—which might be imagined as having significant political, cultural and aesthetic consequences—than about a great overthrow, in revolutionary terms, of the social order, and not in enchanting terms.

There was one important insurrectionist who shared Mitchel's revolutionary tendencies, though in a more sustained and organized form, who has an important part in the violence narrative of these years: James Connolly. Readers of Yeats might be forgiven if they primarily associate Connolly with Pearse, since their names typically appear side by side in Yeats's poetry ("Easter 1916," "Sixteen Dead Men," "The Rose Tree," *The Death of Cuchulain*), but Yeats puts them together more for reasons of scansion and sound than for historical reasons; in fact, Connolly represents quite a different kind of nationalism from Pearse's—and a markedly different approach to violence. Where Pearse was a Romantic, striving in his literary output and political activism toward a mythic ideal of Irishness and enthralled by the notion of generative violence, Connolly was, above all, a militant socialist. His Citizen's Army, an active force in the Rising, was founded in response to the 1913 lockout of Dublin's striking dockworkers, and though he always claimed the two causes to be mutually sustaining and deeply intertwined, he arrived at a position of leadership in the Rising via his labor activism, and there were at times tensions between him and other leaders like Pearse. The outbreak of war, for instance, highlights their contrasting thoughts about violence. Though both staunchly opposed Irish participation in what they viewed as imperial Britain's war, they parted company on the subject of how to understand its violence. Pearse, we recall, used enchanting language to praise war, writing that "the old heart of the earth needed to be warmed with the red wine of the battlefields," while a deeply dispirited, caustic Connolly responded with a fierce articulation of disenchantment. Of the mutual demonizing of warring enemies, he wrote that "it all depends . . . upon whose houses are being bombarded, whose people are being massacred, whose limbs are torn from the body, whose bodies are blown to a ghastly mass of mangled flesh and blood and bones."[61] As for Mitchel, Connolly may not have shared his adulation for the hot torrents of blood unleashed by war, but he revered him as a true revolutionary: "There are no John Mitchels left in Ireland," he wrote in *Workers' Republic* in 1915; "we are not revolutionists. Not by a thousand miles!" (Connolly, 104). In other words, while Connolly was no preacher of creative destruction, he was a leveler, and in that sense he helped to carry forward into the insurrectionary moment an element of Mitchel's destructive ideal.

Mitchel's work demonstrates a trajectory from hate (of the English tyranny over Ireland) to a wider destructive goal, reminiscent of anarchism; this movement, in turn, also illuminates two of Yeats's closely connected and relatively obscure plays, *Where There is Nothing* (1902) and its later incarnation, *The Unicorn from the Stars* (1907).[62] Both plays are notable for their embrace of mystical violence. At the center of both works is a powerful endorsement of destruction, imagined in religious terms. Both dramatize the situation when a young man, full of unorthodox religious fervor, transgresses a range of conventions—dismissing family, mingling with the lowest in the social order (tinkers and beggars), in *Where There Is Nothing* joining and then breaking from a monastery, creating his own renegade order, in *The Unicorn from the Stars* leading a brief anti-British rebellion. Yeats had been reading Nietzsche when he wrote the first play, and one certainly can see in Paul Ruttledge and Martin Hearne, the respective protagonists of the two works, a Nietzschean attitude: heterodox, mystically inclined, defiant of ordinary social codes and constraints, and endorsing a massive overthrow of the social and religious order. In addition to Nietzsche, Katherine Worth also notes, in introducing the plays, the relevance of Blake, Tolstoy, and various occult groups, but she does not mention that Yeats gives voice, especially in *Where There Is Nothing*, to language reminiscent of anarchism.[63] The protagonist Paul, for instance, employs the phrase "pull down" to describe his goal of demolishing the social order, language very close to what we have seen in anarchist writings. "Sometimes I dream I am pulling down my own house," he says, "and sometimes it is the whole world that I am pulling down. . . . I would like to have great iron claws, and to put them about the pillars, and to pull and pull till everything fell into pieces" (*WN*, 59). At this early stage in Act I, Paul is just beginning to formulate his destructive ideal, which will expand and develop over the course of the two plays—from pulling down he will move to extinguishing, and in the later play, Martin employs metaphors of battle, culminating, in the last instance, in an almost nihilistic vision of ecstatic leveling. For Paul, the destructive dream is exemplified in his final sermon (after which he is expelled from the monastery), where he compares destroying the world to blowing out candle after candle: "At last we must put out the light of the Sun and of the Moon, and all the light of the World and the World itself . . . We must destroy the World; we must destroy everything that has Law and Number, for where there is nothing, there is God" (*WN*, 101, 102). And in Martin's terms in *The Unicorn from Stars*, "All is clear now. . . . I am to destroy; destruction was the word the messenger spoke. . . . Ah, if one could change it all in a minute, even by war and violence!" (*WN*, 138).

These expressions of radical violence evoke Mitchel's revolutionary ethos of destruction, the two plays framing this attitude in different ways. In *Where There Is Nothing*, the frame is religious—the "World" Paul wants to destroy is in part a figure for worldliness—and Paul squarely inhabits the mystic's position, to be crucified, as one might have predicted, by the people. In *The Unicorn from the Stars*, the catalyst that turns Martin's urge to destroy into action is the British presence in Ireland, against which he leads a ragtag, doomed brigade. Whether the narrative is mystical or nationalist, however, there is one key element linking these plays to their ancestor Mitchel, but, even more strikingly, showing their distance from him and erecting an obstacle to their being easily read in nationalist terms: "where there is nothing, there is God."[64] Though the desire for nothingness—for a wiping clean and a wiping out—is raised by Mitchel in his creative-destruction diatribe, such a motivation is difficult to reconcile with an activist program of any kind, and certainly not with a national one. Aspiring nations do not want nothingness. The ideal of *nihil* belongs to those hoping to escape from the state, not those committed to its creation.[65]

In *The Unicorn from the Stars*, the problem is reconciled, at least in part, by a turn to allegory. Allegorical reading, in this play, marks a bridge between a destructive ideal and a nationalist one, since it provides an avenue for interpreting Martin's bewildering, otherworldly visions in accordance with the restive mood of the play's vagrant characters, seeking an outlet for action in the real world. Several of them interpret his prophecy in directly nationalist terms, as in this sequence, in which Martin consults a fortune-teller:

> MARTIN: What is it? What is it I have to do?
>
> BIDDY: I see a great smoke, I see burning . . . There is a great smoke overhead.
>
> MARTIN: That means we have to burn away a great deal that men have piled up upon the earth. We must bring men once more the wildness of the clean green earth.
>
> BIDDY: Herbs for my healing, the big herb and the little herb, it is true enough they get their great strength out of the earth.
>
> JOHNNY: Who was it the green sod of Ireland belonged to in the olden times? Wasn't it to the ancient race it belonged? And who has possession of it now but the race that came robbing over the sea? The meaning of that is to destroy the big houses and the towns, and the fields to be given back to the ancient race.
>
> MARTIN: That is it. You don't put it as I do, but what matter? Battle is all.
>
> (*WN*, 145, ellipsis in original)

If Biddy the fortune-teller is plying her trade with all the vagueness it demands, Johnny, a tinker and a rebel, reads in the one-to-one style of the national allegorist. Yet the allegorical model is only partially successful in *The Unicorn from the Stars*. Martin himself does not seem to understand this interpretation—"you don't put it as I do"—and the rebellion he leads is strangely disjunctive. While he chases a mystical message from God, his followers hope to overthrow the British and better their own lives. Martin's obscure mystical vision is intensive to the point of Gnosticism; in looking to pry from such subjective obscurity some real revolutionary fodder, the play's characters take their own formal direction. The result has something in common with works like Wilde's *Vera, or the Nihilists*, discussed in the last chapter for its conjoining of melodramatic with urbane styles; in both plays, the thematics around violence engender disjunctive and irreconcilable sensibilities among different character groupings.

The move to allegory is not complete in these plays, and yet, neither is the darker possibility that hovers around their destructive fantasies: cycles of killing. As we saw in *The Playboy of the Western World*, the biggest threat to a world that praises and enchants violence is that the ideal of generativity will give way to mob mentality and, above all, to a cycle of reprisal. Violent energy is imagined in the works we have been discussing as a generalized frenzy, which takes the form of war or anarchist-like leveling. But such outcomes in a sense represent a byway, a channel, in the Irish imaginary of these years. What transpired in Ireland after the Rising was not a cataclysm of destruction but the targeted terror of reprisal. First came the execution of the sixteen leaders; after the First World War, the British escalated reprisal violence, carried out especially ruthlessly by the Black and Tans, and Irish insurgent forces responded; and finally, reprisal became commonplace in the Civil War, on both sides.

In keeping with this new structure of violence in the world, we can begin to track what we might call a stylistics of reprisal. Keening has its rhythms and structure; generative violence yields a recognizable language of enchantment; and reprisal, too, is not only visible at the level of theme, but also produces its own patterns and formal directives. Yeats's poem "Sixteen Dead Men" provides a point of entry into the reprisal mode, since it is ordered, thematically and structurally, by the idea of back-and-forth violence. The poem was written in 1917, and already registers a pointedly different structure of violence from the generativity of "Easter 1916." It begins:

> O but we talked at large before
> The sixteen men were shot
> But who can talk of give and take,

What should be and what not
While those dead mean are loitering there
To stir the boiling pot? (*Var*, 395)

These lines suggest that the logic of "give and take" belongs only to the living; "those dead men" would naturally not be thinking in such restricted terms (indeed, their stirring of the "boiling pot" might imply a Mitchel-like destruction). Logic itself might be a style of mere mortality, the poem suggests, asking of the limited, living, politicized world: "And is their logic to outweigh/MacDonagh's bony thumb?" Along the lines of "September 1913," "Sixteen Dead Men" would thus seem to promote an economy of excess, condemning a mercantile model of consciousness (and of literary approaches to violence).

But such conclusions, it turns out, are premature, as the poem's final lines envision the dead engaging in their own form of reciprocity:

How could you dream they'd listen
That have an ear alone
For those new comrades they have found,
Lord Edward and Wolfe Tone,
Or meddle with our give and take
That converse bone to bone? (*Var*, 395)

If "our give and take" looks petty and ephemeral in comparison with whatever these heroes might be discussing in their afterworld, still, there is little structural difference between "give and take" and "bone to bone." "Sixteen Dead Men" has a curiously light tone, a singsong quality that reflects its oscillational patterning. Yet that should not obscure the fact that its structure parallels the model of reprisal. It is meter, especially, that creates the reprisal stress. The word "converse" is the pivot; it must be pronounced with the emphasis on "con," rather than "verse," and this oddity in the pronunciation reminds us that the ineluctable return to a this-for-that model really is a function (or a description) of "verse." This verse is fully lodged within a negative ("con") structure, one that insists on setting up con-tests, a world lined up by pro and con. Even after death, the poem indicates, there is no escape from a style that matches bone-to-bone—or eye-for-eye.

Yeats wrote two major poems about reprisal violence, "Nineteen Hundred and Nineteen" and "Reprisals," both of which make significant, moving statements about the relationship of literature to political violence, and employ a language of disenchantment as part of their diverse imaginary. In fact, we might read these poems as responding to earlier and more canonical ones from the enchanting tradition, "Easter 1916" and "An Irish Airman Foresees His Death," respectively. In the latter case, the revisiting is clear and undeniable, in the former more general; for both, Yeats's poetic moves in concord with a general cultural pattern, from a focus on generativity and enchantment to a darker mood where unredeemable, cyclical violence makes urgent claims on the moral and poetic consciousness. These are hauntingly violent poems, punctured by depictions of murder, exceedingly sad and dispirited. "Nineteen Hundred and Nineteen," especially, stands alongside such landmarks as *The Waste Land* and *Guernica*[66] as among the richest accounts of disenchanted violence in the modernist era.[67] Like those works, it needs to be read for its exquisite intertwining of enchantment within a disenchanting idiom, and of resonant, symbolic power within a bleak statement of despair.

More than any other work we have considered in this chapter, "Nineteen Hundred and Nineteen" disenchants violence. After several opening stanzas that critique political hope as naive complacency, the poem catapults us into a present that could never lull or placate:

> Now days are dragon-ridden, the nightmare
> Rides upon sleep: a drunken soldiery
> Can leave the mother, murdered at her door,
> To crawl in her own blood, and go scot-free;
> The night can sweat with terror as before
> We pieced our thought into philosophy,
> And planned to bring the world under a rule,
> Who are but weasels fighting in a hole. (*Var*, 429)

All of the elements of a viscerally disenchanting poetic are here: an image of blood that belies any symbolic or generative associations; the presence of terrifying, unconstrained force; the creation of a violent tableau that punches through the literary work unexpectedly and without consolatory surroundings. A reader might wonder, too, if there is not some contradiction here: how can a "murdered" woman "crawl in her own blood"? The answer is that Ellen Quinn,[68] the woman whose murder by Black and Tans is dramatized in the poem—pregnant, she was also holding a child in her arms at the moment when she was hit—lived for several hours after being shot by the passing Tans, who were drunk in their truck and presumably shot her by mistake: "She was out at the gate watching for [her husband] to come back," an eyewitness wrote, "The lorries passed and shots were fired; the maid ran out and found her lying there. 'Oh, I'm shot!' she said. The whole place was splashed with blood like a butcher's shop. . . . She lived a few hours in terrible pain."[69] Yeats had very likely read these lines, since they were transcribed by Lady Gregory, in one of a series of diary-style weekly columns she contributed to the London-based *The Nation*, all of which chronicle horrendous Black and Tan violence. In the keening tradition, the mother is the emblem of the nation's sorrows; here she represents those sorrows in quite a different way—shockingly, as she writhes in "terrible pain," and without any of the ritual or aesthetic solace offered by the keen.[70] Violence occasions here a terrible collapse of categories, as the mother-mourner becomes instead the victim, and the potential for healing evaporates.

To disenchant, however, is not to depoliticize. The murder of Quinn became, as Cullingford points out, a political lighting rod (Cullingford, 106). Lady Gregory's series of exposés of Black and Tan violence includes language that is nearly unreadable for its graphic description of terrible violence, as she powerfully and bluntly details a situation of intimidation and terror in the community. Yeats's allusion to the murder in his 1921 poem can thus be understood, in part, as a political statement of Republican, anti-British affiliation. It would have been impossible, when the poem was published, to read these lines and not register their disenchantment in partisan terms. And it would be impossible, at any time, to read them and not be sickened and outraged. They thus might be said to occupy a parallel position, in Yeats's poem and in a broader Irish discourse of these years, to Woolf's invocation of the Spanish photographs in *Three Guineas*: a representation of violence that, via its disenchanting visual insistence, promises both to activate and to generalize, creating a violent reaction in the present whose ultimate message is one of universal horror at unmerited victimization in any setting.

Significantly, Yeats embeds this virulently political, historically motivated moment of disenchantment into a stanza (and, more broadly, a poem) that works according to other logics as well. "Now days are dragon-ridden": for all its presentness, the stanza's opening line connotes a generalized state of modern terror, in accord with the poem's original title "Thoughts on the Present State of the World." The "drunken soldiery," of course, will reappear in "Byzantium," another poem with a frenzied, violent feel, yet one whose historicity is muted and rendered dreamlike. The dragon, moreover, with its mythological associations, points ahead to the poem's last stanza:

> Herodias' daughters have returned again,
> A sudden blast of dusty wind and after
> Thunder of feet, tumult of images,
> Their purpose in the labyrinth of the wind;

And should some crazy hand dare touch a daughter
All turn with amorous cries, or angry cries,
According to the wind, for all are blind.
But now wind drops, dust settles; thereupon
There lurches past, his great eyes without thought
Under the shadow of stupid straw-pale locks,
That insolent fiend Robert Artisson
To whom the love-lorn Lady Kyteler brought
Bronzed peacock feathers, red combs of her cocks. (*Var*, 433)

The metaphorics here are abstruse, as Yeats turns for his final image to an obscure corner of Medieval Irish lore, in the form of Artisson.[71] The image of Herodias's daughters, also nontransparent, suggests sexual violence, yet not in the "sudden shudder" tradition. Like the earlier portrayal of Quinn's murdered body, these sisters resist any narrative of generativity, their "purpose" being only "in the labyrinth of the wind." Equally obscure and frightful, the specter of Artisson was described by Yeats, in a note to the poem, as an "evil spirit," as indeed he is. Inevitably, too, Artisson conjures up a Yeatsian cousin, the "rough beast" from the closing lines of "The Second Coming" (written and published two years prior to "Nineteen Hundred and Nineteen"). Both poems close with harrowing visions that meld the historical with the mythic, in the form of a lurching, semiblind being that seems simultaneously to represent and to elude history.[72]

If the rough beast slouching toward Bethlehem offers one form of a monstrous birth, a darkly prophetic answer to the generative violence of the 1916 era (including Yeats's own poem of that tradition), Artisson seems to create havoc with a reading of history as progressive or of violence as productive. He is conjured, after all, from "a sudden blast of dusty wind," not the sexual shudder of climax but the sudden blow that, as we have seen, sets in motion the intimate, visceral experience of historical violence, begun in the body and moving out from there. In several respects, indeed, the poem reads largely as a meditation on the question of historicity. What does it mean to write from and for a historical moment when war is erupting, and when the logic of reprisal is becoming fixed? How can these new realties be squared with such questions as the cultural accomplishments of a civilization, the recent political history of the emerging nation, one's own life's work, and, most generally, the power and limits of the imagination in the face of exceptionally callous, nongenerative violence? Rob Doggett, in a wonderful reading of the poem, sees "Nineteen Hundred and Nineteen" largely as a representation of historical fracture at a very particular moment of political instability, a violent space of national self-definition "between the actual community and the imagined community, between a history waiting to be written and a history that has been written."[73] And Michael Wood, whose splendid meditation *Yeats and Violence* is largely a reading of "Nineteen Hundred and Nineteen," writes that "violence as Yeats understands it [particularly in "Nineteen Hundred and Nineteen"]—whether personal, political, or apocalyptic—is always sudden and surprising, visible, unmistakable, inflicts or promises injury and is fundamentally uncontrollable" (Wood, 20). For our purposes, what is most significant about the poem is the way it simultaneously disengages violence from the modes of thought in which it had been most powerfully lodged in Ireland in the two preceding decades—that of keening and of generative violence, and, to a lesser degree, of destructive utopianism—and asks, in the absence or refutation of these forms, where violence can possibly stand, how it can be part of culture, part of art, part of historical narrative.

Perhaps it will tell us something about the poem's searching and scorching relation to violence that "Nineteen Hundred and Nineteen," for all its referencing of Greek culture, is guided less by such a model—not by Homer, for whom bodies fall and chariots are made, in a cycle of productive war and art—than by Shakespeare's *King Lear*, which is referenced repeatedly in the poem (as in "mock mockers after that/that would not lift a hand . . . To bar that foul storm out" [*Var*, 432]). Yeats's suggestion that violence represents perhaps the most intimate and shattering experience of living in history shares a great deal with Shakespeare's penetrating and exhaustive consideration of violence in *King Lear*, which always sees violence in material terms—acting in the world and on people, destroying and creating. The poem contains some phrases as memorably spare as Lear's own—"What is there more to say?" or "Violence upon the roads; violence of horses"—which seem to stand alone and apart, and it also comprises the Learian bellow, now figured as a caustic assessment of political possibility: "We, who seven years ago/Talked of honour and of truth,/Shriek with pleasure if we show/The weasel's twist, the weasel's tooth." (*Var*, 431). There are, moreover, wonderful images of wild movement in the poem, and dizzying suggestions of flight, as, for instance, "The swan has leaped into the desolate heaven."

Yeats does not ground his swan, whose flight turns instead into a new sign of destruction, reminiscent of the apocalyptic visions of *Where There Is Nothing* and *The Unicorn from the Stars*:

> The swan has leaped into the desolate heaven:
> That image can bring wildness, bring a rage
> To end all things, to end

> What my laborious life imagined, even
> The half-imagined, the half-written page;
> O but we dreamed to mend
> Whatever mischief seemed
> To afflict mankind, but now
> That winds of winter blow
> Learn that we were crack-pated when we dreamed. (*Var*, 431)

Part of the ferocity of "Nineteen Hundred and Nineteen" derives from its sense of self-deception in the past, another Learian motif. As in this stanza, it often melds I's into we's, suggesting that Yeats—in tandem with the cultural project to which he subscribed in the years before reprisal killing and internal war became the norm— ought to have known better, ought to have known not to dream. This is not just pessimism or self-critique; it represents a judgment about a whole approach to cultural and political change, including the theory of generative violence. Indeed, Yeats draws much closer in this poem to Mitchel's destructive idea than to the idea of enchantment, but without the joy or sense of futurity associated with Mitchel. He even uses Mitchel's key term: "Come let us mock at the great/That had such burdens on the mind/ . . . /Nor thought of the levelling wind." Leveling emblematized Mitchel's radicalness, but Yeats's leveling is not revolutionary; its destruction lacks not only euphoria but a motivating political belief. Still, the leveling wind, a pervasive image in the poem, provides an apt metaphor for its mood.

In this poem of reprisal, Yeats returns, over and over, to the whirlwind. He is, of course, famous as a poet of spirals—"Turning and turning in the widening gyre"—and of circling patterns—"of what is past, or passing, or to come" (*Var*, 401, 408). Here those patterns are replaced by a form of wild movement that is troubling and chaotic, even brutal. In the opening stanza, the moon, often for Yeats the instigator of ordering patterns, "pitches common things about." As the poem progresses, we have "those winds that clamour of approaching night," the "wildness" of the swan and its rage, the "winds of winter," "the levelling wind," the "foul storm," the whirlwind imagery surrounding Heordias's daughters, and this stanza:

> When Loie Fuller's Chinese Dancers enwound
> A shining web, a floating ribbon of cloth,
> It seemed that a dragon of air
> Had fallen among dancers, had whirled them round
> Or hurried them off on its own furious path;
> So the Platonic Year

> Whirls out new right and wrong,
> Whirls in the old instead;
> All men are dancers and their tread
> Goes to the barbarous clangour of a gong. (*Var*, 430)

It is curious to find Loie Fuller among the likes of Shakespeare and Phidias in the poem, the only contemporary artist mentioned, and a woman no less. Fuller's performances, with their Asian-inspired dance motifs and their trademark swirling swaths of cloth, created a sensation in Paris in the 1890s and beyond, but did not, I think, suggest permanence, and her joyful presence hardly matches the poem's atmosphere.[74] One wonders why her magically transforming colors would conjure the dragon, except that in this era of reprisal violence, even a formalized, aesthetic spectacle of windlike imagery swirls "the old" back into itself, not only the old of this poem's span (say, seven years ago, or further into the speaker's history, or even back to the time of Phidias) but back to a more primordial past, where the barbarous gong represents a very basic musical impulse. At an earlier moment in Yeats's and Ireland's career, "all men are dancers" might have been a welcome suggestion, along the lines of the various faery works that signal dance as an escape from the drudgery of the world. Instead, the poem's agony swells into every corner of its imagery, the destructive wind an emblem and progenitor of force in a raw and unappeasable form. The swirls that return violence into artifice enact reprisal; they show that even the poem's aesthetic dreams have succumbed to reprisal's indelible logic.

I have suggested that "Nineteen Hundred and Nineteen" revises "Easter 1916" in spirit; its title suggests a corrective (writing out the numbers, the only Yeatsian poem to do so, and of course eliminating the sanguinary Christian reference point), and its wholesale reconsideration of violence casts doubt on the premise of the earlier poem, that moments of convulsive violence can create a lasting aesthetic and cultural legacy. In turning now to Yeats's most direct engagement with reprisal, we find a much more aggressive reengagement with his past history of enchanting violence: "Reprisals" bluntly and bitterly revisits "An Irish Airman Foresees His Death," substituting disenchantment for enchantment. Like "Nineteen Hundred and Nineteen," "Reprisals" was composed between 1919 and 1921, a bleak time for people like Yeats who still held some allegiance to England, and for anyone with a sensitivity to "violence on the roads." In response to the same epidemic of Black and Tan violence that stood behind the "days are dragon-ridden" stanza of "Nineteen Hundred and Nineteen," Yeats wrote a new poem for Robert Gregory, this one without a trace of enchantment.[75] He never published "Reprisals" during his lifetime, in accordance with Lady Gregory's wishes. Readers today will not find it in the most widely read of his collections (M. L. Rosenthal's *Selected Poems and Three Plays*) or in the *Norton Anthology of English Literature*, and this marginality in the canon has perhaps contributed to the relative critical obscurity of reprisal as a significant mode and pattern in Yeats's work, and in the period more generally.

Yeats is well known to have repudiated the style of First World War poetry associated with figures like Owen and Sassoon, writing in his 1936 introduction to the *Oxford Book of Modern Verse* that "I have a distaste for certain poems written in the midst of the great war . . . I have rejected these poems . . . [because] . . . passive suffering is not a theme for poetry," yet "Reprisals" reads uncannily like those lyrics, in both style and content.[76] Like the famous war lyrics, "Reprisals" is structured according to a logic of ruptured belief:

> Some nineteen German planes, they say,
> You had brought down before you died.
> We called it a good death. Today
> Can ghost or man be satisfied? (*Var*, 791)

These opening lines set up the terms that the poem will expand, as it expresses an increasingly troubled sense that the war "that we/Imagined such a fine affair" was in fact an earlier iteration of the horrifying killings perpetrated by the Black and Tans in the postwar years. There is something a little smug in that opening statement—as if bringing down planes had no human content—and the invocation several lines later of "battle joy" suggests that the "we" of the poem had remained stubbornly and startlingly idealistic on the whole question of the war, right through to its end.[77] Now, however belatedly, the mood is angry, and its trajectory of disillusionment culminates in the chilling last lines of the poem: "Then close your ears with dust and lie/Among the other cheated dead" (*Var*, 791). If the war itself is not the precise object of condemnation, the Britain for which it was fought most certainly is, indicating a continuity with other war poems, where the British government, like the war's general staff, is held accountable for the carnage. Too, the poem shares with many disenchanting war texts the selective display of shocking moments of violence, represented in blunt terms ("shot," "murder" "murdering"). And, finally, it envisions the dead rising from their graves to shame the present, another fantasy that was enunciated by many World War One writers. Wrote Sassoon in 1926, "Well might the Dead who struggled in the slime/Rise and deride this sepulcher of crime," while for Yeats the commandment is to "rise from your Italian tomb" and return to the district of Coole, where:

> Half-drunk or whole-mad soldiery
> Are murdering your tenants there.
> Men that revere your father yet
> Are shot at on the open plain.
> Where may new-married women sit
> And suckle children now? Armed men
> May murder them in passing by
> Nor law nor parliament take heed. (*Var*, 791)

The relation to World War One poetry is helpful in showing how closely Yeats hews to a widely available disenchanting idiom, but, of course, the context that gives "Reprisals" its bite is Yeats's own earlier enchantment of violence, as expressed in poems like "An Irish Airman Foresees His Death." There, we recall, death was welcomed for its aesthetic appeal; it was the choice of balance and form, or what Kundera would later call "the unbearable lightness of being." Written in the first person, "An Irish Airman Foresees His Death" had credited its subject with the power to "foresee," indeed to control, his own future; "Reprisals," with its jarring, almost aggressive, second-person voice, retakes that agency from Gregory. Even he, it now seems, has been duped. Invoking Gregory's father reminds the reader of the traditional role of the aristocratic patron in the community, as Yeats idealized it—guardian of its poor and vulnerable, representative of its ethical high ground—and returns Gregory's family situation to the center of the poem's outrage. At this moment of visible English tyranny, Yeats is desperate to imagine an Anglo-Irish aristocracy that could fill the power vacuum, even well past a time when such would be politically conceivable. The poem takes a nostalgic stance with respect to a past when power was firmly held by the Protestant elite. Yet, of course, that power was always intertwined with the British, whose ruthless murderousness in the present casts a long shadow back through the ascendancy. It is an irony for Yeats, if a familiar one in his corpus, that the good guardians (Gregory, his father, their loyal followers) have been nullified and superseded, where the bad guardians (the British) have been emboldened. Politically, the poem thus straddles the line between the Republican passion of "Nineteen Hundred and Nineteen," with which this poem shares a great deal (the Ellen Quinn murder, the drunken soldiery, the Black and Tans operating with impunity) and "An Irish Airman Foresees His Death," which quite literally elevated the aristocracy to a position in the sky. Yeats's poetics of reprisal comes very close, in the end, to the antiwar poetry that would soon become canonical, yet it holds the reins even tighter, refusing at every turn to enchant or mystify, where, as we have seen, those lyrics tended to operate precisely by appropriating an enchanting aesthetic for a disenchanting purpose. And there is good historical reason for this difference: in Ireland after the uprising, reprisal is what followed, historically and imaginatively, from generative violence, and hence its life spelled the death of enchanted violence. "Was it for this?" Yeats had asked in "September 1913," the ineluctable logic of balance facing the poem's lauded economy of excess, while Owen had pressed further, wondering if all human life is not futile ("Was it for this the clay grew tall?"). In "Reprisals," the question is not directly asked, yet its aura is near; it is, perhaps, more an answer than a reiteration of the question: "Then close your ears with dust and lie/Among the other cheated dead."

Yeats's "Reprisals" in many ways epitomizes the literary engagement with the ferocious realities of reprisal, but it is Sean O'Casey whose works are most consistently guided and tormented by its logic. To read them next to Yeats shows how fully the reprisal structure—in theme, tone, stylistics—belongs to this period, in works that represent divergent political and formal modes. O'Casey's most admired works, *The Shadow of a Gunman* (1923), *Juno and the Paycock* (1924), and *The Plough and the Stars* (1926), are all underpinned by the structure of reprisal, and all exemplify an ironic, deflationary attitude toward generative violence.[78] As I have suggested, O'Casey in many ways represents a spirit of opposition to any sanguinary approach to violence. His socialist affiliations are apparent throughout his plays, which exude a deep understanding of the language, spirit, and psychology of the Dublin tenement world where they are typically set—but they have little space for a Romantic view of violence.[79] O'Casey was a disciple of Connolly (a member of the Citizen Army until 1915, when he resigned, not taking part in the Rising) rather than of Pearse, and this difference is manifest at every turn. His plays take generative violence as one more cultural fact to scrutinize and—in his reprisal mode of the 1920s—dismiss.

Most directly engaging with the Rising is *The Plough and the Stars*, whose first half is set in Dublin several months before the events, and whose final, bloody acts take place during Easter Week itself. Without actually scorning the revolutionists, the play nevertheless carries a tone of caustic dismissal of the historic events; there is no transformative beauty here. If this is O'Casey's answer to "Easter 1916," as in some ways it surely is, it is a defiantly anti-meliorist one. Not surprisingly, it drew protests from the Abbey audiences who first viewed it in 1926 (at the same time, the trilogy in general was very successful and helped to revive the fortunes of the Abbey when they began running there).[80] As usual in O'Casey's work, it is women who are given the most interesting and substantial personalities in *The Plough and the Stars*, and their dilemmas dramatize the conflicts of the Rising in the only really salient terms of the play. Most compelling are Nora, the spoiled, selfish young bride of one of the insurrectionists, who desperately tries to keep her husband out of the fight and loses her sanity when he is engulfed in it, and Bessie Burgess, the histrionic, pro-British outlier, whose son is at war in France (by the final act, we learn, he is on his way home with a shattered arm), who also undergoes something of a transformation during the harrowing week of fighting. Nora's madness feels slightly Gothic—sleepwalking in her nightdress, her hair disheveled, with a wild and almost supernatural air—but in general her breakdown is depicted in empathetic and not entirely unrealistic terms. Though a person of limited intellectual and spiritual capacities, Nora is nevertheless genuinely destroyed by the rebellion, by fear and love for her husband. But it is Bessie who gets the prototypical O'Casey treatment. In the first few acts, she is an offensive, Rule Britannia shrew, but in the last act, she turns to caretaking, and selflessly nurses the shell-shocked Nora through harrowing days and nights. In the end, she takes a bullet for her; rushing to pull the raving Nora from the window in fear of British gunfire, she is hit in her stead. But Bessie will be no martyr. Her final lines are as full of unmannered rage as were her diatribes in the first part of the play. She spits antagonism and defiance at Nora and at the audience, who might have been ready to read her in transformative or heroic terms: "Merciful God, I'm shot, I'm shot, I'm shot! . . . Th' life's pourin' out o' me! [*To Nora*] I've got this through . . . through you . . . through you, you bitch, you!" These are her first (shocking) words after being hit, to be followed, a few lines later, by: "This is what's afther comin' on me for nursin' you day an' night . . . I was a fool, a fool, a fool! Get me a dhrink o' wather, you jade, will you? There's a fire burnin' in me blood!" (*CPI*, 258, ellipses in original). Bessie is not about to become a saint. Regretting her sacrifice in bitter terms, she dies entirely unglorified.

Still, there is a running discourse of generative violence in *The Plough and the Stars*, articulated by various men as they rile themselves up for the fight, and as they hope to find some consolation in defeat. Mostly this mode is relayed through Pearse's words. Though mentioned by name in Act III, during the fighting, Pearse's most substantial appearance comes earlier in the play, as the men are rallying to the cause. An unnamed man is seen in shadow in a window above the pub where the action takes place, and his voice is heard intermittently. What we hear in bits and pieces is something of a greatest hits from Pearse's published works, including clips from his oration at Rossa's funeral and his praise of war, both of which we have seen to offer an exemplary language of generative violence. O'Casey is judicious in his treatment of Pearse; using his own words and showing their effectiveness, he gives credence to the idea that generative violence offered the insurrectionists a powerful, motivating idea, supporting them in what they knew would be a losing battle. (That said, the fact that Pearse is seen from the vantage of a pub, scene of prostitutes and other questionable folk, raised hackles among audiences.) In a sense, O'Casey leaves generative violence to the men in the play—some of whom behave with real courage, moved to the end by Pearse's words. All of this really remains at the level of a sketch, however, even caricature, with the fighters entirely out of touch with complex human catastrophes like Nora's mental breakdown or Bessie's rich contradictoriness.[81] From the vantage point of a decade later, *The Plough and the Stars* presents enchanted violence as a rather thin edifice, easily dispatched by the shattering effects of a violence that was never really explained in its terms. For O'Casey, generative violence is, in a word, framed—almost a relic of its era—and hence aptly figured by the silhouette of Pearse, himself framed in a window.

The Shadow of a Gunman, set several years later, in the thick of Black and Tan brutalities, takes terror and reprisal as the state of Dublin existence, and only considers generative violence through layers of irony and literary referentiality. The play takes place over the course of a single day and night in a Dublin tenement, the scene, in the second act, of a Black and Tan raid. There are no real rebels in the play—the Republicans are stowing their weaponry on the premises, but the cast of characters in the play is resolutely on the margins of the national struggle. Nevertheless, the language of Romantic nationalism and generative violence abounds, now stripped of its potency. It has become a kind of shared, armchair vocabulary, a language of violence and nationalism with none of the transformative power imagined by the rebellion writers we have discussed. O'Casey insists that the heroic spirit to which the play continually refers—it opens with a discussion of Shelley—is not so much "dead and gone," as Yeats had thought it in 1913, but a self-promoting fiction. The play borrows its central premise from *The Playboy of the Western World*: that the populace, and especially women, always worships men it (wrongly) believes to be violent. In this case, the false celebrity is Donal Davoren, an indigent poet with no political convictions who is mistaken for a Republican on the run. Given that this misunderstanding awakens the sexual desire of Minnie Powell, the lovely young woman who comes, somewhat implausibly, to inhabit the play's moral center, he is willing to let the misapprehension stand. Donal and his roommate Seumas Shields are skeptical of the whole Republican ideal. As Seaumas explains it:

> I wish to God it was all over. The country is gone mad. Instead of counting
> their beads now they're countin' bullets; their Hail Marys and paternosters
> are burstin' bombs—burstin' bombs, an' the rattle of machine-guns; petrol

is their holy water; their Mass is a burnin' buildin'; their De Profundis is "The Soldiers' Song," an' their creed is, I believe in the gun almighty, maker of heaven an' earth—an' it's all for "the glory o' God an' the honour o' Ireland." (*CPI*, 131)

Amidst the various enthusiasts in the play, the sentiments expressed by Seamus, and to a lesser degree by Donal, stand out as intelligent, reasonable responses to a nightmare situation. And it is, almost literally, a nightmare that transpires in the play's second act, with the raid happening late at night. In the play's crescendo, which takes place offstage, the Black and Tans, having arrested Minnie (she courageously stored a bag of bombs in her room to protect Donal), shoot her in the chest.

For all the emphasis given to Donal and Seumas as they respond to the violent situation around them, the play's presentation of violence hinges not on them, but on Minnie. Early in the play, Minnie seems poised to be caricatured as one more simpleminded, self-deceived patriot, eroticizing violence and imagining herself as a revolutionary hero, while Donal articulates the playwright's own skeptical position:

> MINNIE: Poetry is a grand thing, Mr. Davoren, I'd love to be able to write a poem—a lovely poem on Ireland an' the men o' '98.
>
> DAVOREN: Oh, we've had enough of poems, Minnie, about '98, and of Ireland, too.
>
> MINNIE: Oh, there's a thing for a Republican to say! But I know what you mean: it's time to give up the writing an' take to the gun. (*CPI*, 107)[82]

By 1920, O'Casey suggests, Minnie's attitude has become the stuff of comedy. And yet, when faced with the raid, Minnie is the only person among the tenants to act with courage and integrity. She hides the bombs, stands up to the soldiers, betrays no one, and dies in that spirit. Indeed, Minnie could almost be said to urge the play from its tone of dark comedy toward tragedy, in the direction, that is, of a terrible, transformative beauty—except that O'Casey refuses to promote any such formula.[83] "Oh, it was horrible to see the blood pourin' out, an Minnie moanin'" is the only account given of Minnie's death: disenchantment. And several lines later, the play ends, with Donal appropriately self-lacerating for cowardice ("Oh, Donal Davoren, shame is your portion now") and with Seumas's superstitious comment: "I knew something ud come of the tappin' on the wall!" (*CPI*, 157). In the end, O'Casey is willing to establish Minnie as a figure in the spirit of martyrdom, but not to credit that spirit with any lasting power or meaning. In the absence of any kind of apotheosis, the belief in generative violence ends only in another pool of blood.

Indeed, in O'Casey's world, the further removed one is from the Rising, the more untenable its metaphorics of violence become. *Juno and the Paycock,* the first among this violent trilogy to have been composed and performed, but the latest one in terms of its setting—it takes place two years after *The Shadow of a Gunman,* in an Ireland now at civil war—shows no vestige of belief in generative violence. I have discussed the play already, focusing on its depiction of keening as a shared language of mourning that might also be imagined as a force for change. Here I want to note how fully it imagines a language and structure of reprisal. In the play's final words, uttered in Boyle's inimitable lexicon, O'Casey seems to sum up the condition of Ireland in the midst of civil war: "th' whole worl's . . . in a terr . . . ible state o' . . . chassis! [chaos]" (CPI, 89). But it's not really chassis—not the violence of whirlwinds or leveling winds—that O'Casey chronicles in *Juno and the Paycock.* This is a state of reprisal, eye for eye, bone to bone, and there is nothing chaotic or unpredictable about how that works: first the Tancred boy is shot by the Free Staters; later Johnny, who betrayed him, will be killed by the IRA in retaliation. Nothing, really, could be simpler, and, indeed, the play's whole structure is predictable: we know the family will never get its legacy; we know Mary will be abandoned by Bentham; we know Johnny will die. What determines all of this, I would contend, is not so much O'Casey's indebtedness to melodrama—though Kiberd, for one, makes a convincing case for the centrality of stage melodrama in O'Casey's works in general and *Juno* in particular—as his attachment to a stylistics of reprisal. Such a structure, as we have seen in the case of Yeats's "Sixteen Dead Men," is a style of fatal predictability—as Lady Gregory put it in 1920, "death answering to death like the clerks answering to one another at the Mass."[84] And so we find the back-and-forth:

> JOHNNY: Are yous goin' to do in a comrade?—look at me arm, I lost it for Ireland.
> SECOND IRREGULAR: Commandant Tancred lost his life for Ireland.
> (*CPI,* 84)

With reprisal, the patterning is as inevitable as it is crushing.

This is always, even tautologically, the situation with reprisal: it has no end or, to put it differently, we know exactly how it ends—with more killing. It also has no beginning, or rather, each side contends the other was the original assailant. Politically and personally, the catastrophe of cyclical violence cannot be overstated. For artists, there are really only two possibilities: to express this situation (and this often takes the form of a severe disenchantment) or to imagine some form of imaginative redirection. Girard argues, as we have seen, that the function of sacred violence is to stanch the flow of reprisal's endless call for blood, to redirect reciprocal violence into some different channel, where it can be contained and managed. But this is not really possible in the Irish example, because it was generative violence, imagined in sacred terms, that offered the initial, justifying language, now discredited. With no such imaginative space available, and with the historical present in a nightmarish struggle, writers tended to look back to keening, with its detachment from the violent event itself and its ties to the ancient world, or outward into an architectural or geographic model that might make imaginative sense of the nation's pains. These turns imply an active reconceptualizing, an effort, at the figural and formal level, to break the stalemate of generative versus reprisal violence.

Past, Present, Future: Architectural Allegory

In looking to new imaginative arrangements by way of conclusion, I want to consider two powerful symbols in the iconography of nations, the great tree and, especially, the representative building (usually a house or mansion). There is no more conventional image of a nation than the grand old tree. With regard to the English literature of this period, one thinks readily of the elm in Forster's *Howards End* (1910)—symbol of all that Forster cherishes in mystical, rural England, and all he sees as threatened by homogenization and modernization—or of Woolf's play with the trope in *Orlando* (1928), where the oak tree (along with the gigantic house) provides continuity, comfort, and pleasure over four centuries of novelistic fantasy. In Ireland, the imperative to find unifying national icons was pressing, and the tree offered an obvious choice: organic, ancient, formidable, and nondivisive, it could stand for a united, powerful, richly flourishing Ireland, with roots in the ancient land. We find images of great rooted blossomers not only in Yeats's poetry but throughout the literature of the Gaelic revival, including the nineteenth-century ballad tradition and the literature of the Rising. Standish O'Grady, whose enormously influential *History of Ireland* (1878–81) was read and admired by all the writers we have considered in this chapter, describes Fergus, one of the legendary kings of old Ireland, as "a great sheltering tree," and the image itself seems organic, given that the warriors of Ireland's mythic past, including Cuchulain, are known as "the Red Branch."[85] Or we might point to a poem by MacDonagh entitled "The Oak," from a 1904 volume, in which the tree functions as an obvious allegory for Ireland. "Behold this oak which stands alone/And crowns the crag, and scorns the earth!" it begins, and then details the tree's struggle through adversity (when a mere acorn, it is pecked at by an eagle, and that's just the beginning) on to its ultimate triumph: "It lives, this giant of the hills,/One day to sway in lordly state."[86] What distinguishes MacDonagh's oak, above all, is its capacity for resistance. And this is true more generally, especially with respect to violence; the tree is that which withstands and survives, projecting forward to a glorious future, "one day to sway in lordly state."

Buildings, by striking contrast, become emblems of the shock of violence. Symbolically, they work almost in reverse of the tree, suggestive of all the divisions and vulnerabilities of a nascent nation, sites of personal and family memory, signs of class difference, and ultimately the victims of revolutionary rage. This victimization was real; the destruction of buildings was a central feature in the War of Independence and throughout the Civil War. The First World War left whole towns in ruins, miles and miles of land blasted. Reprisal violence in Ireland was different. It involved targeted destruction, with people attacking individual storehouses, businesses, institutions, and especially homes. The burning of buildings was typically registered in local terms, leaving strange, gaping holes in familiar landscapes, creating pockets of ruins within otherwise functioning locales. Destruction of buildings often took place at night, so that the image of a fiery glow against the dark sky carried its connotations, whether as a cause for celebration or as an image of terror. In the imaginative literature of this period, the burned home worked simultaneously as a realist depiction of reprisal violence, guerilla attack, and civil war, and in allegorical terms as a rendering of the long history of violence in Ireland. Because that toll had so often been taken on the human body, at the same time that the house-as-nation was an inescapable association, the allegory of the destroyed house pointed in two directions: toward a capacious image of the nation, and toward an intensive, individual figuration of the wounded or dead body. Ultimately, the richest and most haunting works in this tradition are characterized by a mutuality and interspersing of these two modes.

During the independence and civil wars, one particularly salient target was the Anglo-Irish estate or "big house," where wealth and power had for centuries been consolidated.[87] The big house, a shrine for Yeats and others with Ascendancy affinities, an admiration for the aristocracy, and a taste for eighteenth-century style, had been a flashpoint in the Irish struggle for decades before the war years. In particular, the land war of the 1870s–'90s, which contributed to the slow dissolution of the estates in the twentieth century, had focused on the Anglo-Irish landlord as the local representative of the despised British landowning system, which created ruthless inequities in wealth and had contributed to the famines of midcentury. If boycotts by laborers and purchasers, as well as Fenian attacks against landlords, held a primary place in the public imagination of the land war—hence overlapping with anarchism in some respects—in the 1919–23 era, the house itself became the object of violence.[88] Thus, in *The Last September* (1929), Elizabeth Bowen's powerful novel of an Anglo-Irish world painfully encountering its own obsolescence—the novel is set in 1920 in an acute period of insurgency against the English—it is the aristocratic Naylor family seat, Danielstown, that takes the ultimate blow.[89] The house, which is full of splendid hollows and spaces of absence (as are the characters themselves), has always been signified by an aura of emptiness. Moreover, as Lady Naylor will say to a neighbor after the death of one of the protagonists, "the house feels empty"—suggesting, via syntax, that the house itself is doing the feeling.[90] This seems right, not so much because Danielstown has functioned in anthropomorphic terms up to now, but because, like the rest of the landscape at this terrific moment of tension before violence—at the violet hour—it is about to do so:

> For in February, before those leaves had visibly budded, the death—the execution, rather—of the three houses, Danielstown, Castle Trent, Mount Isabel, occurred in the same night. A fearful scarlet ate up the hard spring darkness; indeed, it seemed that an extra day, unreckoned, had come to abortive birth that these things might happen. It seemed, looking from east to west at the sky tall with scarlet, that the country itself was burning; while to the north the neck of mountain before Mount Isabel was frightfully outlined. The roads in unnatural dusk ran dark with movement, secretive or terrified; not a tree, brushed by wind from the flames, not a cabin pressed in despair to the bosom of the night, not a gate too starkly visible but had its place in the design of order and panic. (*LS*, 303)

Here again, the violence of reprisal is not chaotic, but designed; not a form of wildness, but of order. When the house is executed, "it seemed . . . that the country itself was burning," but of course, it is not—a crucial distinction in demarcating among different forms of war and terror. If the whole region has paradoxically come to life ("a fearful scarlet ate up the hard spring darkness"), that vividness is a result of the specificity of the destruction. What brings all of this piercing vitality to the world around the burning house is the fact that only individual houses are gone, leaving a gaping vacancy. Now, perhaps, it is the turn of the country to "feel empty."

Yeats, too, registered poignancy and inevitability in the emptiness left in the wake of the big house; like Bowen, he was taken with the idea of the threatened house as image of national violence, and like her, he invested these spaces with emotive life.[91] They reverberate; they "feel" their emptiness—but also, for Yeats, their fullness. "I have looked upon those brilliant creatures," Yeats wrote of the swans at Coole, "and now my heart is sore," and this mournful mood about the loss of the aristocratic estate in the era of land redistribution and reprisal attacks is a recurrent one in his works (*Var*, 322). More than any other single poem, Yeats's sublime "Meditations in Time of Civil War," published in the same volume as "Nineteen Hundred and Nineteen," elaborates this mood and reflects on its meaning and consequences. As its name suggests, the poem is emphatically concerned with the present—concerned, that is, to think about violence in the present moment, and it does so via a "meditation" on a series of built structures. Like Bowen in *The Last September*, the poem takes the big house as an allegory for the nation and for the threatened human body. It includes features common to Yeats's reprisal poems, such as irruptions of disenchanted violence, but its critique is ultimately of a different kind: with the focus shifted from body to building, the poem asks (inconclusively) how a language of violence might function if it is disengaged from the motif of enchantment and the structure of reprisal.

Like all big houses in these years, the "ancestral houses" that entitle the first section of "Meditations in Time of Civil War," are a target of violence; more surprisingly, in this rendering, they are also its product. Yeats imagines the inception of the estate in terms familiar to us from the Homeric model of enchanted violence (and Homer is referenced early in the poem), where, we recall, it is men at war who fuel the artistry of a civilization:

> Some violent bitter man, some powerful man
> Called architect and artist in, that they,
> Bitter and violent men, might rear in stone
> The sweetness that all longed for night and day,
> The gentleness none there had ever known (*Var*, 418)[92]

Here is a central contradiction, one we have confronted repeatedly in this study: that violence and bitterness can bring forth "sweetness" and "gentleness"—Arnoldian terms that connote the intellectual and aesthetic virtues, rather than muscular or potent ones. The creation of homes is metonymically linked with the creation of class ("gentle" of course representing birth as much as sensibility), and both, it would seem, are the product of violence. Later in the poem, Yeats will offer another image of intertwined violence with aesthetics in the form of "a changeless sword," a Japanese emblem of both warfare and artistry. The sword, even more directly than the house, works on the Homeric enchantment model, whereby war and the creation of lasting works of art are reciprocal processes.

The ancestral house, then, is a site of vexed beauty, the lovely product of an ugly past; it is also a place with no active relation to the present. In a poem strongly committed to imagining the particular "times," this obsolescence creates a conundrum. The house may showcase the culture's proud history, but "the great-grandson of that house" is "but a mouse." Even more centrally, its very essence belongs to a mode of existence that Yeats has always insisted is "dead and gone." The opening stanzas of "Ancestral Houses" invoke the economy of excess Yeats affiliated with the Romantic past, in an imagery of overflowing abundance:

> Surely among a rich man's flowering lawns,
> Amid the rustle of his planted hills,
> Life overflows without ambitious pains;
> And rains down life until the basin spills . . . (*Var*, 417)

Yeats makes the lushness as sensory as he can, the l's and s's themselves overflowing. Still, if the language of excess usually adduced to the old martyrs is here marshaled to depict the aristocracy, such a conflation is an act of willful imagining; its ephemerality is everywhere felt. "Mere dreams, mere dreams!" opens the next stanza, as the poet begins to recant his opening invocation of abundance. For the "glittering jet" or "fountain," he now substitutes "some marvelous empty seashell flung/Out of the obscure dark of the rich streams" as symbol of the house (*Var*, 417). One could say much about the resonance of this object, with its Woolfian qualities of sea-made translucence, its whirlpool-like suggestions of changefulness and enchantment, its continuity with (rather than distinction from) the richness of the house in the first lines, its interesting emptiness, and more. The poem is, in sum, anchored at its front end by the ancestral house as a locus for various forms of aesthetic and cultural power, simultaneously created and threatened by the violence that "shadows the inherited glory of the rich" (*Var*, 418).

In the poem, however, the ancestral house—fountain or seashell—quickly gives way to "my house," the title of the next section and the setting of the poem through to its close. Yeats's tower home carries its own symbolic overload, offering a wholly different significatory system from the seat of privilege and "gentleness" that was the big house.[93] On its ground, for instance, "the symbolic rose can break in flower," the rose, as we have seen, being one of several overdetermined symbols for Ireland, mobilized by the Rising poets and by Yeats himself in many of his works. In his stark tower, the poet keeps his own company, in a time of war seeking (and finding) there, "befitting emblems of adversity" (*Var*, 419, 420). It is not only the emblems that are exceptionally fitting; the phrase itself creates an almost perfect circle, a satisfying rendition of the dynamic (if deeply troubled) relation between violence and achievement that the poem largely explores.

Both the ancestral house and the tower, different as they are, stand out as something of a bulwark against the bleak reality of war. We are told, for instance, of an earlier resident who once "founded here. A man-at-arms/Gathered a score of horse and spent his days/In this tumultuous spot," hoping to elude the "long wars and sudden night alarms." Now, of course, that tradition is reenacted by Yeats:

> We are closed in, and the key is turned
> On our uncertainty; somewhere
> A man is killed, or a house burned,
> Yet no clear fact to be discerned (*Var*, 425)

With their affinity to *The Waste Land* ("We think of the key, each in his prison/ Thinking of the key" [*TWL*, 413–14]), these lines have a quintessentially modernist flavor, evoking the psychic imprisonment and sense of linguistic enclosure so often ascribed to early-twentieth-century thought and affect. And yet, of course, it is all quite literal, as the immediate transition to political conditions insists. The key is turned for good reason.

"A man is killed, or a house burned": what kind of difference is expressed in that caesura? The line has a pause in its center, and as we pause with it, we might consider what that "or" is carrying. Perhaps it should be read in a large sense, not only as an additive (men are killed and houses are burned) but, from an imaginative point of view, as a shift. If the "or" functions in this way, then "a house burned" would reflect literal and imaginative conditions different from those of a killed person. The fact that the two halves of the line are imbalanced around the "or" ("a house *is* burned" would be the parallel metric), contributes to this sense of slide. When a man is killed (the present tense resonates), whirlwinds of destruction or cycles of violence ensue. When a house is burned, the consequences are terrible, as the poem sorrowfully attests, but the poetic output might be productive in a different way. Bowen would write, in *The Death of the Heart*, that "the destruction of buildings and furniture is more palpably dreadful to the spirit than the destruction of human life," but the calculus here is somewhat different, as Yeats works to evade the worse/better accounting, while forging in that uncertain space a sense of thoughtful reconsideration.[94] From "A drunken soldiery . . . can go scot free" in "Nineteen Hundred and Nineteen," we move to "yet no clear fact to be discerned"—the former an expression of gruesome injustice, the latter almost a depiction of Yeats's own style. The burning of houses, perhaps, creates a poetic that is more in the meditative than in the weasel-shrieking mode. And yet, such a lull is soon broken, and the following stanza returns to the disenchanting idiom of the reprisal poems: "Last night they trundled down the road/That dead young soldier in his blood" (*Var*, 425).

"Meditations in Time of Civil War" is a poem that does and does not want to be allegorical. Insofar as "a man is killed," the poem rekindles the style and metaphors of "Nineteen Hundred and Nineteen," with the disenchanting language, the self-critique ("We had fed the heart on fantasies"), the invocation of broad destruction ("levelled lawns and gravelled ways"), the wild cry for "vengeance upon the murderers" (of an obscure fourteenth-century templar, in this case), even the final turn to "daemonic images." But when a house burns, another kind of poetry suggests itself, where the life of the house stands in for the killed body, and of course for the nation whose creation and character is at the base of all these conceits. Part of the poem's meditation about civil war, in fact, involves this division between body and house as locus of poetic emphasis. Over and over, it offers the house as the replacement for the body, as, for instance, in the section entitled "My Descendants," where one might expect physical heirs, or at least poems, to be the outcome, but where the stanzas inevitably end instead with the tower: "whatever flourish and decline/These stones remain their monument and mine" (*Var*, 423). There is something powerful and satisfying about "these stones," as there is in the tower's ancient masonry and stony ground, yet stones for Yeats are perhaps always affiliated with death, and moreover the recourse to the house is as conventional a poetic trope as Yeats could find. Architectural metaphors, we might say, provide the imaginative refuge that buildings in the real world also offer, and yet Yeats understands that there is a kind of retreat in this move. "I turn away and shut the door," begins the poem's final stanza, and the question here, as in "Easter 1916," is not only about what the metaphor of the building and door are doing (a sign of the retreat from politics, for instance) but about the poem's formal principles and their consequences: is the architectural allegory simply operating, or is it being offered in the poem for critique? As he asks at the end of "Ancestral Houses," in taking leave of their capacious spaces:

> What if the glory of escutcheoned doors,
> And buildings that a haughtier age designed,
> The pacing to and fro on polished floors
> Amid great chambers and long galleries, lined
> With famous portraits of our ancestors;
> What if those things the greatest of mankind
> Consider most to magnify, or to bless,
> But take our greatness with our bitterness? (*Var*, 418)

The problem with seeing the ancestral house as the nation, or with allowing it to absorb the shocks of violence that surround it historically and in the poem, is that it does not adequately handle "our bitterness." Or maybe the problem revolves around a reading of the last line such that the house takes *away* both the culture's greatness and its bitterness. In that case, the house might do the work of encapsulating and redirecting violence ("take . . . our bitterness") but at the same time siphons off what is best in a culture ("take our greatness"). There is, in the final instance, no free allegory: if the house can replace the pressured body, it does so at the cost of hoarding too much of the nation's soul along with it. And this sense of formal insufficiency reverberates throughout modernism, as attempts to create distanced models for formalizing violence are almost invariably confronted (and toppled) by the body's presence, its sheerness, vitality, insistence, flesh.

Yeats may have been ambivalent in the Civil War period about presenting the representative building as a figure for a nation and for the body, but in his late play *Purgatory* (1938), he returns energetically to the scheme, investing it with a new urgency and showing how fully this metaphor can work to express the conjunction of violence, private desire, and a sense of the future and past as mutually constitutive and consuming. In general and overarching terms, the play can be read as itself an allegory, as its title suggests, with the life span of the person and of the new nation likened to a term in purgatory, still awaiting release and apotheosis, with the killing of the father a sign of the break with England, and so on; and this structure allows an otherwise dreamlike and altogether strange work to be approachable (it is one of Yeats's most anthologized plays). Like many of Yeats's late works, *Purgatory* has the aura of self-summation, and here he turns a ruthless and withering eye on the double frame of house and tree as national figures. With its Beckett-like stage set consisting of "*A ruined house and a bare tree in the background,*" Yeats indicates from the outset that the play's versions of these conventions will be anything but heroic or enchanted (*CP*, 430). Ruin, instead, is the key term. If the house at the center of the play's collective unconscious is Ireland, it is a place of defeat from within, the site of familial purging, where a son kills his father and a father kills his son (*The Playboy* run amok), and where cross-class sex breeds violence and loss; it has long been burned to the ground, a casualty of the drunkenness of its none-too-legitimate owner. On one hand, then, the house represents an Ireland where class miscegenation has bred only vulgarity and violence, and where the nation itself is no more glorious an entity than a patricidal son. The big house is long gone, as the play's primary speaker, the old man, dolefully declares:

> Great people lived and died in this house;
> Magistrates, colonels, members of Parliament,
> Captains and Governors, and long ago
> Men that had fought at Aughrim and the Boyne. (*CP*, 431–32)

For the old man who was born in the house and whose unconscious life it plays out in shadow, the burning down of the house is unforgivable, much worse than murder, which he commits rather freely: "to kill a house/Where great men grew up, married, died,/I here declare a capital offence" (*CP*, 432). In this play about intergenerational struggle—where each is at war with all—the house might have been the source of a national tradition and national memory, in a cosmopolitan key: "There were old books and books made fine/By eighteenth-century French binding, books/Modern and ancient, books by the ton" (*CP*, 432). This function is now left to the unreliable and ever-violent men who wander the roads, revisiting sites of history and personal meaning, only to perpetrate new acts of violence on the spot. In their hands, the reprisal motif comes to ferocious life. Blood demands more blood, as the speaker (in comically gruesome form) relishes the return of an endless family instinct to purge, a wild internalizing of reprisal's logic, culminating in the play with his second intergenerational murder: "My father and my son on the same jack-knife!" (*CP*, 435).

In the voice of the old man, *Purgatory* rants and raves about the whole bloody situation he is damned to replay. *Purgatory* was first performed at the Abbey in 1938, and Yeats appended it to his controversial prose work *On the Boiler* later that year. In the brief preface to *On the Boiler*, he maintains that "in this new publication I shall write whatever interests me at the moment," and it seems appropriate that *Purgatory*, which has something of the feeling of an id to much of Yeats's ego, would be included in this defiant work, which Yeats framed as the uncensored outpouring of a mad old man, and which has upset critics ever since with its eugenic themes and its unrestrained elitism and authoritarianism.[95] And the two works do harmonize, especially in their shared obsession with racial impurity. As he writes in *On the Boiler*, "Since about 1900 the better stocks have not been replacing their numbers, while the stupider and less healthy have been more than replacing theirs. Unless there is a change in the public mind every rank above the lowest must degenerate, and, as inferior men push up into its gaps, degenerate more and more quickly" (*OB*, 18). And in *Purgatory*: "I killed that lad because had he grown up/He would have struck a woman's fancy,/Begot, and passed pollution on" (*CP*, 435). This theme of pollution, in turn, is connected to the architectural metaphors, since in both works the destroyed big house and the racially destroyed nation go together.

For its part, *On the Boiler* also features an ancestral house in decline, this one the Mansion House in Dublin, which Yeats portrays as a great Protestant edifice, now defaced and degraded by its Catholic occupants:[96]

> Let [the Lord Mayor] threaten to resign if the Corporation will not tell the City Architect to scrape off the stucco, pull down the cast iron porch, lift out the plate glass, and get the Mansion House into its eighteenth century state. It would only cost a few hundred pounds, for the side walls and their windows are as they should be, and Dublin would have one more dignified ancestral building. All Catholic Ireland, as it was before the National University and a victory in the field had swept the penal laws out of its bones, swells out in that pretentious front. (*OB*, 10)

It is not at all surprising, given the tendency to equate nations with buildings, that Yeats can easily turn a reasonable suggestion about architectural restoration into a sectarian and class-based diatribe against all he finds objectionable in contemporary culture. The key point, perhaps, is to see how the architectural allegory works: on one hand, by becoming the site of violence, the ancestral building relieves the body of that function, providing a literary analogy to its function in the actual world—this is the structure, to some degree, of "Meditations in Time of Civil War." On the other hand, in its representative role the house takes on all the divisions of the culture—this is what happens in *Purgatory*. In *On the Boiler*, the war between a stately Protestant structure (still solid) and an ugly Catholic façade (easily dismantled) promises continuing disjunctiveness across the new nation, while the house in *Purgatory*, even in ruins, engenders violence and produces trauma, in an ongoing cycle.

And yet, for all the political trouble that the house-as-body or house-as-nation constitutes, there is something deeply attractive, in the midst of historical violence, about the extensive mode it indexes. Perhaps this is why allegory has found a way to adapt to all of the formulae for conceptualizing violence we have discussed—keening, generative violence, and reprisal. "Study that tree," the old man in *Purgatory* commands his son as he kills him, "It stands there like a purified soul,/All cold, sweet, glistening light" (*CP*, 435). Earlier, the old man had enjoined the boy to "Study that house," but there was no similar postscript to suggest sublimity. This tree may not be flowering, nor is it a great-rooted blossomer—Yeats's metaphors stress Arnoldian principles of intellectual purity rather than Pearsean principles of generativity—but, for all that, it cannot help but invoke so many other representative trees in Ireland's recent history. *Purgatory* calls on us to "Appease/The misery of the living and the remorse of the dead"; to do so, it seems, we need to find "cold, sweet, glistening light" where, in the past, we have found enchantment, or reprisal, or leveling winds, or, in the last instance, ruined houses (*CP*, 436). "Here, there were no more autumns," Bowen had written ten years earlier, "except for the trees" (*LS*, 302).

The move to architectural allegory is thus no panacea; it has its own costs and consequences, returning to the subject of violence a very immediate political partisanship. In that sense, it loses its allegorical utility altogether, and indeed *Purgatory* is replete with a claustrophobic sense of implosion or collapse, with death itself figured as "a bundle of old bones" (*CP*, 435). It is not free, moreover, from disenchantment, as, for instance, when the old man reminisces about the original patricide, "They dragged him out, somebody saw/The knife-wound but could not be certain/ Because the body was all black and charred" (*CP*, 432–33). One of the characteristics of the other three forms we have discussed in this chapter—ritual lamentation, generative violence and even reprisal—is that, formally, they do not correlate to any political position; on the contrary, they offer themselves, at least in part, as symbolic forms for overcoming political difference. But with the ancestral house, a sense of division and rivalry is, as it were, built into the very architecture. There is a dual impulse at the root of this play: to lay bare the stark, destructive, indeed primordial lineaments that underlie and determine the creation of a nation; and at the same time, to see such violence in terms of the intimately personal, suggestive life of the unconscious mind, and the family history. For all the play's venom, *Purgatory* enfolds these two realms with passion and power; the audience simultaneously inhabits the tortured and grisly psyche of its violent protagonist and recognizes that such a locale must also be understood by analogy to the nation, via its iconographic stand-ins, tree and house.

Let us conclude by recalling a poem that even more elegantly merges the intensive with the extensive, one that sweeps together many of the principles of violence we have encountered in this chapter, "Leda and the Swan." It is a poem that can, all at once, be generative, allegorical, exultantly destructive, and full of the vengeful energy of reprisal. The sudden blow of the poem's rape, at this point in our discussion, seems almost a primal scene of generative violence, while the poem's allegory is both rewarding (a scene of archetypal power) and imprecise (with all those unanswered questions). It thus differs from *The Unicorn from the Stars*, where allegorical reading suggested an overly-schematic approach, and from *Cathleen ni Houlihan*, which Yeats feared was all too efficacious in its message. The poem's excess of destruction, moreover, is suggested not only in the "shudder in the loins" but in its outcome of "broken wall" and "burning roof and tower." As for reprisal, could anyone do better than Leda, via her daughters? The poem puts it simply, in keeping with reprisal's formal proclivity: "And Agamemnon dead." "Leda and the Swan" thus paints an almost complete picture of the language of violence in the period, except for one thing: it does not keen. There is nothing mournful, in the end, about the propulsive expressions of violence that continually break through in this literary history. They lunge, for better or for worse, into the future. "*Cast a cold eye/On life, on death*," Yeats wrote in the late poem "Under Ben Bulben," scripting his own epitaph, "*Horseman, pass by!*" (*Var*, 640, italics in original).

4. Patterns of Violence
Virginia Woolf in the 1930s

There, couched in the grass, curled in an olive green ring, was a snake. Dead? No, choked with a toad in its mouth. The snake was unable to swallow; the toad was unable to die. A spasm made the ribs contract; blood oozed. It was birth the wrong way round—a monstrous inversion. So, raising his foot, [Giles] stamped on them. The mass crushed and slithered. The white canvas on his tennis shoes was bloodstained and sticky. But it was action. Action relieved him. He strode to the Barn, with blood on his shoes.

—Virginia Woolf, *Between the Acts* (1941)[1]

By the middle of the 1930s, there was no escaping the fact of overwhelming force. To be an artist was to recognize both the vulnerability and complicity of one's medium in relation to the vast movements of violence that were threatening to sweep across all protective boundaries. When Simone Weil proclaimed in 1940 that "violence overwhelms those it touches," and that "each, in contact with force, is subjected to its inexorable action," she also spoke for works of the creative imagination, whose relation to the brute facts of political subjugation seemed increasingly urgent and direct.[2] In an era when fascism and Stalinism were displaying mass spectacles of aestheticized violence and politics, a great many artists felt called upon to create an alternative aesthetic universe, and even those who attempted to stay out of the fray could not easily distance themselves from the encroaching savagery or the sense of artistic complicity with the history of violence. As Woolf asked uneasily in 1933, already acknowledging the growing pressure to confront the suppression closing in around so many civilians, "how can the artist still remain at peace in his studio?"[3]

To write or paint or take a photograph was, in some important sense, to answer violence in an observable form.

Aesthetic works in these years became gripped in an agonistic representational dialectic with violence. As such, their measure of value was bound up with their sense of historical responsibility, and a consciousness about how art and violence interact was constantly pushing to the surface. We have, of course, been tracking such frictions throughout this study, with violence insistently demanding some kind of creative reckoning and writers both embracing and resisting that challenge. What make the 1930s unique are the scale, gravity, and sheer predictability of it all. War was coming, and it was likely to mean violence of unimaginable magnitude. The Spanish Civil War provided a vivid example of that which, as everyone understood, would soon spread and intensify across Europe. Even more radically than in the past, as the scenes from Spain demonstrated, the next war would touch not only soldiers but civilians, the term "total war" having emerged in the interwar period as a lexical reminder of war's reach.[4] Aesthetically, these conditions of the 1930s merged with the lingering (or, perhaps more accurately, revived) memory of the First World War, whose idiom infuses works of this period. And yet, new aesthetic strategies were demanded, developing out from the narratives that had marked the earlier war. That output had prominently included disillusionment, an emphasis on witnessing, the positing of fragmentation as a formal correlative to war-based states of consciousness, and, as we have especially noted, the crisscrossing of enchantment and disenchantment. All of this would be carried forward, but four new elements combined to give particular character to what 1930s works confronted in violence: the immediacy of shattering violence for everyone, not solely for soldiers; a sense of foreknowledge, with world war something already imaginable; a sense, then, of return, as another world war approached, a cataclysm to be repeated and intensified; and an especially strong conviction that art, for better and for worse, was part of the ever-unwinding story of mass violence. As Stephen Spender admiringly wrote in 1938, describing what was already viewed as a signal visual monument of the war in Spain, "*Guernica* affects one as an explosion, partly no doubt because it is a picture of an explosion."[5] *Guernica* figured explosive violence directly, a tableau of its immediate aftermath.

When Giles stamps on a pair of wounded, engorged animals in *Between the Acts*, by contrast, he allegorizes the process of making painting out of bloodshed. The passage is famous among Woolf readers and has been much discussed: an eruption of masculine aggression in the novel, a reminder of the persistent violence of homophobia, an image of paralysis and slow death, a reflection on her darkening state of mind in the period leading up to her suicide, a political allegory of national competition and invasion—all of these and more are encoded in this startling episode. The scene, moreover, was drawn from Woolf's life; in her diary of September 4, 1935, she describes how she and Leonard, walking in Sussex, "saw a snake eating a toad: it had half the toad in, half out; gave a suck now & then. The toad slowly disappearing. L. poked its tail; the snake was sick of the crushed toad, & I dreamt of men committing suicide and cd. see the body shooting through the water."[6] As Woolf's biographer Hermione Lee notes, "the sickening, fascinating sight of the half-dead, half-ingested living corpse" haunted Woolf in the ensuing years, appearing here and there in her personal writing, before its stunning re-emergence in *Between the Acts*.[7]

For all the acknowledged power of the sequence, however, one thing has gone relatively unnoticed: relieving his mental strain in a spasm of violence, Giles also enacts the practice of creating art. His sneakers, here named as "white canvases," refer also to a kind of painterly canvas; the blood that stains them in the moment of killing—a blood painting in effect—remains visible throughout the day, a trace and reminder of the act itself. Woolf's writings are replete with artists and art-works, texts and textuality, and the bloodstained shoes join a crowded ekphrastic field within *Between the Acts*.[8] Yet, in contrast to her earlier writings, which gener-ally smile on the artistic impulse, the posthumous *Between the Acts* puts extreme pressure on the idea of creativity. The novel envisions a range of imaginative ac-tivity, often lingering on expressive origins, but ultimately tilts in the direction of annihilation, silence, and foreclosure. In such a setting, a mere splash of blood on a white surface is easy to overlook, yet its blunt abstraction has a powerful, if quiet, presence in the novel and is, moreover, very much in keeping with the modernist ethos. From Eliot's "jug jug jug jug jug jug" to Yeats's red parallelograms as em-blems of war-filled national histories, the choice of nontranslatable expression over representation had for decades been a hallmark of the era's ethos, and Woolf, while working on *Between the Acts*, was painstakingly writing a biography of her friend, the postimpressionist Roger Fry. *Guernica* itself, along with a number of other paintings, posters, and photographs from the Spanish Civil War, helped to engender a new visual vocabulary surrounding war and violence, and did so, in Picasso's case, in decidedly abstract and allusive terms. Within *Between the Acts*, the possibility of full abstraction is described and praised, as when Lucy Swithin notes that "the Chinese, you know, put a dagger on the table and that's a battle," or at the end of the novel, when Miss La Trobe conceives of a new play to display the history of humanity through "the high ground at midnight . . . the rock; and two scarcely perceptible figures" (*BTA*, 142, 212). The shoes differ from these in car-rying with them the material traces of the violent act. Indeed, as I hope to suggest in my reading of Woolf, there is something iconic about the simple form of blood-artistry suggested by Giles's shoes. Schematic and exemplary, it stands next to such texts as *The Waste Land* and Yeats's reprisal poems as a powerful statement of juncture between literary or visual canvases (whose beauty may not be the defining characteristic) and violence in the world (with its attachment to historical narratives and brute human instincts).

More broadly, it will be the work of this chapter to present Woolf as a great theorist of literary violence. The catastrophe of war reverberates throughout her works, and critics have offered powerful assessments of its presence, at the level of form, character, and language, and have analyzed her affective and agonistic relation to its omnipresence in the modern world.[9] More, readers have credited Woolf's writing, particularly robustly antipatriarchal texts such as *A Room of One's Own* and *Three Guineas*, for its incisive understanding of the violence underlying and determining Western culture.[10] As a feminist who saw the totality of patriarchal violence damaging and compromising many aspects of psychic, social, and artistic life, Woolf was dauntingly insightful. Yet her account of violence goes well beyond the political. Even the framework of psychology, though significantly displayed throughout Woolf's writing (most personally in her memoir *A Sketch of the Past*), does not fully account for the way violence operates in her work. Instead, many of her starkest and most haunting representations of violence are depicted as strange irruptions, whose importance lies more in the way they become absorbed into the text's consciousness than as examples of patriarchal aggression or as traces of abuse in Woolf's own life. As Christine Froula writes, in a superb study that sees Woolf's full body of writing as engaging with questions of war and civilization, asking what it means to imagine art, literature, and culture in a world of massive violence, Woolf's work delivers "a call . . . to become 'one,' to enter history, to think in public and with others about the barbarity and no less the potential of 'this "civilization" in which we find ourselves.'"[11] Beginning with her first novel, *The Voyage Out*, continuing throughout the 1920s and early 1930s, and swelling in her three final works—*The Years*, *Three Guineas*, and *Between the Acts*—episodes of stunning violence are framed, bracketed, eclipsed, dispersed, and above all absorbed into Woolf's textual fabrics. Together, these works demonstrate a completely original strategy for—to return to the snake and toad image—digesting violence into the literary work.

Given the clarity with which Woolf saw the threat of many different kinds of violence, it is especially striking that her overall mode was to imbricate it deeply into her texts and characters, so deeply, in fact, that at times it almost disappears, like the blood on the shoes. For all its intensity, in other words, Woolf's lifelong engagement with violence is marked, in a certain sense, by muteness. "The human soul," writes Weil, "seems ever conditioned by its ties with force, swept away, blinded by the force it believes it can control, bowed under the constraint of the force it submits to" (Weil, 45). Woolf's works persistently display this dynamic. They tell a story of life as the experience of "unseizable force" (as she names it in *Jacob's Room*) and of creativity as a place of neither submission nor resistance, but rather of endlessly varying forms of accommodation, acknowledgment, and rearrangement (*JR*, 137). Violence in Woolf's writing becomes shape, color, trace, or, to give it a single name, *pattern*. An element of form, Woolfian pattern in relation to violence is its own distinct category, a way of thinking in spatial and aesthetic terms about the most visceral, bodily, painful aspects of the mortal condition.

For all the universalism of such thinking, Woolf's treatment of violence, especially in her later works, emerged alongside and in relation to a variety of cultural signifiers that increasingly determined the debates about violence in the 1930s. To unearth and understand these will form the first part of my discussion. As in the short passage when Giles smashes the snake and toad, which is framed around the keyword "action," Woolf's representation of violence is fully engaged with a variety of theories and tropes that circulated among intellectuals, politicians, artists, and journalists of the period. Action, for instance, had by the middle of the 1920s become a political fetish, with special resonance for fascist or protofascist rhetoric, hence carrying distinctly troubling affiliations for the pacifist Woolf. And yet, as works like *Three Guineas* attest, Woolf was not content with merely repudiating or reversing concepts like action. Instead, she engages critically with her culture's central formulations around violence, in a style that pushes, prods, and intervenes rather than erecting its own fixed terms. In addition to the concept of action, several other primary debates and images energized Woolf's works around the problem of violence. There was, first, a large-scale theorizing of war and violence among 1930s intelligentsia, which circulated around the question of whether war and barbarity are endemic to the human condition. Second, the crisis of the Spanish Civil War offered unique and moving visions to answer the carnage of fascism, and this was correlated with a surge of literary activism among many writers of the period, aiming to bolster a politically engaged poetics. And finally, this period made ubiquitous the tendency, in writing across many genres and styles, to present the facts of mass violence in terms of paradox—where wars are fought to end wars, and only violence can be the route to peace.

Indeed, this last feature of her contemporary culture in some ways exemplifies the challenge for Woolf: how to consider one's relation to force without collapsing into the circular structure of paradox, where peace must be folded into violence.

In that model, resistance to violence is futile, and creativity or experiment will always be eclipsed by familiarity. Again, the snake and toad resonate; wrapped in a circle, choking on itself and locked in its cyclical self-death, the pair seems an apt image for what Woolf confronted in the paradoxical logic of violence-for-peace. Like Yeats in relation to generative violence, in engaging this stasis, Woolf saw the dimming of the great power of language itself. It is all the more stunning, then, to find her works straining, paragraph by paragraph, against all the familiar grains, creating an aesthetics of literary violence that continues, as Conrad might have it, to make us see.

Theorizing Violence in the 1930s

"Dear Professor Freud," wrote Albert Einstein in a 1932 open letter, commissioned by the International Institute of Intellectual Cooperation, an arm of the League of Nations, "Is there any way of delivering mankind from the menace of war? It is common knowledge that, with the advance of modern science, this issue has come to mean a matter of life and death for civilisation as we know it."[12] As it happens, Freud's response to this remarkable solicitation was pessimistic—"The upshot of these observations," he declares in his rejoinder, "is that there is no likelihood of our being able to suppress humanity's aggressive tendencies"—yet the exchange itself, symptomatic of its era, points in more open-ended directions (*Why War?*, 47). This was a period in which large questions about war and peace—or aggression and pacifism, or violence and its curtailment—were thrust into the forefront, as writers of all kinds found venues in which to wonder, indeed to agonize, about the seeming inevitability of monstrous war threatening to destroy what many still believed could be a humane world. So Aldous Huxley, in a pacifist encyclopedia published in 1937, would posit a host of claims clustering under the inherency umbrella: that war is "a Law of Nature," that the human species is evolutionarily conditioned to war, that other animals are as violent as man; "Man," he argues, in contradistinction to all of this, "is the only creature to organize mass murder of his own species."[13] In a similar vein, Woolf records in her diary in 1940 an evening conversation with Eliot, Saxon Sidney-Turner, Clive Bell, and others: "our talk?—it was about Civilization. All the gents. against me. Said very likely, more likely than not, this war means that the barbarian will gradually freeze out culture. Nor have we improved . . . Clive also pessimised—saw the light going out gradually."[14] These metaphors—of darkness, barbarism, eclipse, the dimming of civilization—were ubiquitous in these years, made all the more acute by the fact that the contemporary barbarity was emanating from Germany, still viewed by many English intellectuals as epitomizing the West's cultural accomplishments. In all of these discussions, the First World War operated as the defining precursor event, a bloodbath which seemed destined to tell a story not only about itself but about Western culture more generally, as Freud's own writings from the postwar years indicate—the war, after all, having turned Freud into a theorizer of human aggression in the first place, with "Thoughts on War and Peace" written in 1915 and *Civilization and Its Discontents* in 1929. It was in *Civilization and Its Discontents* that Freud made such declarations as "man's natural aggressive instinct, the hostility of each against all and of all against each, opposes the programme of civilization."[15] In *Why War?* as in the literature of the 1930s more generally, there is a powerful, shared sense that a new war would be even more catastrophic and destructive than the last: "given the high perfection of modern arms," writes Freud, "war to-day would mean the sheer extermination of one of the combatants, if not of both" (*Why War?*, 52).

By the 1930s, prominent intellectuals of many sorts were articulating the view that human aggression is one of the driving facts of the world, in its modern incarnation as in the ancient past. A longtime pacifist like Bertrand Russell (jailed for his antiwar activity during the First World War) struggled in this period between believing that people are fundamentally oriented towards peace and giving credence to the idea that the violent drive for dominance has been the underlying motive propelling much of history. In *Power: A New Social Analysis*, published in 1938, Russell argues that "[o]f the infinite desires of man, the chief are the desires for power and glory," and "the fundamental concept in social science is Power, in the same sense in which Energy is the fundamental concept in physics."[16] I think we can see in Russell's "power" something akin to Weil's notion of "force," though his methodology is systematic and historical, rather than epigrammatic and literary. Perhaps the most salient message to emerge from Russell's survey, which scans a broad history and sorts through types of power (such as "Priestly," "Kingly," "Naked," "Revolutionary"), is that power often manifests itself paradoxically, so that, for instance, "periods of free thought and vigorous criticism [when traditional forms of power erode] tend to develop into periods of naked power" (Russell, 97). It is a depressing principle that the best elements in liberal, modern culture inaugurate its most vicious tyrannical outcomes. *Power*, like many other works of these years, stands equivocally between two positions, clearly seeing and cataloging the ubiquity of force, even as it proposes an enlightenment view that reason and humane cooperation might still prevail.[17] In this fundamental dilemma, Russell sounds like the character Peggy in Woolf's *The Years*, a novel published nearly concurrently, as she wavers between hope and despair, wondering about the fate of humankind; are we, after all, "only sheltering under a leaf, which will be destroyed" (*TY*, 388)?

The decades that followed the First World War were exceptional in the outpouring of writing they produced on the subject of the inherent and inextinguishable violence that marks human nature and history, though of course, this kind of question had been probed before. Language that would be employed in the 1930s had germinated for two decades. It can be found, to take just one illuminating example, in a 1910 pamphlet entitled "The Moral Equivalent of War," by the American pragmatist William James. With the threat of war already looming, it seemed that humankind was lurching in the direction of catastrophic violence, and James considers whether there might be some alternative channel into which the warlike tendencies of human beings might be directed. James declares himself a pacifist, and thus it is with regret that he wonders if the goal of ending war will ever be realized, given that "our ancestors have bred pugnacity into our bone and marrow, and thousands of years of peace won't breed it out of us."[18] Writing under a rubric similar to that of the Einstein-Freud exchange—in the form of a pamphlet commissioned by the American Association for International Conciliation—James's object was to consider the moral possibilities for eradicating war. The question of culture is the crux of it: "History is a bath of blood," and yet, he argues, over the millennia, entrenched beliefs about the value of honor, strength, bravery, and community have been so bound up with war as to make it virtually synonymous with those qualities (James, 4). For all his pacifism, James himself seems enthralled, in this short polemic, by the spirit of masculine militarism, and his goal is to recruit the qualities he associates with war in the name of peace and civilian improvement. "Martial virtues must be the enduring cement" of civilian life, he argues, "intrepidity, contempt of softness, surrender of private interest, obedience to command," or again, "the martial virtues, although originally gained by the race through war, are absolute and permanent human goods" (James, 15, 16). James's language is reminiscent of much in Anglo-American adulation of military masculinity at the turn of the century—with all that implies for sexism, homophobia, and the politics of power—and ties in, too, with later iterations (Mussolini: "War alone brings up to its highest tension all human energy and puts the stamp of nobility upon all the peoples who have the courage to meet it"[19]). But what is perhaps most revealing in James's language is the blending of a familiar late-nineteenth-century rhetoric about war's unsurpassable virtues with a dawning awareness of its terrible consequences, the human brutality that it both represents and encourages, and the real imperative to address and overcome the violent instinct in individuals and cultures. In this last sense, "The Moral Equivalent of War" points forward to later decades. Thus Huxley, in his pacifist encyclopedia, includes a heading for "Moral Equivalent of War," in which he directly refutes the logic of virtue that James had extolled; other writers of the 1930s, too, in attempting to understand or oppose militancy, felt compelled to address the truism that war, for all its catastrophe, engenders unique virtue and exemplarity.[20]

Perhaps the key feature of this public reckoning about war was its tendency to conjoin—or, of equal importance, to juxtapose—two kinds of inquiry: a pragmatic approach which focused on how the Western nations might prevent wars, primarily through the expansion and development of international organizations devoted to world peace, and the anthropological or psychological account of violence as a central feature of humankind. In a sense, then, the argument revolved around a duality we have been exploring since the discussion of Stephen's beating in *A Portrait of the Artist as a Young Man*: violence understood in wide, social terms (in the 1930s, this approach was often geopolitical) versus violence understood in primal, originary terms, magnifying the subjective experience (anthropological and psychological). As we have seen over the course of this study, literary works of the period often took an explicit interest in the connection between such matters as the ritual origins of human culture and the realities of violence in the contemporary world. The anthropological angle in modernism has been well documented and its connection to power noted.[21] From Pound's interest in Chinese artistry to Forster's engagement with the spiritual force of Islam and Hinduism, this characteristic geographical promiscuity is inseparable from Western imperial domination, the very ability to conjure such mobility being, in some sense, a legacy of imperial confidence and modes of knowing. And yet there was often courage and genuine urgency in these anthropological incitements. As Marianna Torgovnick nicely sums it up: "we need to see the moderns as they were—as needing the primitive and as inventing the primitive that fit their needs. Their truest greatness may lie in their aspiration after ideas and values and alternative modes of being whose time had not yet come."[22] In the case of war, the sense that the inquiry needed to encompass a broad reckoning with human history and varying cultures met with the development of international associations in Europe and America devoted to preventing war, and so tended to oscillate between a generally pessimistic stance on the inevitability of human aggression and a more hopeful view that the Enlightenment might yet prevail. Perhaps, under the aegis of groups like the League of Nations, there could be an end to war's barbarity. Again, Freud's response to Einstein is symptomatic of the dire and universalist view: "when a nation is summoned to engage in war, a whole gamut of human motives may respond to this appeal," he writes; "The lust for aggression and destruction is certainly included; the innumerable cruelties of history and man's daily life confirm its prevalence and strength . . . Musing on the atrocities recorded on history's page, we feel that the ideal motive has often served as a camouflage for the lust of destruction" (*Why War?*, 43–44).

Equally prevalent were theories that attempted to straddle the two approaches to violence—innate and determining versus aberrant and containable. Leonard Woolf's work from this period is particularly revealing of how such a dual approach might look. His 1935 tract *Quack Quack!* takes an ironic tone as it makes the universalist case. Woolf ridicules the major European politicians of the day— the more bellicose the more absurd, in his view—even as he suggests that there are powerful human tendencies underlying the violence of fascism. Thus he can compare a portrait of Mussolini or Hitler with a Hawaiian statue of a war god, simultaneously mocking the fascist dictators and suggesting continuities among forms of warmongering throughout history and across the globe. In semi-Freudian terms, Woolf sees in dictators "the instincts and emotions of barbarism," and fascism as eliciting atavistic, precivilized emotions and social reactions.[23] By 1939, Woolf's *Barbarians Within and Without* faces even more stark conditions (indeed, between its being completed and printed, the war had begun), with the threat of extreme and annihilative violence not only near at hand, but within one's own ambit of responsibility: "For if civilization is destroyed, it will not be by the Hitlers and Mussolinis and their crude, barbaric violence," he writes, "but by the muddled betrayal of the civilized. It is not the barbarian at the gate, but in the citadel and in the heart who is the real danger."[24] Yet for all the Manichean logic and anthropological suggestiveness in his thinking, Woolf was entirely committed to the idea that states and organizations could, in fact, remake the political world in such a way that war would be increasingly improbable, ultimately refuting the idea that war's violence is endemic or ineradicable. He thus titles the epilogue to his 1940 work, *The War for Peace*, "On Reason," and the primary object of the book is to counter the idea that violence is a necessary and basic feature of human society— in the modern system of nation states as in the ancient world—and hence that war is unavoidable.[25] At stake in all of these works, really, is the question of whether violence ultimately expresses humanity—its infliction the essential fact of power, now and always; its suffering the essential fact of vulnerability, now and always— or whether those binding inevitabilities can be loosened, and a better future can therefore be envisioned.

Virginia Woolf, too, spent much of the 1930s reflecting on the precise nature of violence in the contemporary world, considering its psychic, systemic, and structural qualities. In three scrapbooks she assembled over the course of the 1930s, whose material forms the basis of *Three Guineas*, Woolf can be seen finding her own position with respect to these debates. Several selections, for instance, offer something like the Freudian view of violence as a destructive instinct, including such pieces as a newspaper clipping, in the first scrapbook, on the subject of women's attraction to violent male wrestling matches.[26] Also concerning the idea of elemental human brutality is this passage from Winston Churchill (no hero in the scrapbooks), an excerpt from his *Thoughts and Adventures* (1932):

> The brain of modern man does not differ in essentials from that of the human beings who fought and loved here millions of years ago. The nature of men has remained hitherto practically unchanged. Under sufficient stress,—starvation, error, warlike passion, or even cold intellectual frenzy, the modern man we know so well will do the most terrible deeds, and his modern woman will back him up. (*SB*, 1:49)

Churchill's comments on the essential and unchanging savagery of people are left to stand on their own; as is often the case throughout the scrapbooks, Woolf adds no commentary, and a reader can impute irony where or as it seems appropriate. In this case, one might see a cautious agreement between Woolf and Churchill, as both acknowledge an abiding potential for violence that cannot be concealed by modernity's self-deceptions—unless, of course, the final half line in the selection ("and his modern woman . . .") indicates that Woolf is mostly interested in tracing the sexist underpinnings of Churchill's commentary. If nothing else, what these inclusions show is that Woolf was casting her own withering eye on the broad theorizing of violence that occupied many of her contemporaries, including the way it played out as a consideration of inherency.

Or, to take yet a different kind of example, thinking back to James's formulation about the need for pacifism to find a use for military values like masculinity, heroism, and self-sacrifice, we hear an almost uncannily close echo in another scrapbook entry, this one from a memoir of his dead son by Victor Bulwer-Lytton, 2nd Earl of Lytton, written in 1935:

> We talked of the League of Nations and the prospects of peace and disarmament. On this subject he was not so much militarist as martial. The difficulty to which he could not find answer was that if permanent peace were ever achieved, and armies and navies ceased to exist, there would be no outlet for the manly qualities which fighting developed, and that human physique and human character would deteriorate. (*SB*, 2:8)

There is little ambiguity about Woolf's attitude toward such a statement. What is most telling is to see the continuity of thinking over a full generation: to espouse pacifism, or even to challenge the value of war, is to set oneself against the old patriarchal ideals of manliness.

The theorizing of war and violence in the later modernist years took many forms; in addition to a debate about instinct versus reason, which transpired most pointedly around the onslaught of fascism and the coming of a new war, there was a widespread reckoning with the nature and condition of civilian life, and in particular with the menace of aerial bombardment.[27] The idea that technology would one day make destruction by air a terrifying reality had, as we saw in the case of the dynamite novels of the late nineteenth century, been a part of the British imaginary for decades.[28] After the turn of the century, however, and especially with the experience of the First World War in mind, the concern about what aerial bombardment could do to civilians and their cities intensified; by the middle of the 1930s, the fear of an air war became all but ubiquitous. Airplanes were something of a fetish in the interwar period, with the romanticism that had surrounded the military pilot in the First World War era clinging, often uneasily, to other associations that proliferated in the following decades. Some of these associations were benign, as commercial aviation became a source of public fascination. In fact, the relation of commercial to military flight in this period presented an ongoing dialectic, as suggested in the skywriting-cum-toffee-selling sequence of *Mrs. Dalloway*, in which the attraction of the airplane is composed precisely of its double association with war and with innovative, visually arresting techniques for selling things. Flying was a source of adventure and virtuosity, in the same tradition as mountaineering or polar exploration; like these, adventure aviation in this period was linked to tragedy and failure as much as it was a crucible for human persistence, expertise, and audacity. There is something in this conjunction of epic ambition with catastrophic endings that particularly appealed to the popular British imaginary in this period, as the fascination with polar disasters dramatically shows. Perhaps more than any other single figure, the world-famous Charles Lindbergh provided an aura of popular heroism around the image of flight as adventure. Lindbergh, a romantic figure of the air par excellence, was also a champion of commercial uses for flight, and something of a pacifist in the interwar years. As the victim of a heinous crime, moreover, with the kidnapping and murder of his son, Lindbergh invoked intense public pathos. Similarly, the accomplishments and, more sensationally, the ultimate disappearance of the woman aviator Amelia Earhart in 1937 helped to secure the place of transatlantic flight as one of the signature spheres in which technology, war, adventure, commerce, sensational news, and even gender-bending were yoked and mutually defined.[29]

Most central to the recalibration of the airplane over these years, however, was its increasingly recognized function as a carrier of weapons, the bombs whose power and reach would define the next world war, as they were already defining smaller wars of the mid-1930s. The RAF in fact produced air shows to display its powers to destroy (enemy) cities from the air. As scholars have pointed out, the European imperialist powers engaged in ruthless attacks on colonial subjects during the 1920s and into the '30s, though such attacks were virtually ignored in the European press, with the exception of Mussolini's invasion of Ethiopia. As Susan Sontag puts it, "General Franco was using the same tactics of bombardment, massacre, torture, and the killing and mutilation of prisoners he had perfected as a commanding officer in Morocco in the 1920s. Then, more acceptably to ruling powers, his victims had been Spain's colonial subjects, darker-hued and infidels to boot" (Sontag, 9). But the bombings on European soil presented an entirely different cultural and psychic phenomenon. In fact, as Paul Saint-Amour argues, the muting of colonial violence alongside an enlarging understanding of the threat to European cities in the 1930s was an important element in the interwar consciousness of mass violence, what he calls "the partiality of total war."[30] The interwar period saw a proliferation of works that imagined spectacular scenes of invasion and destruction—often with whole swaths of the nation wiped out—in a sense updating what had been written in the period before the First World War, this time with the emphasis squarely on aerial assault.[31] It is perfectly symptomatic, for instance, to find Woolf including in her scrapbook a devastating description of a 1937 attack by the German military on the southern Spanish town of Almería, along with Guernica one of the most extreme cases of fascist aerial obliteration of civilians during these years (SB, 3:10). Wells—always with his finger on the popular pulse— wrote The Shape of Things to Come (1933), later adapted into a film (1936) which envisioned the world nearly destroyed by an ongoing, massive air war across the globe.[32] Though the novel ends, improbably, with a gesture towards a utopian future, its most memorable images involve the modern world left in ruin by decades of relentless bombing. In Wells's work and elsewhere, the image and idea of the airman as a pure destroyer, indifferent to the mere humanity of civilians thousands of feet below him, began to emerge in competition with the earlier icon of flyboys as aristocrats and sex symbols of the sky. If, for Yeats, the sheer distance represented by the airman had offered an image of metaphysical sublimity, well removed from politics, later years would see that distance as enabling a terrifying indifference to human life, the very inverse of Yeats's idealized view of Robert Gregory. So when Benito Mussolini's son Bruno, a pilot and bomber who helped to destroy Ethiopian civilians and towns during the Italian invasion, described "set[ting] fire to the wooded hills, to the fields and to the little villages" as good sport—"it was all most diverting"—he helped to codify and embody the idea of the bomber as monstrously removed and inhuman.[33] These words are quoted, fittingly, by Russell in *Power*. The idea of aerial bombardment, in sum, provoked concerns in this period ranging across a sweep of categories—military, strategic, psychic, moral, personal, even aesthetic—and occupied thinkers across the disciplines, from professional war planners to imaginative artists, elite as well as popular.

We might note, moreover, that the fixation on aerial assault, and the transformation in thinking about civilians, cities, and safety it entailed, had begun to spread even before the events of the 1930s. Bernd Hüppauf describes the airplane's "profound impact on the perception of the environment" as a "constant reminder that this war [WWI] had also conquered the third dimension, turning Daedalus's dream of escaping from the labyrinth into the nightmare of a complete system of surveillance and threat."[34] Though zeppelin raids in the First World War had been limited in scope, they resonated with the public, permanently altering the idea of separation between civilian and combatant spheres and providing a very clear and direct image of how future forms of devastation would be wreaked. As Saint-Amour dazzlingly argues, almost immediately after the war the idea of the city as liable to destruction, and of its citizens as potential targets, began to characterize not only the thinking of military planners and international organizations but also the formal strategies of interwar modernist novelists, who, as Saint-Amour puts it, "incarnate the novel as air-raid siren." Indeed, "the co-presence in [three major novels of the period, *Mrs. Dalloway*, *Berlin Alexanderplatz*, and *Ulysses*] of an all-encompassing cartographic gaze with a sense of the urban object's radical vulnerability suggests the emergence of a new sub-genre of the city novel in the wake of the Great War: the novel of the total-war metropolis."[35] By the 1930s, then, the significance of aerial bombardment had been well established, the interiorizing and formalizing of an air war having already begun to transform the imaginative range of modernist thinking. Above all, however, it was the Spanish Civil War that brought the idea of aerial destruction into the absolute center of European consciousness, and helped to define the period's aesthetic responses to mass violence.

The Spanish Civil War

When it came to imagining mass violence, the war in Spain set the terms. The paintings, posters, films, and photographs that emerged from it generated a powerful visual vocabulary for representing as well as resisting violence; the journalism and other writing that documented its course (particularly the most notorious atrocities of the insurgent forces) helped to set the tone for testamentary writing about war and genocide well into the twentieth century; and its status as the last front against Hitler and fascism—where democracy *must* make its stand—transformed it into the cause célèbre of its era for writers, artists, and other concerned citizens from around the world. All of this was intensified by the acute and widely shared understanding that the war in Spain represented a "dress rehearsal," to use Ernest Hemingway's term, for what was imminent in Europe and the Far East.[36] Even if the Spanish war itself was actually more complicated than these narratives suggest (a complexity writers like Orwell and Weil attempted to convey), it was, and still is, overwhelmingly understood in stark and polarizing terms, especially by those following the war from outside of Spain. For Woolf in particular, the Spanish war offered, first, a political challenge, as she watched friends and allies join in a concerted effort to help defeat the fascists, a call to arms and politics about which she was deeply ambivalent and in which she was repeatedly entreated to participate. In her scrapbooks, she includes several solicitations from individuals and organizations, as well as pamphlets and manifestos signed by her peers—and in one case by herself (*SB*: 2:34)—and, of course, she frames *Three Guineas* according to such an appeal. Second, and perhaps more importantly, the war offered a personal tragedy for Woolf and her family; her nephew Julian Bell volunteered as an ambulance driver in Spain, and was killed there in 1937. For a war taking place in a part of Europe typically portrayed as far removed from the modernized north, and one not posing a direct threat to England, the Spanish Civil War nevertheless had an enormous place in the consciousness of English people, including Woolf and her circle, at personal, social, cultural, political, and visual levels.

The war became the subject of a huge representational project, first notable as a sign and locus of political commitment. Robert Jordan, Hemingway's alter ego in *For Whom the Bell Tolls* (1940) puts it simply: "He fought now in this war because it had started in a country that he loved and he believed in the Republic and that if it were destroyed life would be unbearable for all those people who believed in it."[37] Hemingway himself covered the war as a journalist, writing over thirty dispatches from Spain, published via the North American Newspaper Alliance in papers across the United States.[38] He also helped to write and produce the propaganda film *Spanish Earth*, released in 1936, which makes an impassioned and eloquent plea for immediate aid to the people of Spain, presented as heroic, dignified, cooperative, and socialist-leaning. *For Whom the Bell Tolls*, in contrast to the film (and to some degree the journalism), steers decidedly away from politics, giving us a protagonist who is "anti-fascist" but otherwise politically evasive, and presenting the Republican forces (with the exception of Jordan) in emphatically nonidealized terms.[39] Published in 1940, the novel postdates the war, and in a sense sums up several years' worth of mourning losses and of celebrating the international outpouring of support that had brought not only Hemingway but writers such as W. H. Auden, Christopher Isherwood, Stephen Spender, and Simone Weil to Spain. As Thomas Mann asked in 1936, "Whose affair is it, if not the creative artist's . . .?"[40]

The participation of artists and intellectuals began early in the war. It took very public shape in the Second Congress of the International Association of Writers, held in three Spanish cities in 1937, and also involved declarations such as the *Left Review*'s 1937 "Authors Take Sides on the Spanish War" forum, which gathered the signatures and written statements from a legion of famous writers. For the Congress, the location in Spain was critical, signifying not only allegiance but also a material, rooted form of participation. The idea of "taking sides" at all is characteristic of the terms employed in the war's activism; as the *Left Review*'s manifesto put it, "It is clear to many of us throughout the whole world that now, as certainly never before, we are determined or compelled, to take sides. The equivocal attitude, the Ivory Tower, the paradoxical, the ironic detachment, will no longer do."[41] The point was not only to descend from the Tower to fight against fascism, but also to make one's writing part of the effort—hence the reference to irony, a stance that crosses over from the personal to the literary. So Auden wrote "Spain" in April 1937 (published initially as a pamphlet), with its famous refrain "but to-day the struggle," to be borrowed by the "Taking Sides" manifesto two months later, which prominently included the phrase "To-day, the struggle is in Spain" (*Cunningham*, 51).

For all the language of absolutes, this drift among public positioning, writing, and voluntarism was always agonistic. Woolf attacked precisely this kind of connection in her essay "The Leaning Tower" (1940), first delivered as a lecture before a working-class audience, in which she complained, as she had in other contexts, about the politicizing of literature. The "leaning tower" writers, as she dubs the generation of Auden, Spender, and their peers, are fatally marred as artists by the political aspirations of their work.[42] For Woolf, writing in a defensive mood, the activism of her younger peers was damaging—rather than generative—to their literary output. And for their part, some of those who were involved in the Spanish Civil War would attempt, in future years, to distance themselves from the certainties of the era. So Auden drew back from "Spain" after the Second World War.[43] As Spender tells the story, in encountering an original pamphlet copy of the poem being sold on the street, Auden scrawled the words "this is a lie" next to its final lines ("History to the defeated/ May say Alas but cannot help or pardon").[44] Or a work like Orwell's *Homage to Catalonia* (1938), whose title and overall concept (a memoir of his months serving with a socialist militia in Spain), would seem to promise a nostalgic look at a time of self-sacrifice and motivation, instead takes a decidedly distant, ironic attitude—the forbidden mode? The book's ambivalent and internally conflicted tone is particularly notable given that it was composed and published while the war was still under way, and hence might have been poised to act primarily as an appeal, along the lines of works like Hemingway's film *Spanish Earth* or Auden's "Spain."

Orwell, Spender, Auden, and Hemingway are just a few; the list is long and varied, and, as these names suggest, prominently includes journalists, whose work in reporting the war was enormously far-reaching and important. We might take, as an emblematic case, the bombing of Guernica in April 1937, which quickly became the most infamous instance of civilian bombing before the Second World War. Guernica ("Gernika" in the Basque spelling), in the north of Spain, was the regional Basque capital, by all accounts a lovely market town. As commentators at the time stressed, it was of no military or strategic value; its almost complete destruction was aimed at its civilian population, and of course at the "morale" of the Spanish people more generally. The town itself was almost entirely razed by the squadron of German airplanes that spent several hours attacking it, thanks to their effective use of incendiary bombs, which set the town ablaze. With its many wooden or partially wooden buildings, it was ready to disintegrate under such a firestorm. The ruthless attack on Guernica caught the world's attention, in part because of the work of foreign journalists who happened to be stationed nearby (in Bilbao) and who arrived in the town within hours of its bombardment. As Ian Patterson writes in his study *Guernica and Total War* (2007), "Had it not been for the presence in Bilbao of some remarkable foreign correspondents . . . the real nature of the events of 26 April might not have been known until decades later. Certainly the bombing of Guernica would never have taken on its symbolic significance."[45] The overwhelming emphasis in these reports was witnessing and presence; to see the destroyed town itself, and to interview its victims, was paramount. At the same time, journalists gave a feel for the fascist enemy, at his post high in the sky, whose motives and tactics were presented as profoundly inhumane, in proportion to the cold calculation that determined all aspects of this kind of attack. Here, for instance, is the English journalist G. L. Steer, the first to report the attack in the British press, describing events in the *London Mercury* (1937):

> It was about five-fifteen. For two hours and a half flights of between three and twelve aeroplanes, types Heinkel 111 and Junker 52, bombed Gernika without mercy and with system. They chose their sectors in the town in

orderly fashion . . . On the shattered houses, whose carpets and curtains, splintered beams and floors and furniture were knocked into angles and ready for the burning, the planes threw silver flakes. Tubes of two pounds, long as your forearm, glistening silver from their aluminium and elektron casing; inside them, as in the beginning of the world in Prometheus' reed, slept fire. Fire in a silver powder, sixty-five grammes in weight, ready to slip through six holes at the base of the glittering tube. So, as the houses were broken to pieces over the people, sheathed fire descended from heaven to burn them up.[46]

Such language was far-reaching. Steer himself was also the unnamed writer of *The Times'* initial reports on the attack (also printed in *The New York Times*), and he included these initial transcriptions from the *London Mercury* in a book on Basque independence published one year later, while other newspapers, journals, and pamphlets also addressed the bombing of Guernica.[47] Reading these lines and others like them, the public was made witness to several key things. First, of course, was the sense of atrocity and outrage at the attack against civilians, whose plight was detailed throughout these writings. Of equal importance, too, was the sheer technological menace of the bombers' virtuosity, directed against meager homes and vulnerable bodies. And finally, it was the systematic quality that defined the Nazi air war in these texts—for instance, that wealthy fascist homes outside of the city were spared while the old and beautiful village was burned to the ground.

Guernica became notorious not only because of the exemplary journalism that revealed its atrocities but because of Picasso's painting, "which soon became an instantly recognizable depiction of the victims of modern war" (Patterson 18). Picasso had been commissioned by the Spanish government earlier in 1937 to contribute a painting to the Spanish exhibit at the Paris International Exposition, in a display that would make a plea to the world for aid in democratic Spain's increasingly desperate cause. In the bombing of Guernica he found his subject, a place and event that were already the scene of acknowledged slaughter and worldwide outrage. Massive in scale, modernist in style, dramatic in emotion, moving in expression, combining the personal and allegorical, the painting was enormously suggestive and effective, and it immediately garnered a sense of authority, though not, it should be stressed, uniform aesthetic admiration. (The opinion pages of *The Spectator* in October 1937 provided a lively debate on the aesthetic merits of the painting, as did art journals of the period.[48]) The Paris display was much visited and reported, and the painting itself, despite its giant size, went on to travel to many cities in Europe and America, including a brief showing in London in 1938.[49] *Guernica* offered one kind of powerful artistic intervention into the war, the larger-than-life vision of a famous artist, whose abstract forms captured both the suffering and dignity of the victims of fascism. The painting seems also an accusation— *"J'accuse"*—an attempt to jar European civilians out of complacency, to insist that they grasp fully the significance of the Spanish war for all of them, by combining specifically Spanish or local iconography (the bull, the rustic and traditional build- ings, the suggestion of the "tree of Gernika" in the far corner), with universal im- ages of horror, vulnerability, and resistance. Too, the painting's palette in layers of gray is highly suggestive of other media. With its coloration and hatching marks, it seems in dialogue with newspapers, even though, unlike many of Picasso's forma- tive cubist works, there is no actual newspaper here—as if to signal that in this case, where the communicative and political stakes are so high, the aesthetic absorption of these rival forms loses its surprise value; the newspaper has its own distinct role in this historical crisis. Moreover, with its grays and sepias, *Guernica* is evocative of photography. For all the contrast between the painting's modernist idiom and mainstream photographic style, that is, its visual language is intertwined with the photography of the period, which, along with journalism, most pervasively medi- ated the war's presence in other settings.[50]

More than the other forms we have thus far noted in this chapter, the rich and diverse photographic archive that emerged from the Spanish war reintroduces the polarities of enchanted and disenchanted violence. It is a visual mode dominated by documentary realism, a genre that tends to take up the dichotomous logic of enchantment and disenchantment with abundant visual clarity. Indeed, it is striking how the photographs of the war tend to fall into those two categories, some stressing the unredeemability and sheer waste of the war's violence, while others envision a spirit of nobility and beauty as a product and legacy of the war's horrors. Woolf's opening gesture in *Three Guineas*, when she depicts herself gazing at gruesome photographs sent by the Spanish government, is helpful to recall in this context—pictures, we might now note, of landscapes very similar to Guerni- ca's.[51] In the *Three Guineas* tableau, we recall, Woolf describes (but does not repro- duce) photographs of ruined houses and bodies, and from this encounter, begins to imagine the lineaments of a universal sentiment against war. The setting is an interesting one. On one hand, she appears to be comfortably situated in the ease and privacy of her English home (this would be Monk's House, the Sussex home where the Woolfs spent much of the 1930s), encountering these pictures of some- one else's home in an unnamed Spanish village, blown to bits. I am reminded of Mary Favret's primal scenario in the expansive condition of "wartime," with the writer at home, looking into the fire in the hearth, thinking and not thinking about war. Here the continuities across the two realms of war and peace (or rather, peace as oncoming war) are unmistakable: Sussex in 1938, like London, was already preparing for an air war—or worse, possible invasion—and, more generally, the idea of a safe and peaceful civilian existence was, as we have seen, disappearing in the public consciousness.[52] If this sense of local threat is left extraneous to Woolf's narrative of viewing the pictures, we might nevertheless ask how their presence in this location might alter them, or, conversely, alter the uneasily quiet English space into which they intrude. Woolf argues in the passage that the photographs generate a visceral reaction; seeing the massacred bodies causes one's own body to experience a "fusion," somewhat like Spender's notion of *Guernica* affecting a viewer in a manner akin to the explosion it depicts. The photos create the necessary horror and shock to incite political engagement—though, as we know from the rest of *Three Guineas*, Woolf was cautious about what kind of political engagement she could support, even toward the goal of abolishing war. To the extent, however, that her own writing might be enlisted in a political cause, it is as part of a chain reaction, a response and answer to these other works of representation and transmission. In the movement through acts of seeing and conveying, the viewer and reader come alive to the destruction being sown in a war happening in a seemingly alternate universe. It is a response conditioned as and calling for affect.[53] Or perhaps, given the aura of preparedness surrounding late 1930s in English culture, it is more accurate to see this "fusion" as premonition, a form of empathy-to-come: in seeing the actualization of extreme violence, those in a state of suspension discover an alchemical connection to its victims. It is a process that depends, vitally, on the visual markers of disenchanted violence.

Indeed, those photographs, icons of meaningless destruction in Woolf's account, came, in our earlier discussion, almost to define disenchanted violence, with their insistence on an ugly destructiveness that cannot be attached to systems or structures of value. Whether Woolf had in mind actual individual photographs or a general style, such disenchanted images from the Spanish war proliferated in these years, and they held an important place in the visual culture of the 1930s, especially during the war, when extremely troubling images of destroyed civilians and cities were enlisted for Republican support. These uses of photography represent complex trajectories across multiple spheres, not only involving the style and content of the photographs themselves, and the channels of reproduction and dissemination (for instance, in partisan newspapers in Spain and across Europe), but also in the responses they engendered, politically, personally, and aesthetically.[54] It should be noted too, that Franco's allies worked to cast doubt on their culpability in the Guernica bombing, maintaining that the town had in fact been destroyed by communists hoping to manipulate public perception and sympathy. It is a tactic that continues up to the present day; the worse the attack on civilians, it seems, the more surreal the forms of conspiracy conjured up in defense. Yet documentation presses against such forces. In the decades that followed the Second World War, documentary images came increasingly to the fore, when marshaling and archiving photographic evidence of bombing campaigns and other acts of horrific violence became a critical aspect of the work of journalists, political actors, and historians. Such photographs were reproduced, discussed, and preserved, and they share with film a central position in the visual legacy of the genocidal and atomic atrocities of the mid-twentieth century.

In the Spanish Civil War, photographs of bombed cities and killed or needy civilians carried a powerful narrative urgency. These visual forms had roots in the disenchanted representational history characterized by Friedrich's photographs from the First World War, a tradition in which the unredeemable, sickening quality of violence is presented in terms of decimated flesh. In the same year that Picasso produced *Guernica*, to take a striking example, the Hungarian-born British journalist Arthur Koestler compiled and published a chilling series of photographs as an appendix to his book *L'Espagne ensanglantée* (subtitled "Un livre noir sur l'Espagne"—"Bloody Spain: A Black Book on Spain").[55] The book is an exposé of fascist atrocities, and though it appears never to have been translated into English (it may have been translated into German), it had enough circulation to get Koestler arrested by the fascists and thrown in prison for six months when he returned to Spain.[56] The photographs assembled in Koester's book, rather like Friedrich's, cover a variety of grisly subjects, including colossally ruined architecture, corpses strewn on deserted streets, and, in several cases, horrendously mutilated bodies, whose very parts have become indistinguishable. Also following Friedrich, Koestler's pictures move in the direction of increasingly difficult viewing—for Friedrich, the culmination came with close-ups of veterans with extreme facial wounds, for Koestler with a collection of pictures of dead children who were killed in an air strike on the town of Getafe in November 1936. There are sixteen pictures in this section, thirteen of which are face-on, close-range pictures of individual children, numbered and tagged. Many are bloodied or visibly gashed, all with mouths gaping open. In fact, these pictures had circulated widely in the six months between the bombings of Getafe and Guernica, disseminated by the Republican government. One photograph of a dead girl, included in Koestler's archive, was used as a Republican poster, and circulated internationally.[57] I do not know if Woolf saw this poster, or this archive of photographs, but they speak a very similar language to the one she invokes at the beginning of *Three Guineas*, all of these photographs working not solely to condemn the fascist forces but also to stamp out any idea of symbolic, cultural, or aesthetic value to be found in the violence of war. Typical of this representational mode, the photographs offer a clinical, seemingly neutral and removed look at the body in ruins, even as they invite a political, activist response. As with Friedrich's archive, these photographs are not, in fact, an objective body of material, standing outside of perspective; on the contrary, their power as disenchanting spurs to action comes from such compositional factors as the relation of intimacy with dead bodies they demand of the viewer, their quality of anonymity, even the indecipherability characterizing many of the bodies they display. As Sontag began declaiming as early as *On Photography*, "Those occasions when the taking of photographs is relatively undiscriminating, promiscuous, or self-effacing do not lessen the didacticism of the whole enterprise. This very passivity—and ubiquity—of the photographic record is photography's 'message,' its aggression."[58] Or, as Emily Dalgarno writes of the Getafe photographs, as printed in a leftist French newspaper: "Two visual codes are at war: whereas the pictures suggest the aesthetics of the family portrait . . . the number displayed below reveals the objectivity of the body count" (Dalgarno, 164). The disenchanting photographs that marked the Spanish Civil War in the public were working actively—to turn body into flesh, person into corpse—and they champion a brutal realism where aesthetics would seem entirely beside the point.

An entirely different ideal is embodied by the most famous photographs of the Spanish Civil War, those of Robert Capa, whose aesthetic of noble Spanish humanity has formed an indelible part of the visual culture of Spain (and the rest of the world) since the 1930s. Capa's photographs are drenched with personal appeal. They are often crisply focused on individual faces, their beauty directly correlated with their often remarkably handsome subjects. Capa's photos of both militiamen and civilians became instantly famous when they burst onto the scene in 1936. They were published and republished in photojournals in many countries, most notably in a special issue of *Life* magazine in 1937, and while Capa's partner Gerda Taro was killed in Spain, her fame muted, Capa went on to a long and distinguished career photographing war and its human consequences. Best known, then as now, is "Falling Soldier," one of a series of photos Capa took one afternoon on a hill in Cordoba, tracking militiamen in a series of exercises that turned fatal. This one captures a soldier at the very instant when he was hit by a bullet and killed, as he is blown backward, his tensed and wracked body and his clenched face reacting to the force of the bullet. Immediately following "Falling Soldier" in the series came another moving image of a man collapsing, in a somewhat more traditional death contour. No doubt because of its compositional shock, "Falling Soldier" has always garnered tremendous attention, as well as controversy. So startling, opportune, and amazing is the shot, indeed, that it has been consistently suspected of having been staged. The debate rages on; though the controversy appeared to have been settled in the 1970s, thanks to the unveiling of the person believed to be the subject of the photograph, recent scholarship attacks the photograph's legitimacy based on its location.[59]

Ultimate authentication aside, the photograph was a visual landmark in the mid-1930s and beyond, and is suggestive of Capa's approach to war's human significance more broadly. Part of what is so astonishing about "Falling Soldier"—actually, about both shots of falling men—is its status as portrait. Here, in the midst not just of war but in the act of being killed in war, the militiaman remains whole and human, his personhood and individuality in a sense enhanced in this picture, even as his body is jolted back by the force of the bullet. Earlier in the series, Capa had captured the group in celebratory pose, upright, enthusiastic, arms in the air, with rifles held high—men of the people dedicated to their work. This spirit, indeed, marks all of Capa's photographs from the war, many of which document civilians, as they face the privations and assaults of the war. He took many photographs during the siege of Madrid (as did other photographers, a host of such pictures being included in Koestler's book), as well as several series tracking refugees. In all of these, the human focus remains both direct and ennobling. Capa captures a sense of elegance and singularity in the features of his subjects, making even the most weathered, lined faces seem vibrantly sensuous. There is, throughout the archive, a sense of presence, even style, in these unbowed civilians. Among Capa's civilian photographs, one gesture is particularly notable: the individual or group staring up into the sky. With aerial bombardment as the overwhelming threat to civilians during the war, this ubiquitous stance is not surprising. It is described in narrative form repeatedly in *For Whom the Bell Tolls*, where the drone of planes almost always precedes their visibility. And so we have an iconographic posture, of civilians craning heads, eyes shaded, staring into the sky, looking at something the viewer herself cannot see, responding to a sound the viewer would never be able to hear.

Capa, of course, taps into a long tradition in European representation of ennobling suffering, which praises and aestheticizes human endurance. His project is essentially Romantic, and his precursors derive significantly from, for instance, French genre painting of the nineteenth century (or English lyrics like Wordsworth's "Michael" and "The Solitary Reaper"). It is a tradition that stressed the hardship of labor, in the context of industrialization and economic injustice, even as the worker's unbroken spirit and body was honored. Here those attributes are transferred from the sphere of labor to scenes of war and bombardment. To the extent that Capa's works can be understood in terms of enchanting violence, then, the terms shift away from the most pervasive formulations we have encountered up to now, in which, for instance, the community of war is imagined as sacred, or in which a regenerative ideal demands that symbolic and aesthetic value emerge from violent events. Instead, it is in the human pathos of endurance and resistance to violence that Capa locates the core of his enchanting visual project. And yet, in his many photographs of people staring into the sky, the dominant emotional register is one of imminence—of destruction to come, perhaps within minutes, or even seconds. For all that they imply of endurance, beauty, and nobility, then, qualities that resonate with the idea of permanence, there is a profound sense of transience and uncertainty in these photographs. To enchant violence, in this part of the Capa oeuvre, is thus, in a strange way, to conjure the shattering of that very ideal, to shadow a moment of continuing human strength with the promise of a horrendous destruction that would look, in the end, more like Koestler's archive of mutilated flesh than Capa's own works of resilient beauty.

These diverse visual creators—Picasso, Capa, those who took, compiled, and disseminated photographs of bombarded cities—believed that by making visible and visceral the barbarity of war and fascism, they could be part of a counteracting force against the most violent regimes and ideologies. Along with poets, journalists, and other writers, they epitomized the activist spirit of the era, constructing a narrative of suffering, resistance, determination, and need that called out for responsiveness from around the world. Yet this kind of activism needs to be distinguished, at least in part, from the idea of "action," which, in the same period, was taking on dramatic connotations of its own. To be involved in the antiwar and antifascist movement was—in the name of peace and justice—to act. But action had also been colonized as an ideal for the right, which fetishized its metaphorics and held it up as the opposite of a weak and despised pacifism. In other words, a complex net of issues around war and action was entangled together in the 1930s, with ideas of activism (or acting) against war and violence coming into contact with very differently weighted beliefs about action, passivity, and pacifism.

Action and Pacifism

"But it was action. Action relieved him." So Woolf describes the particular relief Giles experiences and expresses through stamping on the snake and toad. At its most straightforward, it is a moment of psychic release, depicting, in characterological form, a version of what Eric Leed has called the "drive discharge" model of war and violence. In general terms, the "drive discharge" theory holds:

... that organized spheres of conflict—war, revolution, and warlike sports—function to discharge drives which are blocked from expression in normal social life. War, in an image which seems native to the Age of Steam, provides a "safety valve" for aggressions, drives, and needs that cannot be used in working the social mechanism. Implicitly, the distinction between peace and war is a distinction between necessity and freedom, repression and release, the blockage of vital force inherent in men and groups, and the "expression" of that force in acts which are normally taboo. . . .

War, here, becomes a world of instinctual liberty that contrasts starkly with the social world of instinctual renunciation and the deferment of gratification.[60]

This view, which Leed argues "was a deeply rooted cultural assumption intrinsic to the sense of liberation that many experienced in August of 1914" and which similarly "describes the assumptions of those who, at the end of the [First World] war, feared that the returning veteran had been criminalized, revolutionized, or barbarized by his experience," maps closely onto what we have seen to be a widespread belief in the following decades as well, that human beings are prone to aggression and that there is no way to avoid the slaughter that was beginning to define the modern world, any more than people through the millennia could have prevented their own histories of endless bloodshed (Leed, 6, 7). Giles's frustrations, moreover, are given real credence in *Between the Acts*; the only member of the Oliver circle to be paying close, conscious attention to the dire political and humanitarian situation on the continent, or to be envisioning the destruction that threatens the village and its residents, Giles is perhaps understandably enraged. Discredited though he may be as a violent homophobe—and as a representative of patriarchal capitalism more generally—Giles does embody a twisted and knotted desire to transfer his aggression from the small and local to, one imagines, the fascist and international, a desire that Woolf might expect her readers to share, or at least to understand.

Yet the phrase "it was action" calls up another set of associations, which—unlike the pseudo-Freudian theory of bottled aggression, which both pre- and postdates this era—was more particular to the interwar period, and more specific in its political affiliations. By the 1930s, the cult of action had become a byword for fascism, not only abroad, but in England as well. When "action" comes up in Woolf's novels, it has this tone about it; in the case of Giles, certainly, or in one of Louis's monologues in *The Waves*, when he thinks, "the voice of action speaks," and likens it to aggressive sexual desire, possessed by "an imperious brute."[61] Earlier in the century, the worship of action had helped to characterize avant-garde literary creeds, including futurism and vorticism. Best articulated and epitomized by Marinetti's first futurist manifesto of 1909, this was a language that took its reigning metaphors from motion and activity, declaring that "[u]p to now literature has exalted a pensive immobility, ecstasy and sleep. We intend to exalt aggressive action, a feverish insomnia, the racer's stride, the mortal leap, the punch and the slap," and lauding, among other things, "the beauty of speed."[62] *BLAST*, too, for all its declared differentiation from futurism—its snubbing of automobiles in favor of ships, as an example—notably retains Marinetti's exaltation of action, opting throughout its short run for metaphors of movement and mobility.

As Martin Puchner has shown, these avant-garde manifestos emerged in dialogue with radical political movements, and in the case of "action," it is Italian fascism that is the closest interlocutor.[63] Mussolini always trumpeted action as a fascist value and attribute, and in the early 1930s, he canonized such notions in various texts that helped to codify and rationalize the doctrines of Italian fascism. "Fascism," he writes in one such declaration, "wants man to be active and to engage in action with all his energies."[64] His pamphlet "The Political and Social Doctrine of Fascism," published in English by the Woolfs at the Hogarth Press in 1933 (a text ridiculed by Leonard in *Quack! Quack!*), elevates action explicitly and implicitly, allying it with militarism and opposing it to what Mussolini most reviles, pacifism. "Born of the need for action," in a time marked by "the necessity for action," fascism, he writes, "believes neither in the possibility nor the utility of perpetual peace. It . . . repudiates the doctrine of Pacifism . . . War alone brings up to its highest tension all human energy and puts the stamp of nobility upon the peoples who have the courage to meet it"—and so on, the tract ending with a paean to empire.[65] All of this is highly familiar in the European context—the metaphoric and symbolic associations that underpin such logic, the extreme political usages to which this violent language could be put, the specific consequences in the 1930s and '40s—and these ideas were also disseminated in England in the same period, albeit less consequentially. Oswald Mosely and his British Union of Fascists were the most direct followers of Mussolinian ideology in England, with Mosely's tack to the extreme right escalating through the 1930s. At the beginning of the decade, in 1931, Mosely founded the "New Party," a political movement that was framed more as antiestablishment than fascist.

The party's journal was called *Action*, and in its short run between October 1931 and early 1932, it gave vent to Mosely's increasingly strident voice, but also to a host of other writers who would seem strange company for him.[66] The journal was edited by Harold Nicolson, who also wrote its book reviews, and these included, for instance, a rave report of Woolf's *The Waves* (in its first issue, published on the very day that Woolf's novel came out), reviews of other modernist writers like William Faulkner, and a sustained interest in First World War–related books. Other contributions in every issue included a column by Vita Sackville-West on gardening, film reviews (but not theater, signaling the journal's consciously modern pose), humor, a focus on outdoor pursuits, and, of course, the expected emphasis on politics. The journal's political voice was alarmist, and it resonated with much of the political language of fascism, despite an insistence that it deplored violence. "The Nation Calls for Action at Once," ran its opening issue's leader, and Mosely went on to describe his party in these terms:

> We must create a movement which aims not merely at the capture of political power; a movement which grips and transforms every phase and aspect of national life to post-war purposes, a movement of order, of discipline, of loyalty, but also of dynamic progress; a movement of iron decision, resolution and reality; a movement which cuts like a sword through the knot of the past to the winning of the modern State.[67]

All of this was short-lived and marginal to the overall political life of 1930s England, with the New Party faring execrably in the November elections of 1931, and the journal continuing a course of increasingly conservative ideology, only surviving for a few more months (it was restarted in 1936 under the auspices of the British Union of Fascists, until it was shut down, along with the party, in 1940). Mosely, of course, can claim no ownership of the idea of action, yet the journal I think represents a concise and not immediately discredited example of how the term could work in England in this period, politically and ideologically. Connected to a violent, contemporary worldview, derived from European fascism and feeding directly into movement's like the B.U.F., it marked a pivot where humanist values of thoughtfulness, tolerance, and justice gave way to brutality, racism, and oppression. This whole sensibility, moreover, took shape in a relation of extreme antagonism to pacifism.

The story of pacifism in England in the 1930s is rife with contradictions, as the philosophy found its greatest expression and faced its harshest challenges, all within a few years. Nonviolence and antiwar movements had existed for centuries in England and throughout Europe (the peace historian Peter Brock begins his survey of European pacifism with the early Christians).[68] These were overwhelmingly sectarian, but in the nineteenth century, radical groups opposed to international war and imperialism began to make their own, secular case against violence and aggression. Marx, of course, opposed the wars of nations, and anarchism, too, had always stood against the national world organization that so endemically perpetuates war. Among the different pacifist groups that emerged in England after the First World War, the most prominent was the Peace Pledge Union (P.P.U.), which began in 1934 when a clergyman named Dick Sheppard published a note in the *Manchester Guardian* soliciting postcards from those who would declare themselves opposed to war (*The Times* having turned down his request). Receiving many thousands of these pledges, he organized a movement that grew to several hundred thousand members.[69] All of these groups published their views and membership included many prominent political and intellectual figures (the P.P.U. counted such names as Huxley, Russell, Sassoon, Vera Brittain, and Storm Jameson).[70]

For all this fervency, pacifism stood on very shaky ground in England in the 1930s. Facing the savagery of fascism and the increasingly widespread sense, on the left as well as the right, that war was necessary (or at least inevitable), those who were devoted to nonviolence in general, or to opposing war in particular, were liable to extreme marginalization, indeed to hostility or outright ridicule. By the end of the decade, a number of prominent pacifists had either recanted or recalibrated their positions. Of the strategies employed to avert charges of escapism and worse, the most notable was a recourse to the logic of paradox. When Leonard Woolf in 1940 titled his tract about international politics and democratic survivability under the stresses of fascism *The War for Peace*, he intimated a basic structure of thought that had been a central tenet since Wells's famous coinage of the "war that will end wars" (title of a 1914 polemic, a moniker made famous by President Woodrow Wilson not long after): that the only way to find an avenue to peace—in 1938 as in 1914—was by waging war. To sustain nonviolence, violence. So basic was (and is) this notion, so deeply internalized its logic, that its paradox could pass almost unnoticed throughout the period. Leonard Woolf was not a pacifist, and pacifism itself could not in any coherent way advocate war and violence to attain its end, but it nevertheless became entangled in similar formulations, and, more generally, the period was one in which resisting war and violence seemed more and more elusive and impossible—or more and more attached, in some kind of terrible dialectic, to the achievement of war and violence.

Given how important the Spanish Civil War had become in filtering these questions, we might look to one of its many leftist international volunteers for an interesting rendering of the view that pacifism is always and inevitably bound to violence. Killed in Spain at age twenty-nine, the English communist Christopher Caudwell had just begun a career as an essayist and political theorist.[71] In his essay "Pacifism and Violence," first published posthumously in 1938 in the collection *Studies in a*

Dying Culture, Caudwell makes the case against pacifism as a matter of root economic and social conditions.[72] Within bourgeois capitalism, Caudwell argues, pacifism is nothing more than a form of violence in its own right, just as inaction is only
a disguised (and even self-deluded) form of action. "Man cannot live without acting,"
he writes, "And since man is always acting, he is always exerting force, always altering or maintaining the position of things, always revolutionary or conservative . . .
The web of physical and social relations that binds men into one universe ensures
that nothing we do is without its effect on others."[73] All action, in this account, is
force, and since inaction is embedded in action, to participate in capitalist culture at
all, even in ways that might seem benign or passive, is nevertheless to promote force.
In the case of pacifism, this inherent complementing of opposites means the cloak-
ing of a silent and invisible violence:

> Bourgeois social relations are revealing, more and more insistently, the vio-
> lence of exploitation and dispossession on which they are founded; more
> and more they harrow man with brutality and oppression. By abstaining
> from action the pacifist enrolls himself under this banner, the banner of
> things as they are and getting worse, the banner of the increasing violence
> and coercion exerted by the *haves* on the *have-nots*. He calls increasingly
> into being the violences of poverty, deprivation, artificial slumps, artistic
> and scientific decay, fascism, and war. (Caudwell, 126, italics in original)

What is particularly notable in Caudwell's Marxist formulation is his attack on
those principles of resistance—inaction, pacifism, nonviolence—espoused by
thoughtful, engaged liberals like Virginia Woolf. Too, his comments about the connected nature of the social fabric might remind us of Woolf's own formulations,
laced throughout her writings, of the intimately imbricated web of social, personal,
and psychic connections that knits together the modern world. In Caudwell's rendering, these connections are first and foremost political. There simply is no pacifism under conditions of capitalist inequality; there is only violence.

Even for those working to develop a viable antiwar theory in the 1930s, pacifism
was pressed into a defensive posture, and was open not only to the kind of attack
Caudwell made but also to the war-for-peace formulation rendered inevitable by
the spread of fascism. A particularly eloquent and fervent work, which takes the
route of evading these critiques, is Huxley's *Encyclopedia*, which I have mentioned
in reference to some of the dominant militarist arguments of the period. The *Encyclopedia* sets out the principles of pacifism in a historically extensive, philosophi-
cally cohesive way, dropping back from the particularities of the moment. Adopting
the encyclopedic structure and style—its headings range from "Armaments, Private

Manufacture of" to "Women in Modern War, Position of"—Huxley makes his case against war and violence through a clinical, topic-by-topic analysis, which is cumulatively powerful, while in a sense dodging the dilemmas facing pacifists in the 1930s. He has no subject heading for fascism, for example, instead bundling it with communism, and effectively brushing off both as the "product" of a long history of violence, Western culture's own logical outcome (Huxley, 23). No apologist for the mass violence on the continent, Huxley nevertheless refuses to allow it to alter his own convictions, which look far afield from the present and from Europe for examples of nonviolent political and religious successes. As for the war in Spain, it is mentioned only under the general rubric of civil war, though the atrocities and horrors of aerial bombardment are generously articulated in the *Encyclopedia*, as part of its disenchanting agenda.

Indeed, disenchantment is the dominant mode in pacifist accounts of violence, as one would expect. In the case of the *Encyclopedia*, whose stylistic mandate would seem to disallow too much focus on the flesh, Huxley nevertheless creates headings that invite such emphasis (such as "Chemical Warfare," which includes a detailed and grisly description of how mustard gas attacks the body), and methodically attacks all the conventional terms by which violence is ordinarily enchanted—religious, revolutionary, nationalistic, or even aesthetic. Or, to take a particularly wry example (one which recalls Lytton Strachey's famous rejoinder from two decades earlier), Huxley writes:

> Another favourite question asked by militarists is the following: "What would you do if you saw a stranger break into your house and try to violate your wife?" This question may be answered as follows: "Whatever else I might do—and it is quite likely that I should become very angry and try to knock the intruder down or even kill him—I should certainly not send my brother to go and poison the man's grandfather and disembowel his infant son." And that precisely is what war consists of—murdering, either personally or (more often) through the instrumentality of others, all kinds of people who have never done one any sort of injury. (Huxley, 48)

It is symptomatic of Huxley's approach that he reaches back to the jingoistic formulations of the First World War for his most biting ironies, since the possibility of disenchantment was especially strong, as we have seen, in that period, whereas the contemporary moment invites, by contrast, a potently enchanting idiom.

Other pacifist works of the 1930s took a more direct approach to the violence of the times.[74] In *Why War?*, a pacifist appeal written in 1939, C. E. M. Joad uses vivid, visceral language to drive home the horrors of war, highlighting, as is typical of the disenchanted mode, the vulnerable tissue of the human body. "War, as we now know it," he writes, "is a process whereby mechanisms mangle human flesh. To indulge in it is . . . to enter a shambles in which all the resources of chemical science are concentrated on blinding, burning, poisoning and mutilating living human bodies"; or again, "To-day there is only the naked human flesh that feeds the machine."[75] Though Joad shares with Huxley the desire to offer a bracing account of war's material effects, his work takes an entirely contemporaneous approach to the claims of war and peace, beginning with the international situation at the moment of his writing, and including a late section entitled "The Policy of 'Standing Firm' to Fascism and What It Means." In this penultimate chapter, Joad describes the disheartening experience of attending a pacifist gathering at a Quaker meeting hall, which disintegrated when, in an adjoining room, "a packed audience of excited persons was welcoming with terrific enthusiasm the British members of the International Brigade, just home from Spain" (Joad, 214). Though Joad is careful to speak respectfully of the volunteers, the experience of observing their welcome remains troubling:

> The point for me lay in the contrast between the mild and decorous meeting attended by the few who had come to consider ways of peace, and the uproarious multitude who had come to do honour to the acts of war. The contrast made me pensive. The facts that the multitude belonged to the Socialist Left, and that their meeting place was the headquarters of the Society of Friends, gave point of paradox to my meditations. (Joad, 215)

For Joad, the paradox of pacifists embracing war is one he feels called upon to confront. Socialism is not, of course, synonymous with pacifism, but for Joad there is something definitive about his idea of the left and war: the one must, in order to stay true to its basic tenets and values, oppose the other. It is perhaps symptomatic of the period that Joad's treatise, confident and brimming with moral purpose, ultimately finds itself in an uncomfortable, even alienated position. The pacifist watches, amidst a dwindling circle of friends, as war engulfs not only the continent but his own political movement.

Joad invokes the idea of paradox directly, but there are other measures of paradox in which he more unwittingly engages. Readers of *Three Guineas* will recall Joad's name; he appears there (and in the scrapbooks) as a representative of contemporary misogyny.[76] It is Joad who states, in a memorable footnote, that "Women, I think, ought not to sit down to table with men; their presence ruins conversation, tending to make it trivial and genteel, or at best merely clever" (*3G*, 159). More centrally, Joad is a spokesman in *Three Guineas* for the hypocritical idea that the very highest standards must apply to women's civic participation. Having fought so hard for the vote, Joad declares, women should use their newfound power to advance serious causes, rather than spend their time eating peanuts and ice cream. These are not incidental examples of misogyny and illogic—are men to lose their votes if they do not engage in meaningful political activity?; how absurd to suggest that women have real power; and so on. The fact that Joad, one of the villains of *Three Guineas*, is also an eloquent and committed pacifist indicates an especially problematic situation for Woolf and for her project in *Three Guineas*. In fact, the specific passage Woolf chooses from Joad involves him imploring women to work for peace, and to fight fascism. Along similar lines, when Dick Sheppard made his first appeal for support from fellow nonviolence advocates in the *Manchester Guardian*, inaugurating the P.P.U., he called explicitly for the votes of men, the reasoning being that a peace movement made up primarily of women would have little political force. One could very easily envision a place for this appeal in *Three Guineas*.

The problem of Joad (or Sheppard) represents more than just another ironic study in the logic of patriarchy; its offense and its challenge are structural. If male pacifism comes in the form of subjugation of women, of what use can it be? To answer this question is, of course, part of the imperative of *Three Guineas*. More broadly, though, it belongs to the large dilemma of how people imagined and promoted peace in the 1930s. On all sides, violence crowds out nonviolence: Marxists like Caudwell see pacifism as simply the quiet (or cynical) side of violence; Leonard Woolf and others call for war to bring peace; and feminists might see in pacifism a laudable goal that nevertheless fatally relies on yet more viciousness toward women. And so we reach an impasse, with the idea of action tarnished by its relation to fascism and to other ideals of force and power, but with no obvious pacific alternative. Woolf responded to these dilemmas throughout her late work. Indeed, the whole panoply of public discourse we have examined in this chapter, from debates about the status of violence in the human condition, to the aesthetic response to aerial bombardment, to the limitations of pacifism, find a literary home in her intensely empathetic body of writing.

Virginia Woolf

What, then, does a theory of writing violence look like in Woolf's works? Are there strategies that either develop or persist in her fiction from early novels like *The Voyage Out*, which was largely written before the First World War, to late writings such as *Between the Acts*, produced in the midst of a new war and reflecting the darkening outlook that took its ultimate form in Woolf's suicide? How does the cultural history we have been tracing in this chapter—and more extensively throughout this study—play out across her career? The answer to these overlapping questions is that Woolf accomplished an extremely full and rich assessment of violence over the course of her writing life—the parallels between her first and last novels on this score are remarkable, her career framed around large questions of literary violence—with a result that is essentially twofold. On one hand, she engages many of the strategies and themes that occupied her contemporaries, from an emphasis on disenchantment, to the allegorizing of human violence via animals, to the rendering of the airplane as a singular new threat, to the many debates around the inherence of violence we have seen to concern writers in the 1930s. But there is a second and partially countervailing tendency, a way in which Woolf retreats from the forms for understanding violence that we have been tracking, and these might be categorized under the formal rubrics of dispersal and absorption. Though it is neither feasible nor helpful entirely to separate these two modes—the way she approached her culture's shared tendencies and discourses around violence, the way she created her own unique formal solutions—nevertheless, her works can fruitfully be read both for their relation to a broader culture around violence and for their idiosyncratic turn away from the conventions developing in the public conversation of her day. Ultimately, the violence that Woolf always understood to threaten and encroach on human life comes to be emblematized and activated by several key verbs: bracket, disperse, absorb. From her first novel to her last, and in many nonfictional writings as well, Woolf considers violence in terms of pattern, the shapes and formations it can inhabit within the literary work, almost as if she is creating her own blood painting. Indeed, in all of this, the muting and erasing activity evoked by Giles's shoes is significantly present, as violence is often marked by a mere stain. The central challenge faced by all the writers we have studied—how to find a formal register adequate to the excess and sheer monstrosity of violence—is met in Woolf's writing with extraordinary patience, as each work develops new patterns, shapes, lines, and depths where violence can reside, or be contained, or find sharp new visibility. Woolf is, in this sense, a little like her creation Mrs. Ramsay, confronting "this thing that she called life," a force that is "terrible, hostile, and quick to pounce on you," and yet, "she said to herself, brandishing her sword at life, Nonsense."[77] Brandishing her sword at her own lifelong nemesis—violence—Woolf created a countermovement; if violence in her writing is often like a wave, the texts she shapes are like the obscure patterns left, however temporarily, on the battered sand.

"July 19th, 1939. I was forced to break off again, and rather suspect that these breaks will be the end of this memoir": as critics have noted, the Second World War impinged on Woolf's attempt, in *A Sketch of the Past*, to write her personal history.[78] The war was the motivating force behind this sketch—she began each entry with a description of bombers and invasion threats—but it also profoundly interrupted and disrupted the effort:

> June 8, 1940. . . . Shall I ever finish these notes—let alone make a book from them? The battle is at its crisis; every night the Germans fly over England; it comes closer to this house daily. If we are beaten then—however we solve that problem, and one solution is apparently suicide (so it was decided three nights ago in London among us)—book writing becomes doubtful. But I wish to go on, not to settle down in that dismal puddle. (*MB*, 100)

The disruptions converge here in 1940, when not only her writing but her life is at stake. These are extreme, terrifying, and moving statements, signifying debilitation—interruptions that herald only endings. Yet they also crystallize a theme that, in less abortive form, had always permeated Woolf's work, the idea that violence presents a profound dislocation, around which literary works take their shape. In the memoir, the interrupting presence of the ongoing war gave form to the very past Woolf was writing. It created a heightened sense of magic and refuge in memory, for instance, and it also imposed its *own* structure of irruptive violence onto the past, the never-quite-safe haven of personal history. In this retrospective moment, in other words, the pattern of interrupting violence became one of the defining forms around which the individual life would be understood and narrated. And so Woolf offers in *A Sketch of the Past* a handful of crux events from her earliest memories, which, in this late and anxious writing, she describes as both formative and representative of her aesthetic consciousness. There is rapture and ecstasy, ignited by a blowing curtain in the Cornwall nursery, or focalized by the sight of a flower, complete and perfect.[79] There is terror and self-hatred, generated by her half-brother's sexual assault, or by the sight of a boy in the park whose face is marked and disfigured. There is early reckoning with death, and also with suicide. There is the stunning awareness of a latent pacifism, when the young Virginia finds that she is incapable of fighting with her brother, and allows him to pummel her (*MB*, 66, 71, 78, 71). In *A Sketch of the Past*, undertaken when Woolf had finally read Freud (or at least when she had acknowledged having read him), she writes back through her life and career, suggesting a personal dimension to the perception and endurance of violence. Even when lifted out of this explicitly psychologized frame, moreover, Woolf insisted on seeing violent events, to which a person is randomly, bewilderingly subjected, as pivotal elements in the aesthetic imagination.

Late in her life, Woolf's writing tilts steeply towards this violence, as readers often note. Diary entries register bleakness, foreclosure, and real sadness: on March 24, 1940, she writes, "I remember the sudden profuse shower one night just before war wh. made me think of all men & women weeping"; January 9, 1941 opens, startlingly, "A blank"; on January 26, she writes, simply, "we live without a future"; and the list goes on. (At the same time, it should be noted that Woolf's diary in these years is not merely a record of depressed sentiments, filled as it is with her habitual wit and brio, and rebounding often into notable expressions of pleasure.)[80] Short prose works of the late 1930s, too, became a forum for considering the viability of liberal or pacifist strategies for confronting violence, and more largely, for weighing the possibility, in some basic sense, of survival. Thus one of Woolf's last pieces, "Thoughts on Peace in an Air Raid," takes the Blitz as an opportunity to imagine, in the future, a gentle demilitarizing of Western masculinity, as Woolf muses on how, through the creative and educative capacity, women might work to mitigate the "subconscious Hitlerism" of their culture.[81] Or in Woolf's final, unfinished essay "Anon" (initially envisioned as a full-length work), she erases the author altogether, in a gesture that is simultaneously self-annihilating and breathtakingly lovely and elevating:

> The voice that broke the silence of the forest was the voice of Anon. Some one heard the song and remembered it for it was later written down, beautifully, on parchment. Thus the singer had his audience, but the audience was so little interested in his name that he never thought to give it. The audience was itself the singer . . .[82]

Above all, the last three extended works of her career, *The Years*, *Three Guineas*, and *Between the Acts*, iterate and reiterate an increasing consciousness of overwhelming force. In form as well as theme, these texts present a world where waves of violence wash over us—in the crush of wars, in the organizing facts of patriarchy, in the history of a family.

The metaphor of the wave, indeed, is exemplary, providing a neat illustration of the way Woolf sets violence in tension and also dialogue with literary form, noting its power, engulfing it in her texts, erasing it even as she thrusts it into view. Woolf employed the wave metaphor abundantly over the course of her career, often to represent the terror of an indifferent, harsh world. In *To the Lighthouse*, water and wave are mesmerizing, beautiful, and evocative; but they are also the trigger of an almost ontological threat to the human condition. Thus in the famous dinner scene, the small party finds its shelter together in an island-like oasis, battered and encroached upon by the watery world around it. Or, earlier in the novel, in a moment of quiet reflection, Mrs. Ramsay is suddenly frozen in fear, for she finds that the "monotonous fall of the waves on the beach . . . remorselessly beat the measure of life, made one think of the destruction of the island and its engulfment in the sea" (*TTL*, 15–16, ellipses added). *Jacob's Room* has Betty Flanders, her son off at the front, wonder if the booming sound in the night might be the guns: "'Not at this distance,' she thought. 'It is the sea'" (*JR*, 154). And in *The Years*, written a decade and a half later, a scene set in a First World War air raid evokes the familiar metaphor: "The guns were still firing, but far away in the distance. There was a sound like the breaking of waves on a shore far away" (*TY*, 293). Waves in Woolf's work signal destruction and engender terror, at the same time that they are an emblem of extreme aesthetic patterning, as in the novel of that name. The metaphor of the wave, in other words, explicitly and closely ties violence to form (Betty Flanders, for her part, shifts quickly from guns to a more artful and imaginative image: "Again, far away, she heard the dull sound, as if nocturnal women were beating great carpets" [*JR*, 154]). The ubiquity of waves in Woolf's writing underscores how important the intertwining of violence with aesthetic creation is for her, but also how elusive; the waves denote, but also, true to their structure, wash away the stain of violence.

Early Patterns: *The Voyage Out*

As early as her first novel, Woolf had developed her sense that there can be no separating aesthetic projects from intense, brutal episodes of violence and suffering. Indeed, in *The Voyage Out* (1915), Woolf makes her protagonist Rachel Vinrace into something of a repository for the experience and expression of violence, a collecting point for the many otherwise disparate and inchoate passages about violence that abound in the novel. These range from incidental suggestions and unidentified statements to more extended sequences, as when the English company aboard the *Euphrosyne* spots a fleet of warships from the deck. What unifies these disconnected passages in *The Voyage Out* is a consistent circling back from the suggestion of violence to Rachel, who exemplifies a quality of deep susceptibility and malleability. Allied especially with animals, Rachel is the pivot point for the text's reflections on that which is physical, vulnerable, precarious. There are two especially resonant such passages, one strange and oblique, the other piercing and vivid. In the first, which appears just several pages into the novel, the group aboard the ship alludes to a herd of goats, drowned at sea:

[Mr. Pepper] professed himself surprised to learn that although Mr. Vinrace possessed ten ships, regularly plying between London and Buenos Aires, not one of them was bidden to investigate the great white monsters of the lower waters.

'No, no,' laughed Willoughby, 'the monsters of the earth are too many for me!'

Rachel was heard to sigh, 'Poor little goats!'

'If it weren't for the goats there'd be no music, my dear; music depends upon goats,' said her father rather sharply, and Mr. Pepper went on to describe the white, hairless, blind monsters lying curled on the ridges of sand at the bottom of the sea, which would explode if you brought them to the surface, their sides bursting asunder and scattering entrails to the winds when released from pressure, with considerable detail and with such show of knowledge, that Ridley was disgusted, and begged him to stop.[83]

Among other oddities of this passage is the fact that in the final draft of the novel, Woolf gives no explanation of what it might mean. Rachel's dreaminess about goats is complemented by Pepper's explicitness about flesh, but in neither case do we learn the provenance of these dead beasts who seem to amalgamate actual dead goats with the larger horrors and mysteries of what might rest at the bottom of the sea. In an earlier draft, the narrator had noted, several pages after this conversation, that Rachel's father "was a sentimental man who imported goats for the sake of empire."[84] When the final draft eliminates the clarifying fact that Vinrace is a goat importer, it leaves the passage to stand alone as a strange aside, where mangled animals or monsters at the bottom of the sea are simply depicted, for no obvious reason, at the same time that they are vaguely associated with Rachel, who empathizes with the goats and who is closely linked, throughout the novel, with images of drowning.

All of this culminates, horrifically and tragically, when Rachel experiences fever as a form of suffocation under water, returning her almost to a prenatal state of fluid existence, and also to the poor little goats:

At last the faces went further away; she fell into a deep pool of sticky water, which eventually closed over her head. She saw nothing and heard nothing but a faint booming sound, which was the sound of the sea rolling over her head. While all her tormentors thought that she was dead, she was not dead, but curled up at the bottom of the sea. There she lay, sometimes seeing darkness, sometimes light, while every now and then some one turned her over at the bottom of the sea. (*VO*, 322)

In the typical allegorical usage, violent imaginings of animals stand in for their human counterparts. Here, however, Woolf closes the circuit, giving us a picture of Rachel's fevered and suffering interior life every bit as vivid as the depiction of the goats' bodies that had so disgusted Ridley. As in Yeats's poems, allegory drops to symbol, metaphor to identity. The vitality and heat of violence seems simply to burn through the structural boundaries separating signified from signifier, person from animal. Lurking in the background of all of this, and tying together its divergent imagery, is not only Rachel, but also the disenchantment of the body more generally, revealing itself as flesh. So Helen, in a visit upriver, becomes "acutely conscious of the little limbs, the thin veins, the delicate flesh of men and women, which breaks so easily and lets the life escape compared with these great trees and deep waters. A falling branch, a foot that slips, and the earth has crushed them or the water drowned them" (*VO*, 270). The novel is always circling around such frail flesh.

The scenario of the goats/monsters—a moment of excessive animal mutilation, interiorized by Rachel and later played out as her own private drama, connected with drowning—has trenchancy in the novel, a kind of recurrence effect. It comes back in a tableau of behind-the-scenes hotel activity, a sequence reminiscent of such other modernist accounts of the underbelly of bourgeois life as Dorian Gray's nights in the opium dens, Stephen Dedalus's wanderings in the squalid Dublin streets, or Franz Biberkopf's life in seedy Berlin.[85] Rachel, ambling through the halls of the hotel, happens upon a scene of employees at their work:

> Two large women in cotton dresses were sitting on a bench with blood-smeared tin trays in front of them and yellow bodies across their knees. They were plucking the birds, and talking as they plucked. Suddenly a chicken came floundering, half flying, half running into the space, pursued by a third woman whose age could hardly be under eighty . . . the bird ran this way and that in sharp angles, and finally fluttered straight at the old woman, who opened her scanty grey skirts to enclose it, dropped upon it in a bundle, and then holding it out cut its head off with an expression of vindictive energy and triumph combined. The blood and the ugly wriggling fascinated Rachel, so that although she knew that some one had come up behind and was standing beside her, she did not turn round until the old woman had settled down on the bench beside the others. (*VO*, 238–39)

Even more directly than with the goats, Rachel stands in the position of spellbound spectator. In this episode of identity and radical difference, Woolf has her protagonist watch women who seem her exact other: in age, class, work, language, and attitude. It is a scene of female community, as the women talk and work together, and also, of course, of dramatic violence. For her part, Rachel would seem to identify primarily with the chickens, since it is their "blood and ugly wriggling" that transfixes her, and since she is generally associated in the novel with suffering beasts who have in store for them a grisly fate.

Yet when the tableau is resurrected in Rachel's illness, it is the beheading women, rather than the animals, who appear. "She opened [her eyes] completely when [Terence] kissed her," in a moment of relative consciousness, "But she only saw an old woman slicing a man's head off with a knife. 'There it falls!' she murmured" (*VO* 320). It seems that the paradigm that substitutes animal violence for a human counterpart is going askew in *The Voyage Out:* far from allaying the textual pressure of presenting human vulnerability, the sequence with the chickens has lodged in Rachel's consciousness, with powerful and ongoing consequences. The images of beheading that torment her throughout her illness doubtless represent her own castrating urges, but mostly are experienced as reiterated horror, with the phrase "there it falls" announcing the returned vision. Indeed, Rachel continuously occupies all three positions: she is the woman with the knife, she is the writhing hen, and she is also the bystander, who happens in on the bloody scene and can never quite dispel it from her mind or body.

Over time, Woolf will make the presence and absorption of violence more and more oblique; the characterological emphasis, which places Rachel at the center of the novel's violent imaginings, recedes, and violence will come in less direct and reiterated spectacles. In the novel's closing pages, Woolf adumbrates what will become her central system for engaging violence, to refigure it as pattern. Here is St. John, numb after the misery and tragedy that has so fully consumed him, allowing the welcome indifference of the hotel to lull him into tranquility:

> As he sat there, motionless, this feeling of relief became a feeling of profound happiness. Without any sense of disloyalty to Terence and Rachel he ceased to think about either of them. The movements and the voices seemed to draw together from different parts of the room, and to combine themselves into a pattern before his eyes; he was content to sit silently watching the pattern build itself up, looking at what he hardly saw. (*VO*, 352)

In these closing paragraphs of her first novel, Woolf makes a complex gesture, on one hand suggesting that form (here called pattern) provides an escape and release from the pressures of suffering and death, but on the other hand, depicting this tendency in troubling terms, as St. John disengages himself, shuns intimacy, and takes pleasure in envisioning people's relations as entirely aesthetic. It is as if, in this closing movement, as St. John gazes abstractly into the hotel, Woolf gazes out onto a different horizon, of modernism's future, and also of her own career, during which she will register violence as pattern. Or rather, in a strange, hall-of-mirrors way, Woolf seems not so much to be looking forward as backward—at herself now, finishing her first novel, which in retrospect anticipates a career of striving to find the appropriate balance between expressing the great human events defined by violence (including suffering, death, loss, and physical trauma) and refiguring these in purely formal terms.

The 1920s: *Jacob's Room, Mrs. Dalloway, To the Lighthouse*

Woolf makes a dramatic gesture in this direction—of formalizing death and violence, of questioning the prominence of character, and of holding her own moves open to radical critique—in the first of her 1920s novels, *Jacob's Room*, the work that marks her major break with conventional form, soon to be followed by two novels whose distinguishing formal experiments also emerge around the dark shape of violence, *Mrs. Dalloway* and *To the Lighthouse*.[86] *Jacob's Room* makes the question of annihilating violence its central dilemma: how to write (or read, or know, or desire) a man who is, in some essential way, always on his way to death. Predetermined to die in the war, Jacob will never be given a completely full or knowable character, as if he is, from his very boyhood, on the verge of disappearing. At every level, Woolf posits her protagonist as elusive, with both major and minor characters responding to him in terms of this central, personal enigma. People "endow [him] with all sorts of qualities he had not at all," he "looked quiet, not indifferent, but like some one on a beach, watching" he is "distinguished looking," "the silent young man."[87] With all this vagueness about him, it is not surprising that characters turn to simile, noting his resemblance to different types—admirals and generals, frequently, and works of stone, relentlessly. He is "like one of those statues . . . in the British Museum" (*JR*, 67), classical, monumental marbles that are both lifelike and lifeless, and associated above all with war. Women are especially tormented by Jacob's indeterminacy, which seems to match his noncommittal habits and general inscrutability. Jacob's self-sufficiency is part of his defining quality of distance and drift; it is also, in this novel that takes the university circle as a site of remarkable intimacy and community, an aspect of that hermetic masculine culture which erects its own barriers against women. Thus they cope: Fanny Elmer, desperate during Jacob's long absence in Greece and Turkey, visits the British Museum, squeezing out a residue of recognition and satisfaction from "the battered Ulysses . . . enough to last her half

a day" (*JR*, 150), while Clara Durrant gets by on excruciating patience, reminiscent of the kind of agonized waiting suffered by Jane Austen's young women. But
this is no Austen novel; as in *The Voyage Out*, which promises us a young woman's bildungsroman knitted into the domestic novel and then shockingly kills off
both protagonist and genre, so, here, the generic preparations are in place to
bring recompense after all that waiting, yet no such consolation is forthcoming.[88]
In *The Voyage Out*, the generic end-jam comes as a cruel jolt; here, it is foreclosed
in advance and comes as no surprise at all.

For all the unknowability about Jacob, there is one thing we know from the
beginning: he will die in the war. As readers cannot fail to note, his name Flanders
alerts us from the start to the place where his life will end, and even his first name
comes freighted with loss and a sense of erasure. When "Ja-cob, Ja-cob" is called to
the young boy on the beach at the novel's opening, it does not produce the boy, any
more than it will when Bonamy repeats the gesture at the end of the novel—
"Ja-cob, Ja-cob" is a cry of loss and mourning, a communal wail in advance of and
after the calamity, akin, in some ways, to the Irish keen that simultaneously mourns
the losses of the past and prepares for the violence to come.[89] The blankness at the
center of that broken name is like many other images of emptiness in the novel—
"listless is the air in an empty room" goes the refrain—culminating in the novel's
final and eponymous room, so full of objects, missing their subject (*JR*, 31, 155). The
objects in Jacob's empty room, moreover, are themselves constructed of emptiness
and of loss, not only his old shoes, whose literal shape is one of molding to a
missing body, but also numbers of letters that litter his table. Well before the novel's
ending in Jacob's room, we have already been reminded that letters embody a kind
of death, that "to see one's own envelope on another's table is to realize how soon
deeds sever and become alien" (*JR*, 79). Bookended by death, the novel is relentless
in insisting on the determinism of this whole twisted narrative of the young life
headed for slaughter. We begin with Betty weeping, and we end with the shock of
death, almost as if the cycle is working in reverse. Betty's tears in the opening
sequence make a blot on her writing paper, suggesting from the start that grief
fundamentally thwarts and distorts writing, and yet, in one and the same passage,
Woolf suggests an aesthetic reparation, for the tears "made all the dahlias in her
garden undulate in red waves and flashed the glass house in her eyes, and spangled
the kitchen with bright knives" (*JR*, 3). If this altered form of seeing represents
some kind of compensation, it is not therefore pacific; every element that passes
before Betty's tearful eyes suggests death and violence, from the bright knives, to
the glass assaulting her eyes, to the bloodlike red waves. In this compacted gesture
at the beginning of the novel, Woolf promises a text that will enmesh its aesthetics

238 AT THE VIOLET HOUR

with violence, even as it will seek to keep alive the human aspects of loss, the widow
whose husband is under the ground, the mother whose son will die in war.

The novel is indeed thoroughly engrossed by death, presenting a catalogue of
mortality. People die; we know that, but here it happens unexpectedly—"Accidents,"
Betty rues as early as the novel's second paragraph, "were awful things"—and, at
the same time, with devastating predictability (*JR*, 3). And it is not only people
who die in *Jacob's Room*. When "a tree has fallen," it is "a sort of death in the forest,"
the land "seemed to lie dead," young children kill their butterflies, and so on (*JR*,
25, 85). Death is rigorously physical in this novel, from the sheep's jaw that mes-
merizes Jacob on the beach in the novel's impressionistic opening sequence to the
full inventory of burial and memorial apparatuses—tombstones, graveyards,
bones, bodies that are never properly mourned (like Betty's brother, who may or
may not have drowned long ago), monuments, statues, names of the dead en-
graved on all manner of stones. Tombstones are especially ubiquitous, appearing
even in such seemingly random locations as the bizarre cargo in a passing truck.
Or perhaps it is not random; Sassoon, for one, noted in his memoir that there was
something especially conspiratorial and invidious about the coffins prepared in
advance of the Somme. As Froula notes, it is as if the full history of Western civilization had made the novel's outcome—Jacob's never-narrated death in the war—
not only inevitable, but necessary: "*Jacob's Room*," she writes, "traces an inexorable
yet reasonless reduction of masculine subjects to dead bodies," as Jacob comes to
take his expected place in the line of patriarchs. All of the men are caught in the
cycle, the narrative being set by Jacob's surrogate father Captain Barfoot, who "represents the long history of collective violence into which Jacob will be conscripted"
(Froula, 70, 71).

For the novel is as consumed with war as it is with the broader category of
death. The imagery of war comes in many forms—starting with Barfoot ("he was
lame and wanted two fingers on the left hand, having served his country" [*JR*, 18]),
moving through references to admirals and other war leaders, including the various statues and monuments, inevitably oriented around war and warriors, that
constitute the public landscape of the novel, increasingly involving the visible or
aural presence of massing soldiers, and culminating in the political discourse that
brings a declaration of war. War is present by suggestion from the earliest moments in the novel, and its urgency becomes greater and greater as the novel progresses, moving from an undercurrent to a torrent, as soldiers and military music
come to predominate the scene, whether in Greece or in London. The aura is of a
gathering storm, as if the cultural history of the West had, all along, been building
to its ultimate import, fulfilling itself. The circularity of the novel's beginning and

ending suggests a narrative of violent realization (now we know what it really means to call for a boy who will never answer), and also offers a pattern for reading cultural history: at the end, we come back to the beginning. We have seen how origins were understood in the 1930s as a story of the ineluctable return to barbaric violence, and here, too, there is an unwelcome suggestion that even literary beginnings are fields of death. It was after all the Trojan War that began the Western literary tradition, providing the language, as we have repeatedly noted in this study, for fully integrating war with beauty, horror with value.

Homer's Trojan War is also the event that Simone Weil would name as founding the idea of "force," and this is pertinent to Woolf's meditation on the long and recurrent history of war in *Jacob's Room*. Metaphors of wind and darkness are especially potent as signifiers of an uncontrollable power that will destroy indiscriminately and extensively: "Violent was the wind now rushing down the Sea of Marmara between Greece and the plains of Troy . . . Now it was dark. Now one after another lights were extinguished. Now great towns—Paris—Constantinople—London were black as strewn rocks," or again, "But the wind was rolling the darkness through the streets of Athens, rolling it, one might suppose, with a sort of trampling energy of mood which forbids too close an analysis of the feelings of any single person, or inspection of features" (*JR*, 140, 142). Like Yeats in "Nineteen Hundred and Nineteen," Woolf employs wind to signify force itself, the very limit of human value, individuation, and meaning. The darkness here is obliterating, with all that is valuable in civilization flickering out and becoming extinguished (a motif we will find again in *To the Lighthouse*, *The Years*, and *Between the Acts*). Here, as in Weil's formulation, the humanity of people ("the feelings of any single person," one's "features") is leached away, as the individual is fated to become no more than a thing, a strewn rock. Woolf circles around this terrible possibility, first giving Bonamy "a very queer feeling . . . of force rushing round geometrical patterns in the most senseless way in the world" (*JR* 133). This notion of a senseless force, akin to the destroying wind, is expanded by the narrator into a communal sense of the world's workings: "It is thus that we live, they say, driven by an unseizable force. They say that the novelists never catch it; that it goes hurtling through their nets and leaves them torn to ribbons. This, they say, is what we live by—this unseizable force" (*JR*, 137). The logic of force is of inexorability, the structure is of interconnection, and the content of this iteration of force is highly suggestive, comprising battleships and submarines, "banks, laboratories, chancelleries, and houses of business," buses and policemen, even the human body itself: "When [the policeman's] right arm rises, all the force in his veins flows straight from shoulder to finger-tips; not an ounce is diverted into sudden impulses, sentimental regrets, wire-drawn distinctions" (*JR*, 136–37). If Budge the policeman will be a figure of satire in Miss La Trobe's pageant, here he embodies the trajectory of Western culture, which ends, in this particular segment, with the Durrants and their guests "talking about Germany" (*JR*, 137). Even if force may be said (ironically) to elude novelists, this passage offers something of an allegory for *Jacob's Room* itself: this text too is composed of "geometrical patterns," its own construction could be legible as a writing of "unseizable force," and the passage gestures ahead to what will become a signature of Woolf's fiction in subsequent novels, her metaphors of connection providing a diffuse unity within her novelistic worlds. And yet, for all this emphasis, Woolf's stance on the value of the insight about force is equivocal, the speaking voice ("they say") reflecting a questionable communal sentiment, of the sort that crops up often in her fiction (notably, in the brackets of *To the Lighthouse* and the villagers' idiom in *Between the Acts*), always with some combination of pointedness and banality, poetry alongside conventionality.

It cannot be accidental that Woolf takes her novel to task at the moment when it seems to express itself most directly. As the visual shifts ushered in by Betty's tears had suggested at the outset, Woolf is exceptionally conscious of the way her novel takes violence as its aesthetic engine. There is a kind of inhumanity about this novel, a cruelty even, as Woolf refuses to give Jacob any real fullness of character, the episodic and fragmentary structure of the narrative correlating with a distinctly partial, unfinished protagonist. In setting him up for violent death, it seems, Woolf has built obliteration into his very being. At its most extreme, we might even say that the novel's formal proclivities, its construction of patterns and shapes (on the page, in the way we are able to know characters, in the structure of parallelism at beginning and end), is pitted against its humanity. To keep true to its vision of people as little bits of historical flotsam, the novel leaves its own creations empty, hollow. Even Jacob's mother and best friend fall short, their closing thoughts in his empty room hardly commensurate with the loss at hand. Bonamy's cry of "Jacob! Jacob!" is poignant and powerful, but his more intellectual reaction to the room bespeaks a shocking distance from it all—"What did he expect? Did he think he would come back?"—and especially the verb, "he mused" (*JR*, 155). The novel exacts a trade, in some basic sense, between its formalism and its humanity, as suggested by the destructive wind—to recognize its power is to lose sight of (and interest in?) the individual. Such a configuration also arose at the end of *The Voyage Out*, when the ability to see people as shapes, life as pattern, offered solace from the actual facts of humanity, sickness, loss, and death, but at a cost.[90] It is especially interesting—and ironic—that this economic logic should so define a novel that takes as its starting and ending point the utterly incalculable pain and waste of a young man's death in war.

At this novel's heart is a terrible pain, a wound. It comes in part, no doubt, from the layering of the war story onto Woolf's own past, with Jacob a figure for her brother Thoby, who had died when he was only twenty-six (after a trip to Greece). It is a wound that does not show overtly, unlike the manifestly injured Captain Barfoot. Nor is it in the form, exactly, of a blot, akin to the spreading ink that mars Betty's letter and causes her visual world to ripple. It is a stain, the deep mark of violence on the world that never really disappears, as seen during a sailing and swimming expedition: "when Jacob had got his shirt over his head the whole floor of the waves was blue and white, rippling and crisp, though now and again a broad purple mark appeared, like a bruise" (*JR*, 39). These purple marks in the water will return in Woolf's writing; there is something in their shape that is fundamentally evocative of violence and threat, of the way a whole, gigantic narrative of world violence is always just beneath the surface, just out of view. In this scene of male bathing—ground zero, as Fussell has shown, for signifying the vulnerable flesh of the war's soldiers—there is much that is peaceful and beautiful, yet the benign qualities always follow a qualifier ("as if wisdom and piety had descended . . .," "as of a man calling pilchards . . .," "as if old men smoked by the door . . ." [*JR*, 39]), bespeaking an extreme tentativeness about what kind of peace can coexist in relation to the world's bruise. More, in this novel published in the same year as *The Waste Land*, Woolf gives us her own violet hour (it will not be the last in her writings): "Strangely enough," the narrator remarks after Jacob reemerges from the water, "you could smell violets, or if violets were impossible in July, they must grow something very pungent on the mainland then" (*JR*, 39). Notwithstanding the tour-guide tone (a notable instance of what Froula has nicely dubbed the "essayist-narrator" voice), there is something enormously strange and haunting in the presence of violets here, their aural proximity to violence and also the soft beauty they connote, making similar gestures to Eliot's etherealizing violet in *The Waste Land*. At one and the same time, Woolf gives us the wound and its antidote, an image of ugliness that nevertheless conjures its own sweet intensity. If the purple mark in the water allows for the enchanting powers of violet to contain and mute its meaning, however, such constructs become impossible when it is Jacob himself who is the direct and immediate victim of violence. There, it seems, the artfulness, or perhaps artificiality, of the novel's heightened form, cued to death and loss, ensures not enchantment but erasure.

To the Lighthouse inherits both of these violence protocols from *Jacob's Room*, the creation of visual patterns that obliquely express terrible episodes of violence (the bruise) as well as the development of artful formal mechanisms constructed to manage death. This latter takes its most crystallized and famous form in the actual bracketing of death and violence in the "Time Passes" section of the novel.[91] The brackets are startling, callous, and indifferent; they divert and diminish. Death, they seem to say, is not the decisive, world-changing event we have always imagined; when people die, they simply become asides. And so, after lavishing attention on Mrs. Ramsay's every turn of consciousness over the many pages of "The Window," and after evincing a spirit of deep and rich empathy for her (despite her flaws, which it also emphasizes), the novel can kill her off not only within a parenthetical, but within a dependent clause. The first reading of Mrs. Ramsay's death in brackets always provokes a gasp, calling for a necessary rereading. At the same time, the brackets have nearly the reverse effect: they create little frames around their content, setting off, memorializing, protecting. The brackets shock— as death itself always shocks—but they also temporize. They remind us that it is ultimately the survivors who require attention, death and loss mattering primarily insofar as they become part of the consciousness of the living. Moreover, the brackets are effusively literary; they align the brutal facts of life with the way such facts are known and understood, in language, in this case the formal trope of parentheses. Mrs. Ramsay is the most notable casualty of the brackets, but Prue and Andrew are also lost in such spaces, and, indeed, the "Time Passes" sequence itself is a kind of bracket, as the novel skates the thin line between its two more robust segments, "The Window" and "The Lighthouse."[92] Windows, too, have bracket-like shapes, and the novel is replete with images and scenarios—the dinner scene, Lily's painting of the purple triangle, the "shape" that, in Lily's view, Mrs. Ramsay creates as a confrontation to chaos—that replicate and enlarge the idea of encirclement as a principle and formal concept which both wards off and contains death. The bracket as encirclement signals the terrible arbitrariness of violent or sudden death, but also emphasizes basic, human strategies for living, in the face of the many ruthless reminders of mortality that structure the novel.

Mrs. Ramsay dying unexpectedly one night, Prue in childbirth, Andrew blown up in the war—these are sensational and grievous matters for the parentheses, punctuating "Time Passes" and determining its sorrowful character, as well as setting the stage for the rest of the novel, which works toward reparation, but there are other brackets with stranger content, and these offer somewhat different suggestions about the relation of literature to violent loss. In the case of the bracket that relays that Augustus Carmichael has become a famous poet, the description of his success is followed by this comment: "The war, people said, had revived their interest in poetry" (*TTL*, 134). Here the content within the parenthetical is connected to Woolf's intention in using brackets, since both are concerned with how literature makes formal sense of violence. In reference to the war and Augustus, Woolf is of course being ironic about the vogue for war poetry.[93] Though herself supportive of a number of the famous soldier poets (in her writing, through the Hogarth Press, and in the larger Bloomsbury context), there is always the possibility, with Augustus, of his being something of a lightweight—we never know—the tone of the bracketed language intimating that the surge in taste for war poetry might have been as much about easy solutions and sentimental emotionality as it was about genuinely confronting war (or reading serious poetry). If Woolf's own experiments, as in the brackets, are both challenging and surprising, the culture of war-poetry consumption, by contrast, was in many ways nostalgic and undemanding.

The brackets represent a highly self-aware aspect of the text's consciousness; artful and formal, requiring that we see them on the page as much as read them, they offer commentary on the novel's other formal moves. As windows, for instance, they comment on "The Window," enhancing its thematics, but also suggesting a certain artifice in the novel's use of such figures. Tonally, too, they are equivocal, playing a choral role, catching the contemporary idiom ("people said"), raising a question of authorial cat and mouse: can the narrator really disappear at these crucial moments, muting herself behind a general social voice? In this sense, they recall *Jacob's Room*, but in a more contained fashion, as one would expect of bracketed passages. The brackets in fact comment on themselves. Of particular significance as a metabracket, defiantly reconstituting the brackets' most notable functions, is this one, which stands as its own tiny chapter (VI) in "The Lighthouse":

> [Macalister's boy took one of the fish and cut a square out of its side to bait his hook with. The mutilated body (it was alive still) was thrown back into the sea.] (*TTL*, 180)

On one hand, this ministory, in comparison to the deaths of Mrs. Ramsay, Andrew, and Prue, is inconsequential. This is a fishing expedition, after all, and the use of fish as bait would hardly be shocking to Woolf's readership, much less to the characters of *To the Lighthouse*. Graphic and unflinching, it represents an instance of the hard-bitten, Scottish, working-class ethos that Mr. Ramsay so admires and that, as critics have noted, casts a somewhat conventional, even essentialist, eye over the local inhabitants of the island.[94]

And yet, here is the wounded body; more than any other passage in the novel, including the devastating parenthetical sequences conveying death, this one delivers the quivering flesh. With the brackets working in their distinctively doubled way, they wind a secure cordon around their content, pinioning the flesh into this one spot; at the same time, they draw special attention to that flesh, hence opening the door to its presence in the novel. What floods in is the disenchanted reality of the mortal body—the body as victim, cut and discarded by an entirely unsympathetic young man, not only mutilated but desecrated. By contrast, when Andrew and his peers are killed in the war, the novel's language remains distant and conventional, reminiscent of journalistic or official renderings of such events during the war years:

> [A shell exploded. Twenty or thirty young men were blown up in France, among them Andrew Ramsay, whose death, mercifully, was instantaneous.] (*TTL*, 133)

Among the great fictions of the war was that of the instantaneous (hence presumably painless) death, one of those lies that underlay the dialogue between the military and the civilian population. "Twenty or thirty," meanwhile, reminds us of the callousness and insincerity of contemporary reports, even those disseminating comforting fictions. Commenting, then, on the habitual language used to depict and also to evade the reality of war deaths, the passage simultaneously participates in and stands aside from such protocols. But one thing is clearly avoided, and that is the flesh.

Woolf, then, is pulling no punches; she is vividly clear in attributing to the fish's body the disenchanted ugliness that she will not give to the dead soldiers (or to Mrs. Ramsay, or Prue). She turns to the animal body—and one with distinctly nonhuman attributes—for the disenchanting presence. In the typical use of animal allegory, as we have seen, an animal stands in for a person (or for some segment of the population), the depiction of violence in a sense relieving the pressure on the human body to bear the representational weight of its own potential suffering. In *The Voyage Out*, Woolf partially revised that mode. Rachel's identification with the goats and chickens (her own conscious identification as well as the reader's identification of her with these animals) seemed to determine and demand her tragic end, as, dying of fever, she lay drowning in visions of violence reminiscent of what she had seen or imagined with the animals. In *To the Lighthouse*, the allegory would seem to operate more conventionally: we see the fish mutilated; we consider the human body subjected to violence. And yet, the effects are complex, disorienting, subversive. Coming as it does in the midst of the novel's final section, which is devoted to unification and resolution, its abrupt appearance acts as a fresh disruption, a return (formally as well as atmospherically) to "Time Passes," with its ethos of destruction, undoing, and loss. In resurrecting the earlier brackets, in turn, the fish passage raises a question as to whether those earlier scenarios were quite accurate, with regard to the wounded and suffering body. It relays that ground-zero quality that Spillers associated with the most victimized of all people (the slave woman), and thus forces the earlier, more conventional recordings into a dubious light. Too, the passage creates its own cycle of infinite regress, drawing a parallel between the fish and the text; a square or window inside the novel, like all the bracketed passages, this one announces another square, inside the fish itself. The square of fish *is* the bracket; it is a statement and metaphor for the text's stylistics. Thus the novel's signature formal mechanism for relaying death, loss, tragedy, suffering, and violence—the brackets—becomes the very essence (the destroyed body) it has been deployed, at least in part, to evade. When fish becomes flesh becomes text, it sends disenchantment hurtling back to those earlier moments when violence was relayed more evasively, through euphemistic, idiomatic language. In a strange way, in fact, the fish passage is the least contained within its bracket, perhaps because it has no real relation to the plot; purely an image—of violence, of the violated body, of the text—it effectively disperses its meaning throughout the novel.

To the Lighthouse is, after all, full of fish and fishing references (as are nearly all of Woolf's works), with Woolf evoking a Christian association of Jesus with fish, littering the novel with lines of poetry that allude to the sea and its tragedies, organizing the last section around a sea voyage (Cam looking dreamily into the water recalls Rachel Vinrace, among others), and on from there. Critics have fruitfully analyzed these rich associations, suggesting, among other things, that the fish becomes a metaphor for a subversive femininity.[95] What the square of fish flesh does is to layer something disturbing into all of this, so that the text seems infused with the threat of disenchanted violence. The body as flesh, the irruptive power of violence— these form a substratum in the novel, always partially effaced. Early in "The Window," Minta chattily conveys her fear of bulls, thinking, in vaguely Freudian terms, that "she must have been tossed in her perambulator when she was a baby" (*TTL*, 74). It is an innocuous enough reference—though one could certainly unpack the image of the bull, with its suggestions of masculine violence. When the perambulator as incubator of traumatic memory reappears, however, the sense of consequence intensifies. Now it is in James's rendering, as he tries to measure the justice of his (violent) hatred of his father:

> Suppose then that as a child sitting helpless in a perambulator, or on some one's knee, he had seen a waggon crush ignorantly and innocently, some one's foot? Suppose he had seen the foot first, in the grass, smooth, and whole; then the wheel; and the same foot, purple, crushed. But the wheel was innocent. (*TTL*, 185)

Anticipating the passage where Giles stamps on the snake and toad, this one, too, presents a searing visual image (appropriately, since it is a description of a visual image scored into the child's consciousness, recalling Joyce's language surrounding the beating of Stephen's hands). In *To the Lighthouse*, the crushed foot stands beside the fish as the only other reference to mutilated flesh, and although it comes as part of a thought experiment (hence aligned with the philosophical exercises of Mr. Ramsay and his followers), it nevertheless has real visual resonance. The word "crush" is used twice in the passage, and the structure of thought indicates a particularly intensive imaginative experience, almost as if we could see pain—start with the foot in its whole and unblemished state, see the wheel (turned weapon, as in Elaine Scarry's account of torture), then return to the foot, now smashed. Moreover, the mashed purple foot casts a shadow back on Lily's purple triangle, and on Mrs. Ramsay more generally, while the reference to infantile terror recalls Minta's less concentrated reflections about her preconscious past. Again, a seemingly contained image of the flesh forcefully impinges into other parts of the novel, staining them, we might say, the way Giles's shoes remain colored by the residue of blood.

The purple stain, in fact, becomes emblematic of Woolf's simultaneous inclusion and muting of ghastly violence in *To the Lighthouse*. Here, for instance, is a passage characteristic of the more harrowing sequences in "Time Passes," depicting a view out to sea during the war:

> [There was] something out of harmony with this jocundity and this serenity. There was the silent apparition of an ashen-coloured ship for instance, come, gone; there was a purplish stain upon the bland surface of the sea as if something had boiled and bled, invisibly, beneath. (*TTL*, 133–34)

Expanding on the suggestion made in *Jacob's Room*, "Time Passes" is full of such imagery. This passage, for instance, culminates in the novel's most wildly despairing language, where the war years are imagined as a time of brutality and idiocy, the light of reason having gone extinct, when "gigantic chaos streaked with lightning could have been heard tumbling and tossing," and "it seemed as if the universe were battling and tumbling, in brute confusion and wanton lust aimlessly by itself" (*TTL*, 134, 135). Indeed, these sequences in "Time Passes" press up against the terseness and conventionality of the bracketed passages, offering an alternative language for the violent reality both styles convey. For its part, the metaphor of the purplish stain on the water is visceral and indelible, and it also offers—along with the mutilated fish—an image for how violence operates in the novel: just out of view, only available as an "as if," yet terrible, threatening, sad, disenchanting. Connecting across the text to Mrs. Ramsay as a purple triangle and to the crushed purple of the foot, it helps to weave violence into the textual fabric.

One is reminded again, with this sequence of purple and violence, of Eliot's use of violet in *The Waste Land*. *To the Lighthouse*, it seems, has its own violet hour, its own set of associations by which purple stands for the most disenchanted, visceral effects against the body, and also for the aesthetic work marshaled on the other side: the work of submerging and muting, but also of telling and making visible, ultimately of absorbing violence into a textual world where beauty and ugliness jostle for supremacy, along the lines, perhaps, of the novel's most overt image of artistry, Lily's painting:

> Beautiful and bright it should be on the surface, feathery and evanescent, one colour melting into another like the colours on a butterfly's wing; but beneath the fabric must be clamped together with bolts of iron. (*TTL*, 171)

Those bolts of iron have always seemed an image of strength, solidity, and longevity, to counter the sweetness and light of the painting's (feminine) beauty; but in the shadow cast by the irruptive violence we have been tracking, they also sound like instruments of torture and imprisonment. Even Lily's painting, the definitive ekphrastic object among Woolf's works, and one seemingly removed and abstracted from the flesh, in its own way partakes of the violent suggestiveness made manifest in the fish and shaded in purple.

Mrs. Dalloway, similarly canonical and sharing many formal features with the later novel, offers its own bracketing structure in the person of Septimus Warren Smith.[96] It seems straightforward enough that Septimus embodies the war. He is, of course, one of its former soldiers, representative of millions of men who returned home to England (and to all of the warring nations), bearing with them many wounds, repositories of a history of violence that noncombatants might never fully understand. Shell-shocked and entirely unable to resume normal civilian life, Septimus is exemplary, too, in acting as a fundamental disruption of his home culture—hence the psycho-medical forces arrayed around him. Surrounded, moreover, by violent imagery (flames, most notably), keeping company with the dead, and sending his wife Lucrezia into a state of her own near-traumatic anxiety, Septimus is a repository for the war's violent residue, far from dissipated five years after the armistice. David Bradshaw has movingly argued that *Mrs. Dalloway* is "a commemorative text which memorializes the dead of the First World War in a variety of ways, even as it dissents from the necrolatry of the state," and, more, that "there are moments of observance in the text which are almost ceremonial in their reverence and dignity."[97] And it is not only the war: "Death is defiance," thinks Clarissa about Septimus's suicide, and as he sits on the window sill, drinking in life's pleasure for one last instant before his plunge, he stands for all the sensitive, vulnerable people for whom "human nature" is experienced as an assault, and whose difference and unhappiness cannot, it seems, be tolerated in the world.

The novel is intensely empathetic to Septimus, Clarissa's deep and spontaneous understanding of him in its last pages suggesting a form of identification that the reader herself has been asked to extend to this troubled and yet fundamentally appealing protagonist. (We might note, nevertheless, that Clarissa's response is, in its own way, limited, with a narcissistic, callous quality about it, just as Clarissa's great strength as a facilitator of human contact can also be derided, as it is by Peter Walsh, as merely the accomplishment of a "hostess.") Septimus's violent life, both representative of a generation and intensely individual, is indeed one of the most heartbreaking in modernism. The novel began as a short story, "Mrs. Dalloway in Bond Street," yet as a novel, it shaped itself equally around Septimus's madness, and the connection between his mental struggle and Woolf's own has always been noted ("I adumbrate . . . a study of insanity and suicide; the world seen by the sane and insane side by side," Woolf wrote in her diary in 1922.).[98] Still, for all his poignant imbrication in Woolf's own story, Septimus is not really an alter ego (or double, foil, or scapegoat) for her or for Clarissa, though the two are formally and imagistically linked throughout the novel; he is formed fundamentally by the war's violence, and his life tells *its* story. This type of historical ventriloquism, as Leed has shown, represents the general pattern for First World War soldiers suffering from shell shock; to decipher their symptoms was to learn how modern mass warfare writes itself into the soldier's bruised consciousness. Even beyond this, with his load of trauma, his broken and cryptic attempts at language, and his profound separation from the ordinary goings-on of the postwar world, Septimus also becomes a figure for modernism—for its states of consciousness and its formal commitments. It is a disheartening analogy, in a way; threatened by coercion on all sides and experiencing the world as assault, Septimus is thoroughly consigned, even before his suicide, to a futureless stasis.

If Septimus most distinctly embodies the threat and reality of mass violence, other traces abound in the novel. Most notable, as critics have stressed, is the entire patriarchal establishment represented by Drs. Bradshaw and Holmes. Formidable and threatening, the politico-medical structure in the novel is even more coercive in its modern form (Bradshaw) than in its conventional, Victorian style (Holmes). Either way, the insistence on "conversion" reaches beyond Septimus, indicating a form of subjection that cuts across different categories of experience and can be practiced by different kinds of would-be convertors. So we have, for instance, Miss Kilman—lonely, hungry, and herself sympathetic as a victim of wartime hysteria—bent on conversion, and in that sense exerting (or hoping to exert) a measure of force in the world. Or there is Richard, not the patriarchal boor of his namesake in *The Voyage Out*, but nevertheless carrying patronizing political overtones. Or the Bradshaws: Lady Bradshaw is not an attractive character, to be sure, but Woolf presents her, nonetheless, as another victim of her husband ("there had been no scene, no snap; only the slow sinking, water-logged, of her will into his" [*MD*, 109]). One could continue in this vein; the novel's characters, from its most central to its entirely peripheral, belong to a kind of force field, where exertions and violent tendencies from one direction can be felt, in lesser and greater degrees, in another. Given how pronounced is the imagery of connectedness in the novel—in the form of a great fabric or mist, as Clarissa variously thinks, or in the spectacles of shared watching represented by the car and airplane—such a vision of violence aptly extends the text's overall thematics.

Yet this image of violence as part of the great push and pull of the novel's (or London's) shared consciousness raises questions—as we have found so many times in this study—about its aesthetic status. In texts like "Easter 1916" and *The Waste Land*, at the moment when violence is most thoroughly and gorgeously imbricated in the literary text, it is, in a sense, lifted back out, to be seen as jagged and discomforting, demanding that we ask what the effect is or should be when the blast of destruction stands as the bedrock of a text's—or a culture's—artistic achievement. Such questions are also implied in one of *Mrs. Dalloway*'s most memorable sequences, that of the airplane sweeping through the London sky, an object of war (from the recent past and surely again in the future) marshaled in the name of a new mission, advertising toffee. It is an overdetermined sequence, a favorite of critics, this skywriting exploit that lifts the eyes of the citizens of London, in awe, confusion, and pleasure, uniting them in concentration, and momentarily diverting them from the patriotic emotions engendered by the great personage in the grey car. Remarkable in many ways—a grand theater of textuality, a comment on the artifice of all forms of signification, a wonderful evocation of how the new spaces of modern life create incredible distances and simultaneously breach them, a scene that mimics in the populace a child learning to read—the sequence also showcases just how intricately the life of violence has been absorbed into the civilian sphere. As we have seen, the airplane had already, by the 1920s, established itself as a major technological legacy of war. Even if the gesture of looking up at the sky, which dominates the sequence, had not yet assumed the full import it would have by the time of the Spanish Civil War, when it came to epitomize the perilous civilian condition, still, as Saint-Amour has stressed, the tense and involuntary move of upward looking reflects the period's dawning awareness of the air as the site of warfare, an active and fundamentally threatening sphere, whereby the city and its populace become targets for the lofty and dehumanized gaze of aerial bombers. The skywriting episode coheres the novel's mood of recent trauma, a kind of group shell shock that always registers the airplane as potential weapon, in what Saint-Amour calls a "sense of suspended, future-conditional violence" (Saint-Amour, 142).[99]

For all its violent suggestiveness, however, the airplane in the toffee sequence is acting under the rubric of commerce; it is, as Jennifer Wicke notes, "emblematic of all writing under the sign of mass culture."[100] Indeed, as Michael North has shown, Woolf based the skywriting sequence on an actual happening in June 1922—the first ever commercial skywriting in London, and hence a dramatic public spectacle, in which the airplane spelled out the name of the newspaper that also conspicuously covered the event in its pages, the *Daily Mail*. In shifting from newspapers to toffee, Woolf's airplane flaunts its commercial inconsequence all the more conspicuously.[101] Flamboyantly it displays its wares, its birdlike drops and rises undertaken in the name of a type of creation—an elemental writing, which of course spells out a familiar commodity, or, more accurately, an item of small decadence—akin, in that sense, to the chocolate éclair Miss Kilman buys at the Army and Navy store, another instance of military surplus feeding, as it were, the demands of the civilian populace. All of this belongs to a commercial London that has emerged from its wartime privations; as the novel testifies from its first page to its last, the city is flourishing, with its populace on a sustained shopping spree. The airplane, along with the Army and Navy stores, makes it literal: the war is over, the whole enormous infrastructure of war can now be reconstituted in and for commerce. Buying and selling exuberantly function as antidotes to war, affirming and creating where war devastates and destroys. So Lady Bexborough "opened a bazaar, they said, with the telegram in her hand, John, her favourite, killed" (*MD*, 3). And yet, as Lady Bexborough herself demonstrates, the war is not really over, the destruction and tragedy it spawned not so much ended as dispersed and ingrained—those habitual Woolfian forms of admitting violence into the textual consciousness. Moreover, the British economy in 1923 was not entirely booming, with industrial action and unrest having carried over from the immediate postwar period, culminating in the 1926 General Strike, an event that was much more powerful in defining the mid-1920s than is sometimes remembered. Too, as Woolf and her peers had acknowledged for years, war and commerce were never oppositional categories in the first place. The image of the war profiteer (often represented, in Britain as in Germany, as Jewish) was a staple villain in the period, with Pound, Eliot, and others imbuing their poetry, prose, and private writings with this kind of anti-Semitism. Even those wary of too-easy caricatures, much less of anti-Semitism, strongly suspected a profit motive among many powerful men endorsing and directing the war. Sassoon, in his famous Soldier's Declaration, referred both to military and capitalist aggressors when he declared: "I believe that the War is being deliberately prolonged by those who have the power to end it."[102]

Perhaps all of the novel's war-related commercial activity, then, is just another sign of the war's ultimate profitability. In a series of essays Woolf wrote for *Good Housekeeping* in the early 1930s (later collected as *The London Scene*), which represent her most sustained reflection on the city and its commerce, she shows herself highly attuned to the double nature of urban commercial exuberance. On one hand, she revels in the sheer energy of the city, and in the seeming infiniteness of its capitalist creativity, where demand and supply spin an endless spiral of production and more production, engendering not only objects but aesthetic effects. In the great London warehouses, for instance, she finds compelling patterns:

> Indefatigable cranes are now at work, dipping and swinging, swinging and dipping. Barrels, sacks, crates are being picked up out of the hold and swung regularly on shore. Rhythmically, dexterously, with an order that has some aesthetic delight in it, barrel is laid by barrel, case by case, cask by cask, one behind another, one on top of another, one beside another in endless array down the aisles and arcades of the immense, low-ceiled, entirely plain and unornamented warehouses.[103]

The pleasure of form is very clear in this passage, which mirrors in its cadences the rhythmic symmetries it describes. On the other hand, Woolf intimates that there are real costs and hidden pains standing behind the commodities at which she marvels, a whole world of work and transportation and, in some cases, exploitation demanded for every ivory umbrella handle.

Mrs. Dalloway shares this tone and spirit to an important degree. For all its tremendous pleasure in the June day—"what a lark, what a plunge"—the novel, like its protagonists (Clarissa, Septimus, Rezia), has something of the anorexic or ascetic about it, and plunging, as we know, turns out to be the sign of suicide. The skywriting, in its way, is an excessive frivolity, marking a disequilibrium between the magnificence and power of the airplane, on the one hand, and the lightness and inconsequentiality of this one's particular aim, on the other. As Yeats and Wilfred Owen have each phrased it, in reference to the great violent events of the times, "was it for this . . .?" Once again, it is this crux relation between balance and excess that motivates the modernist text's most spellbinding formal maneuvers around violence; the airplane becomes an emblem of that desire, and also of its always falling short. For all its significatory power, the flight leaves in its wake a vague aura of disappointment and uncertainty (Clarissa's query "What are they looking at?" is the last thing we hear about the plane [MD, 29]). The airplane straddles the line between the view that culture can absorb and redirect the technologies of violence (somewhat akin to Leonard Woolf's political stance a decade later that war and violence need not be the drivers of human history) and a bleaker notion that there always lurks, in these objects, the reality of killing and death, just as Septimus reads in every tree fiber or car window the signs and signals of his dead war friends.

By the mid-1920s, Woolf had come to see the airplane as a primary player in the whole dialectic of war, violence, commerce, and aesthetics. *Orlando*, too, her last novel of the decade, features an airplane at a critical moment, at the very end of the novel. Delivering Shel to the modernized Orlando, the plane shoots in, melodramatically and self-consciously playing the deus ex machina. In the twentieth century, Woolf seems to say, we turn to the airplane as our ultimate metaphor, our combined image of savior and destroyer, our overdetermined technological fetish. For all the undertones of war that *Mrs. Dalloway*, especially, resuscitates, the evocations surrounding the airplane in these 1920s novels are also of gusto and confidence; though intimated as a looming threat in the world, the airplane nevertheless operates largely as an expression of literary exuberance (in that sense, it is akin to Conrad's treatment of dynamite, where, we recall, the extravagance of Stevie's death became an occasion for literature, after considering the limits posed by an exploded body, to show its dazzle). Yet in Woolf's three major works of the 1930s, this tone of aviational pleasure evaporates; in each, the airplane, true to the period's zeitgeist, becomes an image of the complete vulnerability of the civilian population. In fact, if the skywriting in *Mrs. Dalloway* was an instance of Woolf's textual dance around violence, in these later works the airplane operates, conversely, as that which *creates* the urgent need for literary strategies around violence, so direct, severe, and disenchanting is its threat. Each novel features the violent realities of the airplane: *The Years* in an air raid sequence set in London during the First World War, *Three Guineas* in the Spanish photographs, and *Between the Acts* in the fleet of planes that burst across the sky near the end of the novel, bifurcating the Reverend Streatfield's sentence as he entreats the village audience to donate money to his church. Woolf's airplanes now fully express the 1930s imaginary, their artistry or literary flair deeply compromised by what they have come to do.

Overwhelming Force: *The Years, Three Guineas, Between the Acts*

In *The Years*, a novel inflected by the Spanish Civil War and the contemporary mood of impending catastrophe, the air raid sequence expresses two decades of gestating discomfort about what it means to be targeted by bombers. The scene is set in 1917, as the characters—Eleanor, Sara, Maggie, Renny, Nicholas—gather for dinner; disrupted by the sirens, they migrate to the cellar, then reascend after the all clear, resuming their evening. On one hand, the characters are nonchalant about the air raid, proclaiming themselves unbothered, slipping easily back into wonted activities once the raid has ended, concerned primarily about whether the sleeping children were roused by the noise. On the other hand, the raid cuts apart and disrupts the life of the group: "there had been a complete break," the narrator declares, "none of them could remember what they had been saying."[104] As in *A Sketch of the Past*, where the war continually intervenes and thwarts the possibility of writing (even as it acts as an inducement to write the memoir), here, too, the presence of the Germans overhead severs the stream of conversation and thought, an idea that will be made literal by the squadron of planes in *Between the Acts*. In keeping with this notion of disruption, moreover, there is the serious question of whether these raids are, in fact, lodging themselves in people's consciousness. As Sara notes of the sleeping children: "But they may have dreamt" (*TY*, 294). These experiences of generalized violence might find a home deep in the psyche, they might live there unrecognized, they might be obliquely felt and expressed. The life of dreams perhaps betrays what the stiff upper lips of civilians, responding to a culture of wartime resolve, aim to disavow, the power of violence to traumatize, infiltrate, shape.

Ultimately, the raid poses itself as a question: Does it change, disrupt, and distort? Or does it leave everyone, finally, exactly the same? Sara notes, and the text confirms, that the old conversations do in fact return (endlessly), hence perhaps overriding the immediate sense of "complete break." And no one can answer the question of dreaming. The sequence might also be understood in the context of the contemporary debate about whether war is or is not endemic to human nature, whether it fundamentally defines us or is, instead, an aberration that can be eliminated by a supreme effort at international cooperation. Much in the novel certainly tends in the direction of annihilation and chaos, as in the preamble to the year 1908, which again portrays a cold wind as a metaphor for intense violence: "Uncreative, unproductive, yelling its joy in destruction . . . Triumphing in its wantonness it emptied the streets; swept flesh before it; and coming smack against a dust cart standing outside the Army and Navy Stores, scattered along the pavement a litter of old envelopes; twists of hair; papers already blood smeared . . ." (TY, 146). Its destruction imagined almost as intent, the brutal wind, like its counterpart in *Jacob's Room*, recalls Yeats's leveling wind as nightmare in "Nineteen Hundred and Nineteen," suggesting an aura of frightening force, human in power yet without agency. In terms of the air raid, Renny, a Frenchman and the most politically engaged person in the room, betrays a sentiment of savage anger during the raid itself (he is a bit like Giles from *Between the Acts* in that regard). Nevertheless, Renny summarizes the experience in unemotional terms: "I have spent the evening sitting in a coal cellar while other people try to kill each other above my head" (TY, 295). His summation is resigned, equivocal, noncommittal. There is irony in his statement, yet also a tone of unreality. It suggests, in its resignation and impersonality, that these insane violent happenings cannot be addressed in any meaningful way by the civilians in their cellars, much less eradicated by people working above ground for peace.

Notably, Renny characterizes the killing in detached terms, with "other people" aiming to kill "each other" rather than targeting him and his family, and, more generally, the novel seems intent on placing violence at a slight remove from its characters, or, better, on seeing it in a constant interchange with more sustaining forces, such as beauty and calm. So Sara and Maggie, at home in their flat in a rough London neighborhood, hear harsh sounds from their window, but these are suffused with loveliness: "The night was full of roaring and cursing; of violence and unrest, also of beauty and joy" (TY, 189). On the evening of the air raid, too, Eleanor experiences the dark London night, counterintuitively, in especially friendly terms: "She had a sense of immensity and peace—as if something had been consumed" (TY, 298). And the novel itself, which, like *Orlando*, ends at the "present day," closes in stunningly optimistic terms: "The sun had risen, and the sky above the houses wore an air of extraordinary beauty, simplicity and peace" (TY, 435). It is a breathtaking closure (for a novel whose actual year of completion was 1936[105]), with its allusion to Wordsworth's sublime 1802 poem about the beauty of the London morning, "Lines Composed upon Westminster Bridge," a canonically romantic image of the city at peace.[106] As Favret has shown, however, Romanticism's idiom of domestic calm is often writ as only one half of the complex interplay with distant war; Woolf's channeling of Wordsworth is perhaps closer in spirit to that earlier peace than might at first be suspected—a one-year lull in the Napoleonic wars, to be followed, in 1803, by the threat of invasion. Such expressions of peace might always carry war in them, incipiently and tragically. Or we might read these last lines in *The Years*, whose tone is virtually the opposite of the closing lines of Woolf's subsequent novel, *Between the Acts*, as a wish or plea, as when the group in the air raid lift their glasses to "a New World," or when, in the culminating pages of the novel, narrator and characters welcome the literal dawn and herald the new day.

For all their poignancy, such performatives have about them a certain strained willfulness, a consciousness of their fictionality. In the case of the air raid toast, Woolf alludes to the spirit of utopianism that, in both the First World War years and the 1930s, relied on the paradox that war could—indeed was needed to—make peace: war to end wars, as we have seen. It was a structure of thinking that her novels might relay, given how widespread was its logic, but could never entirely endorse. In the novel's last lines, moreover, it is difficult not to read the still and peaceful city as all the more vulnerable and open to attack, that moment of suspension captured in Capa's photographs of civilians looking up at the sky. The novel itself looks up at the sky, as the characters literally look out the window at the dawn. Woolf's Wordsworthian echoes seem, if not ironic, then deeply sad, a reaching out and back towards the kind of calm splendor and tranquil strength that in 1936 could never replicate what one might have claimed for London in 1802, when Wordsworth could describe the city's openness to the sky—however this might invite a quiet and oblique engagement with a distant war—as a central feature of its majesty, and could do so, moreover, from the vantage of a location of special interest to those who might want to bomb the city, a bridge.

Woolf's treatment of air warfare in *The Years* is consistent with the novel's larger approach to violence, which it both admits and radically denies. With its chronicling of the Pargiter family over a half century, the novel invites a focus on major historical events, such as wars and the deaths of world leaders; death, especially, functions as the selection principle and organizing motif of the historical span. The Irish national drama plays an ongoing role in the novel's imaginary, with Parnell's death echoing in ways that evoke Joyce and other Irish modernists. And the Pargiter women, in their different styles, stand up against the brutality of their times. Rose, an obscure member of the Woolfian feminist pantheon, is a defiant suffragist; as a young woman, she goes to jail for breaking windows. Delia champions the Irish cause (and mourns Parnell). And as the novel moves into the 1930s, Kitty, always an enemy of raw power, makes her case against force, which is becoming more and more ubiquitous and endemic. These women offer voices of small resistance, tinny echoes in the large public sphere. As Peggy, one of the younger generation, thinks:

> But how can one be "happy," she asked herself, in a world bursting with misery? On every placard at every street corner was Death; or worse—tyranny; brutality; torture; the fall of civilisation; the end of freedom. We here, she thought,

are only sheltering under a leaf, which will be destroyed. And then Eleanor
says the world is better, because two people out of all those millions are
"happy." (*TY*, 388)

Though the novel quickly moves from these late reflections towards its tenuous af-
firmation of peace, Peggy's question might stand for the text's own: what is the value
or truth of focusing on one person, one family even, given the greater panorama of
suffering and brutality engulfing the world? It is a question of and for the novel in
general, the genre that has done the most to lift the fates of "two people" out of the
"millions," insisting, at its very core, that the happiness of one pair does matter.
Governed by this spirit of self-annihilation, *The Years* anticipates *Between the Acts*
in suggesting that, with tyranny, brutality, and torture announcing themselves on
every corner, the novel is resigning, unable any more to assert its fundamental,
defining principles. The threat of real futility is near, literature itself looking "like a
serpent that swallowed its own tail" (*TY*, 129).

At the same time, the Woolf who wrote *A Room of One's Own*, with its famous
denunciation of novels that preach political creeds (or "Modern Fiction," or "The
Leaning Tower"), even in late 1936 cannot bend her novel under the sweep of force.
Though she gestures towards the massive movements of violence defining "the
years," for the most part, her strategy is gamely to carry on with the novelistic
function she has undertaken, to tell the family story. She is a bit like Eleanor herself, in that sense—Eleanor, who despite a cramped and virginal life, too much of
which is spent caring for her father, has a real energy and spirit which carry her
through the decades almost triumphantly. Moreover, the cry for peace at the end
of the novel might be taken as a plea for the novel itself, premised as all are (and
most literally this one) on the idea of new days, on the particular aspect of willing
suspension of disbelief that presses us to imagine continuity past the moment of
the book's closure. Yet the novel's treatment of violence is not solely a matter of the
oscillation or competition between acknowledging mass violence and defiantly
refusing to succumb to it; instead, Woolf creates small, almost invisible pockets
where violence can reside and tell its story. If *To the Lighthouse* perfected the
strategy of bracketing—that is, of giving a view to violence that is framed or surrounded, even as that view sheds light intermittently on swaths of the novel, in a
manner akin to the lighthouse beam—here Woolf takes that motif a step further,
condensing the place of violence into extremely packed spaces, where its history
can be read only by scrutinizing.

The strategy begins, not surprisingly, with the body, and especially with the
hand. After its ritual description of the weather, the novel opens with "Colonel

Abel Pargiter," patriarch of the family, "sitting after luncheon in his club talking." The setting is a hermetic world of Victorian masculinity, where "his com-
panions in the leather armchairs were men of his own type, men who had been
soldiers, civil servants, men who had now retired," and who "were reviving with
old jokes and stories now their past in India, Africa, Egypt . . ." (*TY*, 4). As one
might expect from this description, loaded with those Victorian habits, obses-
sions, and blind spots that so infuriated Woolf and her peers, Abel belongs fully
to Woolf's parents' generation—yet without her particular family's intellectual
proclivities—in which women provide domestic comforts for men at the ex-
pense of their own fulfillment, and where a patriarchal atmosphere reigns in the
home, stifling and partially silencing the children. An unattractive figure, with
his mistress (Mira) and his military, colonial past, Abel would seem to offer a
starting point from which future characters can only improve and bloom, as
indeed they do.

And yet, Colonel Pargiter is most memorable for an injury that marks the violent tendencies of his era onto his own body, a mutilated hand. The hand seems to
invade the early portions of the novel, mentioned no fewer than three times in its
first few pages. And invasion seems the right metaphor, as the hand's initial appearance comes in the context of Abel's sexual advances on Mira: "The Colonel
began to stroke her neck. He began fumbling, with the hand that had lost two
fingers, rather lower down, where the neck joins the shoulders," in a phrase that
will be repeated verbatim on the next page (*TY*, 8, 9). The injured hand functions
in a variety of simultaneous registers: it marks Abel as both a representative and a
victim of his aggressive past; it brings home the colonial violence of "India, Africa,
Egypt"; it links that colonial mode of force with Abel's unsettling relationship with
Mira; it acts as a visual reminder of the violability of the body, hence the potential
for disenchanted violence; and it recalls, in its truncated way, the "withered stumps
of time"—and of limbs—that had marked so many injured men from the First
World War. Abel, let us be clear, was no First World War conscript or deluded
volunteer, no victim in the sense that Woolf's generation understood the soldiers
of their era to be, having received his injury instead in the quintessential war of
colonial force: "He had lost his two fingers of the right hand in the Mutiny, and the
muscles had shrunk, so that the right hand resembled the claw of some aged bird"
(*TY*, 13). The Mutiny (or first Indian war of independence, in 1857, when the British
responded to a rebellion initiated by sepoys with a policy of extreme repression)
exemplifies the mid-Victorian violence spree around the world, Abel's two lost
fingers a pittance in comparison with the harsh tactics employed by the British in
stamping out the insurgency. Nevertheless, Abel's injury remains an almost unique

physical symbol in Woolf's works, which strenuously avoid almost any inclusion of physical scarring and deformation of its primary characters (Captain Barfoot presents one other such character, and incidental figures with mutilated or otherwise deformed bodies make brief appearances here and there). Abel's own children, following their father's (and Woolf's) lead, keep quiet about the injury, though "the shiny knobs of the mutilated fingers fascinated Rose" (*TY*, 13).

The shrunken hand, the shiny knobs, the missing fingers: when they appear, they seem to bring a violent past flooding back into the novel, akin to the square of fish in *To the Lighthouse*, and the injury, moreover, reproduces and disperses itself across the text, with scarred hands cropping up repeatedly. Mrs. Porter, the elderly woman whom Eleanor visits as part of her charity work, has hands that are "knotted and grooved like the gnarled roots of a tree," and those hands, symbolic of her physical pain, seem to burn into Eleanor's shoulder, where she grips the younger woman (*TY*, 99). Within the Pargiter family, there is, first, a scar on Morris's hand ("the white scar where he had cut himself bathing"), especially visible at his most public moments, such as when Eleanor views him admiringly at the law courts (*TY*, 110, 202). More troubling are the white marks on Rose's wrist, testament to an early attempt at suicide. It is a kind of family inheritance, the wounded hand, a signal of a whole violent landscape—colonial force, sexual power relations, the tremendous stifling of women—yet one that is left undernarrated, just as the Pargiter children remain mute on the subject of their father's deformity. In focusing on the hand, of course, Woolf taps into a rich field for the symbolism of violence. In the rector's beating of Stephen Dedalus's hands, as we saw, hands signaled both fracture and healing, as Joyce posited the origin of language and creativity at the moment when Stephen was beaten on his hands, unjustly and painfully. In *The Years*, the injured hand is also the injur*ing* hand (Stephen and the rector conflated), closing the circle. The Colonel's mutilated hand is first seen in the scenario with Mira, where its groping action and the odd decapitating imagery ("where the neck joins the shoulders") hold undertones of an unspecified violence; Mrs. Parker is very much a victim of social and economic inequality, and she also transmits her pain to Eleanor; Rose's self-inflicted wound layers infliction into victimization; even Morris, though nothing like his father as a symbol of patriarchal power, shows his scar most notably at the courts, where he forms part of the same judicial establishment whose submerged violence Woolf does so much to expose in *Three Guineas*, a companion text to *The Years*. Even Kitty, who spends her life deploring force, always makes the same gesture when she thinks about it: she lifts her hand and slams it down. All touch, the novel seems to indicate, is violent touch.

Yet perhaps the most significant inheritor of the colonel's wound is an unlikely figure, Sara. One of Abel's nieces—cousin to Eleanor and the other Pargiter children— Sara is in some ways akin to Isa in *Between the Acts*. Like Isa, she lives in her own lyrical world, creating a running, private poem out of everything she observes and experiences. Like Isa, too, she has a deep sensitivity to violence in the world, even as she is, in a sense, protected by her thick wall of private consciousness. Markedly unlike Isa, Sara is not integrated into the normative life of wife and mother (there is no stockbroker husband, no family home); as a young woman, she lives with her sister, and, after Maggie's marriage, seems to float alone through London, singing her private melodies. Significantly, the first thing we hear of Sara, before we enter her rich interior world or watch her pirouetting, is that she has a "slight deformity . . . She had been dropped when she was a baby; one shoulder was slightly higher than the other" (*TY*, 122). The deformity upsets Abel, makes him "squeamish"—an interesting bit of narcissistic failure to self-identify, since, of course, it reflects back on his own injured body. Like Minta in *To the Lighthouse*, who traces her fear of bulls to a fantastical event in infancy, here the crippling moment also happened in babyhood, though this one is more real, and more unsettling. Sara's mother may have a special attachment to her because of her injury, yet the event and its ramifications remain shrouded. "But they might have dreamt," Sara will say of her sister's children in the air raid, and she, too, might trace her psychic life to whatever kinds of childhood trauma both led to and followed from her injury. Perhaps; yet none of this is really allowed into the novel, which almost entirely circumvents Sara's deformity, as she herself is said to skip happily along as a child, unbothered by it.

Instead, the novel registers the shocks of violence, such as the one suggested by Sara's body, in strange ripples. The wounded hands are passed along, injured and injuring, but only seen in glances—Morris, for instance, shows his scar when he moves his hand across his brow, or in some other similar gesture, so that one glimpses it only fleetingly. And for Sara, her injury is best adumbrated in a startling and oblique passage:

> She curled herself up with her back to the window. She had raised a hump of pillow against her head as if to shut out the dance music that was still going on. She pressed her face into a cleft of the pillows. She looked like a chrysalis wrapped round in the sharp white folds of the sheet. Only the tip of her nose was visible. Her hip and her feet jutted out at the end of the bed covered by a single sheet. (*TY*, 144–45)

It is a strange description, difficult to envision. I find in this odd moment—which follows upon an evening spent reading *Antigone*, a quintessential text of violence for Woolf throughout her career—an extrapolating or dispersing of Sara's injury onto her surroundings. Consider, for instance, this list of words: "hump," "cleft," "sharp," "jutted." The first of these alerts us to the connection with Sara, her own hump, while the others each suggest wounds and wounding. It is a deeply uncomfortable sequence (even if it describes an act of comfort, going to sleep), registering the facts of violence as a series of jagged points and clefts. It evokes death, with the white sheet suggesting a shroud—and it points back to Sara's reading of *Antigone*, since she had focused in her reading on the dead body, whose consecration is Antigone's mission and the source of her defiance of the state. At the same time, the simile in the passage is of incipient life, in the image of the chrysalis. Indeed, the intertwining of death or wounding imagery with the promise of new life mimics what the novel as a whole also confronts, whether in the air raid sequence or in the novel's closing pages, when it simultaneously presents the brute facts of violence and tyranny, and raises its voice in a hymn to peace. Violence in *The Years*, in these ways, is much like one of its other spectral manifestations, an owl with a mouse in its talons that swoops in and out of vision during one of the Pargiter family reunions. Simultaneously everywhere and nowhere, it impinges and retreats, it is absorbed and enfolded, it resides on the body and then hides itself, it juts out and is re-covered.

In *The Years*, Woolf creates an expansive panorama of violence, even as she disperses and mutes it, lifting her voice to a tenuous peace; in *Three Guineas*, written just after and growing out of a similar set of preoccupations, Woolf offers her most direct account of force, in a vision of Western culture as a product of deep and unending violence. Violence is right on the surface in *Three Guineas*, as attested by the narrator's opening encounter with the Spanish photographs. As we have seen, the photographs signal disenchanted violence; they belong to the same representational family as Friedrich's visual archive of wounded veterans, asking to be taken as nothing more nor less than records of war's brutal attack on the flesh. In a very real sense, the photographs set the task of *Three Guineas*. To answer their visual challenge ("a crude statement of fact addressed to the eye"), to create a complementary idiom that will work alongside their gruesome visuality in making the case against war, to turn the eyes away from the maimed bodies and landscapes without in any way reenchanting war and violence—these are the imperatives of Woolf's polemic.[107] The text will meet them in terms decidedly its own. Taking on the great questions about violence of its day, *Three Guineas* answers both directly and stylistically, through its patterns.[108]

As Woolf's scrapbooks attest, *Three Guineas* is the product of years of reckoning with her culture's often skewed and self-denying attitude towards war and other violent events and tendencies.[109] The foundational catastrophe for Woolf is the First World War, whose legacy is everywhere in *Three Guineas*. Wilfred Owen provides the book's primary terms for critiquing war ("war is inhuman . . . war is . . . insupportable, horrible and beastly"), and it is the First World War that gives the text its overall understanding that war is an unmitigated catastrophe, not only for its participants but for the whole of civilization (*TG*, 12). Very much in keeping with its era, moreover, *Three Guineas* imagines the world situation of the late 1930s as promising a repetition and intensification of that earlier slaughter. In *Three Guineas*, Woolf engages directly with the theorizing of violence that we have seen to preoccupy her contemporaries, rising to the demand of creating new formal mechanisms to match the violent conditions of the times. She takes on such contemporary questions as whether war is endemic to humankind (shifting the terms to argue that if war is inherent, it is only so in men) and whether there is anything valuable about war (we know Woolf's answer to that one); she sets the scene around the violent events in Spain, specifically the ruin left by aerial bombardment; and she tackles, in especially creative terms, the problems of action and passiveness.[110]

Among the organizing antinomies of *Three Guineas*, there is no opposition more ringing than the central one dividing violence from peace—or, put differently, dividing the purveyors of convention (which, in this text, is a form of violence) from those who experiment. On one side are the fathers. The tyrant or dictator is the prototype:

> He is a man certainly. His eyes are glazed; his eyes glare. His body, which is braced in an unnatural position, is tightly cased in a uniform. Upon the breast of that uniform are sewn several medals and other mystic symbols. His hand is upon a sword. He is called in German and Italian Führer or Duce; in our own language Tyrant or Dictator. And behind him lie ruined houses and dead bodies—men, women, and children. (*TG*, 142)

The portrait is exact, another mimed photograph in the text, along with the description of the Spanish photos and the inclusion of a raft of actual pictures of public figures in their fancy getups. This one, like the description of the Spanish photographs, would be highly familiar in 1938, a composite image of the tyrant from across Europe (and the globe, in our time). And yet the primary argument of *Three Guineas* is that the dictator represents an extreme case only; his avatar is everywhere in Western culture, not only there (Germany, Italy, Russia), but here, in Britain, the father in nearly every home, the judge, the university don, even the pacifist (as we have seen, with Joad, one of the period's most prominent pacifists, showing his stripes in *Three Guineas* as a hypocritical sexist). All patriarchs share with the dictator a deep-seated love of power. Behind the dictator lie dead bodies and destroyed landscapes; behind these less obviously threatening men lie subjugated women and girls, a whole history of silencing and thwarting. Crucially for this text, that is, when it comes to violence, "the public and the private worlds are inseparably connected . . . the tyrannies and servilities of the one are the tyrannies and servilities of the other" (*TG*, 142).

On the other side are the experimenters, those who challenge and forego the dominant desires of power and prestige, who act through unique and creative channels, who eschew acclaim and self-promotion, who punch through the wall of conventional thinking to make real changes, even if only on a tiny scale. Though *Three Guineas* is a generally downbeat text, the word "depressing" figuring regularly (as in "these are the facts and they are depressing"), when it comes to the idea of experimenting Woolf is full of optimism, even joy. Here, for instance, is her utopia of an experimental university, a place of learning that would jettison all of those habits and proclivities that she believes contribute to war:

> Obviously then, it must be an experimental college, an adventurous college. Let it be built on lines of its own. It must be built not of carved stone and stained glass, but of some cheap, easily combustible material which does not hoard dust and perpetrate traditions. Do not have chapels. Do not have museums and libraries with chained books and first editions under glass cases. Let the pictures and the books be new and always changing. Let it be decorated afresh by each generation with their own hands cheaply. . . . It should teach the arts of human intercourse . . . The aim of the new college, the cheap college, should be not to segregate and specialize, but to combine. It should explore the ways in which mind and body can be made to co-operate; discover what new combinations make good wholes in human life. (*TG*, 33–34)

The passage radiates with utopian promise, with pleasure and hope, energized by verbs like "combine," "explore," "co-operate" and "discover," and conveying the exhilaration of adventure. Even in this partial excerpt, the word "new" is used three times. One almost feels the relief in throwing off the old, dusty cover of tradition. At the same time, Woolf has her dogma, her "do not" and "do not"; this is no anarchic celebration of individual creativity. In both the emphasis on newness and in her polemical rejection of convention, the passage recalls one of her most famous manifestos, "Modern Fiction," which exhorted writers to do away with all the literary conventions ("no plot, no comedy, no tragedy, no love interest or catastrophe in the accepted style") to find their way to "life" by following new rules.[111] In the fifteen years that separate these two visions of experimentation, however, much has changed; there it was writers—working in their own names, with posterity in mind—who were called upon to make it new, while here it is an anonymous group of women, who reject fame and influence; there it was writing, that singularly individuated profession, that offered a route to intellectual revolution, while here we have an institution, with bricks and mortar.

Above all, what has changed, I think, is that by the 1930s Woolf had been betrayed by her male modernist peers, many of whom had come to embrace fascism and other authoritarian ideals. Unquestionably, the literary clarion call of "Modern Fiction" was answered (and also anticipated) by a host of writers, many of them men, many connected to Woolf's circle; and yet, in their masculinism and adulation of force, these same artists—by the logic of *Three Guineas*—have contributed to the brutal, violent condition of the world. Woolf never names Eliot, Pound, Lawrence, Yeats, or any comparable writers in *Three Guineas* (though she does offer her habitual dismissal of Wells). And yet it is abundantly clear, in passages such as the utopian university description, that she has transferred her hopes for radical protest and creative transformation from her (male) modernist peers— those brave anticonventionalists of the early 1920s out to change the world with their pens—to an imaginary cast of anonymous people, mostly women, whose work will be prosaic rather than dazzling, collaborative rather than individual, indeed almost invisible. Her decision in the text, moreover, to embrace a number of Victorian women (Gertrude Bell, Mary Kingsley, Josephine Butler, even Florence Nightingale is named)—women who opposed the vote in their day and, in the case of Bell, played a role, through her work in Iraq, in cementing British imperial power, who for most of Woolf's career stood for all that needed to be overcome and superseded in her parents' generation—this choice suggests, again, that Woolf is looking for new alignments, backing away from her signature celebration of her artist peers in favor of a more equivocal tradition of women, most of whom could not reasonably be termed "modern."

In this revaluing of experiment, Woolf tackles the question of action, developing her own model of activism that, she hopes, will succumb neither to the noxious quality of "action" as it was imagined in this period nor to the paradoxes of pacifism. As is often discussed, the final turn in *Three Guineas* is toward what Woolf dubs a society of "outsiders," those whose disaffiliation from nation and other conventional sites of loyalty positions them to oppose and critique patriarchal and patriotic values, to make small cracks in the wall of masculinism and subjugation. Woolf cites several such efforts—a mayor who refuses to knit socks for soldiers, a sports team for women whose leader refuses to award trophies—actors on small stages, working in modest ways to confront entrenched and powerful forces in their culture. In this call to outsiders, Woolf works out a complex logic around action. It would seem that *Three Guineas* is all for activation—as we have seen with the Spanish photographs, or, for instance, in passages like this one: "We who have looked so long at the pageant in books, or from a curtained window watched educated men leaving the house at about nine-thirty to go to an office, returning to the house at about six-thirty from an office, need look passively no longer" (*TG*, 61). Tied to the servile and confined life of the private home, female passivity is a thing of the past, to be joyfully discarded as women become active members of the public world.

But, of course, Woolf quickly complicates the story, questioning the value of joining men in their professional work (following the procession, as she terms it), and with that revaluation comes a recalibration of passivity. The text is full of calls for renunciation—of honors, money, privilege, power, fame—and, perhaps surprisingly, points repeatedly to the life of Jesus as a salutary example of such willing sacrifice. And yet, despite a leaning in this direction, hers cannot be entirely the logic of paradox: that in passivity there is the greatest action, in renunciation the greatest power. Woolf does call for a kind of active passivity or passive activism, but the intention is to confront in these formulations the logic of violence itself, by slipping out of its dominant formal arrangements. The text thus describes a variety of measures one might take in the quest to answer the Spanish photographs. Some are direct in relation to war (for women not to adulate war, never to shame men who refuse to fight), others oblique. There are exhortations to writers, to educators, to those working in the name of peace or women's equality, and to ordinary citizens, who in *Three Guineas* are credited with having perhaps the greatest potential for pressing change, albeit in latent form: to opt out, abstain, and refuse, and hence, in their own way, to pressure, demonstrate, and perform. Above all, she invites all of her readers to experiment; perhaps by creating a form of passive activism her experimenters will "break the ring, the vicious circle, the dance round and round the mulberry tree, the poison tree of intellectual harlotry" (*TG*, 99).

Indeed, as this passage reminds us, the dominant characteristic of violence in *Three Guineas* is that it comes as repetition, an endless, regressive experience of return. As Woolf asks, in her first iteration of the cyclical motif:

> If we encourage the daughters to enter the professions without making any conditions as to the way in which the professions are to be practiced shall we not be doing our best to stereotype the old tune which human nature, like a gramophone whose needle has stuck, is now grinding out with such

disastrous unanimity? "Here we go round the mulberry tree, the mulberry tree, the mulberry tree. Give it all to me, give it all to me, all to me. Three hundred millions spent upon war." (*TG*, 59)

This rhythm, harkening back not only to a children's nursery rhyme but also to Eliot (who borrowed it for "The Hollow Men"), returns over and over in the text, with emendations and alterations, always stressing the same thing: the incessant quality of violence, its similarity across time and space, so that one sees the continuities among all forms of tyrannical behavior, all forms of suppression. Violence is always raw and unique, but when looked at through the prism of history, it is also fundamentally numbing, almost hypnotically repetitive. And so, as the text reaches its close and the brutality of the contemporary moment again rises to the forefront, now audible where it had been visible in the case of the Spanish photographs,

> . . . we seem to hear an infant crying in the night, the black night that now covers Europe, and with no language but a cry, Ay, ay, ay, ay . . . But it is not a new cry, it is a very old cry. We are in Greece now . . . That is the voice of Creon, the dictator. . . . And he shut [Antigone] not in Holloway or in a concentration camp, but in a tomb . . . It seems, Sir, as we listen to the voices of the past, as if we were looking at the photograph again, at the picture of dead bodies and ruined houses that the Spanish Government sends us almost weekly. Things repeat themselves it seems. Pictures and voices are the same today as they were 2,000 years ago. (*TG*, 141)

This is really the crux of *Three Guineas*: to expose the deep affinities among forms of violence (Creon and Hitler, the dictator abroad and the father at home, old wars and new ones). And like Sophocles, for whom the cyclicality of human life is the basis for tragedy, Woolf presents these commonalties and cycles across history as totally crushing, something like *The Waste Land*'s invocation of these repeated narratives of brutal violence that have always made a waste of human experience.

It is thus especially significant that, in constructing her own experiment in opposing war, Woolf adopts a similar set of patterns. The text is, firstly, very repetitive. It employs certain phrases and expressions over and over (Owen's "beastliness, insupportability, and folly of war," the mulberry tree rhyme), it circles back to particular narratives or tableaus (the Spanish photographs, *Antigone*), and its overall structure is itself a form of modified repetition (the three appeals, one guinea for each). Readers who are not fond of *Three Guineas* might indeed describe Woolf's text as itself sounding a bit like that broken gramophone. If *Three*

Guineas goes in circles, however, it does so—like each iteration of the mulberry tree rhyme, or like the answer to each solicitation—in a spirit of modification. Hence the odd disjunction at the end of each iteration of the rhyme. If the ouroboros from *The Years* or the snake/toad mass in *Between the Acts* makes vivid the idea of circle-as-futility, *Three Guineas* wants to find some kind of revisionary energy in these patterns of circling and cycling violence. "Ignorant as we are of human motives and ill supplied with words," Woolf writes of historical change and progress, "let us then admit that no one word expresses the force which in the nineteenth century opposed itself to the force of the fathers. All we can safely say about that force was that it was a force of tremendous power" (*TG*, 138). Force against force: this is the only possibility, and yet, of course, the positive force in question must be entirely unlike its homonym; it must be nonviolent and noncoercive. (We might note how much repetition there is even within a single sentence, as here, with the word "force" used four times.)

What Woolf imagines, finally, as the counterpoint to the endless circle of subjugation is a counter-circling, which involves its own form of destruction ("a force of tremendous power") but in a spirit that is liberatory and inclusive. There are several such visions in the text, responses-in-kind to the dominant pattern of recurring violence. They answer and complicate the mulberry tree, repeating its structure but undoing its meaning. So, for instance, the experimental college passage ends with a vision of deconstruction, as both actual and ideal models of the university are sent to the pyre:

> "Take this guinea and with it burn the college to the ground. Set fire to the old hypocrisies. Let the light of the burning building scare the nightingales and incarnadine the willows. And let the daughters of educated men dance round the fire and heap armful upon armful of dead leaves upon the flames. And let their mothers lean from the upper windows and cry, 'Let it blaze! Let it blaze! For we have done with this "education"!'" (*TG*, 36)

I say "deconstruction" because, for all its flames and burning, the vision is not exactly one of destruction (the creative destruction of anarchism, for instance, has a different theory behind it, in part because anarchists aimed to burn actual buildings). If the old colleges are secure in the real world, the imaginary ones also cannot be destroyed, because they are constructed precisely to be rebuilt by each generation, to be combustible and temporary. The utopian college, in other words, incorporates the fiery dance into its conception; it is meant to be burnt. Significant, too, is the central place of the mothers in this vision of counter-circling. They lean from the windows and cheer on their daughters; in a later iteration, they "laugh from their graves," again encouraging the younger women: "'It was for this that we suffered obloquy and contempt! Light up the windows of the new house, daughters! Let them blaze!'" (*TG*, 83).[112] It *was* for this! Woolf takes a leap of faith in answering Owen, Yeats and others who had wondered whether the Enlightenment had gone dark, imagining continuity and mutuality from mother to daughter, in a striking departure from her more renowned attitude of generational conflict. A cycle demands another cycle; if violence comes in the form of return, so too must its antidote. Woolf thus renews the agonizing question of reprisal, yet resisting its nightmarish, bloody logic. For their part, the daughters here circle around "the new house, the poor house, the house that stands in the narrow street" and chant "'We have done with war! We have done with tyranny!'" (*TG*, 83). With their bacchic energy and unleashed feminine strength, these women anti-warriors invite an Irigarian or Cixousian reading, pointing, indeed, to a protest spirit that recalls the 1960s more than the 1930s. It is instructive, too, to think back to the burnt buildings that comprised the landscape (allegorical and real) in the later Irish works we have discussed. The freight and sorrow of those lost structures came in relation to their historical significance, their carrying of tradition; in knocking religion off its stand, Woolf can delight in these incinerations—fanciful even if they are not, in Yeats's terms, "mere dreams."

Most centrally, what the chanting, burning passages show is how thoroughly the confrontation with violence in *Three Guineas* matches and absorbs the structure of violence itself. Antiviolence has to consume violence, to swallow it. The image of swallowing has figured before in this study, in *The Waste Land,* where it represented the stunted and muted music that even horrific histories of violence construct ("O swallow, swallow . . ."), and it will return in *Between the Acts,* as Bart Oliver hums the same line from Swinburne's (and Eliot's) poem, as well as in the snake-toad dyad. Here, the idea of consumption has a double cadence: first in the image of burning and bonfires, a material and literal consuming, and second in the text's formal move of counter-circling, where one kind of violent process (the world history of violence) is absorbed or ingested into another one. As with Woolf's treatment of passivity and action in the text, the structure here is dialectical, with the polarities of violence and antiviolence mutually engendering and transforming. It is also formal, in a literal sense. The actual form that violence takes, the destructive circle, is met and overtaken by another version of itself.

There is, moreover, yet another kind of circling in *Three Guineas,* which emerges only at the text's close, and this one is meant, perhaps, to swallow both of its predecessors: "But that would be to dream—to dream the recurring dream that has haunted the human mind since the beginning of time; the dream of peace, the dream of freedom" (*TG*, 143). That Woolf closes *Three Guineas* with the idea of peace recalls *The Years*, whose final lines were almost defiant in their desire to envision peace in the midst of the violence that was so thoroughly dispersed through world and text. Peace and violence in *The Years* always move in tandem, whether in the loveliness of evenings that are stalked by terror or in the lifting of eyes toward the sky, in a gesture that evokes both bombardment and the utopian belief in a better future. In *Three Guineas*, the similarity and yoking of violence with peace is formal, with the structure of return and circularity defining all at once the numbing horror of the mulberry tree, the energy and enthusiasm of women's resistance, and the undercurrent of hope that makes its quiet countersong.

And it is figured as song, for the voices credited with pushing forward the dream of peace are "the voices of the poets, answering each other" (*TG*, 143), an echoing conversation that itself echoes one of Woolf's most compelling accounts of the great urge to write, Orlando's summation of her centuries-long desire for voice:

> Was not writing poetry a secret transaction, a voice answering a voice? . . . What could have been more secret, she thought, more slow, and like the intercourse of lovers, than the stammering answer she had made all these years to the old crooning song of the woods, and the farms and the brown horses standing at the gate, neck to neck, and the smithy and the kitchen and the fields, so laboriously bearing wheat, turnips, grass, and the gardens blowing irises and fritillaries?[113]

Writing is always romantic in *Orlando*, a basic human response to the natural world. It is an urge figured organically, an answer to woods and cows and gardens, even if such organicism is best experienced from the luxury of 365 rooms of one's own, and even if it takes a few centuries to write a finished poem. Something of that romantic model is retained even in *Three Guineas*, where the echo chamber of voices is audible over the "bark of the guns and the bray of the gramophones" (*TG*, 143). Or is it? For all the relief and pleasure of Woolf's nod to the poets and their dream of peace at the end of her text, the serpent is always swallowing its tail in *Three Guineas*. Woolf is pinned down in and by her own patterns, where the circularity of violence and its counterforms seems, finally, engulfing.

It is not surprising that the most visible literary antecedent in both *The Years* and *Three Guineas* is *Antigone*; though all of the Greek dramatists steeped their plays in violence, Sophocles is remarkable for having by far the bleakest vision, his characters locked in a losing battle with fate, their mortality figured as a prison. In *Antigone*, it is not only the relation of male dictator to female resister that is so relevant to Woolf's critique, but also Antigone's punishment, to be buried alive, walled in a circular chamber, a metaphor for the cramped, stunted human condition for Sophocles, and of the mulberry tree of ever-returning subjugation for Woolf. In fact, the very form of drama in Woolf's last works becomes associated with the stark mortal reckoning epitomized by Sophocles. *Between the Acts*, above all, embraces dramatic form as a way to present life on the verge of—and indeed defined by—catastrophic violence. In fact, every formal strategy for engaging violence we have tracked in Woolf's writing appears in *Between the Acts*, a novel whose belief in the power and efficacy of literature—a voice calling to a voice—is dimmed and compromised. Violence now can be found in all of the Woolfian forms: as spectacle, irruption, shape; in the body; scored into the landscape; absorbed and dispersed. In *Between the Acts*, as in *Antigone*, life itself is modeled on the patterns that violence takes.

We see it in the name; in the shift from *Pointz Hall* to *Between the Acts*, Woolf indicates the depth of the novel's engagement with violence as pattern. Acts, acting, action—all are implicated in Woolf's exploration of the formal, rhythmic structures of violence in the world. What are "the acts"? Most obviously, the acts in Miss La Trobe's pageant, which, for its part, is a spur for the novel's characters to recognize themselves as actors, as part of the play's—and the world's—large cast. "You've stirred in me my unacted part," Lucy feels of Miss La Trobe's production, while Bart reports that "our part . . . is to be the audience. And a very important part too" (*BTA*, 153, 58). Though introduced amusingly, the role of audience is a serious proposition in the novel, suggesting the Greek idea of chorus (Greece itself being repeatedly invoked, as with the barn, which reminds people of a Greek temple [*BTA*, 26]). Mrs. Manresa performs her part energetically, and for Giles, the pleasure of basking in her light comes because she makes him "feel less of an audience, more of an actor" (*BTA*, 108). Others among the assembled group feel violated and uncomfortable in the spotlight, fidgeting and complaining about their treatment. La Trobe will pressure these impulses as hard as she can, forcing her audience to confront itself with uncomfortable silence—"She wanted to expose them, as it were, to douche them, with present-time reality" (*BTA*, 179)—or with jarring mirrors—"So that was her little game! To show us up, as we are, here and how" (*BTA*, 186)—and even with a lecturing voice on the megaphone accusing the audience of hypocrisy. The whole question, indeed, of the relation between acting on a stage and acting in the world remains strained in the novel (with *King Lear*, the play that most famously articulated this relation, hovering allusively in the background), in part because La Trobe's play intends to vex that very line, in part because the pressure of the historical moment is so intense—"reality too strong"—as constantly to be felt in the midst of what is supposed to be a simple "village entertainment." The airplanes are the most potent example of such painful confusion of these categories, forcefully intruding onto the village scene; they very literally split apart language (slicing between "opp" and "portunity" in Streatfield's appeal), an extremely mild anticipation of what their German counterparts, in Giles's frustrated understanding, will soon do: "rake that land into furrows; planes splinter Bolney Minster into smithereens and blast the Folly" (*BTA*, 53). As Gillian Beer has noted in "The Island and the Aeroplane," the planes at the end of *Between the Acts*, with their exact V formation, are unambiguously warplanes, and in that sense they contrast with the looping, diving airplane of *Mrs. Dalloway*, whose status on the threshold between military threat and commercial exuberance was the essence of its significatory overdrive. Preceded by their sound, as we have seen always to be the case (here initially mistaken for music), the airplanes signal war as directly as is possible in 1939; and though these British planes are meant to defend rather than menace the community below, their message is of destruction more than protection.

Indeed, from the vantage of the sky, the land in *Between the Acts* is already scarred by violence, as each wave of inhabitants (or invaders) has left its marks in the very texture of the landscape: "From an aeroplane, [Bart Oliver] said, you could still see, plainly marked, the scars made by the Britons; by the Romans; by the Elizabethan manor house; and by the plough, when they ploughed the hill to grow wheat in the Napoleonic wars" (*BTA*, 4). If a novel like *Orlando* figured historiography in terms of succeeding social and literary styles, and if La Trobe's pageant elaborates literary history as a procession (a favorite metaphor for Woolf in these years), here, in the opening pages of *Between the Acts*, the ages again come in clear sequence, this time very literally marked by violence. The history of the locale is figured in this short passage as something of an ongoing battle between the land and the invaders who have followed one another—even the great narrative of agriculture is filtered through war—a notion that contrasts with the sentiment of changelessness experienced by those looking comfortably at the view from the protected terrace. Will the scars of the current generation, the novel seems to ask, be the blasted landscape left by bombs? One thinks of the dynamite tradition, where the gash in the landscape marked a nihilistic vision yet was also the site of productivity, something of a literary point of origin. In a text consumed by history—where even in short sequences, an enormous variety of operations for both memory and history can be elaborated—this iteration stands out for the harshness of its vision. It also encodes with particular power the idea of muted, silent histories of violence, of the sort Rhys would later impute to the broad movements of British culture. Such a blunt accounting for life and history as scarring and recurrent warfare anticipates the novel's conclusion, where Isa and Giles become an inverted Adam and Eve, whose enmity, at the end of the June day, might be said to stand in for the whole race's history of violence: "But first they must fight, as the dog fox fights with the vixen, in the heart of darkness, in the fields of night" (*BTA*, 219).

For its part, the audience of villagers, playing out its choral function, weaves the contemporary situation into its communal voice. On one hand, this would seem an exceptionally insulated and inwardly focused community. Giles, for one, feels "rage with old fogies who sat and looked at views over coffee and cream when the whole of Europe—over there—was . . . bristling with guns, poised with planes" (*BTA*, 53). Here, on the brink of war, in time of extreme international tension and sweeping violence, the locals gather to watch their pageant, seemingly oblivious, comparing barns and past village plays, enacting their own habitual performances. And the sense of localness is everywhere stressed. Figgis's guide, we are told, is as accurate in 1939 as it was in 1830, suggesting an impermeability about the community. Page the reporter is another quintessentially local figure, as central to the village cast as is Albert the idiot, a gossip columnist in a novel that weighs the newspapers heavily as the source of information from the world beyond the village. On the other hand, Giles is not really accurate in his condemnation of his family and the other local people; it may be reluctant and partial, but the community does in fact invite all kinds of externals, including the troubling events on the continent, into its consciousness. Lucy might think herself far from the sea, but we are told emphatically that it is actually only thirty-five miles away, and this proximity analogizes to the deceptive nature of the village's insularity. The protective hollow where the villagers gather is not, as the narrator indicates and the villagers at some level seem to understand, particularly protective. Examples of its porousness abound. The library, a room to which characters return now and again over the course of the day, and whose contents are described with both irony and affection, certainly seems a haven from the now, representing a repository for family history, its accrued volumes expressing different eras, tastes, and personalities, akin to the literary history on view in the pageant. At the same time, the library is full of contemporary cheap novels bought at the London train station for the three-hour ride, or, in Woolf's wonderfully alliterative terms, "the shuffle of shilling shockers that week-enders had dropped." (Interestingly, "dropped" is a verb associated more with bombs than with books.) The library, in fact, is as much given over to the present as it is to the past. As for the house—synecdoche for family, community, and nation, and the ultimate site of shelter—it is repeatedly characterized as a "shell," the merest of protective coverings, itself to be opened up in the final moment, when "the curtain rises." An evocative image, as in Yeats's

"Meditations in Time of Civil War," the shell can be, all at once, an image of lustrous beauty, wrought by the sea; a delicate ornament; a mere relic and ruin left of a once-living creature; the thinnest of shelters; or, disrupting the metaphoric chain entirely, the agent that destroys all of this, the artillery shell.[114]

More generally, the village is actually not nearly as static and contained as it seems to project, or perhaps to desire. Streatfield laments, about movies and motorbuses, that they lure away his congregants, but they are also technologies that very effectively usher the outside world into the village. Movie houses in particular, which were affiliated in this period with newsreels as much as with entertainment, held a prominent role in helping to create a national narrative about news events, and eventually about the war. And it was emphatically a national dialogue, since newsreels in British cinemas in the 1930s, unlike the films shown there, were entirely British-produced and oriented; interestingly, moreover, the moviegoing population in this period was largely working-class, making the cinema, as the historian Nicholas Pronay argues, "exceptional among all the products of twentieth-century technology in that it reached the poorer elements in the community first before spreading upwards . . ."[115] It may be, in other words, that the newsreel in this period had begun to offer a narrative about world events alternative to that found either in newspapers or in the library's volumes; still, in *Between the Acts*, these are incidental suggestions. The newspaper, by contrast, is omnipresent.[116] "For her generation," Isa thinks, "the newspaper was a book" (*BTA*, 20).[117] The paper indeed crosses all the generations; it is also read by the oldest member of the family, Bart (who uses it, too, to scare little George), and, akin to the cards, letters, shilling shockers, and even the filleted sole, its regular arrival signals an ongoing relationship between home and away, country and city, as the pageant itself also indicates. Modernization in general is a major topic in the villagers' idiom, from a running commentary on refrigeration and aerodromes to the fact that the play's proceeds have been slated to electrify the church (an irony, needless to say, since by the time of the novel's writing such illumination would have been rendered moot by air raid conditions).

Further countering Giles's critique, the villagers' commentary is laced with a latent understanding of the severity of the political situation abroad, and of the vulnerability of their world at home. The combination of localness (even triviality) with acknowledgement of terrible violence renders the village dialogue at once anxious, grimly comic, and, in its own way, powerfully evocative: of a moment of dawning awareness, where the reality of what is to come, of what is, for millions of people, already at hand, is only half internalized or articulated. Characters think directly about invasion ("what's the channel, come to think of it, if they mean to invade us?") or about what the airplanes signify ("the aeroplanes, I didn't like to say it, made one think . . .,") or about the victims of persecution ("And what about the Jews? The refugees . . . the Jews"), seeming to recognize the profound temporality and fragility of the present (*BTA*, 199, 121, ellipses in original). Lucy, certainly the most detached of the family members from contemporary events, imagines a prehistory in which England was not separated from the continent (a view that comes courtesy of Woolf's old straw man, Wells), making literal and geographical the connectedness that underlies her spiritual habit of "one-making." And it is Lucy, too, who sees a leaf on the pond and thinks it the shape of Europe, with other leaves representing different continents or nations, "Islands of security, glossy and thick," emphasizing the lull and lure of the great fiction that England is a protected (or sceptered) isle (*BTA*, 205). Highly expressive of these contradictory emotions and proclivities, the choral voice of the novel veers and verges, at times conveying a quality of (modernist) pastiche that intermingles high with low, serious with silly, political with personal, among other dichotomies. So we have, for instance:

> "What we need is a centre. Something to bring us all together . . . The Brookes have gone to Italy, in spite of everything. Rather rash? . . . If the worst should come—let's hope it won't—they'd hire an aeroplane, so they said . . . What amused me was old Streatfield, feeling for his pouch. I like a man to be natural, not always on his perch . . . [*extra ellipsis mine*] . . . But I was saying: can the Christian faith adapt itself? In times like these . . . At Larting no one goes to church . . . There's the dogs, there's the pictures . . . It's odd that science, so they tell me, is making things (so to speak) more spiritual . . . The very latest notion, so I'm told, is nothing's solid . . . There, you can get a glimpse of the church through the trees . . ." (*BTA*, 198–99, ellipses in original).

As in the overdetermined sequence with the mirrors—to be read, I think, with at least a degree of tongue in cheek—here Woolf seems in part to be parodying modernism itself, which, like all other linguistic forms in *Between the Acts*, falls precariously on the verge of obsolescence. At the minimum, Woolf shows a willingness to be playful with her own serious concerns—the idea of nonchurchgoing, we recall, was presented as vital political engagement in *Three Guineas*, while the "latest notion . . . is nothing's solid" comes straight out of Woolf herself (via Bergson, or Pater, or Montaigne). There is a kind of poetry, moreover, in the shared narrative voice in these segments of the novel (as in the pseudo-rhyming of "pouch" with "perch," say), interwoven with the gramophone's music and the language of the play, at the same time that Woolf's almost Popian use of figures like litotes or juxtaposition

274 AT THE VIOLET HOUR

gives voice to her own frustration with the smallness of country life. These passages, moreover, might be read as the community's collective unconscious, and they reveal a tense competition between the desire for insularity—for the comfort of what is known and understood—and the reality of worldwide interconnection, a tension in sync with the novel's most abundantly stated opposition, between unity and dispersal, or, in its own shorthand, "un-dis."

For the acts—to return to the title—are, of course, the wars. Woolf wrote *Between the Acts* in the midst of the Blitz, and the sense of profound precariousness—the possibility that all Woolf loved and valued could be wiped out—is everywhere in the novel. Famously antipatriotic, Woolf in these last years of her life articulated a sense of love and emotion about England proportionate to the extreme threat to its buildings, its landscape, its very life, and especially to London. As Lee movingly writes:

> Like many other writers witnessing the city in these weeks . . . Virginia described the destruction of "her" London eloquently and with strong personal feeling. She wrote about it a little in letters, never in essays or fiction, but mainly to herself in the diary, in a shocked, rapid, jagged, intensely observant language. It was some of her most powerful writing, about some of the most painful things she had ever witnessed. (Lee, 728)

In *Between the Acts*, set in 1939, the potential for civilian catastrophe is writ as incipience, in keeping with the dominant mode of the 1930s; it anticipates the Blitz instead of recording it.[118] And yet Woolf's emotion about the destruction all around her determines the novel's tone, which is as much in the key of sorrow as of ominousness. The world of *Between the Acts*, that is, simultaneously crouches in fear and lifts its voice in sorrow. If Giles imagines the whole area smashed and destroyed, other voices seem to weep for such violence as if it has already happened. And so, in the midst of the pageant, a herd of cows, mourning a lost calf, "took up the burden . . . All the great moon-eyed heads laid themselves back. From cow after cow came the same yearning bellow. The whole world was filled with dumb yearning. It was the primeval voice sounding loud in the ear of the present moment" (*BTA*, 140). The primeval voice speaks repeatedly in *Between the Acts*, always in some way reflecting the oncoming violence of the present. With the wailing cows, moreover, Woolf returns to animal allegory, the cows very directly expressing a sorrow that belongs, more properly, to the human audience. Not long after this nonhuman expression, a rain shower douses the audience, and it too is presented as an image of collective mourning: "Down it poured like all the people in the world weeping. Tears. Tears. Tears" (*BTA*, 180). These are, of course, instances of the "pathetic fallacy," yet they escape the charges of artificiality or sentimentality that modernism might be expected to level, in part because they accurately reflect something very real in the contemporary consciousness, as Woolf felt and filtered it. In March of 1940, as we have seen, she recorded a moment like this in her diary: "Not a sound this evening to bring in the human tears. I remember the sudden profuse shower one night just before the war wh. made me think of all men & women weeping" (*Diary*, V, 274). Pointz Hall, too, expresses in its spaces the shared sentiment of loss and mourning, and, as in *Jacob's Room*, of foreshadowing as well as felt pain: "Empty, empty, empty; silent, silent, silent. The room was a shell, singing of what was before time was; a vase stood in the heart of the house, alabaster, smooth, cold, holding the still, distilled essence of emptiness, silence" (*BTA*, 36–37). There is beauty in this emptiness, as there is in the song of the cows or the rain, a strange loveliness even at moments of heart-breaking pressure. And the characters, too, express a sense of sadness—Isa, Miss La Trobe, William Dodge—which is often aesthetically rich and productive (as with Isa's poetic rendering of the world, or Miss La Trobe's artistry), and which Giles tersely names for all of them: "I'm damnably unhappy" (*BTA*, 176).

The flood of sadness in the novel is profoundly humanizing, but in a strange way, the grim ubiquity of violence also presses the novel in a different direction, towards an anti-characterology and near nihilism that threatens to undermine the novel itself, a generic self-destruction more severe than what we saw in *The Years*, though similar in spirit.[119] In that novel, we recall, it was the ubiquity of tyranny and violence that pressed the text into a mode of declamation that, in Woolf's own view, is fatal to art ("On every placard, at every street corner was Death . . ."). Here, the question of novelistic limitation takes a different form—of a drama that has already been written. Drama of course is ubiquitous in *Between the Acts*. First we have the pageant itself, which, though distinct from the novel, at times merges into its stream, as when the description of the gramophone or megaphone becomes indistinguishable from the novel's narration. And the audience picks up the pageant's tune and intonations; as Isa puts it, "It's the play . . . the play keeps running in my head" (*BTA*, 105). Permeating its audience, the pageant invites an uneven reaction. At times, it has transformative power, as in the last moments before the community disperses, when the play continues to cast a spell on the scene ("Each still acted the unacted part conferred on them by their clothes. Beauty was on them. Beauty revealed them" [*BTA*, 195–96]); at other times, as we have seen, La Trobe aims to unsettle and antagonize her viewers, a village version of Artaudian discomfort. What I want to stress about the pageant's dramatic effects, however, is the way it sets the stage, literally and figuratively, for the novel to act out a different kind of drama. The novel marks the moment of oncoming tragedy; it stands just on the threshold of the main act of massive violence, which it both presages and mourns. It leads up to the act; at the end of the novel, the curtain rises.

In other words, for all the emphasis on the acts and acting, the novel actually assigns itself the place of the interim, of "betweenness." The place in the hollow, of quiet and calm before the storm, of incipience and fear, betweenness is an expression of that which both expands in the intervals and shrinks in the face of the acts. It concerns the actors just before and after they play their parts—as they dress and undress in the bushes, so to speak—a time of preparation and anticipation. The novel depicts a state of tension in the before and between, which is also felt as lethargy, or perhaps rest: "They stared at the view," goes one of many such depictions, "as if something might happen in one of those fields to relieve them of the intolerable burden of sitting silent, doing nothing, in company" (BTA, 65). The state of betweenness has its pleasures, too, its beauty and poignancy. Here, for instance, is little George, as a child able to dig deeply into his immediate time and place, to inhabit the in-between with intensity and keen sensitivity: "The flower blazed between the angles and the roots. Membrane after membrane was torn. It blazed a soft yellow, a lambent light under a film of velvet; it filled the caverns behind the eyes with light. All that inner darkness became a hall, leaf smelling, earth smelling, of yellow light" (BTA, 11). For their part, the villagers also acknowledge the appeal of resting in the moment before and after, when, for instance, they hesitate before leaving the grounds, enjoying their time of unity before the inevitable dispersal. This state of betweenness is both capacious and ready to be obliterated, like the view, which Giles thinks of as eminently destructible even as he also acknowledges its permanence and serenity. To be between is not to have to act, to be Hamlet rather than Lear. It is to remain in the present.

And yet, as Woolf has always implied, the present is never really possible to inhabit ("it had become," Mrs. Ramsay thinks of the dinner scene as she steps out the door, "already the past" [TTL, 111]). In Between the Acts this instability is not only ontological or existential; it is also historical. The present, now inescapably understood as "between" two wars, is eclipsed by what is coming. Woolf figures this annihilating force as a shadow, like the giant silhouettes that pervade the final paragraphs of the novel ("The great hooded chairs became enormous . . . The window was all sky without colour" [BTA, 219]), or in Isa's evocative terms: "The future shadowed their present" (BTA, 114). Harking back to Eliot's early poetry, as she so often does, Woolf, too, gives us a shadow that marks betweenness, yet for her, there is no flourishing on the cusp of restrictive categories, like Eliot's shadow in "The Hollow Men" ("Between the idea/And the reality/Between the motion/And the act . . . Between the conception/And the creation/Between the emotion/And the response . . ."); in *Between the Acts*, the future that shadows the present is all menace.[120] One might note, here, Woolf's heavy and affective reaction to a solar eclipse (1928), which she described in the essay "The Sun and the Fish": the sun is darkened, and "This was the end. The flesh and blood of the world was dead; only the skeleton was left. It hung beneath us, a frail shell; brown; dead; withered." Even after the sun remerges and brings an enormous optimism with it, "still the memory endured that the earth we stand on is made of colour; colour can be blown out; and then we stand on a dead leaf . . ."[121] Anticipating her 1930s imagery—the precarious leaf that will not shelter in *The Years*, the shell of a home in *Between the Acts*—the projection of annihilation takes the form, as always, of shape, color, visual pattern.

The present is fraught, too, by a different kind of temporal logic, that of the long history (and prehistory) of humankind, which Woolf figures in *Between the Acts* as an essential violence; it is her most sustained contribution, along with *Three Guineas*, to the 1930s conversation about whether war and violence are endemic to human life. The suggestion of some kind of elemental barbarism is intimated early in the novel, with Lucy reading and musing about prehistory, "when the entire continent, not then, she understood, divided by a channel, was all one; populated, she understood, by elephant-bodied, seal-necked, heaving, surging, slowly writhing, and, she supposed, barking monsters" (*BTA*, 8). For all the fantasy and imaginative appeal of these musings ("she supposed" reminding us that Lucy's inventiveness is filtering and transforming her reading), the adjectives and verbs here (elephant-bodied, seal-necked, heaving, surging, writhing, barking) recall those terrifying passages in both *To the Lighthouse* and *The Years* where the whole universe seemed embroiled in a violent semiotic, where "gigantic chaos" ruled and the "light of reason" had flickered out. And *Between the Acts* has its own version of such overarching chaos, which it figures primarily in terms of an attenuated and broken communicability. The novel dramatizes the failure of communication and intimacy at nearly every level, from the image of Isa tapping uselessly on the glass at her unheeding children, to the actors' words being lost in the air, to the many sequences that show the village and family communities as fragmented and at odds: "dispersed are [they]." Moreover, to return to Wells's textbook, what Woolf does not mention in *Between the Acts* is where it ends: with the First World War, which Wells treats as a major cataclysm in human history, and to which he devotes far more pages than to any other event in his broad catalogue. *The Outline of History*, in other words, moves from one kind of barbarism (albeit an imaginatively evocative and fantastical one) to another. Miss La Trobe, too, looking to the future, finds the distant past. Already beginning to construct her next play, she sees this new one arising from "the mud," where "the intolerably laden dumb oxen plod . . ."; it is elemental in shape, another outline of history (as is the pageant, as is the novel itself). "There was the high ground at midnight; there the rock; and two scarcely perceptible figures" (*BTA*, 212). It is a setting that for La Trobe is "fertile," productive of "words without meaning—wonderful words," a breath of hope and promise in a world become increasingly shadowy.

And yet, for all the richness and relief accompanying La Trobe's vision of prehistory, it also heralds the novel's conclusion, a far more sobering sequence:

> Left alone together for the first time that day, they were silent. Alone, enmity was bared; also love. Before they slept, they must fight; after they had fought, they would embrace. From that embrace another life might be born. But first they must fight, as the dog fox fights with the vixen, in the heart of darkness, in the fields of night.
>
> Isa let her sewing drop. The great hooded chairs had become enormous. And Giles too. And Isa too against the window. The window was all sky without colour. The house had lost its shelter. It was night before roads were made, or houses. It was the night that dwellers in caves had watched from some high place among rocks.
>
> Then the curtain rose. They spoke. (*BTA*, 219)

Woolf imbricates many literary and cultural references into her concluding lines, both external and internal to the novel—most directly Conrad, but also Matthew Arnold, the novel's own Miss La Trobe, and those many writers of the 1930s who had worried about the essential violence always ready to erupt in destructive chaos and slaughter. Moreover, Woolf's sentences here are uncharacteristically short and blunt. They are also repetitive ("And Giles too. And Isa too . . ."), her language mimicking in form what it describes, a radical reduction in the creative power. The passage is similar, in that sense, to what we saw in "Easter 1916," where the language of generative violence became lulling and circular, forcing out alternative modes of thought, checking the imaginative capacity. Where Yeats makes this linguistic lethargy equivocal and seductive, Woolf sees the lights going out; it is the only really dark and terrifying ending to any of her novels. Even *The Voyage Out*, in some ways the closest in spirit to *Between the Acts*, pushes past Rachel's death, to conclude instead in the indifferent space of the hotel, impervious to the losses it witnesses. And so St. John relaxes, after the intense grief of Rachel's illness:

> All these voices sounded gratefully in St. John's ear as he lay half-asleep, and yet vividly conscious of everything around him. Across his eyes passed a

procession of objects, black and indistinct, the figures of people picking up their books, their cards, their balls of wool, their work-baskets, and passing him one after another on their way to bed. (*VO*, 353)

At the conclusion of *Between the Acts*, there is no quiet forgetting of calamity; on the contrary, many of the novel's defining forms of creativity are squeezed out and diminished, in a trajectory that takes its final direction when the novel relinquishes itself to drama. Such a move transpires at several levels, not only in thematic terms, but also in its generic borrowing, as it partakes of many features it attributes to drama: characters figured as cast; the audience playing a choral role; the contained setting; the twenty-four-hour time span; the refrains and repetitions that give a sense of formal cohesion to the play/novel; and, of course, the final curtain. Given the depth and diversity of the theatrical referencing, and given the imaginative appeal of the pageant for late modernism, as Jed Esty has described it, such an overlap seems fruitful. The problem is that, in *Between the Acts*, the essence of the novel's (or play's) humanity is drained, so that characters become stock characters, relationships fall into clichéd categories, people act out their roles with a wearisome predictability, even the most intimate relations are anchored on formulated phrases. "Surely," as Isa sums it up, "it was time someone invented a new plot, or that the author came out from the bushes" (*BTA*, 215).

In *Between the Acts*, the rubric of wearying repetition is expansive. The acts, first, signal the repeating sequence, as do the annual production of the pageant itself and its allied rituals. "Every summer, for seven summers now, Isa had heard the same words; about the hammer and the nails; the pageant and the weather. Every year they said, would it be wet or fine; every year it was—one or the other" (*BTA*, 22). The swallows are in on the repetitive mode, returning every summer (and provoking the interesting philosophical question of whether, if they are not the same actual birds, their annual migration actually counts as a return). Lucy, whose "one-making" takes the form of giant circling excursions, continually seems to read the same passage from Wells, just as she asks herself every year whether to move to Kew. If these forms of repetition are perfectly benign, the novel is nevertheless clouded by the idea of war as an ever-repeating cycle, and by the structure of return as annihilative. And so we have an exceptionally startling passage, as the family and guests are looking at the view: "The flat fields glared green yellow, blue yellow, red yellow, then blue again. The repetition was senseless, hideous, stupefying" (*BTA*, 67). There are a number of curious features in this brief and brutal passage. First, it is one of those narratorial moments that unfixes the subject whose feeling is being recorded; it seems to belong to the text as a whole. Mrs. Manresa is being described in the immediately preceding lines, but if it is her thought, it is not hers alone.[122] Second, the lines jarringly contrast with everything that has been said up to now about the view, whose signal characteristic is that it invites universal affection (even Giles, who imagines it blasted apart, "loved" it). And finally, it is very strange and disorienting to find such a painterly, aesthetic moment—the undulating colors, the interesting mixing—and one tuned to the familiar and revered, depicted in such aggressive and repellent terms. In its very surprise, it is a profoundly clarifying moment. Repetition in some basic way means violence; its presence shocks and sickens.

What counteracts the monstrousness of repeated violence is pattern—an alternate style of pattern that mitigates the forcefulness of repetition. If the view passage startled with its unexpected revulsion, its counter-passage, just several pages earlier, had offered a wonderfully exuberant image of the surroundings:

> The other trees were magnificently straight. They were not too regular; but regular enough to suggest columns in a church; in a church without a roof; in an open-air cathedral, a place where swallows darting seemed, by the regularity of the trees, to make a pattern, dancing, like the Russians, only not to music, but to the unheard rhythm of their own wild hearts. (*BTA*, 64–65)

It is a marvelous moment, a surge of lightness and joy in a novel that tends toward the sorrowful. The dancing swallows call up many evocations, from Yeats's "Among School Children" to the sensation of the Ballets Russes in the 1920s, while the roofless church, a modernist Tintern Abbey, manages to skirt all that Woolf loathed about religion, while inviting in what she could still afford to love—its architecture, for instance, and its sheer, unanchored uplift. Moreover, the reference to Greece in this passage, unlike the Sophoclean mode that stresses the imprisonment of the human condition ("They were all caught and caged; prisoners" [*BTA*, 176]) evokes what British culture had always idealized about the ancient landscape—a fantasy that, in their own time, the classical temples had been open to the sky, their columns supporting no roof. But what is most strange about the passage is how precisely Woolf delineates the nature of the trees' regularity, the specificity of their pattern. They are ordered, but not too much so, architectural but open; the whole tableau establishes a perfect balance between form and formlessness, repetition (or regularity) and freedom. Indeed, it is tempting to see in this glorious moment the achievement of a goal we have followed throughout these pages: to find a language that will precisely delineate violence's excess, without lapsing into an economic style of balance and counter-balance, or, conversely, succumbing to the lure of waste and self-sacrifice.

This contrast between repetition and pattern is the crux of it for Woolf, as it is for modernism more broadly, the difference between violence as overwhelming force and violence as something that must be acknowledged, but can also be managed and accommodated, by formalizing it in some way—weaving it into the text, or bracketing it, or embodying it, to name several styles we have encountered. In the pre-1930s novels we have considered (*The Voyage Out, Jacob's Room, Mrs. Dalloway, To the Lighthouse*), violence was formalized, in the most explicit sense; it was imbricated in the primary formal mechanisms of the text. As we move into the three late works, that possibility is threatened—but here is the key point: it is threatened, particularly in *Three Guineas* and *Between the Acts*, by form itself. In *The Years*, Woolf created an especially muted and oblique pattern for violence; and yet *The Years* suggests that when some threshold of world violence has been crossed, this formal solution no longer suffices, and the novel as genre ceases to suffice. With *Three Guineas*, the repetitiveness of violence becomes the text's own stylistic driver; its strategy is to take up the circular rhythm, in effect swallowing up the terrible problem of repetition (violence) by a desired form of circularity (the bacchic dance or the recurrent dream of peace). Of course, one only dreams of peace because one is confronted by war, and so the pattern is regressive, mutually engendering (like the snake and toad). In *Three Guineas*, in other words, repetition and pattern are closely linked; Woolf's vision of breaking the violent cycle involves more circling, absorbing and refiguring the pattern that had been deadly and depressing with new energy and intention. *Between the Acts* pushes the furthest, asking: is history no more, finally, than repeated acts of violence? We can do nothing to intervene in the acts; and it is not even clear that can we imagine forms and patterns that, as in her previous novels, might incorporate violence without entirely succumbing to its force.

"Surely," as Isa says, "it was time someone invented a new plot." It may be an impossible task for this novel, a rhetorical rather than genuine appeal. If there were to be a new plot, it would have to be Isa's to create, Miss La Trobe's plays being too fully invested in what has already been written. Isa is always at work on her own narrative: she writes poetry concealed in an accounting book; she very consciously scripts herself (as lover to the man in gray, for instance) and others ("the father of my children"), and she constructs an ongoing poem over the course of her day, a rhythmic reflection on the rich sensory and intelligible world around her. Like many other artist figures throughout Woolf's fiction, Isa is a stand-in for Woolf, not so much because her output resembles the novel (much less for reasons of character similarity) but because the deep psychic attitude she betrays—to approach her world, an often bracingly difficult one, punctuated by loneliness and frustration, in a spirit of aesthetic creativity and exuberance—resembles Woolf's own lifelong accomplishment.

The challenge for Isa comes with the intrusion of violence. It enters with the newspaper. Where Giles reads about international finance, and the villagers are drawn to stories about the royal family—and where, for everyone, the lead-up to war provides the subtext—Isa reads a story of a rape:

> "The troopers told her the horse had a green tail; but she found it was just an ordinary horse. And they dragged her up to the barrack room where she was thrown upon a bed. Then one of the troopers removed part of her clothing, and she screamed and hit him about the face . . ."
>
> That was real; so real that on the mahogany door panels she saw the Arch in Whitehall; through the Arch the barrack room; in the barrack room the bed, and on the bed the girl was screaming and hitting him about the face, when the door (for in fact it was a door) opened and in came Mrs. Swithin carrying a hammer. (*BTA*, 20, ellipsis in original)

Strange as it sounds, it is a true story; coverage appeared in *The Times* on successive days in June 1938.[123] "That was real": Isa's response, reverberating with the realness of disenchanted violence, anticipates and conditions the reader's. Crucially, though, there follows a mutation from this very realness, as the rape language refuses to stay static, joining the thought stream, and Isa embraces that "imaginative reconstruction of the past," so often constitutive of the novel's female characters (*BTA*, 9). More than any other single event depicted in the novel, the story of the raped girl, lured in by the fantastical idea of a horse with a green tail, permeates Isa's imagination, transforming her interior monologue. It returns over the course of the day, always with Isa's own emendations; she will soon have the girl hitting the soldier with a hammer, having incorporated Lucy's unthreatening hammer (used to nail up the placard about the pageant) into the violent narrative. In the actual trial and news coverage, a recurring question involved the girl's complicity; here, there is no doubt that this is a rape, and Isa, in her vision, gives the rape victim the opportunity to hit back in a meaningful way, with a weapon. It may be, indeed, that Isa's arming of the girl represents her own unfulfillable wish to smash back at men, a repressed and reversed narrative of female rage that recalls Rachel Vinrace's identification with the women beheading the chickens. We might also note, again, the recurrence of the primitive weapon to join our bayonets, here the hammer.

Mostly, however, the intrusion of this blunt moment of visceral violence, sexual and disenchanted, disrupts Isa's internal equilibrium, her poetic form of self-regulation; but it also adds something, a realness that is, in a strange way, anchoring for Isa. When, for instance, Isa listens to Lucy and Bart having their annual conversation about the weather on pageant day, her interior monologue concludes: "The same chime followed the same chime, only this year beneath the chime she heard: 'The girl screamed and hit him about the face with a hammer'" (*BTA*, 22). The effect of this shocking intrusion into the lulling sequence is mixed. In part, it depersonalizes and generalizes: this year's sequence of wet-and-fine—1939's—is different from all previous ones, underpinned by brute violence. The description comes from Isa's personal iconography, but it speaks to the world situation. It is also jolting: if the conversation about the weather acts as a soporific (like the effect of a large lunch on a warm day, such as the one that puts Bart to sleep on the terrace), the presence of the rape shocks Isa's language, and the novel's, into alertness. It acts internally the way Giles wishes to act on the villagers around him, to force the pressing reality of violence into view, disrupting the rituals that order and shape their day. As the Giles comparison suggests, this jolting function is twofold. On one hand, it pains Isa's own interior life, which is constantly pressured by the memory of her reading about the rape. On the other hand, it counters the repetitive ritual, which, as we have seen, mirrors and anticipates the massive violence of the wars. In other words, her internalization and absorption of one narrative of violence (the rape) in part counteracts another, broader one (the history of world violence, emblematized by the two wars, and by repetition). In that sense, the rape is almost a comfort, a form of violence that can still be assimilated. It thus recalls *The Secret Agent*, which, in shifting to Winnie's melodramatic story of domestic violence from Stevie's ambiguous one of dynamite explosion, found available literary conventions. Woolf drives the point home a little later in the novel, when Isa, in the midst of a particularly troubled thought sequence, turns to the raped girl as part of her retreat from public violence and apathy: "On, little donkey, patiently stumble," she encourages herself, "Hear not the frantic cries of the leaders who in that they seek to lead desert us. Nor the chatter of china faces glazed and hard. Hear rather the shepherd, coughing by the farmyard wall; the withered tree that sighs when the Rider gallops; the brawl in the barrack room when they stripped her naked . . ." (*BTA*, 156). It is a difficult sequence to understand; why would she "hear rather" the sounds in the background of the rape? Perhaps because "the brawl in the barrack room when they stripped her naked" belongs to the tradition of formalizing violence with which Woolf has always worked. It scans, for one thing. And it represents Isa's imaginative absorption and redirection of violence as part of her personal poem, a synecdoche, in the end, for Woolfian textuality.

The passage, moreover, comes as close as Isa's narrative ever will to modernism, and particularly to Eliot, whom she echoes stylistically (one hears the timbre, especially, of such lyrics as "The Journey of the Magi" and "Sweeney among the Nightingales"); in fact, the rape functions in Isa's consciousness, and in the novel more generally, in a manner akin to Eliot's amalgamation of the rape of Philomela in *The Waste Land*. In both cases, the rape allusions return repeatedly; are interwoven very thoroughly into the textual fabric and consciousness; work in relation to larger narratives of world violence (primarily war); and put particular stress on the division between enchanted and disenchanted violence. In Eliot's poem, we recall, the rape of Philomela provoked an especially dense and layered reflection on the way violence becomes the foundation on which many aesthetic forms are based, often leaving behind only trace reminders of its original catastrophe. Here, things are much rawer; the rape is "real," a contemporary event given in material detail, a violent attack figured as palpable (and the bizarre inclusion of the green-tailed horse only heightens this sense of its viscerality). This raw quality fits with the temporality of violence in *Between the Acts*—oncoming, shadowing, squeezing out the present moment—in contrast to *The Waste Land*, which stands instead as a postwar monument, dedicated, in part, to mourning and healing. And yet, the commonalties are striking; perhaps, indeed, it is this intertextual connection that calls up the Swinburne poem "Itylus" in *Between the Acts*, from which Bart—an unlikely reader of Swinburne—hums several lines, including, "Swallow, my sister, O sister swallow" (*BTA*, 109). It is, of course, the same one Eliot borrows in *The Waste Land* to suggest how deeply violence is embedded in literary culture and history, and reminds us, as in Eliot's poem, that tales of brutal violence can be transformed, though long historical and literary passages, into lyrical refrains, almost nonreferential bits of music. More generally, what the parallel between *The Waste Land* and Woolf's novel helps to show is that these narratives of violent rape fundamentally display and challenge the relation between art and violence. Woolf reveals that for Isa, the rape, though shocking and terrible, is also invigorating; it shakes up her language, just as it breaks the somnambulatory quality of the day. It does not enchant—Woolf will never allow that—but it does revive; it demands recognition.

The rape sequence, then, becomes a critical, transformative element in Isa's and the novel's poetic consciousness, insisting on its presence; as such, it stands as a complement and counterforce to the other moment when violence and creativity are interlocked, Giles's stamping on the snake and toad. The passage, as we have seen, reflects the contemporary conversation about violence in several ways (the questions of inherent human violence, the status of action), and also resurrects many of Woolf's own preoccupations, as reflected in her earlier works (the circularity of violent happenings, animal allegory). I have suggested, moreover, that the blood on the shoes represents an instance and refraction of artistic creation, or, we might say, of form itself. In other words, it allegorizes Woolf's own writing, which repeatedly offers the equivalent of a splash of blood as a distillation of its own processes for accommodating violence—the purple stains or bruises in *Jacob's Room* and *To the Lighthouse*, the wisps of cloud left by the airplane in *Mrs. Dalloway*, the wounded hand in *The Years*, to name a few cases.[124] The blood on the shoes, then, becomes emblematic: it stands for Woolf's ob-servations about how violence and art mutually inseminate, in her own work as in that of many other artists (including Eliot). As the novel moves more and more in the direction of gestural violence, the patterns that Woolf has created in the past show their artificiality, they anatomize themselves. Are they no more than a stain of blood on the shoes? Moreover, with the artist visible—violent, aggressive, homophobic, frustrated, as well as impotent, helpless, passive—his artistry seems all the more com-promised. Indeed, the elemental quality of the entire configuration aligns it with the other primal moments in the novel, a trajectory that ends in the novel's final para-graphs, with their grimacing, frightening cadences.

The rape and the shoes suggest a reckoning with violence that not only looks out at the world, but also back at Woolf's career, and these are not the only such self-referential moments in *Between the Acts*. Lucy, too, articulates an aesthetic model that recalls Woolf's earlier works, particularly at the end of the novel, when she spies the ancient fish in the pond. It is a favorite Woolfian image, one that has resonance as early as *The Voyage Out*, and comes in a passage that also evokes such canonical figures as Lily Briscoe:

> Then something moved in the water; her favorite fantail. The golden orfe followed. Then she had a glimpse of silver—the great carp himself, who came to the surface so very seldom. They slid on, in and out between the stalks, silver; pink; gold; splashed; streaked; pied.
>
> "Ourselves," she murmured. And retrieving some glint of faith from the grey waters, hopefully, without much help from reason, she followed the fish; the speckled, streaked, and blotched; seeing in that vision beauty, power, and glory in ourselves.
>
> Fish had faith, she reasoned. (*BTA* 205)

Is this, then, the vision that counters what Isa and Giles, in their separate iterations, show about the complicity of art with violence? Woolf poses the possibility that Lucy's vision, like Lily's in *To the Lighthouse*, might offer a real alternative to the shadowy mood epitomized by both the rape and the bloody shoes (and in *To the Lighthouse* by the sound of waves or the purple stain). It is an especially welcome passage, moreover, because fish in *Between the Acts* have generally not fared well: they come filleted, or with gills full of blood, or at the end of two crisscrossed fishing lines (*BTA*, 21, 48). And yet, the freedom and beauty of the fish in the pond are circumscribed by Lucy's own limitations—"Fish had faith, she reasoned"—as Woolf puts the brakes on her as a viable visionary for this novel (as, in an earlier passage, when her admirable proclivity for "one-making" is undermined by her childlike image of God as a giant head). The novel seems disinclined to give Lucy any real or sustained imaginative reach, instead, as we have seen, tending to stereotype and circumscribe all of its characters, Lucy included; she is all faith, Bart all skepticism, neither sufficient. Just as *Three Guineas* indicated that Woolf had moved away from her male modernist peers as sources of experimental inspiration, here it is Woolf's own former modernist expressions of hope and beauty that she presents as tired and self-deceived. Instead, the rape language and the shoes have a resonance and honesty in the present that distinguishes them from insufficient visions such as Lucy's. They are distinct, too from the novel's many images of violence in the past, wonderfully compact and layered as those are, such as the passage about the scarred landscape, or another in which is framed—literally, in a glass case—"a watch that had stopped a bullet on the field of Waterloo" (*BTA*, 7).

Isa and Giles, in their disparate ways, initiate images of violence and creation that have a depth of metatextual layering one expects of a final novel. "In the history of art," Edward Said notes, quoting Adorno, "late works are the catastrophes."[125] If we return to *The Voyage Out*, we can see that Woolf has moved almost one hundred and eighty degrees in her understanding of character and violence: there, it was Rachel who became the recipient and focal point, constellating the episodic, detached spectacles of violence that peppered the novel; here, the protagonists themselves act out the dialectic between art and violence, making their own canvases in blood. There is nothing enchanted about such complicity, but nor are we in *Three Guineas*, with its positing, in the Spanish photographs, of a thoroughly disenchanted view. Indeed, the division between enchanted and disenchanted violence, which we have seen to energize the literature of modernism to no small degree, itself seems beside the point. Miss La Trobe had ended her pageant with self-reflection, "Ourselves," and Woolf's version of that imperative, at least in part, involves a searing look at how and where and in what form violence has inhabited her literary oeuvre. And though Woolf may not be one for self-dramatizing gestures, when she ends her novel with a rising curtain, she indicates something that all three of her final works have intimated: a new story is ready to be told. Woolf cannot, of course, know the extent and contours of the worldwide violence that will follow her death. What she does know is that it will not be she, or modernism, that will find the language for writing those painful truths.

Conclusion

The cover of the *New Yorker* on September 24, 2001, was almost completely black. Looking closely, one could discern faint shadows of the twin towers shaded in the dark, just a hint of figuration in the blank, black field. It was a dramatic gesture, and one that answered remarkably well to the enormous public questions about art and culture that circulated in that intense, uncertain, memorable period immediately after the attacks: what kinds of representational statements would, could, or should be made? How would the aesthetic domain be touched by the attacks, and would artists step forward with their own defining visions? How would the responses of local people to the events overlap or jar with reactions from other parts of the country and the world? Of course, these questions have spun and widened in the decade since 2001, and have spread across the globe, as war has followed war. But the immediacy of the *New Yorker*'s response can be taken as paradigmatic of one primary answer to the shock of massive violence epitomized by 9/11: restraint, blankness, emptiness. These were responses cued to the salient fact of this particular crime, that the bodies themselves were incinerated, crushed, vanished. One of the most sobering and memorable images from the day is of the local hospitals readying themselves, once the towers had begun to burn, for huge numbers of injured people, instead remaining nearly empty. The visual spectacles of 9/11 have been seen by billions, but with the exception of a few stunning photographs featuring falling bodies, which appear as specks against the enormity of the towers, no one has ever seen the bodies of the dead.[1] The violence of the attacks was instantly recognized as historic and transformative, and the absence of flesh made its own imaginative claims.

Or perhaps it is the lost flesh itself that makes patterns. There are photographs from Hiroshima that show geometrical patches against a wall or on stone steps; they look like human silhouettes, or perhaps just blotchy grey shapes. But what they show, it seems, are the remains of annihilated bodies, portraits.[2] It is hard to imagine shadows so full of visceral truth, so meaningful in both historical and physical terms, so chilling as these Hiroshima traces. Absence of bodies, of people, of narratives: this has been the reality of the second half of the twentieth century, determining the full range of imaginative life. The Jews of Europe did not vanish in the same sense that bodies did in the atomic flashes or on 9/11; the attempt to erase them was, rather, the steady work of years, the massive project of a party and an anti-Semitic tradition bent on annihilation. In the memorial culture that has developed all over the world in response to these events—the genocides, wars, targeted attacks, and mass upheavals that have defined the second half of the twentieth century—we find a countercurrent, what Woolf might call "the force which . . . oppose[s] itself to the force" of tyranny, an effort at communal, archival, narrative, architectural, and aesthetic levels to combat the erasure of human beings and their histories.[3] There is, in this massive memorial endeavor, no single or dominant style. On the contrary, as James Young reminds us, familiarity is the enemy of memory; if memorials are going to stir and awaken the imagination, they need to be active and disruptive, capable of defamiliarizing what is known and expected.[4]

Nevertheless, in the broad memorial effort, and more generally in the literary and artistic project attached to the mass violence of the second half of the twentieth century, one central principle remains always at the forefront: whatever representation can accomplish, it will never capture the enormity of the violence it is remembering. The problem of excess is greater than ever—the sheer number of the shoes in the landmark Auschwitz exhibit provides searing visual testimony—and one of the most enduring aesthetic responses has been to make visible that very incommensurability. As Tim O'Brien writes, "in the end, really, there's nothing much to say about a true war story, except maybe 'Oh.'"[5] This is not to say that "true" war stories don't get told (O'Brien's own body of work is testament to the ongoing, unfinished, intensely fruitful commitment to that project) but rather that they are relentlessly framed according to a consciousness of disequilibrium. One thinks of W. G. Sebald, whose works are built around great funds of absence, tales of postwar migrations and reconstitutions that refuse to name or narrate the war's violence. Or of Michael Ondaatje's *The English Patient* (1992), which tells its war story in and through breach: in books, in walls, in memory. Or of Toni Morrison, whose narratives are almost always oriented around the foundational traumas of slavery. Or of Samuel Beckett, at the midpoint of the century, writing war and violence into his denuded, bare stages, *Waiting for Godot* (1952), among other things, readable as an allegory for the violence of the Second World War, including atomic explosion. Or of Kurt Vonnegut, who for decades felt the difficulty (and compulsion) of producing a novel about the firebombing of Dresden; in the end, for all the eccentricity of *Slaughterhouse-Five* (1969), Vonnegut found the most powerful epithet for mass destruction in the seemingly banal phrase "so it goes," and the most apt visual markers for the destruction of Dresden to be simple descriptions, marked by metaphors that stress the absolutely elemental: "There was a fire-storm out there. Dresden was one big flame. The one flame ate everything organic, everything that would burn. . . . Dresden was like the moon now, nothing but minerals. The stones were hot. Everybody else in the neighborhood was dead. So it goes."[6]

All of this spareness, emptiness, void, and geometry is, as we have seen, a deep and important aspect of modernism, which built much of its formal edifice on the grounds of awful violence. Each chapter has illuminated an aspect of the elemental impulse, the desire to purge from the surfeit of physical and psychic overload generated by violence, to find instead an idiom that is lean and sharp—as sharp, perhaps, as the "bright knives" that Betty Flanders's tears make of her visual surroundings. Modernism looks at violence and finds incredible deformations of human bodies, landscapes, and culture. What it offers are compacted bits of language that express these terrible realities: the shovel, the blood painting, the purple stain, the sudden blow, the withered stumps of time. These markers function as emblems, standing in for something larger and themselves notable as figures, always inviting a deeper look, a historical eye, a desire to uncover whatever grisly brutality the world has fostered and concealed, a willingness to imagine the unimaginable. There is, in these efforts, an ethos of slimness and trenchancy, a desire to create literary insignias that will do at least four things at once, like the story of Philomela layered into *The Waste Land* or the square of fish in *To the Lighthouse*: make violence visible through some abstract form; demand, in that gesture, a vigilance in reading the world, so that the raw and painful reality of violence will always be known and felt, that it will shame, that it will be unceasingly alive; nevertheless to contain the spread of violence within the text, mitigating its toxicity, insulating the literary work to some degree from the gruesome power that violence carries, and enabling exceptional forms of beauty to emerge from its violent content; and lastly, to open the text to critique on grounds of these very approaches. One thinks, again, of Tim O'Brien, who makes the body of "the man I killed" into a kind of artwork, with the wound over the man's eye in the shape of a star, a butterfly resting on his neck, "and even in the shade a single blade of sunlight sparkled against the buckle of his ammunition belt" (O'Brien, 142).

The star over the man's eye, the butterfly, the sunlight, the man's "long shapely fingers"—these are only part of the story, however, which is equally infused with a horrendous physical reality that seems to push the literary work away from its patterning impulse, insisting instead on rendering violence's surfeit directly, without flinching ("the skin at his left cheek was peeled back in three ragged strips . . . his neck was open to the spinal cord and the blood there was thick and shiny and it was this wound that had killed him" [O'Brien, 139]). The look is clinical, the facts overwhelming. "So many," *The Waste Land*'s Unreal City voice notes in wonder, "I had not thought death had undone so many," and it is true; the First World War inaugurated the consciousness of vast hordes of killed and wounded, numberless dead, millions and millions, only to be surpassed by the slaughter of the Second—and on from there, winding down the century's killing fields (*TWL*, 62–63). Representation has kept pace, with every visual and literary genre contributing to the onslaught of violence in the aesthetic domain. Much in the contemporary world's fetish for blood, gore, killing, torture, and death seems only tangentially related to what we have been studying in this book, where the hallmarks have been restraint, uneasiness, and often awe at the power of violence (rather than a sense of easy access or manipulability). There is, however, at least one important thread of continuity from modernism to the blood-drenched tide of current taste, namely the disenchanted tradition, which, as we have seen, offers itself as testimony: this is what violence looks like, this is what it does. Here we have Ellen Quinn, crawling in a pool of her own blood, the most salient figure in Yeats's poetry to stand for the dark vortex of reprisal, thoroughly epitomizing the disenchanted view. Stevie's exploded remains represent another benchmark; whatever Conrad's metaphors might scramble to accomplish in the wake of Stevie, there is always the forensic aspect of his fragmented body, that which is gleaned by studying the parts dispassionately, surveying the carnage. To begin with the corpse and end with the crime has always been central to mystery genres, and the motif has been vastly extended into the present— television crime drama, to take the most obvious example, is unthinkable without the detailed examination of the corpse. And yet the terms have shifted when it comes to the immersion in fleshly horror. Where in modernism the anatomical or medical look at the ruined body was kept within tight bounds, a sign of meaninglessness and waste, today it is seen as the initial ground of understanding, a necessary aspect of reckoning with killing, as O'Brien's accounting for his victim's wounds attests.

In very sober and real terms, the body's forensics represent the primary fact of every attack that leaves as wreckage exploded people: the body as tissue, organ, cells. Brian Turner, a combatant in the Iraq War, gives us such flesh in his 2004 poem, "Here, Bullet": "If a body is what you want," he begins, "then here is bone and gristle and flesh."[7] Gristle: it is hard to imagine anyone in fact wanting this rendition of the human body, so alimentary, so revolting (the inverse, in some sense, of Leopold Bloom's delight in organs). It is a poem of imagined answers and completions, the poet's language defiantly rounding out the bullet's damage, catalogued in robustly anatomical terms. From the "gristle and flesh" that conjures a grotesque meat eating, the poem moves to a more biological idiom (aorta, valves, synaptic gaps, adrenaline), suggesting the medical endeavor that stands— perversely and yet humanely—at the other end of war's violence, the attempts to fix and heal that follow the body's shattering by bullets and bombs.[8] Among other extensions and completions the poem addresses is the continuity with modernism, the era that forged the idea of soldier-poet—Turner's "the barrel's cold esophagus, triggering/my tongue's explosives" a direct legacy of Owen's "incurable sores on innocent tongues." Owen and Turner are soldiers, yet their understanding of how flesh, war, language, and loss engage and produce one another in the scene of war belongs equally to the civilian world, whose protection from the violence of combat has eroded steadily over the hundred years since the First World War. As Jean Rhys reminds us, it is those standing in the shadows of the traditional historical imagination, the subjects (rather than agents) of war, empire, and injustice, who in many ways are the inheritors of modernism—not of its canonicity, perhaps, but of its insights, that violence lurks and defiles even the stateliest of edifices, the smoothest of surfaces.

The explosion of bodies—in a central market, pizzeria, mosque, United Nations headquarters, anywhere—and the bodiless void of the World Trade Center present two extremes of physical presence and absence in the wake of violent attack in our current era; contrasting with both of these, and in a sense falling in between them, is a configuration we have repeatedly encountered in this study, the moment of touch. It has often anchored these readings, beginning with Stephen Dedalus and the prefect, the touch that can be a sign of healing, or of callous and inhumane brutality, or of the way any intimate violent interaction between two people gestures beyond them to broader categories and narratives. To consider two people touching as a fundamental unit in the story of violence in the twentieth century is to change the scale, back from the numberless hordes, to reestablish the individual's ordinary imaginative span as the essential one in apprehending violence. The hand, the personal encounter, the closeness of sympathy with grievous violence: these infuse something distinctly archaic, elemental, and universal into the violent encounter. In modernism, as we have seen, there can be tremendous generativity in these conflations, an anthropological energy that fosters a sense of primacy in violent origins. Later in the twentieth century, modernism itself might be asked to help produce such outcomes, as in *Apocalypse Now* (1979), which siphons its intellectual and atmospheric fuel from Conrad and Eliot, and which makes a glorious—indeed glamorous—case for the enchanting possibilities inherent even in the ugliest and most venal forms of mass violence.[9] More to the point, the film wants to secure a space, within its expansive war landscape, for the intimate meeting, the moment when violence and touch become one. There are many such expressions in *Apocalypse Now*'s lengthy and extravagant final sequence at the Kurtz compound, culminating in Willard's spectacularly intimate killing of the colonel. It is an attack very much by hand, the silhouette of man hacking at man with an enormous knife set against the villagers' ritual slaughter of a bull.[10] Coppola's elevation of such hand-to-body killing as a sign of relative purity may seem atavistic, heavy-handed, ethnocentric, even a bit insane (and Eleanor Coppola's memoir of the making of the film presents Francis as having something of a nervous breakdown along the way, himself entering a private world of excess and egomania to match those of his characters), but it is nevertheless astute about its precursor moment, the modernist period, which continued to see in the intimate violent encounter an aura of something vital and primary, if not enchanted or glorified.[11] To be sure, Coppola is engaged in an eloquent and grand project of literary inheritance and supersession, but the larger point is to see how the paradigms we have been studying are carried forward, whether in lavish, highly literate fashion (as in *Apocalypse Now*) or more invisibly, as later writers have sought their own emblematic motifs, fitted to a half century when the garish display of violence has become more and more commonplace.

Violence and touch in Coppola's film trigger an enchantment response, yet this is not a universal move in the later twentieth century any more than it was for modernists; in fact, to be able to touch without even a spark of sympathy might be seen as humanity's very nadir. So in *Survival in Auschwitz* (*Ger*, 1947), Primo Levi recalls a moment when touch has been drained of even the dregs of human civility, and sees in that denuding a full expression of Nazi evil:

> The steel cable of a crane cuts across the road, and Alex catches hold of it to climb over: *Donnerwetter*, he looks at his hand black with thick grease. In the meanwhile, I have joined him. Without hatred and without sneering, Alex wipes his hand on my shoulder, both the palm and the back of the hand, to clean it; he would be amazed, the poor brute Alex, if someone told him that today, on the basis of this action, I judge him and Pannwitz and the innumerable others like him, big and small, in Auschwitz and everywhere.[12]

There is no shortage, in Levi's writing, of sadism, gruesome inhumanity, or unimaginable indifference; if this story stands out as exemplary in his memory, it is because the structure for engendering feeling is so markedly available and perverted, the possibility of sympathetic or curative touch so entirely abandoned. The distorting of objects and structures that promise security into the most vicious purveyors of violence is, as Elaine Scarry has shown, the hallmark and basis of torture—the use, say, of common household items as mechanisms to impart pain and engender fear.[13] Or, to return to 9/11, the employment of airplanes as weapons represents the most acute and visible sign of such transformation from the ordinary and benign into the unrecognizable and deadly. We saw a gesture in this direction in *The Secret Agent*, with the Professor's potential as a suicide bomber extending and intensifying his power (force) across space and into the future. The airplane as weapon, moreover, closes the loop of associations around the airplane that we have seen to form a rich and contradictory part of the post–First World War imaginary, reaching a height in the 1930s, to be followed finally by the Second World War's obliterative bombing campaigns. Paul Virilio sees such conflations as definitive of perception itself in the later twentieth century, where the camera's eye and the weapon's targeting mechanisms express and propel one another, becoming part of one imaginative unit:

> From the first missiles of World War Two to the lightning flash of Hiroshima, the *theatre weapon* has replaced the *theatre of operations*. Indeed the military term "theatre weapon," though itself outmoded, underlines the fact that *the history of battle is primarily the history of radically changing fields of perception*. In other words, war consists not so much in scoring territorial, economic or other material victories as in appropriating the "immateriality" of perceptual fields. As belligerents set out to invade those fields in their totality, it became apparent that the true war film did not necessarily have to depict war or any actual battle. For once the cinema was able to create surprise (technological, psychological, etc.), it effectively came under the category of weapons.[14] (Emphasis in original)

Virilio is equivocal about when to pinpoint the historical moment where violence and seeing come to inhabit the same intellectual and cultural domain. Here the Second World War is the locus, but elsewhere he will fix the era of the First as the moment when "the target area had become a cinema 'location', the battlefield a film set out of bounds to civilians" (Virilio, 11), and in that historicizing he agrees with other scholars, like Bernd Hüppauf, who writes that "the origin of this process of abstraction, which finally led to images of the Gulf War devoid of the space necessary for human experience, but highly fantastic and playful, can be traced back to the late nineteenth century. Its period of consolidation and first culmination was World War I, particularly in aerial photography."[15] Paul Fussell, too, in marking the imaginative transformations ushered in by the war, sees the trenches propelling a rerouting of the entire perceptual and cognitive capacity, to be expressed in literature, in colloquial speech, in the full range of memory and thought.

The early-twentieth-century writers at the center of this book, certainly, have struggled to give a voice to violence that would be adequate to what they see as its overwhelming scale and threat, impinging on structures of epistemology and perception, as of understanding and belief. At the same time, the very idea of adequation, the sense that there can be an imaginative or formal structure to balance and approximate violence, has always come fraught with misgiving. To take, for instance, the inevitable recourse to an economic model (this for that) is, perhaps, to give in to the capitalist logic whose indifference and voracity is responsible for war, empire, and injustice in the first place. This conundrum has provoked many of the writers in this study (most pressingly, Yeats and Woolf), and it does not, moreover, disappear in the later parts of the century. Writing his way from victimization to protest after being badly wounded in Vietnam, Ron Kovic, in *Born on the Fourth of July* (1976), offers the failed logic of barter as a culminating statement of despair and defeat: "The blood was rolling off my flak jacket from the hole in my shoulder and I couldn't feel the pain in my foot anymore, I couldn't even feel my body. I was frightened to death. I didn't think about praying, all I could feel was cheated . . . All I could feel was the worthlessness of dying right here in this place at this moment for nothing."[16] It is the "for nothing" in Kovic's assessment that clinches his near-nihilism, that the struggle he has chronicled will have had no payoff, no return, no meaning. And indeed Kovic cannot devote the last word of his memoir to this recognition of the complete wastefulness of war, framed in terms of a poor trade. He concludes, instead, in an entirely different idiom, with a hymn to his childhood, an oddly aestheticized mélange of memory and music that harks back not only to his own past in 1950s Long Island, rendered in the haze of nostalgia, but also to a literary past he never mentions, modernism. In borrowing prototypically modernist forms (pastiche, stream of consciousness) as an alternate statement of the ultimate meaning of massive violence and the individual life story, Kovic's memoir, like Coppola's film, suggests something other than straightforward influence. What it suggests is that the formal experiments by which many modernists engaged violence retain some of their appeal and power even in these new settings, and even when they are no longer associated with a fixed period in literary history. In part, this appeal comes from the fact that modernist efforts to accommodate violence have roots in much older traditions (with enchantment and disenchantment, especially), reaching back in literary culture all the way to the *Iliad*, where war and art belong to one field, one endeavor. The attraction comes, too, because there is something resilient about the way modernism simultaneously placed violence at the center of its consciousness and found ways to reframe, contain, and aestheticize it, without needing to glorify or valorize it.

At the same time, when set against the stunning technological and representational developments of the second half of the twentieth century, and into the twenty-first, modernism itself can feel anachronistic on the subject of violence—indeed, in the case of Coppola, it is imagined specifically as the site of connection to an ancient world, a catalyst for the contemporary to reach out and back from its own time of routinized killing into a zone where violence might be understood, through its affinity with the long past, to represent and confer sacredness, sublimity. More generally, however, literary culture in recent decades has taken its cues from the ubiquity of visible violence that characterizes our era—its dispersal, via technology, into every household, in a seemingly unstoppable expansion. Rushdie's conceit in *Midnight's Children* (1980) of a connection among the one hundred at the level of frequency, which brings often terrifying violence directly into their shared consciousness, presages the later emphasis on networks and interconnection that has come to pervade in the digital era. Another later-twentieth-century form to have acquired surprising trenchancy in the conception of violence is the graphic novel; appropriate to the visuality of contemporary culture, texts like *Maus* (1986) and *Persepolis* (2000) have generated a powerful new idiom, fueled by the juxtapositions and abrasions in form and content they create.[17] Animated film, too, pried from the preserve of children, has come into its own as a resonant style for considering the range of historical, personal, social, psychic, and aesthetic consequences of violence (as in *Waltz with Bashir*, the 2008 Israeli film). These are new developments altogether, sharing with the modernist works we have studied a serious, ongoing effort to find languages appropriate to the magnitude of the violence they chronicle, but departing in most other ways—in form, tone, sensibility, reigning conceits, imagined audience.

Above all, where contemporary literature seems to have shifted tracks from modernism is in its relation to the globe. As we have seen, technologies such as the airplane led writers in the early twentieth century to see the world, along with other units such as the city, as grimly interconnected by potential destruction, and this understanding of violence as a phenomenon that cuts across and reconstructs the lineaments of the globe has been greatly deepened in later decades; one thinks of *Gravity's Rainbow* (1973), another epic formulation, which confers on its rockets the principle of potentially universal connectivity. Well beyond America and England, the last fifty years have seen a much amplified exploration of the scales and forces that violence can take, often in the context of colonial and postcolonial deformations of individuals, communities, nations, and ecologies. One explanation for the expanded comprehension of how violence works, at the global and often invisible level, is thus a straightforward one: more and more of the literary world is being shaped by those who would never have been in a position to miss the reality of world violence. With new vistas of writing, communication, connectivity, and narrative opening, the place of violence in determining the contours of imaginative life has come fully out of the shadows. If writers such as Woolf found tremendous challenge in maintaining the integrity of the literary text in the face of a violence understood as geographically unbounded as well as historically extensive, later writers take these conditions as their base and groundwork. They also begin with a fully renovated cartography. As critics have amply discussed, the hierarchies that fix center and periphery have long faltered, and the British Isles have come to inhabit their actual size and scale in a world conceived in global, or even planetary, dimensions.

At the same time, *At the Violet Hour* has noted, over and over, an anticipation of this very shift in scope and authority. For all its sense of artistic mission and cultural power, modernism saw the future as outside of its grasp. In each phase of the violence narrative we have been studying, we have found this idea: that the form and force of violence will always catapult it out of the imagination of the present, so that it will come to stand, instead, as the very principle of an unknowable future. At the end of a novel, or a career, or a national saga of war and loss, what we find is not a curtain falling but one rising, as Woolf makes literal in the last work in this study, *Between the Acts*. "In my beginning is my end," Eliot would write not long before Woolf's death, seeing in the temporal collapse of past, present, and future an emblem for the cycles of violence and beauty that had always concerned his poetry, and the works more generally of modernism. In the encounter with violence, indeed, ends and beginnings seem unusually mutual, signs and avatars of one another. And yet, for all this commingling of chronologies, the rising curtain onto a bleak future is, in its way, a decisive image to represent the condition of writing about violence. Something will always exceed the present, the current writer, the instant in time; violence's defining fact of excess applies also to temporality. The violet hour is, after all, a marker of how time passes. As Capa's photographs of civilians warily scanning the sky remind us, there is an ineradicable imbalance between the present (of bodily integrity, of life) and the future (of destruction, of death). It is a principle of incipience, with the present carrying with it the weight, as it were, of the future. And it is a principle of ignorance, with the present feeling its way toward a future whose violence will, in the end, always find a way to surpass even our worst imaginings.

Notes

Introduction

1. Matthew Arnold, *Culture and Anarchy* (Cambridge: Cambridge University Press, 1990), 6.

2. For a deft recent work on modernism and technology, see Enda Duffy, *The Speed Handbook: Velocity, Pleasure, Modernism* (Durham: Duke University Press, 2009).

3. As Perry Meisel puts it, "Modernism is, in all its historical manifestations, the recurrent desire to find origins or ground despite the impossibility of ever doing so for sure." See Perry Meisel, *The Myth of the Modern: A Study in British Literature and Criticism after 1850* (New Haven: Yale University Press, 1987), 4.

4. W. G. Sebald, *On the Natural History of Destruction*, trans. Anthea Bell (New York: Modern Library, 2003), 53.

5. Wilfred Owen, *The Poems of Wilfred Owen* (London: Chatto, 1990), 170.

6. Walter Benjamin, *Illuminations*, trans. Hannah Arendt (New York: Schocken, 1968), 84. Elaine Scarry's *The Body in Pain: The Making and Unmaking of the World* (Oxford: Oxford University Press, 1985) was the pathbreaking study in this area, and has strongly influenced my thinking. For several compelling works that consider how violence finds a voice despite the limitations Scarry has articulated, see Santanu Das, *Touch and Intimacy in First World War Literature* (Cambridge: Cambridge University Press, 2005); James Dawes, *The Language of War: Literature and Culture in the U. S. from the Civil War through World War II* (Cambridge, MA: Harvard University Press, 2002); and Drew Gilpin Faust, *This Republic of Suffering: Death and the American Civil War* (New York: Knopf, 2008).

7. Robert Buch, *The Pathos of the Real: On the Aesthetics of Violence in the Twentieth Century* (Baltimore: Johns Hopkins University Press, 2010), 18.

8. In attending to the moment of violent encounter, one inevitably faces several possible methodological and ideological objections. There is, first, the problem of contributing to a thematics of voyeurism. In her study of spectatorship and slavery, Saidiya Hartman explicitly disavows the focus on the "routine display of the slave's ravaged body" in favor of more dispersed and concealed realms of violence, a choice that for Hartman is both laudable and

fruitful: Saidiya Hartman, *Scenes of Subjection: Terror, Slavery, and Self-Making in Nineteenth-Century America* (Oxford: Oxford University Press, 1997), 3. Broader critiques have been inaugurated, for instance, by Rob Nixon, whose concept of "slow violence" demands a very different temporal scheme from one generated by the moment of infliction, by Ian Baucom, who locates the almost silent, almost invisible murder of slaves as a new nexus for configuring the imaginative scene of what he calls "the long twentieth century," and by Slavoj Žižek, who has argued that to focus on the violent event (what he calls "subjective violence") is itself a political (and perhaps he would even say violent) move, since it obscures deeper, systemic forms of violence in the culture at large ("objective violence"). All of these points are well taken, Žižek's stance being the most generally construed—that there is never a pure and free ground against which violence manifests as entirely unique and aberrant. See Rob Nixon, *Slow Violence and the Environmentalism of the Poor* (Cambridge, MA: Harvard University Press, 2011), Ian Baucom, *Specters of the Atlantic: Finance Capital, Slavery, and the Philosophy of History* (Durham: Duke University Press, 2005), and Slavoj Žižek, *Violence: Six Sideways Reflections* (London: Profile, 2008). Despite the utility of these critiques, there are good reasons to track carefully the focus on the violated body, in part because to do so helps us to understand, as distinct from overlook, these less visible forms of violence as well.

On the topic of the witness and testimony, some of the most encompassing, stirring, and influential scholarly works over the last several decades include Giorgio Agamben, *Remnants of Auschwitz: The Witness and the Archive* (New York: Zone, 2002); Cathy Caruth, *Unclaimed Experience: Trauma, Narrative, and History* (Baltimore: Johns Hopkins University Press, 1996); Caruth, ed. *Trauma: Explorations in Memory* (Baltimore: Johns Hopkins University Press, 1995); Terrence Des Pres, *The Survivor: An Anatomy of Life in the Death Camps* (Oxford: Oxford University Press, 1980); Shoshana Felman, ed., *Literature and Psychoanalysis: The Question of Reading: Otherwise* (Baltimore: Hopkins University Press, 1982); Felman and Dori Laub, eds., *Testimony: Crises of Witnessing in Literature, Psychoanalysis, and History* (New York: Routledge, 1992); Geoffrey Hartman, ed., *Holocaust Remembrance: The Shapes of Memory* (Cambridge: Blackwell, 1994); Marianne Hirsch, *Family Frames: Photography, Narrative, and Postmemory* (Cambridge: Harvard University Press, 1997); Hirsch and Leo Spitzer, *Ghosts of Home: The Afterlife of Czernowitz in Jewish Memory* (Berkeley: University of California Press, 2010); Primo Levi, *Survival in Auschwitz: The Nazi Assault on Humanity*, trans. Stuart Woolf (New York: Simon and Schuster, 1996); Levi, *The Drowned and the Saved*, trans. Raymond Rosenthal (New York: Random House, 1989); Emmanuel Levinas, *God, Death, and Time*, trans. Bettina Bergo (Stanford: Stanford University Press, c.2000); Ruth Leys, *Trauma: A Genealogy* (Chicago: University of Chicago Press, 2000); Leo Spitzer, *Hotel Bolivia: The Culture of Memory in a Refuge from Nazism* (New York: Hill and Wang, 1998); and Jay Winter, *Remembering War: The Great War between Memory and History in the Twentieth Century* (New Haven: Yale University Press, 2006).

9. As is always the case with "modernism," my usage carries field qualifications: I am using the term primarily as it derives from literary history, though I also discuss visual culture, and my focus is on the British Isles, which of course is nonidentical with other modernisms. I hope that the models I am tracing in this book will resonate beyond (and in some cases specifically challenge) national traditions or borders.

10. The pandying episode represents one of the most overtly autobiographical sequences in the Clongowes segment of *Portrait*. For discussion of the episode with respect to Joyce's young schooling experiences, see Bruce Bradley, *James Joyce's Schooldays* (New York:

St. Martin's 1982), especially 69–78. See also Richard Ellmann, *James Joyce* (Oxford: Oxford University Press, 1983), 28.

A different context for the passage involves practices of punishment within British and Irish schools more generally, and one could set it alongside other works in the modernist period that critiqued the Victorian school for its brutality and philistinism. For discussion of these issues in a Dublin and Jesuit context, see Patrick J. Ledden, "Education and Social Class in Joyce's Dublin," *Journal of Modern Literature* 22:2 (Winter 1998–99): 329–47, and Jim Muller, "John Henry Newman and the Education of Stephen Dedalus," *James Joyce Quarterly* 33:4 (Summer 1996): 593–603. For discussion of the Victorian school more broadly, see John Chandos, *Boys Together: English Public Schools 1800–1864* (New Haven: Yale University Press, 1984); J. A. Mangan, *The Games Ethic and Imperialism: Aspects of the Diffusion of an Ideal* (New York: Viking, 1985); Mangan and James Walvin, eds., *Manliness and Morality: Middle-Class Masculinity in Britain and America: 1800–1940* (Manchester: Manchester University Press, 1984); and David Newsome, *Godliness and Good Learning: Four Studies on a Victorian Ideal* (London: Murray, 1961).

11. James Joyce, *A Portrait of the Artist as a Young Man* (New York: Penguin, 1993), 51–52.

12. In a rich and engaging reflection, Michael Wood writes (about Yeats) that "there is a moment within violence that is also non-narrative and seemingly prior to the law and the human subject." He goes on to suggest the word "turbulence" as an apt one to characterize violence in much of Yeats's work. See Michael Wood, *Yeats and Violence* (Oxford: Oxford University Press, 2010), 19–20.

13. We might, for instance, consider Tolstoy's reflection in *War and Peace* about the inverse relation between power and bodily vulnerability in war, or Scarry's analysis in *The Body in Pain* of the defining feature of power in the Hebrew Bible being a disembodied God in relation to a radically embodied people.

14. Critical accounts of "the body" have been a major topic over the last several decades. One dominant strain, for which Judith Butler's works from the 1990s can be seen as leading articulations, takes the body as a construct, inseparable from, and fundamentally determined by, a host of factors that, in a sense, create the person from the inside out. See especially Judith Butler, *Gender Trouble: Feminism and the Subversion of Identity* (New York: Routledge, 1990) and *Bodies That Matter* (New York: Routledge, 1993). For a deconstructive approach to violence (also representative of its critical era), in which the body is dematerialized and language is the focus, see Nancy Armstrong and Leonard Tennenhouse, eds., *The Violence of Representation: Literature and the History of Violence* (New York: Routledge, 1989). Moving in a different direction, a smaller and less cohesive cohort of scholars has challenged the constructionist thesis. Coming from such diverse perspectives as human rights, Holocaust studies, postcolonial studies, and a variety of New Historicist and materialist positions, critics have recommitted to a sense of priority about the body's material presence. I will refer to a number of these theorists over the course of my study.

15. Analysis of what kind of space is opened up in the intimate moment when oppressor meets oppressed (or colonizer meets colonized) has been addressed by cultural and literary critics over the last several decades. For a canonical formulation, see Homi K. Bhabha, *The Location of Culture* (London: Routledge, 1994), 84–92 and 102–22.

16. Within a broad field, several useful and rich discussions of Joyce and colonization are Vincent J. Cheng, *Joyce, Race, and Empire* (Cambridge: Cambridge University Press, 1995); Seamus Deane, *Celtic Revivals: Essays in Modern Irish Literature, 1880–1980* (London: Faber,

1985); Enda Duffy, *The Subaltern* Ulysses (Minneapolis: University of Minnesota Press, 1994); Jason Howard Mezey, "Ireland, Europe, The World, The Universe: Political Geography in *A Portrait of the Artist as a Young Man*," *Journal of Modern Literature* 22:2 (1999): 337–48; and Emer Nolan, *James Joyce and Nationalism* (New York: Routledge, 1995).

17. In depicting this interlocking of subjective with extensive violence, one precursor from a different national tradition comes especially to mind: Fyodor Dostoevsky, who has a shadowy presence throughout modernist accounts of violence. In some cases (such as Raskolnikov's dream of the mare in *Crime and Punishment*), later writers will make direct reference to Dostoevsky. More generally, a number of the themes, historical topics, and formal mechanisms I will be discussing figure in Dostoevsky's works as well (especially *The Devils, Crime and Punishment,* and *The Brothers Karamazov*). Still, for all the over-laps, there are important formal and contextual differences separating Dostoevsky from the early-twentieth-century British writers who followed him. To take just one example: if the double murder at the outset of *Crime and Punishment* (with its widely dispersed ramifica-tions throughout the novel) might stand at the cornerstone of many later considerations of brute violence, Dostoevsky's verbose style of realism in the novel, the novel's gender con-structions, and its ultimate Christian framework mark important differences from the later English tradition. It is tempting to read Raskolnikov in protomodernist terms; but what do we do about Sonya?

18. For discussion of what kinds of purpose the Victorian novel sought to serve, see Amanda Claybaugh, *The Novel of Purpose: Literature and Social Reform in the Anglo-American World* (Ithaca: Cornell University Press, 2007).

19. For incisive and diverse readings of allegorical usage, see Gordon Teskey, *Allegory and Violence* (Ithaca: Cornell University Press, 1996). For more comprehensive accounts of allegory in literary history, see Theresa M. Kelley, *Reinventing Allegory* (Cambridge: Cam-bridge University Press, 1997), and Jon Whitman, ed., *Interpretation and Allegory: Antiquity to the Modern Period* (Leiden: Brill, 2000).

20. Bainard Cowan, "Walter Benjamin's Theory of Allegory," *New German Critique*, 22 (Winter 1981): 110. For elaborate treatment of Benjamin and allegory, see Baucom, *Specters of the Atlantic.*

21. In a brief discussion, Fredric Jameson has noted that allegory comes to the fore not in modernism, which adhered to the symbol, but in postmodernism. See Fredric Jameson, *Postmodernism, or, the Cultural Logic of Late Capitalism* (Durham: Duke University Press, 1991), 167–68.

22. W. B. Yeats, *The Variorum Edition of the Poems of W. B. Yeats* (New York: MacMillan, 1957), 441. Cited hereafter in text as *Var.*

23. For a richly historicized reading of the poem, attuned to many of these issues, see Elizabeth Cullingford, *Gender and History in Yeats's Love Poetry* (Cambridge: Cambridge University Press, 1993), 140–64.

24. See Edward Said, "Yeats and Decolonization," in Terry Eagleton, Fredric Jameson, and Edward Said, *Nationalism, Colonialism, and Literature* (Minneapolis: University of Minnesota Press, 1990).

25. Terrence Des Pres, *The Survivor: An Anatomy of Life in the Death Camps* (Oxford: Oxford University Press, 1980), 69–70, emphasis in original, ellipses added.

26. Paul Fussell, *The Great War and Modern Memory* (London: Oxford University Press, 1975), 61.

27. Olive Schreiner, *The Story of an African Farm* (London: Penguin, 1995), 258.

28. Horses and the First World War remain a compelling combination. For a wonderful Canadian novel featuring horses and war, see Timothy Findley, *The Wars* (Toronto: Penguin, 1977). Witness, too, the 2012 Stephen Spielberg film *War Horse*, and the book and hit play that preceded it.

29. The foundational text, which inaugurated the field of animal studies, is Peter Singer, *Animal Liberation* (New York: Avon, 1977). Influential works with a more literary emphasis include Jacques Derrida, *The Animal that Therefore I Am* (New York: Fordham University Press, 2008); Donna Haraway, *Primate Visions: Gender, Race, and Nature in the World of Modern Science* (New York: Routledge, 1989); Haraway, *When Species Meet* (Minneapolis: University of Minnesota Press, 2008); and Cary Wolfe, *Animal Rites: American Culture, the Discourse of Species, and Posthumanist Theory* (Chicago: University of Chicago Press, 2003). For a survey of the state of the field circa 2009, see the articles in the section "Animal Studies," *PMLA* 124:2 (March 2009): 472–575.

30. Alfred Döblin, *Berlin Alexanderplatz: The Story of Franz Biberkopf*, trans. Eugene Jolas (London: Continuum, 2004), 103.

31. Violation derives from the Latin verb *violare*, "to treat with violence, to outrage, dishonor, injure, etc." (*OED*).

32. Most obvious are the overlaps between body and mind; trauma allows for little distinction between bodily and mental disturbance, and offers a vocabulary for considering their interpenetration. The realms of past and present also intertwine, especially in the notion of recurrence, where the past is relived in and as the present. Even the ontological categories of self and other come under scrutiny in trauma, since, for example, the witnessing of atrocity can be as traumatizing an event as the direct experience of it. In Freud's remarks on trauma in *Beyond the Pleasure Principle*, he stresses that the trauma victim is always a spectator, never the person wounded. For some of the most influential and moving accounts of trauma, see note 8 above. For a critic who expresses skepticism about the utility and ethical implications of trauma as a signifier beyond actual traumatization, see Kali Tal, *Worlds of Hurt: Reading the Literatures of Trauma* (Cambridge: Cambridge University Press, 1996).

33. Judith Butler, *Precarious Life: The Powers of Mourning and Violence* (London: Verso, 2004), xii.

34. For an especially concise and helpful review of some of these strategies, see Elizabeth Frazer and Kimberly Hutchings, "Argument and Rhetoric in the Justification of Political Violence," *European Journal of Political Theory*, 6:2 (2007): 180–99.

35. Quoted in *The New York Times*, September 30, 2001.

36. Interestingly, the German word "gewalt" is translated as both "force" and "violence."

37. Weil's politics are not easy to summarize: a sometime socialist, anarchist, and Bolshevik (all self-described), she is known for her pacifism, but also, in partial contradiction, she participated in the General Strike of 1933 and volunteered in the Spanish Civil War. And despite her being Jewish, several essays in the late 1930s indicate an insensitivity and anti-Semitism that is hard to understand. For discussion of Weil and politics, see Mary G. Dietz, *Between the Human and the Divine: The Political Thought of Simone Weil* (Totowa, NJ: Rowman and Littlefield, 1988) and Christopher J. Frost, *Simone Weil: On Politics, Religion, and Society* (London: Sage, 1998).

38. Or, in Paul Virilio's terms, "war is a symptom of delirium operating in the half-light of trance, drugs, blood and unison. This half-light establishes a corporeal identity in the

clinch of allies and enemies, victims and executioners—the clinch not of homosexual desire but of the antagonistic homogeneity of the death wish, a perversion of the right to live into a right to die." Virilio, *War and Cinema: The Logistics of Perception*, trans. Patrick Camiller (London: Verso, 1992), 5.

39. Simone Weil, *The* Iliad *or the Poem of Force*, trans. James P. Holoka (New York: Peter Lang, 2003), 45.

40. The essay was first published in two issues of the journal *Cahiers du Sud* in December 1940 and January 1941, though there remains confusion about exactly when it was written. The editors of a pamphlet edition (translated by Mary McCarthy) date the essay's composition to the summer of 1940 (hence after the fall of France), while others leave unspecified its precise composition date. See Simone Weil, *The* Iliad *or the Poem of Force*, trans., Mary McCarthy (Wallingford, PA: Pendle Hill, 1976), 2; Simone Pétrement, *Simone Weil: A Life*, trans. Raymond Rosenthal (New York: Pantheon, 1976); and, following her, Dorothy Tuck McFarland, *Simone Weil* (New York: Frederick Ungar, 1983).

41. George Orwell, *1984* (New York: Penguin, 1977), 267.

42. For discussion of these issues, see Laura Winkiel, *Modernism, Race, and Manifestos* (Cambridge: Cambridge University Press, 2008).

43. Filippo Marinetti, *Selected Writings* (New York: FSG, 1972), 42.

44. See Marjorie Perloff, *The Futurist Moment: Avant-Garde, Avant Guerre, and the Language of Rupture* (Chicago: University of Chicago Press, 1986).

45. Wyndham Lewis, ed. *BLAST* 1914 (repr. Santa Rosa: Black Sparrow, 1997), 7.

46. For English writers of the modernist years, Nietzsche was an anxiety-of-influence figure. Nearly everyone had a strong opinion, for or against, acknowledged or unacknowledged. In celebrating violence and disdaining Christian values of subjection, pacifism, and self-sacrifice, works such as *The Genealogy of Morals* and *Thus Spake Zarathustra* offered to subsequent generations a philosophy of violence (and of history *as* violence) that remained influential for decades.

47. Fussell, *The Great War and Modern Memory*, 35.

48. Margot Norris, *Writing War in the Twentieth Century* (Charlottesville: University of Virginia Press, 2000), 1.

49. Virginia Woolf, *Mrs. Dalloway* (San Diego: Harcourt, 1997), 100.

50. D. H. Lawrence, *Aaron's Rod* (New York: Penguin, 1976), 139.

51. In the Iraq and Afghanistan wars (2001–present), journalists have focused a good deal on injured soldiers. Even before a scandal involving inadequate care and resources at Walter Reed Hospital brought added attention to the subject (spring 2007), this journalistic focus, which cuts across medical, technological, psychological, and broadly social categories, suggests real potential for breaking the wall of silence that generally surrounds injured war veterans.

52. I discuss some of the effects of bodily injury in the postwar period in the final chapter of *Modernism, Male Friendship, and the First World War* (Cambridge: Cambridge University Press, 2003). See also Joanna Burke, *Dismembering the Male: Men's Bodies, Britain, and the Great War* (Chicago: University of Chicago Press, 1996).

53. On the subject of the bomb as a turning point in the history of killing, see the eclectic and fascinating work by Sven Lindqvist, *A History of Bombing*, trans. Linda Haverty Rugg (New York: The New Press, 2000).

54. See Trudi Tate, *Modernism, History, and the First World War* (Manchester: Manchester University Press, 1998).

55. For the effects of DORA, see Samuel Hynes, *A War Imagined: The First World War and English Culture* (London: Bodley Head, 1990). For discussion of modernism and propaganda more generally, see Mark A. Wollaeger, *Modernism, Media, and Propaganda: British Narrative from 1900–1945* (Princeton: Princeton University Press, 2006).

56. See, for instance, Cassandra Laity, "T. S. Eliot and A. C. Swinburne: Decadent Bodies, Modern Visualities, and Changing Modes of Perception," *Modernism/Modernity* 11:3 (September 2004), 425–48.

57. The bayonet, in other words, puts a slight check on one of the twentieth century's recurring fantasies, a product of the First World War which has not since lost its hold—the retrospective nostalgia for one-to-one combat over modern mass warfare. One might think here of General Patton, especially as imagined in the 1970 film *Patton*.

58. George Orwell, *Burmese Days* (San Diego: Harvest, 1962), 59. Of course, we are trusting the narrator's translation. Cited hereafter in text as *BD*.

59. Nixon, *Slow Violence and the Environmentalism of the Poor*.

60. For discussion of the timber industry in Burma ("the land of teak" as it was known), see Raymond L. Bryant, *The Political Ecology of Forestry in Burma, 1824–1994* (Honolulu: University of Hawaii Press, 1997).

61. For all its withering critique of empire, there is almost no history in *Burmese Days*. As its name suggests, the novel sits, marking time, in a slow present. There are, however, coded references. I read, for instance, a listing of earthquake dates by an otherwise silent Burmese servant as a version of a covert nationalist history (*BD*, 182–83). At the time of the novel's publication (1934), anti-British activity was on the rise in Burma.

62. "History" means many things. In this portion of the introduction, and again in the first chapter, I am laying out imaginative models for comprehending and articulating violence in the past. In chapters 2, 3, and 4, I develop cultural histories of violent events, a different methodology.

63. See, especially, Richard Slotkin, *Regeneration through Violence: The Mythology of the American Frontier, 1600–1860* (Middletown: Wesleyan University Press, 1973).

64. Dominick LaCapra, *History and Its Limits: Human, Animal, Violence* (Ithaca: Cornell University Press, 2009), 92–93.

65. For discussion of the digging and naming nexus devolving from a new understanding of the Biblical Adam in the seventeenth and eighteenth centuries, see Joanna Picciotto, *Labors of Innocence in Early Modern England* (Cambridge, MA: Harvard University Press, 2010).

66. Philip Fisher, *Hard Facts: Setting and Form in the American Novel* (Oxford: Oxford University Press, 1985).

67. See Baucom, *Specters of the Atlantic*.

68. See Mary A. Favret, *War at a Distance: Romanticism and the Making of Modern Wartime* (Princeton: Princeton University Press, 2010).

69. Jean Rhys, *Wide Sargasso Sea* (New York: Norton, 1982). A related notion—and compelling provocation—is Jennifer Wenzel's "Past's Futures," as explicated in a lecture by that name delivered at Columbia University, April 2011.

70. The actual massacre for which the town is named was a convoluted affair, involving fratricide and treachery, and some celebrity. It did not involve the killing of (or by) slaves.

71. It could be objected that the unnamed male narrator (aka Rochester) cannot be trusted, especially on the subject of sensory input, and in a more developed reading of the novel, these sensory observations would need to be registered in their full, political terms (such that, for instance, the islands' beauty, which is often figured by still pools, is feminized, hence ready for attack by Rochester). Even so, one can never discount the value of beauty in *Wide Sargasso Sea*.

Chapter 1

1. As suggested in the Introduction, a different kind of argument about how killing creates culture is developed by Philip Fisher (Fisher, *Hard Facts: Setting and Form in the American Novel* (New York: Oxford University Press, 1987)). With respect to the colonial era, Fisher argues that one central "hard fact" of literary and cultural history—the killing of Native Americans—enabled the imaginative possibility of freedom. As he says of James Fennimore Cooper's *The Deerslayer*:

> The stages of [Leatherstocking's] life are marked by beginnings stained with violence. As biography *The Deerslayer* gives Leatherstocking two features that allow him to begin his life: first, he has taken an adult name and left youth behind. The cost is one dead Indian. Second, he has been endowed with recovered freedom, radical freedom (at the cost of a massacre). Now his history begins. (Fisher, 86)

2. See, especially, "Science as a Vocation" and "The Protestant Sects and the Spirit of Capitalism," both in Max Weber, *From Max Weber: Essays in Sociology*, trans. H. H. Gerth and C. Wright Mills (New York: Oxford University Press, 1958) 129–56, 302–22. Schiller's actual phrase is accurately translated as "de-divination" rather than "disenchantment."

3. See Akeel Bilgrami, "Occidentalism, the Very Idea: An Essay on Enlightenment and Enchantment," *Critical Inquiry* 32 (Spring 2006): 381–411.

4. The debate about enchantment, disenchantment, and secularism is robust, spurred in part by Charles Taylor's important work *A Secular Age* (Cambridge, MA: Harvard University Press, 2007). Two recent volumes that include many of the major voices in this conversation are Michael Warner, Jonathan VanAntwerpen, and Craig Calhoun, eds., *Varieties of Secularism in a Secular Age* (Cambridge, MA: Harvard University Press, 2010), and George Levine, ed., *The Joy of Secularism: 11 Essays on How We Live Now* (Princeton: Princeton University Press, 2011). See also Joshua Landy and Michael Saler, eds., *The Re-enchantment of the World: Secular Magic in a Rational Age* (Stanford: Stanford University Press, 2009). For summaries of Weber and his influence, particularly for contemporary theory, see Nicholas Gane, *Max Weber and Postmodern Theory: Rationalization versus Re-enchantment* (London: Palgrave, 2002), and Andreas Michel, "Differentiation vs. Disenchantment: The Persistence of Modernity from Max Weber to Jean-Francois Lyotard," *German Studies Review*, 20:3 (October 1997): 343–70.

5. See Georg Lukács, *The Theory of the Novel: A Historico-Philisophical Essay on the Forms of Great Epic Literature*, trans. Anna Bostock (Cambridge, MA: MIT University Press, 1973).

6. The machine, of course, can function in contrary ways with respect to these issues. Often demonized as the primary agent in disenchanting the world, the machine was also lauded, by (certain) modernists, as the model for futurity's special aesthetic promise. In the visual field, perhaps the most arresting modernist portrayal of machine aesthetics—and dystopics—is Fritz Lang's 1927 film *Metropolis*.

7. Paul H. Fry, *The Poet's Calling and the English Ode* (New Haven: Yale University Press, 1980), 3.

8. Percy Shelly, *The Poetical Works of Shelley* (Boston: Houghton Mifflin, 1975), 378.

9. The phrase "natural supernaturalism," as readers will recognize, belongs to M. H. Abrams, *Natural Supernaturalism: Tradition and Revolution in Romantic Literature* (New York: Norton, 1971). For an argument that modernist poets represent an unacknowledged and anxious revival of Romanticism, see Carol Christ, *Victorian and Modern Poetics* (Chicago: University of Chicago Press, 1984).

10. For discussion of enchantment and modernism, see Susan Johnston Graf, "An Infant Avatar: The Mature Occultism of W. B. Yeats," *New Hibernia Review* 9:4 (Winter 2005): 99–112; Timothy Materer, *Modernist Alchemy: Poetry and the Occult* (Ithaca: Cornell University Press, 1995); Alex Owen, *The Place of Enchantment: British Occultism and the Culture of the Modern* (Chicago: University of Chicago Press, 2004); Helen Sword, *Ghostwriting Modernism* (Ithaca, NY: Cornell University Press, 2002); Leon Surette, *The Birth of Modernism: Ezra Pound, T. S. Eliot, W. B. Yeats, and the Occult* (Montreal: McGill-Queen's University Press, 1993); and Surette, ed., *Literary Modernism and the Occult Tradition* (Orono, ME: National Poetry Foundation, 1996).

11. Owen, *The Place of Enchantment*, 13, 16.

12. See Jay Winter, *Sites of Memory, Sites of Mourning: The Great War in European Cultural History* (Cambridge: Cambridge University Press, 1995).

13. My usage is thus unique, yet I have chosen to maintain the terms enchantment and disenchantment for two reasons. First, there is no substitute for "enchantment," which, in addition to the meanings already discussed, carries echoes of magic and the supernatural. Second, in the modernist period itself, the term had begun to be used in some of the ways I will be suggesting. Weber I have mentioned, and in chapter 3, I will consider Yeats, who, for instance, uses the term "enchanted to a stone" in "Easter 1916," his most famous reflection on generative violence. Conrad, in one of his late novels (*Victory*, 1915), makes much of the idea of enchantment (his protagonist's nickname is "enchanted Heyst") using the term to invoke the allure of the East. Yet the idea of enchantment in the early twentieth century, unlike myth, was still uncertain and its usage sporadic, allowing for more critical flexibility.

14. If *King Lear* references abound in this study, that is because the play so exquisitely and painfully exemplifies some of the movements I am discussing. Jonathan Arac has drawn my attention, for instance, to the fact that "scalding," a word used repeatedly in the pandying episode in *Portrait*, has its most memorable usage in Lear's description of his own tears ("mine own tears/Do scald like molten lead," IV. 7: 48–49). See William Shakespeare, *King Lear* (New York: Penguin, 1999) 120. More generally, the play's extended reflection on the way excessive violence both strips bare and acts as a powerful generative engine (for language, for consciousness) suggests a signal precursor to the kinds of movements I am tracking, along an enchantment/disenchantment axis, in the twentieth century,

15. Elaine Scarry, *The Body in Pain: The Making and Unmaking of the World* (New York: Oxford University Press, 1985), 137.

16. Rupert Brooke, *The Poems of Rupert Brooke* (London: Black Swan 1989), 133.

17. See George Mosse, *Fallen Soldiers: Reshaping the Memory of the World Wars* (New York: Oxford University Press, 1990).

18. Sigmund Freud, *Totem and Taboo: Some Points of Agreement between the Mental Lives of Savages and Neurotics*, trans. James Strachey (New York: Norton, 1989), 192.

19. Mark Manganaro, for instance, has argued that in the early twentieth century, two competing forms of anthropology developed, the Malinowskian endeavor to root anthropology in the immersive fieldwork of the eyewitness observer, and the cultural comparatist approach, where the scholarly field is the library and the work expands outward in space and backward in time. Frazer and Freud belong to the latter tradition, as does Eliot. See Mark Manganaro, *Myth, Rhetoric, and the Voice of Authority: A Critique of Frazer, Eliot, Frye, and Campbell* (New Haven: Yale University Press, 1992).

20. For discussion of ancient Greece in the Victorian cultural imagination, see Richard Jenkyns, *The Victorians and Ancient Greece* (Oxford: Blackwell, 1980); Jenkyns, *Dignity and Decadence: Victorian Art and the Classical Inheritance* (Cambridge, MA: Harvard University Press, 1992); Frank M. Turner, *The Greek Heritage in Victorian Britain* (New Haven: Yale University Press, 1981); and Turner, *Contesting Cultural Authority: Essays on Victorian Intellectual Life* (Cambridge: Cambridge University Press, 1993).

21. For discussion of Jane Harrison's importance for literary modernism, see Martha C. Carpentier, *Ritual, Myth, and the Modernist Text: The Influence of Jane Ellen Harrison on Joyce, Eliot, and Woolf* (Amsterdam: Overseas Publishing Association, 1998).

22. Sorel's influence on modernism has been demonstrated by Michael Tratner, *Modernism and Mass Politics: Joyce, Woolf, Eliot, Yeats* (Stanford: Stanford University Press, 1995). See also Dan Edelstein, "The Birth of Ideology from the Spirit of Myth: Georges Sorel among the *Idéologues*," in *The Re-enchantment of the World*, 201–24, and Rod Mengham, "From Georges Sorel to *Blast*," in *The Violent Muse: Violence and the Artistic Imagination in Europe, 1910–1939*, eds. Jana Howlett and Rod Mengham (Manchester: Manchester University Press, 1994), 33–44.

23. Jack J. Roth, *The Cult of Violence: Sorel and the Sorelians* (Berkeley: University of California Press, 1980).

24. Georges Sorel, *Reflections on Violence*, trans. T. E. Hulme (New York: Huebsch, 1914), 137.

25. Max Weber, *From Max Weber*, 334.

26. Hannah Arendt in *On Violence* (1969) offers several provocative definitions, of some relevance to Sorel's ideas of force and violence. From the vantage point of the 1960s student revolts, Arendt looks across the spectrum of political movements and systems that have been propelled by violence. If Sorel claimed a distinction between violence and force, for Arendt the divide is between what she calls "violence" and "power." Power, in her view, is political; it is "the essence of all government," the product of joint human action. "Power is never the property of an individual: it belongs to a group and remains in existence only so long as the group keeps together." Violence, by contrast, "is by nature instrumental," a matter solely of means, always in need of justification, unlike power, which "needs no justification, being in the very existence of political communities." One can hear, even in these condensed formulations, how utterly dismissive Arendt is of the tendency to enchant violence. Violence could not possibly be generative in her scheme, since it is a mere instrument, ancillary not only to power (the structure of governments) but also to authority, which derives from the respect accorded to particular persons or institutions. "Power and violence are opposites," she writes; "where the one rules absolutely, the other is absent. Violence appears where

power is in jeopardy, but left to its own course it ends in power's disappearance." See Hannah Arendt, *On Violence* (San Diego: Harvest, 1970), 44, 51, 52, 56.

27. Girard waves away "Frazer and the Cambridge Ritualists" for missing what he sees as the central feature of Greek and all primitive cultures, namely "the sacrificial crisis and its resolution," but to my reading, Girard's text seems less like a radical corrective than a descendent of the earlier writers. René Girard, *Violence and the Sacred* (Baltimore: Johns Hopkins University Press, 1979), 96.

28. Frantz Fanon, *The Wretched of the Earth*, trans. Richard Philcox (New York: Grove, 2004), 44.

29. For discussion of Marx's (relative lack of) interest in violence, in contradistinction to Fanon's, see Arendt, *On Violence*.

30. For discussion of gender issues in Fanon's work, see Gwen Bergner, "Who Is that Masked Woman?: Or, the Role of Gender in Fanon's *Black Skin, White Masks*," *PMLA* 110:1 (1995 January): 75–88; Chantal Kalisa, "Black Women and Literature: Revisiting Frantz Fanon's Gender Politics," *Literary Griot: International Journal of Black Expressive Cultural Studies*, 14:1–2 (Spring–Fall 2002): 1–22; Desiree Lewis, "Myths of Motherhood and Power: The Construction of 'Black Woman' in Literature," *English in Africa* 19:1 (1992 May): 35–51; and Bart Moore-Gilbert, "Frantz Fanon: En-Gendering Nationalist Discourse," *Women: A Cultural Review* 7:2 (Autumn 1996): 125–35.

31. *Black Skin, White Masks* (Fr., 1952, Eng., 1967), especially, draws a devastating portrait of colonial subjectivity as a product of racial and class hierarchies that cut across metropolis and island, men and women.

32. As Jean-Paul Sartre noted in his preface to the 1961 edition, Fanon "shows perfectly clearly that this irrepressible violence is neither a storm in a teacup nor the reemergence of savage instincts nor even a consequence of resentment: it is man reconstructing himself" (Fanon, lv). Unlike Fanon, Sartre takes up the prominent stereotypes that surrounded violent black masculinity in the early 1960s (primitivist, simultaneously fearsome and unthreatening), even as he follows Fanon in elevating violent action as the key to postcolonial self-development.

33. Georges Bataille, *The Tears of Eros*, trans. Peter Connor (San Francisco: City Lights, 1989), 52. Cited hereafter in text as *Tears*.

34. Hortense J. Spillers, *Black, White, and in Color* (Chicago: University of Chicago Press, 2003), 206.

35. Virginia Woolf, *Three Guineas* (San Diego: Harcourt, 1966), 10–11.

36. I will discuss some of these issues more fully in chapter 4.

37. For discussion of Fenton, see Susan Sontag, *Regarding the Pain of Others* (New York: Farrar Straus Giroux, 2003). Elaine Hadley addressed Fenton's photographs in the broader context of journalistic representation of the Crimean war, in a lecture delivered at Columbia University, March 2011. For another lively discussion of these images, see Errol Morris's article in the online edition of *The New York Times* at http://opinionator.blogs.nytimes.com/2007/09/25/which-came-first-the-chicken-or-the-egg-part-one/.

38. See Sontag, *Regarding the Pain of Others*.

39. For discussion of Friedrich's text, within the context of the competing uses of photography that emerged in Germany in these crucial postwar years, see Dora Apel, "Cultural Battlegrounds: Weimar Photographic Narratives of War," *New German Critique* 76

(Winter 1999), 49–84. See also Bernd Hüppauf, "Experiences of Modern Warfare and the Crisis of Representation," *New German Critique* 59 (Spring-Summer 1993): 41–76.

40. Ernst Friedrich, *War against War!* (Seattle: Real Comet Press, 1987), 22.

41. "On its appearance, *Témoins* raised a storm of controversy and received more than two hundred reviews throughout Europe and the United States," the editors of the English reprint of *War Books* write. See Ernest Marchand and Stanley J. Pincetl Jr, foreword to *War Books: A Study in Historical Criticism* by Jean Norton Cru (San Diego: San Diego State University Press, 1976).

42. On the subject of listening, the "boy" of line 2 might be imagined to be the speaker's own youthful self, or perhaps one of the boys whose experience at the hot gates the poem depicts; or, again, the boy's reading can be understood as conjuring the tableau that follows it—first "waiting for rain," now in it.

43. T. S. Eliot, *The Complete Poems and Plays 1908–1950* (New York: Harcourt, 1967), 21.

44. Eliot's deep reading in Aeschylus is well established; *Agamemnon* in particular is referenced as the epigraph for "Sweeney among the Nightingales," composed just before "Gerontion." I have not noted any critical discussion of *Agamemnon* in relation to "Gerontion," however.

45. Aeschylus, *Aeschylus I: Oresteia*, trans. Lattimore (Chicago: University of Chicago Press, 1953), 52.

46. War and postwar (*Iliad* and *Odyssey*), always the double concerns of Greek civilization, are enfolded here too. For a wonderful reading of the poem's reflection on the consequences of the war in the form of the Versailles treaty, and its Keynesian critique, see Vincent Sherry, *The Great War and the Language of Modernism* (New York: Oxford University Press, 2003), 207–16.

47. An interesting intertext here is Yeats's poem "Nineteen Hundred and Nineteen," written two years later and sharing a good deal in sprit with "Gerontion," which also takes the destructive wind as a guiding motif.

48. James Campbell, "Combat Gnosticism: The Ideology of First World War Poetry Criticism," *New Literary History* 30:1 (1999): 203–15.

49. We might note, too, the title of a memoir of the period, *Disenchantment*. See C. E. Montague, *Disenchantment* (New York: Brentano's, 1922).

50. Siegfried Sassoon, *The War Poems* (London: Faber, 1983), 100.

51. For a dazzling reading of the poem, see Meredith Martin, "Therapeutic Measures: *The Hydra* and Wilfred Owen at Craiglockhart War Hospital," *Modernism/Modernity* 14:1 (2007): 35–54. See also Martin, *The Rise and Fall of Meter: Poetry and English National Culture, 1860–1930* (Princeton: Princeton University Press, 2012), chapter five.

52. Wilfred Owen, *The Poems of Wilfred Owen* (London: Chatto, 1990), 117, 152, 112; Sassoon, *The War Poems*, 100; Isaac Rosenberg, *The Collected Poems of Isaac Rosenberg* (New York: Schocken, 1949), 84.

53. For discussion of the voyeuristic side of war criticism, see Adrian Caesar, *Taking it Like a Man: Suffering, Sexuality and the War Poets: Brooke, Sassoon, Owens, Graves* (Manchester: Manchester University Press, 1993). See also Terry Castle, "Courage, mon amie," *London Review of Books* 24:7 (April 2002) 3–12. And for an especially empathetic reading of war poetry that takes the display of violence as an ethical imperative, see Marian Eide, "Witnessing and Trophy Hunting: Writing Violence from the Great War Trenches," *Criticism* 49:1 (Winter 2007): 85–104.

54. Erich Maria Remarque, *All Quiet on the Western Front*, trans. A. H. Wheen (New York: Fawcett, 1996), 286–87.

55. Homer, *The Iliad*, Trans. Richmond Lattimore (Chicago: University of Chicago Press, 1951) 126.

56. The tradition of linking *The Waste Land* to the war goes back to its initial publication in 1922. Despite an ahistorical bent among early reviewers, who stressed the poem's universal themes, and Eliot's own demurring against historical interpretation, readers nevertheless have long seen the poem as an epochal statement of the postwar condition, carrying with it echoes of war. Paul Fussell helped to canonize that position in 1975, giving Eliot a central place in his story of modernity as a product of the war, while the new historicist turn in the 1980s opened new avenues for reading the history in grittier detail. I will make reference over the course of this discussion to several studies that engage the place of war and postwar in the poem.

57. Even before he wrote *The Waste Land*, and throughout his career, Eliot was a rampant enchanter and disenchanter, able to beautify and to bludgeon within a drumbeat. As the famous opening lines of "The Love Song of J. Alfred Prufrock" have it, "Let us go then, you and I/When the evening is spread out against the sky/Like a patient etherised upon a table": T. S. Eliot, *The Complete Poems and Plays, 1909–1950* (New York: Harcourt, 1967), 3. But no other work approaches *The Waste Land* in its extensive consideration of art and violence.

58. The poem's presiding mode is one of self-contradiction, and much of the most exciting Eliot criticism works to explicate this spirit. So, for instance: *The Waste Land* purveys a profound dread and loathing of femininity; *The Waste Land* allows Eliot to inhabit and perform his own repressed femininity. *The Waste Land* cries out for regeneration and reform of the modern wasteland; the poem revels in the waste of the land, taking real pleasure in the corporeal realities of contemporary urban decay. *The Waste Land* embraces the high history of Western art and civilization as a powerful authorizing force; *The Waste Land* undoes and subverts the most revered cultural monuments, presenting them in the fragments they have become. Excellent examples of criticism that takes its cues from the poem's self-divisions include Harriet Davidson, "Improper Desire: Reading *The Waste Land*," *The Cambridge Companion to T. S. Eliot*, ed. A. David Moody (Cambridge: Cambridge University Press, 1994), 121–31; Christine Froula, "Eliot's Grail Quest, or, The Lover, the Police, and *The Waste Land*," *Yale Review* 78:2 (Winter 1989): 235–53; Colleen Lamos, *Deviant Modernism: Sexual and Textual Errancy in T. S. Eliot, James Joyce, and Marcel Proust* (Cambridge: Cambridge University Press, 1998); and Michael Levenson, "Does *The Waste Land* Have a Politics?" *Modernism/Modernity* 6:3 (1999): 1–13.

59. T. S. Eliot, *The Waste Land* (New York: Norton, 2001), 313–21. Cited hereafter in the text as *TWL*; numbers refer to lines in the poem.

60. For an attentive discussion of "Death by Water," see Jewel Spears Brooker and Joseph Bentley, *Reading* The Waste Land: *Modernism and the Limits of Interpretation* (Amherst: University of Massachusetts Press, 1990).

61. Such magnetism is surprising, however, for two reasons: first, because the lines were written, in only slightly different form, before the composition of the rest of the poem (in French, in the 1918 poem "Dans le Restaurant"), and because the alterations within *The Waste Land* manuscript are especially striking with respect to "Death by Water." It was this section that Pound most ruthlessly sheared, its eight lines a mere snippet of Eliot's original

ninety. In this deleted section of "Death by Water," Eliot had devised, among other things, a surprisingly coherent first-person narrator, a sailor reminiscent of such seafarers as Homer's Odysseus, Virgil's Aeneas, and Coleridge's Ancient Mariner. See T. S. Eliot, *The Waste Land: A Facsimile and Transcript of the Original Drafts* (San Diego: Harcourt, 1971). Cited in text hereafter as Eliot, *Fasc.*

62. Eliot, *Complete Poems and Plays*, 132, 133.

63. The Bleistein "Dirge" recalls Clarence's dream in *Richard III*, an allusion notably omitted from Eliot's notes. In a nightmare of drowning,

> Methoughts I saw a thousand fearful wracks,
> A thousand men that fishes gnawed upon,
> Wedges of gold, great anchors, heaps of pearl,
> Inestimable stones, unvalued jewels,
> All scattered in the bottom of the sea.
> Some lay in dead men's skulls, and in the holes
> Where eyes did once inhabit, there were crept
> (As 'twere in scorn of eyes) reflecting gems,
> That wooed the slimy bottom of the deep
> And mocked the dead bones that lay scattered by.

For Clarence, who accurately foresees his own impending murder, the transformation performed by the sea on the drowned body represents a mockery, the jewels juxtaposed against the lifeless skull, now bereft of eyes. See William Shakespeare, *Richard III* (New York: Penguin, 2000), 38.

64. James Joyce, *Ulysses* (New York: Vintage, 1986), 41–42.

65. Eliot had read "Proteus" in *The Little Review* before completing *The Waste Land*.

66. In addition to *The Tempest*, Eliot refers extensively to Wagner's *Tristan and Isolde*. Both plays highlight not only themes of ache and loss with respect to the sea, but also other forms of enchantment, such as trickery and magic spells. More generally, Eliot's poem taps into a broad imaginary about the seas and oceans, an area that has recently emerged as a subject of critical interest. Drawing on work on slavery and diaspora, political theory, animal studies, and ecocriticism, scholars have illuminated the historical, ideological, and aesthetic underpinnings of western approaches to the seas. For an excellent survey of the field, see the articles in the section "Oceanic Studies," *PMLA* (May 2010): 657–730.

67. For a concise and historically astute analysis of the associations around the Smyrna merchant, see David Roessel, "'Mr. Eugenides, the Smyrna Merchant,' and Post-War Politics in *The Waste Land*," *Journal of Modern Literature* 16:1 (1989): 171–76.

68. See, especially, John Peter, "A New Interpretation of *The Waste Land* (1952)," *Essays in Criticism* 19:2 (April 1969): 140–75; James E. Miller, *T. S. Eliot's Personal Waste Land: Exorcism of the Demons* (University Park: Pennsylvania State University Press, 1977); and Christine Froula, "Eliot's Grail Quest."

69. In the letter, Eliot praises the *Daily Mail* for its "attitude on nearly every public question of present importance." With respect to Turkey in particular, he writes, "On the Turkish question, and on other matters of foreign policy, you have manifested a temperance, sanity, and consistency which can but rarely be attributed to the Press—virtues, however, in which the Press ought to lead the public. In an age when the intellect is eclipsed alternately

by passion and apathy, such virtues can hardly be over-estimated" (T. S. Eliot, letter to the *Daily Mail*, January 8, 1923).

70. For many centuries, the debate about Homer's birthplace centered, as it does today, on Smyrna versus the island of Chios. Homer is said to have ended his life on Chios, but the question of his birth is uncertain. In the period of *The Waste Land*, the dominant theory was that Homer most likely came from Smyrna and/or composed the *Iliad* there. See, for instance, Denton J. Snider, *The Biographical Outline of Homer* (Saint Louis: William Harvey Miner, 1922).

71. Paul Fussell, *The Great War and Modern Memory* (London: Oxford University Press, 1975).

72. For an especially thoughtful and expansive discussion of this fact, see Allyson Booth, *Postcards from the Trenches: Negotiating the Space between Modernism and the First World War* (New York: Oxford University Press, 1996).

73. Rupert Brooke was the most famous such figure. For discussion of Brooke's death and burial, see John Lehmann, *Rupert Brooke* (London: Weidenfeld and Nicolson, 1980).

74. One generic context in which *The Waste Land* might be read is the pastoral, and particularly the pastoral elegy. Most canonical as sources are Shelley's "Adonais" and Milton's "Lycidas." For a discussion of the pastoral tradition with respect to the war, see Sandra M. Gilbert, "'Rats Alley': The Great War, Modernism, and the (Anti) Pastoral Elegy," *New Literary History* 30 (1999): 179–201. For thorough discussion of the trope of lost youth, see Paul Fussell, *Great War*; Adrian Caesar, *Taking it Like a Man*; Peter Parker, *The Old Lie: The Great War and the Public-School Ethos* (London: Constable, 1987); and Martin Taylor, introduction to *Lads: Love Poetry of the Trenches* (London: Constable, 1989).

75. The manuscript of the poem contains three further references to violet, very much in the spirit of the four that remain in the final draft, and these are layered into one long segment: "So through the evening, through the violet air . . .," "Oh, through the violet sky . . .," "The Shrill bats quivered in the violet air . . .," and, for good measure, "In the calm deep water where no stir nor surf is/Swims down and down;/And about his hair the seaweed purple and brown." See Eliot, *Fasc.*, 113–15.

76. Woolf's novels are also filled with violets; they are ubiquitous. I have found no repeated or regular signifying system, though their affiliation with mourning is often evoked. Wilfred Owen's version is a poem entitled "Purple." Meanwhile, other associations for the word *violet* and the color purple abound, including those clustering around flowers (widespread in English poetry of the nineteenth century); the light spectrum (which ends in violet); and, in the twentieth century, with queer identities.

77. The soldier name Albert carries generalizing associations, along the lines of (but not as fully as) Tommy.

78. See Paul Morrison, *The Poetics of Fascism: Ezra Pound, T. S. Eliot, Paul de Man* (New York: Oxford University Press, 1996), 90–95.

79. For thorough discussion of the Philomela story in the context of patriarchal violence, see Patricia Klindienst Joplin, "The Voice of the Shuttle Is Ours," *Rape and Representation*, eds. Lynn A. Higgins and Brenda R. Silver (New York: Columbia University Press, 1991), 35–64.

80. We do not know the date, even roughly, when *Pervigilium Veneris* was composed. Various times between the second and fifth centuries have been suggested. See the Loeb edition, *Catullus, Tibullus and Pervigilium Veneris* (Cambridge, MA: Harvard University Press, 1976), 343–46.

81. Although Eliot does not reference "Itylus" in the notes to *The Waste Land*, we know that he had considered the poem carefully, since he discusses it directly in his 1920 essay, "Swinburne as Poet." See T. S. Eliot, *Selected Essays* (New York: Harcourt, 1964), 281–85.

82. Algernon Swinburne, *The Complete Works: Poetical Works, Vol. 1* (New York: Russell and Russell, 1968), 187–89.

83. "Jug jug" represents a standard Elizabethan rendering of the nightingale's song.

84. One might immediately object to Eliot's use of the phrase "So rudely forc'd" as a description of the rape—such an artful and stylized rendition of what, in Ovid's telling, is recounted in anything but delicate terms. It is worth noting, in this context, a sense of hesitation on the part of the editors of the Norton Critical Edition of *The Waste Land*: in the segment on Ovid, the editors include Tereus's cutting out of Philomela's tongue, but they skip over the next sentence in Ovid's narrative, in which we read "Even after his crime, though the story is scarcely believable,/ Tereus debauched that bleeding body again and again." Certain violations seem too atrocious even for scholarly mention. See Ovid, *Metamorphoses*, trans. David Raeburn (London: Penguin, 2004), 237, and T. S. Eliot, *The Waste Land, A Norton Critical Edition* (New York: Norton, 2001), 48.

85. For reference to Eliot's praise of the water-dripping lines (in a letter to Ford Madox Ford), see B. C. Southam, *A Guide to The Selected Poems of T. S. Eliot* (San Diego: Harcourt, 1984), 187.

Chapter 2

1. A number of the most inflammatory anarchist works, which have always circulated in clandestine form, are only readily available online. For these, I use web addresses in my citations. For "La Ravachole," see http://www.marxists.org/reference/archive/ravachol/la-ravachole.htm

2. The *OED* defines "sensational" as follows: "Of works of literature or art, hence of writers: Dealing in 'sensation' [. . .], aiming at violently exciting effects. Also of incidents in fiction or real life: Calculated to produce a startling impression." As these terms ("violently exciting effects," "startling impression") indicate, it appears to be endemic to the "sensational" to consider the personal, social, and ethical consequences of its effects. The term entered usage in the early 1860s, alongside the literary phenomenon of the sensation novel. For discussion of some of these issues, see Patrick Brantlinger, "What Is 'Sensational' about the 'Sensation Novel'?," *Nineteenth-Century Fiction* 37:1 (June 1982): 1–28; Ann Cvetkovich, *Mixed Feelings: Feminism, Mass Culture, and Victorian Sensationalism* (New Brunswick, NJ: Rutgers University Press, 1992); and D. A. Miller, *The Novel and the Police* (Berkeley: University of California Press, 1988).

3. I am primarily interested in the broad, public ramifications and representations of dynamite violence. Hence I discuss works, for the most part, that circulated beyond the immediacy of radical circles: published fiction, essays, and manifestos; journalistic accounts from the mainstream press; and anarchist memoirs. It should be noted, however, that anarchists were copious producers of radical journals. For an excellent analysis of the way anarchism was represented in the mainstream press, see Haia Shpayer-Makov, "Anarchism in British Public Opinion 1880–1914," *Victorian Studies* (Summer 1988): 487–516.

4. Dynamite was also associated with Fenians, who preceded anarchists in their usage of it. I will discuss some overlaps between Fenians and anarchism in the next chapter. Here my focus is more specifically on anarchists.

5. Margaret S. Marsh, *Anarchist Women, 1870–1920* (Philadelphia: Temple University Press, 1981), 6.

6. Friedrich Nietzsche, *On the Genealogy of Morals and Ecce Homo*, trans. Walter Kaufmann (New York: Vintage, 1967), 326. As Kaufman notes, the phrase was taken from an 1886 review of Nietzsche's book *Beyond Good and Evil*.

7. Paul Avrich, *The Haymarket Tragedy* (Princeton: Princeton University Press, 1984), 166.

8. I have chosen, throughout this chapter, to use the masculine pronoun in my reference to anarchists. For ease of reading, I find it preferable, and a majority of the works I will be discussing take the masculine gender of the anarchist for granted. However, women were present in the anarchist movement to no small degree—Emma Goldman being the most famous—and the dynamite fiction of the period often had a marked gender theme, with beautiful women anarchists, for example, featured as seductresses. For discussion of women and radical movements of the period, see Marsh, *Anarchist Women*; Avrich, *Anarchist Portraits* (Princeton: Princeton University Press, 1988), 214–28; Alex Houen, *Terrorism and Modern Literature: From Joseph Conrad to Ciaran Carson* (Oxford: Oxford University Press, 2002), 34–93; and on Goldman in particular, Candace Serena Salk, *Love, Anarchy, and Emma Goldman* (New Brunswick: Rutgers University Press, 1990) and Bonnie Haaland, *Emma Goldman: Sexuality and the Impurity of the State* (Montreal: Black Rose Books, 1993).

9. For the most comprehensive study of the dynamite novel, see Barbara Arnett Melchiori, *Terrorism in the Late Victorian Novel* (London: Croom Helm, 1985). A recent work, covering some of the same ground as the present study but published too late for consideration, is Deaglán Ó Donghaile, *Blasted Literature: Victorian Political Fiction and the Shock of Modernism* (Edinburgh: Edinburgh University Press, 2011). For a rich, historicized account of many of these issues, including their relation to Conrad, see Houen, *Terrorism and Modern Literature*, 34–93. For a brisk but helpful survey, see Bernard Porter, *The Origins of the Vigilant State: The London Metropolitan Police Special Branch before the First World War* (London: Weidenfeld, 1987), 98–113. See also Arthur F. Redding, *Raids on Human Consciousness: Writing, Anarchism, and Violence* (Columbia: University of South Carolina Press, 1998).

10. I will discuss aerial bombardment in chapter 4. For a selection of writings germane to this chapter's concerns and time frame, see I. F. Clarke, ed., *The Tale of the Next Great War, 1871–1914: Fictions of Future Warfare and of Battles Still-to-Come* (Liverpool: Liverpool University Press, 1995).

11. Peter Brooks, *The Melodramatic Imagination: Balzac, Henry James, Melodrama, and the Mode of Excess* (New York: Columbia University Press, 1985); Elaine Hadley, *Melodramatic Tactics: Theatricalized Dissent in the English Marketplace, 1800–1885* (Stanford: Stanford University Press, 1995). See also Ben Singer, *Melodrama and Modernity: Early Sensational Cinema and Its Contexts* (New York: Columbia University Press, 2001).

12. All the major news media, dailies as well as weekly/monthly periodicals, covered anarchist events. Papers such as *The Times* treated anarchist attacks as a staple topic. A perusal of *The Times* from the mid-1880s to the mid-1890s, in particular, betrays an exceptionally consistent interest in the subject, with "outrages" reported and discussed almost daily.

13. John Henry Mackay, *The Anarchists: A Picture of Civilization at the Close of the Nineteenth Century*, trans. George Schumm (Brooklyn: Autonomedia, 1999), 73.

14. The most famous mention of anarchy in British modernism comes in Yeats's "The Second Coming" ("mere anarchy is loosed upon the world"). What is striking, from the

anarchy/anarchism point of view, is how the "anarch" of an earlier draft of the poem—something that suggests the figure of the anarch*ist*—becomes transformed into a more general moniker for chaos and destruction. For Yeats's draft, see William Butler Yeats, *Michael Robartes and the Dancer: Manuscript Materials*, ed. Thomas Parkinson (Ithaca: Cornell University Press, 1994), 133–46.

15. Émile Zola, *Germinal*, trans. Havelock Ellis (New York: Vintage, 1994), 253, 146.

16. E. Douglas Fawcett, *Hartmann the Anarchist; or, the Doom of the Great City* (London: Edward Arnold, 1893), 109.

17. For helpful overviews of anarchism, see Avrich, *Anarchist Portraits*; David Miller, *Anarchism* (London: J. M. Dent, 1984); and George Woodcock, "Anarchism: A Historical Introduction," in Woodcock, ed., *The Anarchist Reader* (Hassocks: Harvester, 1977), 11–56. For English anarchism, see John Quail, *The Slow Burning Fuse: The Lost History of the British Anarchists* (London: Paladin, 1978). See also David Goodway, *Anarchist Seeds beneath the Snow: Left Libertarian Thought and British Writing from William Morris to Colin Ward* (Liverpool: Liverpool University Press, 2007).

18. Thus we note a theoretical difference between Bakunin, the most important exponent of anarchism in the 1860s and '70s, and Karl Marx, which led to a famous break at the founding of the First International (1864).

19. Peter Kropotkin, *Kropotkin's Revolutionary Pamphlets*, ed. Rojer N. Baldwin (New York: Benjamin Bloom, 1968), 284.

20. Peter Kropotkin, *Mutual Aid: A Factor of Evolution* (Montreal: Black Rose Books, 1989), 5.

21. See Avrich, *Portraits*, "Kropotkin's Ethical Anarchism," 53–78.

22. For discussion of the origin and development of propaganda by deed, see Caroline Cahm, *Kropotkin and the Rise of Revolutionary Anarchism 1872–1886* (Cambridge: Cambridge University Press, 1989), and Ulrich Linse, "'Propaganda by Deed' and 'Direct Action': Two Concepts of Anarchist Violence," in *Social Protest, Violence, and Terror in Nineteenth- and Twentieth-Century Europe*, eds. Wolfgang J. Mommsen and Gerhard Hirschefield (New York: St. Martin's 1982), 201–29. For a brief, but very astute, summary, see Miller, *Anarchism*, 98–101.

23. Mikail Bakunin, *Bakunin on Anarchism*, ed. and trans. Sam Dolgoff (Montreal: Black Rose, 1980), 334. Bakunin characterized the formula in 1870 in these terms: "Now we all have to embark together on the revolutionary ocean, and henceforth spread our principles no longer by words but by deeds—for this is the most popular, the most powerful and the most irresistible form of propaganda" (quoted in Cahm, 76). Or, in an 1873 letter to a Swiss federation of anarchists, "This is the time not for ideas but for action, for deeds" (Dolgoff, 352).

24. Quoted in Cahm, 78.

25. Avrich uses the phrase "clean sweep" in reference to the words of the militant Italian anarchist Luigi Galleani, and Norman Sherry finds a number of resonant usages that might have contributed to the employment of such language in *The Secret Agent*. See Avrich, *Portraits*, 169, and Sherry, *Conrad's Western World* (Cambridge: Cambridge University Press, 1971), 279.

26. For discussion of the conference, see H. Oliver, *The International Anarchist Movement in Late Victorian London* (London: Croom, 1983), 10–17.

27. The question of whether Conrad was familiar with *A Girl Among the Anarchists* remains open; for a convincing account that the Rossettis' novel may have influenced him,

see David Mulry, "Popular Accounts of the Greenwich Bombing and Conrad's *The Secret Agent*," *Rocky Mountain Review* (Fall 2000): 43–64.

28. Isabel Meredith, *A Girl Among the Anarchists* (Lincoln: University of Nebraska Press, 1992), 188.

29. For a succinct and pointed rendering of this argument, see Jeffory A. Clymer, *America's Culture of Terrorism: Violence, Capitalism, and the Written Word* (Chapel Hill: University of North Carolina Press, 2003), especially 14–20. Émile Henry quoted in Woodcock, *Anarchist Reader*, 192.

30. Joseph Conrad, *The Secret Agent: A Simple Tale* (Cambridge: Cambridge University Press, 1990), 31. Cited hereafter in text as *SA*.

31. G. K. Chesterton, *The Man Who was Thursday* (London: Penguin, 1986), 12.

32. In French, the term was "*propagande par fait*," the word "fait" meaning both "act" and "fact," and this conjunction of action with accomplished fact has added connotations. The suggestion is that violent action immediately changes the structure of opposition between the insurrectionists and the world they seek to effect, because facts represent an already altered world.

33. Joseph Conrad, "The Informer: An Ironic Tale," *The Collected Stories of Joseph Conrad* (Hopewell, NJ: Ecco, 1991), 326. Cited hereafter in text as *CS*.

34. Shpayer-Makov, "Anarchism in British Public Opinion," 492.

35. We might note, too, that even into the twentieth century, when the novel was written, anarchism was still very much alive in the press, a fact sure to be available to Chesterton, who, in addition to his enormous volume of books, also wrote weekly columns in several newspapers, and even published his own journal, the *G. K.'s Weekly*.

36. Some believe Nechaev collaborated with Bakunin on the "Catechism." For consideration of the relationship between Bakunin and Nechaev, see Avrich, *Portraits*, "Bakunin and Nechaev," 32–52.

37. The intertwining of science and anarchism falls under the more general rubric of Victorian dreams and dystopias about the nature and direction of science. Anarchists like Kropotkin saw themselves as guided by "natural science," and bomb technology was a fetish for anarchists, while the public saw in the revolutionary embracing of dynamite something sinister about scientific progress itself ("infernal machines" was a common usage). For discussion of some of these issues, see Houen, *Terrorism and Modern Literature*, 34–54.

38. For English anarchists, Ravachol became a lightning rod, almost a metaphor for the extreme edge of anarchist commitment to propaganda by deed. See Quail, *Slow Burning Fire*, 140–43.

39. Qtd in Woodcock, *Anarchist Reader*, 195–96.

40. http://www.sscnet.ucla.edu/history/franks/classes/131b/perm/radicalsdocuments. html For another translation, see http://www.nbp-info.org/library/SergeiNechaevKat.htm

41. See Mackay, *The Anarchists*, 48–49.

42. N. G. Chernyshevsky, *What Is to Be Done?* tr. Michael R. Katz (Ithaca: Cornell University Press, 1989), 280.

43. Alexander Berkman, *Prison Memoirs of an Anarchist* (New York: Schocken, 1970), 7–8. Berkman's masculinism is not unique among male anarchists, though it is striking. Despite a lifelong intimacy with the feminist Emma Goldman, for instance, he persists in referring to her, in his *Memoirs*, as "the Girl." More generally, notwithstanding anarchism's

opposition to social codes and laws and its affinities with nihilism—a movement with a strong feminist bent—anarchists often look conventional when it comes to gender. In *Under Western Eyes*, Conrad's most thorough treatment of Russian revolutionary characters and motives, he hones in on some of these contradictions, ruthlessly parodying what he views as the revolutionists' hypocrisy on the subject of female emancipation.

44. In later works, Berkman attempts to mute this furor somewhat, and to place violence in a more submerged position with respect to anarchism's goals and methods. As he writes in 1926, "You have heard that Anarchists throw bombs, that they believe in violence, and that Anarchy means disorder and chaos. . . . No, my friend, it is capitalism and government which stand for disorder and violence. Anarchism is the very reverse of it; it means order without government and peace without violence": Alexander Berkman, *What is Anarchism?* (Edinburgh: AK, 2003), 138.

45. The fact that Berkman is of Jewish origin does not seem to lessen the power of the Christian thematics.

46. Frank Harris, *The Bomb* (Portland, OR: Feral House, 1996), 26.

47. Stepniak, *Underground Russia: Revolutionary Profiles and Sketches from Life* (Westport: Hyperion Press, 1973), 39–40, 42. . . . In addition to drawing a portrait of the terrorist, Stepniak's extremely engaging and readable tract also includes profiles of a number of famous revolutionaries. Stepniak also wrote a novel entitled *The Career of a Nihilist* (1889).

48. See Oscar Wilde, *The Complete Plays of Oscar Wilde* (London: Methuen, 1988). Wilde was not alone in presenting Russian terrorists sympathetically. Though the British government was allied with the czarist government, and though the English press reacted with outrage at the assassination of the czar in 1881, many English writers expressed sympathy with the revolutionaries. In *Under Western Eyes*, Conrad creates in Razumov (the counterrevolutionary spy) a decidedly mixed protagonist, but the revolutionist Victor Haldin is offered as an idealist, whose martyrdom the novel, for all its blistering irony, never fully repudiates.

49. Wilde's title character might have been modeled on several historical Veras who received the attention of the English press, perhaps Vera Zasulich, who shot the governor of Saint Petersburg in 1878, or Vera Figner, a member of the group who eventually succeeded in assassinating the czar; or perhaps Wilde's choice of a quintessentially Russian female name is meant to suggest something generic about her, an emblem of female revolutionary energy. For discussion of some of these issues, see Sos Eltis, *Revising Wilde: Society and Subversion in the Plays of Oscar Wilde* (Oxford: Clarendon, 1996), 27–54. See also H. Montgomery Hyde, introduction to *The Complete Plays of Oscar Wilde*, 21–23.

50. For all Wilde's fame as an ironist, he held on to some of melodrama's trappings and character types, as in *The Picture of Dorian Gray* (1891), and throughout his life continued to admire revolutionaries, as indicated in "The Soul of Man under Socialism." As late as *De Profundis*, he praises Kropotkin:

> Two of the most perfect lives I have come across in my own experience are the lives of Verlaine and of Prince Kropotkin: both of them men who passed years in prison: the first, the one Christian poet since Dante, the other a man with the soul of that beautiful white Christ that seems coming out of Russia.

Oscar Wilde, *The Letters of Oscar Wilde*, ed. Rupert Hart-Davis (New York: Harcourt 1962), 488.

51. My claim that Wilde's play accords with popular representations of anarchists is based on my reading of the anarchist/terrorist as a figure of some complexity on the cultural scene. Eltis, by contrast, argues that in terms of contemporary drama, Wilde's play is unique in portraying nihilists in a positive light. See Eltis, 34–44.

52. George Griffith, *The Angel of the Revolution: A Tale of the Coming Terror* (London: Routledge, 1995), 14. The novel was first published serially in 1893 and in book form in 1895.

53. For an historical example, Emma Goldman describes a scene at a public gathering in which several Spanish anarchists "opened their shirts and showed the horrible scars of burned flesh" (quoted In Oliver, 115).

54. In the film *Metropolis* this theme is given wide expression, as the workers' underground bodies literally feed the machines, and the radical leaders make good use of the rhetoric of bodily flesh providing the building material for the undeserving wealthy.

55. P. Kropotkin, *The Conquest of Bread* (New York: Benjamin Blom, 1968) 6. See also Marshall S. Shatz, ed. *The Essential Works of Anarchism* (New York: Quadrangle, 1972).

56. Berkman, *Prison Memoirs*, 3.

57. Anarchists had a particularly strong animus against the legal system.

58. Essay quoted in W. C. Hart, *Confessions of an Anarchist* (London: G. Richards, 1911), 139.

59. For discussion of the essay, the trial of Niccol, and the full historical context, see Quail.

60. In London, of two anarchist clubs, one was German (the Autonomie) and the other Jewish (Berner Street), and a Yiddish journal, *Arbeter Fraynd*, was published out of the East End. For engaging discussion of Jewish and Italian anarchist circles in the United States, see Avrich, *Portraits*, "Sacco and Vanzetti: The Italian Anarchist Background," 162–75, and "Jewish Anarchism in the United States," 162–75.

61. Conrad, *Collected Stories*, 309, 312.

62. We should perhaps note that the story ends in an enigmatic fashion, with the suggestion that perhaps Mr. X was no anarchist at all, more like a practical joker.

63. Henry James, *The Princess Casamassima* (New York: Penguin, 1987), 34.

64. In this sense, *The Princess Casamassima* is less of an outlier in James's canon than is sometimes thought, insofar as his signature style involves the circling around of gaps and aporias (in speech, meaning, understanding).

65. In *The Melodramatic Imagination*, to which I earlier made reference, Peter Brooks makes a convincing argument that James's works operate according to what he calls "the melodrama of consciousness." "The reasons for outward and inward melodrama in James are the same," he writes, "his desire to make ethical conflict, imperative, and choice the substance of the novel, to make it the nexus of 'character' and the motivation of plot" (Brooks, 159). A brilliant reading of James's full oeuvre, Brooks's analysis of James as creating a melodramatic substratum to his seemingly ironized, complex surface is not focused on a given text or topic but, conversely, demonstrates a nearly ubiquitous stylistics and structure of meaning-making (a "moral occult") in James's works.

66. The canonical treatment of Conrad's politics remains Avrom Fleischman, *Conrad's Politics: Community and Anarchy in the Fiction of Joseph Conrad* (Baltimore: Johns Hopkins University Press, 1967). For an earlier, still widely read account, see Irving Howe, *Politics and the Novel* (London: Stevens, 1961). For the most thorough and influential discussion of Conrad's sources for *The Secret Agent* and his other revolutionary novels, see Norman

Sherry, *Conrad's Western World* (Cambridge: Cambridge University Press, 1971). For more recent discussions, of particular interest vis-à-vis anarchist violence, see James F. English, "Anarchy in the Flesh: Conrad's 'Counterrevolutionary' Modernism and the *Witz* of the Political Unconscious," *MFS* 38:3 (1992): 615–30; and Ian Watt, "The Political and Social Background of *The Secret Agent*," in *Essays on Conrad* (Cambridge: Cambridge University Press, 2000). See also Houen, *Terrorism and Modern Literature*.

67. For discussion of Conrad's use of disfigurement as an image of materiality in a multifarious sense, see Michael Fried, "Almayer's Face: On 'Impressionism' in Conrad, Crane, and Norris," *Critical Inquiry* 17:1 (Autumn 1990): 193–236.

68. For discussion of Conrad's knowledge of anarchism and the Greenwich Park outrage, see Fleishman, English, Watt, and Sherry. See also Jacques Berthoud, "*The Secret Agent*," in *The Cambridge Companion to Joseph Conrad*, ed. J. H. Stape (Cambridge: Cambridge University Press, 1996), 100–21.

69. In Milan, in 1898.

70. *The Times*, February 16, 1894

71. For a brilliant discussion of this motif, see Fleischman, 185–214.

72. For the canonical establishment of who's who in *The Secret Agent*, see Sherry, *Conrad's Western World*. Though I differ with Sherry on some of his conclusions, his overall scheme of showing how Conrad picked and chose among historical personae to create his portraits is highly illuminating.

73. It seems likely that Conrad came upon the narrative of the Greenwich bombing as the brainchild of the Russian embassy, frustrated with Britain's lax laws and hoping to goad public opinion, from Ford Madox Ford, who appears to have heard such rumors from his anarchist connections.

74. For discussion of Conrad and Dostoevsky, see Keith Carabine, *The Life and the Art: A Study of Conrad's "Under Western Eyes"* (Amsterdam: Rodopi, 1996), 64–96; Martin Halliwell, *Images of Idiocy: the Idiot Figure in Modern Fiction and Film* (Aldershot: Ashgate, 2004); Paul Kirschner, "The French Face of Dostoevsky in Conrad's *Under Western Eyes*: Some Consequences for Criticism," *Conradiana* 30:3 (Fall 1998): 163–82; and David R. Smith, "Conrad and Dostoevsky," *Conradian* 15:2 (January 1991): 1–11.

75. See English, "Anarchy in the Flesh." The flesh motif is pervasive in the novel. Many of the novel's characters are extremely fat, often to the point of disability (Verloc, Michaelis, Sir Ethelred, Winnie's mother), the theme of corporeality spreads in various directions, as with the repeated invocations of Cesare Lombroso's theory of degeneracy, which was framed in terms of the phrenological capacity to read the face and body, and the novel closes with the twin images of the Professor as a corrosive threat to the bodies of all Londoners and Michaelis's utopia of the future as a giant hospital.

76. For discussion of the Ripper phenomenon, see Gary Corille and Patrick Luciano, *Jack the Ripper: His Life and Crimes in Popular Entertainment* (Jefferson, NC: McFarland, 1999); Perry Curtis Jr, *Jack the Ripper and the London Press* (New Haven: Yale University Press, 2001); and Judith Walkowitz, *City of Dreadful Delight: Narratives of Sexual Danger in Late-Victorian London* (Chicago: University of Chicago Press, 1992), 191–228.

77. S. Stepniak, "The Dynamite Scare and Anarchy," *The New Review* 6 (May 1892): 541.

78. Conrad also attacked sensationalism in "The Loss of the *Titanic*." See Joseph Conrad, *Notes on Life and Letters* (London: Dent, 1934), 287–307. Cited hereafter in text as *NLL*.

79. Of interest here is a nearly contemporaneous phenomenon transpiring on the other side of the world, in the Spanish-American War of 1898, during which the role of the press expanded, and around which the question of media representation became tensely knotted. See Bill Brown, *The Material Unconscious: American Amusement, Stephen Crane, and the Economics of Play* (Cambridge, MA: Harvard University Press, 1996).

80. Frederic A. Sharf, Anne Nishimura Morse, and Sebastian Dobson, *A Much Recorded War: The Russo-Japanese War in History and Imagery* (Boston: MFA Publications, 2005), 2.

81. Conrad, *Notes on Life and Letters*, 111–12.

82. See Elaine Scarry, *The Body in Pain: The Making and Unmaking of the World* (New York: Oxford University Press, 1985).

83. A number of critics have observed the split quality of *The Secret Agent*, and have considered the move to Winnie and domestic violence. In a well-known commentary, Irving Howe argues that the second half of the novel marks an increasingly caricatured portrait of humanity. For Howe, Conrad's irony is too encompassing in this novel, and the shift to Winnie's drama in the second part of the text catalyzes a form of parody that turns the whole panorama into a kind of grim urban puppet show (Howe, *Politics and the Novel*). More recently, two excellent feminist critiques have worked from the observation of a fundamental shift in the novel, in both style and thematics, in which the detective novel (with its particular preoccupations and cultural markers) cedes to the domestic novel (with its own forms of violence). See Wendy Moffat, "Domestic Violence: The Simple Tale within *The Secret Agent*," *ELT* 37:4 (1994): 465–89, and Rishona Zimring, "Conrad's Pornography Shop," *MFS* 43:2 (1997): 319–48. For discussion of the domestic drama as, in effect, a way to work out broader anxieties surrounding anarchism, see Eileen Sypher, "Anarchism and Gender: James's *The Princess Casamassima* and Conrad's *The Secret Agent*," *Conradiana* 9:1 (Winter 1988): 1–16.

84. For discussion of this sequence, see Joseph McLaughlin, *Writing the Urban Jungle: Reading Empire in London from Doyle to Eliot* (Charlottesville: University Press of Virginia, 2000), 133–67.

85. The notion of "vigilance" is repeatedly invoked in the novel's opening chapters, tapping into a wider Victorian preoccupation with policing. For discussion of these issues, see Miller, *The Novel and the Police*; David Philips, *Crime and Authority in Victorian England: the Black Country, 1835–1860* (London: Croom Helm, 1977); Porter, *The Origins of the Vigilant State*; and Philip Thurmond Smith, *Policing Victorian London: Political Policing, Public Order, and the London Metropolitan Police* (Westport, CT: Greenwood Press, 1985).

86. Joseph Conrad, *Lord Jim* (New York: New American Library, 1981), 11.

87. Joseph Conrad, *Joseph Conrad's Letters to R. B. Cunninghame Graham* (Cambridge: Cambridge University Press, 1969), 169. Zdzislaw Najder makes an interesting case for reading the novel in terms of a subverted—what we might call a deconstructed—melodrama. He writes, for instance: "The narrative . . . goes against the melodramatic grain of the subject matter. The course of action does not resolve the conflicts but makes them more complex and ambiguous; instead of simple contrasts we are faced with manifold deceptions, misunderstandings and ambiguities." See Zdzislaw Najder, "Joseph Conrad's *The Secret Agent*, or the Melodrama of Reality," *New York Literary Forum* 7 (1980): 161.

88. Joseph Conrad, *Nostromo* (New York: Penguin, 1960), 127.

89. Here one might consider Fredric Jameson's notion of Conrad's "political unconscious." Jameson's reading of Conrad stresses a stylistics that does not so much repress the

322 NOTES TO PAGES 125–135

historical as create a space of ambiguity and division at precisely the point where history threatens to assert itself. See Fredric Jameson, *The Political Unconscious: Narrative as a Socially Symbolic Act* (Ithaca: Cornell University Press, 1981), 206–80.

90. For the decisive reading of *Great Expectations* in this vein, see William A. Cohen, *Sex Scandal: The Private Parts of Victorian Fiction* (Durham: Duke University Press, 1996).

91. Sherry has suggested a possible model for the Professor as suicide-bomber, the Fenian Luke Dillon, who was known, apparently, to have kept a ready explosive device on his person to ward off arrest. However, it is not entirely clear that Conrad knew about this. See Sherry, *Conrad's Western World*, 283–85.

92. See Francis Fukuyama, "The End of History?" *The National Interest* (Summer 1989).

93. D. H. Lawrence, *Kangaroo* (New York: Penguin, 1980), 353.

94. Lawrence makes almost the identical move in an essay of the same year, 1923, entitled "Surgery for the Novel—Or a Bomb," in which he expresses not the least bit of interest in bombs, but he does offer this thought experiment, as a cure for the novel's malaise: "Supposing a bomb were put under the whole scheme of things, what would we be after?" D. H. Lawrence, *Selected Literary Criticism* (New York: Viking, 1956), 117.

Chapter 3

1. Georges Bataille, *The Accursed Share: An Essay on General Economy, Volumes II & III*, trans. Robert Hurley (New York: Zone, 1993), 85.

2. Something like this might be said about the First World War, but what differentiates the Irish rebellion from the war, in this regard, is that its literary and political expression can be understood in more finite terms, bounded by national and temporal parameters. Also, a note on terminology: in accordance with ordinary usage, I employ "the Rising" specifically to refer to the events of Easter week, 1916. Other terms (insurrection, insurgency, rebellion, anticolonialism, etc.) refer to broader phenomena in the period and beyond.

3. Anna MacBride White and Norman Jeffares, eds., *The Gonne-Yeats Letters, 1893–1938* (London: Hutchinson, 1992), 372.

4. W. B. Yeats, *The Variorum Edition of the Poems of W. B. Yeats* (New York: Macmillan, 1957), 393. Cited in text hereafter as *Var*.

5. *Gonne-Yeats Letters*, 384.

6. With respect to the critical tradition, several extraordinarily insightful works have influenced me in writing this chapter, and I will refer to these over the course of my discussion: Elizabeth Cullingford, *Yeats, Ireland and Fascism* (New York: New York University Press, 1981); Seamus Deane, *Celtic Revivals: Essays in Modern Irish Literature, 1880–1980* (London: Faber, 1985); Declan Kiberd, *Inventing Ireland: The Literature of the Modern Nation* (Cambridge, MA: Harvard University Press, 1995); David Lloyd, *Anomalous States: Irish Writing and the Post-Colonial Moment* (Dublin: Lilliput, 1993); and Michael North, *The Political Aesthetic of Yeats, Eliot, and Pound* (Cambridge: Cambridge University Press, 1991), 21–73. For biography, the current standard is R. F. Foster's *W. B. Yeats: A Life*, 2 vols. (Oxford: Oxford University Press, 1998 and 2003). A later addition to this canon, which appeared after all but the final revisions of this book, is Michael Wood, *Yeats and Violence* (Oxford: Oxford University Press, 2010).

7. In *Where There Is Nothing* and *The Unicorn from the Stars*, the principle of excessive giving motivates the protagonists, who find richness in squander and reward in selflessness.

The phrase, "where there is nothing, there is God," at the core of both works, makes this paradoxical point. In "Poetry and Tradition," Yeats wrote that the aristocracy has the greatest potential to make "beautiful things," because, as he says, "their place in the world puts them above the fear of life . . . because Providence has filled them with recklessness." He adds, paraphrasing Wilde, "All the most valuable things are useless." See W. B. Yeats, *Essays and Introductions* (New York: Macmillan, 1961), 251. Cited in text hereafter as *EI*.

8. Yeats would later concede that he had failed, in "September 1913," to recognize the vitality of romantic nationalism, as it would be embodied in the Rising. In a note to "September 1913," he wrote that "'Romantic Ireland's dead and gone' sounds old-fashioned now. It seemed true in 1913, but I did not foresee 1916. The late Dublin Rebellion, whatever one can say of its wisdom, will long be remembered for its heroism. 'They weighed so lightly what they gave,' and gave too in some cases without hope of success. July 1916" (*Var*, 820).

9. Theobald Wolfe Tone, *The Autobiography of Theobald Wolfe Tone, 1763–1798, Volume 1* (Dublin: Maunsel, 1893?), 39.

10. John Mitchel, *Jail Journal: 1876* (Washington, DC: Woodstock, 1996), 89. Cited in text hereafter as *JJ*.

11. Padraic (*sic*) H. Pearse, *Collected Works: Political Writings and Speeches* (Dublin: Maunsel and Roberts, 1922), 25. Cited in text hereafter as *PWS*.

12. Virginia Woolf, *To the Lighthouse* (San Diego: Harcourt, 1981), 149.

13. For an engrossing discussion of elegy, which treats it as a form of mourning, with psychoanalytic functions, see Peter Sacks, *The English Elegy: Studies in the Genre from Spenser to Yeats* (Baltimore: Johns Hopkins University Press, 1985). In his focus on the elegy, Sacks does not discuss the central role played by women in mourning traditions.

14. The topic of ritual lament in the Greek tradition has occupied classical scholars. See especially Margaret Alexiou, *The Ritual Lament in Greek Tradition* (Cambridge: Cambridge University Press, 1974); Gail Holst-Warhaft, *Dangerous Voices: Women's Laments and Greek Literature* (London: Routledge, 1992); Richard Martin, *The Language of Heroes: Speech and Performance in the Iliad.* (Ithaca: Cornell University Press, 1989); and Gregory Nagy, *The Best of the Achaeans: Concepts of the Hero in Archaic Greek Poetry* (Baltimore: Johns Hopkins University Press, 1979). For a brisk summary of the tradition, in the context of several passages from the *Iliad*, see Maria C. Pantelia, "Helen and the Last Song for Hector," *Transactions of the American Philological Association* 132:1–2 (2002): 21–27.

15. Nicole Loraux, *Mothers in Mourning, with the Essay "Of Amnesty and its Opposite,"* trans. Corinne Pache (Ithaca: Cornell University Press, 1998), 35.

16. Jay Winter, *Sites of Memory, Sites of Mourning: The Great War in European Cultural History* (Cambridge: Cambridge University Press, 1995), 113.

17. One thinks of Cindy Sheehan, the mother of an Iraq war soldier who was killed in combat in 2004; she became the leader of an antiwar movement.

18. For discussion of mourning in Ireland as an energizing element in political, cultural, and national life, see Duncan Greenlaw, *Borders of Mourning: Remembrance, Commitment, and the Contexts of Irish Identity* (Dublin: Maunsel, 2004).

19. A well-known anecdote claims that Yeats originally sent Synge to Aran, a site of pilgrimage in the heyday of the Gaelic revival (though this account has been disputed). It was their first meeting, in Paris, and Yeats depicts himself as poised to give advice to the younger writer:

I said: "Give up Paris. You will never create anything by reading Racine, and Arthur Symons will always be a better critic of French literature. Go to the Aran Islands. Live there as if you were one of the people themselves; express a life that has never found expression." I had just come from Aran, and my imagination was full of those grey islands where men must reap with knives because of the stones. (Yeats, *EI*, 299)

20. Linguists, too, were drawn to the Aran Islands. Despite the widespread fiction of an untouched land, entirely secluded from modernizing Europe, the Aran Islands were often visited by travelers looking precisely for such purity, and by linguists from all over Ireland and other parts of the world.

21. John M. Synge, *The Aran Islands* (Evanston: Northwestern University Press, 1999), 36–37. Cited in text hereafter as Synge, *AI*.

22. John M. Synge, *Collected Works, Volume III, Plays, Book I* (London: Oxford University Press, 1968), 25–26. Cited in text hereafter as *CW III*.

23. See, for instance, Thomas Davis, *Essays and Poems* (Dublin: M. H. Gill, 1945), 93–109. We might also note, in this regard, John Mitchel's introduction to a collection of poems by Clarence Mangan, which presents Mangan's verse, in part, as embodying what I am calling the keening mode: "The very soul of his melody," writes Mitchel, "is that plaintive and passionate yearning which breathes and throbs through all the music of Ireland." See John Mitchel, introduction to *Poems of James Clarence Mangan*, by James Clarence Mangan (Dublin: O'Donoghue, 1903), xxxvii.

24. W. B. Yeats, *The Collected Plays of W. B. Yeats* (New York: Macmillan, 1952), 56. Cited in text hereafter as *CP*.

25. It is perhaps not surprising to find Pearse comfortably amalgamating these two traditions, since it became his goal, by the time of the Rising, to embrace a full span of nationalist positions. For instance, though he was initially critical of *The Playboy of the Western World*, by 1913 he called Synge "a man in whose sad heart there glowed a true love of Ireland," and regretted the initial disparagement (*PWS*, 145).

26. For discussion of this paradigm—the proud mother who sacrifices her sons for the good of the nation or revolution, or, more generally, "mothering the nation"—in various historical periods and national traditions, see Nancy Armstrong, *Desire and Domestic Fiction: A Political History of the Novel* (New York: Oxford University Press, 1987); Lynn Hunt, *The Family Romance of the French Revolution* (Berkeley: University of California Press, 1992); George Mosse, *Nationalism and Sexuality: Respectability and Abnormal Sexuality in Modern Europe* (New York: Howard Fertig, 1985); and Mary Ryan, *Empire of the Mother: American Writing about Domesticity* (New York: Harrington Park Press, 1985).

27. Padraic (*sic*) Pearse, *Collected Works of Padraic H. Pearse: Plays, Stories, Poems* (New York, Stokes, 1917), 44. Cited in text hereafter as *PSP*.

28. Seamus Deane, for instance, usually a generous (as well as brilliant and capacious) reader of different literary styles among Irish writers, has little to say in praise of O'Casey's works. There is, he writes, "a coarsening element in his work related to his attempt to make sense of contemporary political situations in the light of an imperfectly conceived moral system" (Deane, *Celtic Revivals*, 108). And David Lloyd—also prolific as a period synthesizer—does not mention O'Casey at all in *Anomalous States*.

29. Sean O'Casey, *Collected Plays, Volume One* (London: MacMillan, 1967), 86. Cited in text hereafter as *CPI*.

30. The passage also carries classical associations: the image of the fondled head, desecrated in war, recalls Hector in the *Iliad*; the sense of parallelism in warring families has broadly Greek associations; the scales of sorrow suggest Zeus.

31. By "physical force tradition," I mean the view that parliamentary and political means alone would never secure independence and that violence/insurgency must play a role in the national struggle. In the nineteenth century, it was John Mitchel, above all, who represented this tradition. I will discuss Mitchel in part iii, "Reprisal."

32. Pearse's language about the war has been noted by critics. It functions, for instance, as the basis for Deane's appraisal of Pearse as a writer in the heroic, even "chivalrous," tradition. See Deane, *Celtic Revivals*, 63–74.

33. Thomas MacDonagh, too, stressed the resurrection in many of his poems, such as in the 1904 volume, *April and May*, whose preface explains that "most of [the poems] embody the thought of this Season, and Death in Life, and Resurrection." See Thomas MacDonagh, *April and May; with Other Verse* (Dublin: Bryers and Walker, 1904). Plunkett and Mac-Donagh write a form of devout Catholic verse, but their near-obsession with the crucifixion and resurrection also points to a broader overlap between national and religious idioms, in a conflation that took its ultimate form in the Rising.

34. A ubiquitous image in Yeats's works, the rose has been discussed widely. For several focused discussions, see Jonathan Allison, "The Rose, the Reader and Yeats's Intentions," *Yeats: An Annual of Critical and Textual Studies* 13 (1995): 3–10; Wayne K. Chapman, "Yeats and the Rose of Sharon," *English Language Notes* 29:3 (March 1992): 51–53; and Donald R. Pearce, "The Systematic Rose," *Yeats Annual* 4 (1986): 195–200.

35. Aubrey de Vere, *Poems from the works of Aubrey de Vere* (London: Catholic Truth Society, 1904), 102.

36. I am using Pearse's translation; see Padraic (*sic*) Pearse, *Collected Works of Padraic H. Pearse: Songs of the Irish Rebels and Specimens from an Irish Anthology* (Dublin: Maunsel, 1918), 25. Lest anyone wonder at the erotic language of most of the poem—it is not overtly national until the final stanza—Pearse noted, "Its passionate love phrases are of course allegorical" (25). The poem circulated under several names, "The Little Dark Rose," "Róisín Dubh" (in Gaelic), and in somewhat different form as "Dark Rosaleen." This last was the title given by Mangan in his widely read iteration. The final lines of that version run as follows:

> O! the Erne shall run red
> With redundance of blood,
> The earth shall rock beneath our tread,
> And flames wrap hill and wood,
> And gun-peal, and slogan-cry,
> Wake many a glen serene,
> Ere you shall fade, ere you shall die,
> My Dark Rosaleen!
> My own Rosaleen!
> The Judgment Hour must first be nigh,
> Ere you can fade, ere you can die,
> My Dark Rosaleen!

See James Clarence Mangan, *The Poems of James Clarence Mangan* (Dublin: O'Donaghue, 1903), 5.

37. Joseph Mary Plunkett, *The Poems of Joseph Mary Plunkett* (London: Unwin, 1916), 59–60.

38. The reverence for Shelley in this period is particularly notable. In addition to developing a Romantic idiom that was influential for this generation of poets and intellectuals, Shelley also wrote several revolutionary pamphlets in favor of Irish emancipation. See Paul O'Brien, *Shelley and Revolutionary Ireland* (London: Redwords, 2002).

39. Interestingly, this printing of the poem is not mentioned in *The Variorum Edition*. As for Lionel Johnson, he and Yeats were friends from Yeats's years in the Rhymers' Club in London. Yeats included "The Ways of War" in *Poetry and Tradition* (*EI*, 258).

40. Here is Pearse:

> I turned my back
> On the dream I had shaped,
> And to this road before me
> My face I turned.
>
> I set my face
> To the road here before me,
> To the work that I see,
> To the death that I shall meet. (*Poems of the IRB*, 25)

41. Another crux question involves the timing of the poem's publication: having written it and circulated it privately in the heat of the post-Rising months, why did Yeats wait four years before publishing it? Foster plausibly suggests political considerations: under some suspicion of being "pro-German," for his support of Roger Casement (who attempted to procure arms from Germany and was executed by the British), Yeats did not feel it advisable to publish a poem viewed at the time as highly pro-Nationalist. (See Foster, Vol. 2, 59–65.) Also, there was the continuing issue of Hugh Lane's bequest to the National Gallery: Lane, an Anglo-Irish collector of impressionist art who died in 1915 (aboard the *Lusitania*), had left his collection, in a codicil to his will, to Dublin. Yet the organization responsible for city government, the Dublin Corporation, prevaricated and nearly lost the collection to London, whose National Gallery eagerly offered to build a wing for it. Yeats wrote several poems about this mess, and his concern with it may have made him wary of large political statements in this period.

42. This omission might be said to correspond to the historical fact that Yeats himself was not in Ireland when the Rising occurred (he was in England, no less) and was taken completely by surprise.

43. See Kiberd, *Inventing Ireland*, 216–17.

44. See Meredith Martin, *The Rise and Fall of Meter: Poetry and English National Culture, 1860–1930* (Princeton: Princeton University Press, 2012).

45. Cullingford, *Yeats, Ireland and Fascism*, 85.

46. Foster treats the fascism question rather quietly, seeing Yeats's politics in the thirties as entirely subject to other urgent poetic and personal questions.

47. Conor Cruise O'Brien, *Passion and Cunning: Essays on Nationalism, Terrorism, and Revolution* (New York: Simon and Schuster, 1988), 8–61. The 1913 dockworkers strike and subsequent lockout was a galvanizing event in Irish labor politics of the period.

48. Jonathan Allison, "Introduction: Fascism, Nationalism, Reception," in *Yeats's Political Identities: Selected Essays* (Ann Arbor: University of Michigan Press, 1996), 1.

49. Michael Tratner, *Modernism and Mass Politics: Joyce, Woolf, Eliot, Yeats* (Stanford: Stanford University Press, 1995), 150.

50. For discussion of the war and Ireland, see Fran Brearton, *The Great War in Irish Poetry: W. B. Yeats to Michael Longley* (Oxford: Oxford University Press, 2000); Adrian Gregory and Senia Paseta, eds., *Ireland and the Great War: "A War to Unite Us All?"* (Manchester: Manchester University Press, 2002); Keith Jeffery, *Ireland and the Great War* (Cambridge: Cambridge University Press, 2001); and Nuala C. Johnson, *Ireland, the Great War and the Geography of Remembrance* (Cambridge: Cambridge University Press, 2003).

51. In constructing these refrains, Yeats may have been thinking, among other things, of Wilde's play *Salome*.

52. For discussion of sexual politics over the span of Yeats's works, see Marjorie Howes, *Yeats's Nations: Gender, Class, and Irishness* (Cambridge: Cambridge University Press, 1996).

53. For discussion of some of Yeats's techniques in the context of a broader modernist ambivalence about theatricality, see Martin Puchner, *Stage Fright: Modernism, Anti-Theatricality, and Drama* (Baltimore: Johns Hopkins University Press, 2002), 119–38.

54. *The Playboy* began its life in polarizing terms. Indeed, many readers of modernism today know only this about the play: that it incited riots. Early detractors included not only the audience members who disturbed its first performances, but also others, including reviewers, who deplored its representation of the Irish populace, along with its notoriously scandalous language (it was the uttering of the word "shift" in the third act that set off the riot on the first night). For analysis of the disturbances as part of a larger discussion of the theater and the public in this period, see Paige Reynolds, *Modernism, Drama, and the Audience for Irish Spectacle* (Cambridge: Cambridge University Press, 2007).

55. In addition to his reading of Synge in *Inventing Ireland* (166–88), see also Kiberd, *Synge and the Irish Language* (London: MacMillan, 1979).

56. Kiberd, for instance, has noted that despite this conventional linkage of violence with masculine sexual desirability, Synge's representation of masculinity and femininity in the play is quite unconventional, even radical.

57. J. M. Synge, *The Playboy of the Western World and Other Plays* (Oxford: Oxford University Press, 1998), 104–5. Cited in text hereafter as *Playboy*.

58. One might consider, in this regard, the concluding paragraphs of "The Dead," where Joyce also imagines a unifying national consciousness around the prospect of death. Whether the spellbinding ending of "The Dead" and *Dubliners* ultimately envisions a paralyzing, deathlike stasis or a purifying transformation is left open.

59. W. B. Yeats, *The Letters of W. B. Yeats* (London: Rupert Hart-Davis, 1954), 690.

60. The term leveler has historical connotations as well, to which Mitchel perhaps alluded. The Levellers were a seventeenth-century English dissenting group, dedicated to reform of the franchise, religious rights, and the prison system; they were often misportrayed by their contemporaries as wildly radical (proto-anarchists hoping to overthrow the social order).

61. James Connolly, *Collected Works, Volume Two* (Dublin: New Books, 1988), 52.

62. Unlike some of his pairs of plays, such as *A Full Moon in March* and *The King of the Great Clock Tower*, both of which Yeats included in the collected edition, he opted to omit *Where There Is Nothing*, which he felt had been superseded by *The Unicorn from the Stars*, which he co-wrote with Lady Gregory. The two are quite different, and, as the editor of *Where There Is Nothing* argues, there is good reason to make the earlier play available.

63. Katharine Worth, introduction to *Where There Is Nothing and The Unicorn from the Stars*, by W. B. Yeats (Washington, DC: Catholic University of America Press, 1987). Cited in text hereafter as *WN*. In his autobiography, Yeats mentions having met "the Anarchist Prince Kropotkin" at the home of William Morris, in whose circle Yeats moved for a time. See W. B. Yeats, *The Autobiography of William Butler Yeats* (New York: MacMillan 1953), 86. For discussion of Morris's influence on Yeats, see Cullingford, *Yeats, Ireland, and Fascism*, 16–28.

64. Yeats makes an oblique reference to Mitchel in *The Unicorn from the Stars*: one of the beggars sings a song about being arrested and deported, "For to plough Van Diemen's Land," the penal colony where Mitchel served his fourteen-year sentence (Yeats, *WN*, 142).

65. That nihilism had wide appeal in nineteenth-century Russia is as one would expect: to the tyranny of the absolutist state, nihilism stands in perfect opposition. It seems that the early emphasis on nihilism was something Yeats wanted to disown, as he distanced himself from the first play and built a robust national plot into the second version, perhaps at the behest of Lady Gregory, who collaborated in the rewriting.

66. I will discuss *Guernica* in the final chapter.

67. For a wonderful reflection on "Nineteen Hundred and Nineteen," see Wood, *Yeats and Violence* (indeed, his volume is slightly misnamed, since it is primarily a study of that poem).

68. For discussion of whether her name was in fact Ellen or Eileen, and for more details about the shooting and inquest, see Wood, 20–22.

69. *The Nation* (London), November 13, 1920, 216.

70. The symbolism of the mother was clearly important to Yeats. Had he been looking primarily for gruesome injustice, he might have found it in a column of Gregory's from a month later, where she reports on the horrendous murder of two boys from a small town in the west of Ireland (Shanaglish). In one account she quotes a witness saying, "the flesh was as if torn off the bones," and in another "the body of one was 'all charred and most of the skull badly fractured, part of it being missing. The flesh was hanging on the legs and arms'" (*The Nation*, December 18, 1920, 413, 414).

71. Herodias was the wife of King Herod, and their most famous daughter was Salomé, a figure who hovers in the background of those of Yeats's plays that feature a woman dancing around a severed head. As for the plural "daughters," the reference is less certain. Yeats had mentioned Herodias's daughters in his note to "'The Hosting of the Sidhe," as figures for wild movement, and as illustrations of the tendency for a populace to transpose mythical beings from one era to another: "Sidhe is . . . Gaelic for wind, and certainly the Sidhe have much to do with wind," he explains; "They journey in whirling winds, the winds that were called the dance of the daughters of Herodias in the Middle Ages, Herodias doubtless taking the place of some old goddess" (Yeats, *Var*, 800).

72. For a wonderful reading of Artisson as a figure who is "at once common and occult, public and private, destructive of the aristocracy and yet, as the epitome of violence, constitutive of it as well," who is, indeed "one of Yeats's greatest images," see North, *The Political Aesthetic of Yeats, Eliot, and Pound*, 61.

73. Rob Doggett, "Writing Out (of) Chaos: Constructions of History in Yeats's 'Nineteen Hundred and Nineteen' and 'Meditations in Time of Civil War,'" *Twentieth Century Literature* 47:2 (Summer 2001): 142–43.

74. Yeats would have seen Fuller in Paris in 1890. See Foster, Vol. 1, 109.

75. In addition to these two poems, Yeats also wrote a more traditional elegy for Gregory, "In Memory of Major Robert Gregory," which ends with the heartbreaking stanza:

> I had thought, seeing how bitter is that wind
> That shakes the shutter, to have brought to mind
> All those that manhood tried, or childhood loved
> Or boyish intellect approved,
> With some appropriate commentary on each;
> Until imagination brought
> A fitter welcome; but a thought
> Of that late death took all my heart for speech. (*Var,* 327–28)

76. W. B. Yeats, introduction to *The Oxford Book of Modern Verse, 1892–1935* (Oxford: Oxford University Press, 1978), xxxiv. Yeats omitted Owen, but included several war poems by Sassoon and Herbert Read.

77. On Yeats's relation to the war, Foster takes the embittered, sulky poem "On Being Asked for a War Poem" as the key statement:

> I think it better that in times like these
> A poet's mouth be silent, for in truth
> We have no gift to set a statesman right;
> He has had enough of meddling who can please
> A young girl in the indolence of her youth,
> Or an old man upon a winter's night. (*Var,* 359)

In a 1914 letter, moreover, Yeats described his response thus: "It is merely the most expensive outbreak of insolence and stupidity the world has ever seen . . . and I give it as little thought as I can" (quoted in Foster, Vol. 2, 5). On Yeats and the war, see T. R. Henn, *W. B. Yeats and the Poetry of War* (Oxford: Oxford University Press, 1967), and Samuel Hynes, "Yeats's Wars," *Sewanee Review* 97:1 (Winter 1989): 36–55. For Ireland and the war more generally, see note 50 above.

78. I hope readers will not find it confusing that I have chosen to discuss the plays out of their chronological order. Since I am arguing that generative violence gives way, imaginatively, to reprisal, it seemed helpful to present the plays in terms of their internal time frames (1916, 1920, 1922) rather than in their compositional order. They were composed in relatively quick succession, in any case.

79. There are, however, two counterexamples, where O'Casey employs a robust language of generative violence; both of these, significantly, focus on heroic labor. First is a 1919 history of the Citizen Army (a labor-based militia founded after the lockout of 1913, which eventually merged with the Irish Volunteers and played a central role in the Rising), of which he was a member until 1915. See P. O Cathasaigh [i.e., Sean O'Casey], *The Story of the Irish Citizen Army* (Dublin: Maunsel, 1919). And the second is the late play *The Star Turns Red* (1940), which features the heroic figure of "Red Jim," who, along with other loyal communists, courageously fights against a fascist-supported state. See Sean O'Casey, *Collected Plays, Volume Two* (London: MacMillan, 1950). For an assessment of O'Casey and the representation of violence, see Bernice Schrank, "Sean O'Casey and the Dialectics of Violence," in *Shadows of the Gunmen: Violence and Culture in Modern Ireland,* eds. Danine Farquharson and Sean Farrell (Cork: Cork University Press, 2008), 38–62.

80. See Reynolds, *Modernism, Drama, and the Audience for Irish Spectacle*, 199–206.

81. If this conflict reminds readers of some similar issues in First World War literature, where there is a rift between supporting the war and recognizing the depth of psychic response to battle and war loss—one thinks of *Journey's End*, for instance—such a parallel is not far from the mark. O'Casey's next play, *The Silver Tassie* (1928), which focuses on a disabled war combatant, takes up this exact dynamic.

82. Notably, Yeats's *Cathleen ni Houlihan* is set in 1798.

83. O'Casey and Yeats at times seem like nemeses; initially allies, they had an eventual (and highly public) falling out over Yeats's rejection of *The Silver Tassie* for the Abbey in 1928. As Kiberd notes, moreover, O'Casey ridiculed "Easter 1916," titling a chapter in his autobiography "A Terrible Beauty is Borneo" (Kiberd, *Inventing Ireland*, 224). For discussion of the conflict with O'Casey over *The Silver Tassie*, see Foster, V. II, 367–72.

84. *The Nation*, December 4, 1920, 333.

85. Standish O'Grady, *History of Ireland, Volume I: The Heroic Period* (New York: Lemma, 1970), 116.

86. Thomas MacDonagh, *April and May*, 37.

87. For discussion of the big house in Irish literary history, see Vera Kreilkamp, *The Anglo-Irish Novel and the Big House* (Syracuse: Syracuse University Press, 1998).

88. The word "boycott" in fact dates from the late nineteenth century. It was the successful disruption of the estate belonging to one Captain Boycott that gave the practice its name, and also, incidentally, helped cement the early political fortunes of Parnell.

89. For an especially luminous discussion of *The Last September*, with resonance here for its argument about how colonial violence was imagined in the period within a larger frame of stunted progress, see Jed Esty, "Virgins of Empire: *The Last September* and the Antidevelopmental Plot," *Modern Fiction Studies* 53:2 (Summer 2007): 257–75. See also Kreilkamp, *The Anglo-Irish Novel and the Big House*, 141–73. For Bowen's reflections on the subject, see her essay "The Big House," in Elizabeth Bowen, *The Mulberry Tree* (London: Virago, 1986), 25–30.

90. Elizabeth Bowen, *The Last September* (New York: Random House, 2000), 300. Cited hereafter in text as *LS*.

91. Some of this poignancy is undoubtedly personal, as evident in her 1942 memoir named for her family estate, *Bowen's Court*.

92. Bowen makes a similar point about the surprise and paradox of finding the origins of beautiful, refined big houses in the violent, unruly men who built them in the eighteenth century: "These country gentlemen liked sport, drink and card-playing very much better than they liked the arts—but they religiously stocked their libraries, set fine craftsmen to work on their ceilings and mantelpieces and interspersed their own family portraits with heroicized paintings of foreign scenes" (Bowen, *Mulberry Tree*, 27).

93. The actual tower is Ballylee, which Yeats purchased in 1916 and where he lived intermittently until 1928. It is featured in many of his poems of these years, and gives its name to both a single poem, "The Tower," and to the volume.

94. Elizabeth Bowen, *The Death of the Heart* (New York: Random House, 2000), 270.

95. W. B. Yeats, *On the Boiler* (Dublin: Cuala, 1971), 8. Cited in text hereafter as *OB*.

96. The Mansion House, built in 1710 and acquired soon after as the official residence of the Lord Mayor of Dublin, has a central place in the events of the revolutionary period,

including the 1919 signing of the Declaration of Independence and meeting of the first Dáil session there. Architecturally, Yeats objected to a metal canopy added in 1896 to the entry area in honor of Queen Victoria's (controversial) visit to Dublin. In the 1930s, a plan to demolish the Mansion House was discussed, but never enacted.

Chapter 4

1. Virginia Woolf, *Between the Acts* (San Diego: Harcourt, 1969), 99. Cited in text hereafter as *BTA*.

2. Simone Weil, *The Iliad or the Poem of Force*, trans. James P. Holoka (New York: Peter Lang, 2003), 57, 61.

3. Virginia Woolf, *The Moment and Other Essays* (San Diego: Harvest, 1976), 228.

4. The term "total war" became common in the years immediately leading up to the Second World War, though it came into usage two decades earlier. Its popularization as a term is often credited to the German General Ludendorff's memoir of the First World War, *The Total War* (*Der Totale Krieg*, 1936). An earlier extended usage is Léon Daudet, *La Guerre totale* (Paris: Nouvelle Librairie Nationale, 1918). For discussion of the concept, see Roger Chickering and Stig Forster, eds., *Anticipating Total War: The German and American Experiences, 1871–1914* (Cambridge: Cambridge University Press and Washington, DC: German Historical Institute, 1999).

5. Cited in Valentine Cunningham, ed., *Spanish Front: Writers on the Civil War* (Oxford: Oxford University Press, 1986), 220–1.

6. Virginia Woolf, *The Diary of Virginia Woolf, Volume Four, 1931–1935* (New York: Harcourt, 1982), 338.

7. Hermione Lee, *Virginia Woolf* (New York: Vintage, 1999), 655.

8. Woolf casts the net wide in depicting art and its production in the novel—with Miss La Trobe's pageant occupying nearly a third of the novel's pages, a marked emphasis on the artistry of and within Pointz Hall, various characters inhabiting artist-like roles, and a running comparison of life to theater.

9. Criticism that engages Woolf and war will be cited throughout this chapter. For an important inaugural study, see Mark Hussey, ed., *Virginia Woolf and War: Fiction, Reality, Myth* (Syracuse: Syracuse University Press, 1991).

10. Considerations of violence in the twentieth century do not often focus on Woolf. For a discussion that takes her as a central voice, particularly with respect to gender, see William A. Johnsen, *Violence and Modernism: Ibsen, Joyce, and Woolf* (Gainesville: University Press of Florida, 2003).

11. Christine Froula, *Virginia Woolf and the Bloomsbury Avant-Garde: War, Civilization, Modernity* (New York: Columbia University Press, 2005), 32. Froula's study is majestic and exhaustive. I came to it only after having written the bulk of *At the Violet Hour*, and was pleased to note a shared viewpoint and, in some cases, overlapping selections of materials. I will reference Froula's work throughout this chapter.

12. Albert Einstein and Sigmund Freud, *Why War?*, trans. Stuart Gilbert (Paris: International Institute of Intellectual Cooperation, 1933), 11–12.

13. Aldous Huxley, *An Encyclopedia of Pacifism*, in Robert A. Seeley, *The Handbook of Non-Violence* (Westport, CT: Lawrence Hill, 1986), 6.

14. Virginia Woolf, *The Diary of Virginia Woolf, Volume Five, 1936–1941* (San Diego: Harcourt, 1984) 268. Several of the richest and most thorough considerations of this theme—the idea of an ongoing opposition between civilization and barbarity as a founding feature of interwar

culture—are Froula, *Virginia Woolf and the Bloomsbury Avant-Garde*; Samuel Hynes, *A War Imagined: The First World War and English Culture* (London: Bodley Head, 1990); and Daniel Pick, *War Machine: The Rationalization of Slaughter in the Modern Age* (New Haven: Yale University Press, 1993).

15. Sigmund Freud, *Civilization and its Discontents*, trans. James Strachey (New York: Norton, 1989), 82.

16. Bertrand Russell, *Power: A New Social Analysis* (New York: Norton, 1938), 11, 12.

17. Weil joins the debate in these terms as well, arguing against the view that nations have unalterable dispositions (warlike or pacific), seeing instead the possibility of international cooperation as a feasible bulwark against war. See "The Great Beast: Some Reflections on the Origins of Hitlerism," in Simone Weil, *Selected Essays: 1934–1943*, trans. Richard Rees (London: Oxford University Press, 1962), 89–144.

18. William James, "The Moral Equivalent of War" (New York: American Association of International Conciliation, 1910), 6.

19. Benito Mussolini, *The Political and Social Doctrine of Fascism*, trans. Jane Soames (London: Hogarth, 1933), 11.

20. Huxley, *An Encyclopedia of Pacifism*, 56.

21. For a selection of anthropologically themed studies of modernism, see Elazar Barkan and Ronald Bush, eds., *Prehistories of the Future: The Primitivist Project and the Culture of Modernism* (Stanford: Stanford University Press, 1995); Jed Esty, *A Shrinking Island: Modernism and National Culture in England* (Princeton: Princeton University Press, 2004); Susan Hegeman *Patterns for America: Modernism and the Concept of Culture* (Princeton: Princeton University Press, 1999); Marc Manganaro, *Modernist Anthropology: From Fieldwork to Text* (Princeton: Princeton University Press, 1990); Cary J. Snyder, *British Fiction and Cross-Cultural Encounters: Ethnographic Modernism from Wells to Woolf* (New York: Palgrave Macmillan, 2008); Marianna Torgovnick, *Gone Primitive: Savage Intellects, Modern Lives* (Chicago: University of Chicago Press, 1990); and John B. Vickery, *The Literary Impact of the Golden Bough* (Princeton: Princeton University Press, 1973). For summary of this material, see Manganaro, "Modernist Studies and Anthropology: Reflections on the Past, Present, and Possible Futures," in *Disciplining Modernism*, ed. Pamela L. Caughie (Houndmills, UK: Palgrave Macmillan, 2009), 210–20, and Patricia Rae, "Anthropology," in *A Companion to Modernist Literature and Culture*, eds. David Bradshaw and Kevin J. H. Dettmar (Malden, MA: Blackwell, 2006), 92–102.

22. Torgovnick, *Gone Primitive*, 174.

23. Leonard Woolf, *Quack Quack!* (London: Hogarth, 1935), 109.

24. Leonard Woolf, *Barbarians Within and Without* (New York: Harcourt, 1939), 138.

25. See Leonard Woolf, *The War for Peace* (London: Routledge, 1940).

26. *SB*, 1: 21. The scrapbooks are available in full online, at *Virginia Woolf: Reading Notes for* Three Guineas: *An Edition and Archive*, http://www.csub.edu/woolf/tgs_home.html. Citation will be by volume and page, abbreviated in text as "*SB*."

27. The idea of a civilian/combatant distinction has perhaps never been firm. Mary Favret makes the case that as far back as the end of the eighteenth century, any seeming safety wall between war and peace was beginning to erode. See Favret, *War at a Distance: Romanticism and the Making of Modern Wartime* (Princeton: Princeton University Press, 2010). Also germane is Susan Sontag, *Regarding the Pain of Others* (New York: Farrar, Straus, Giroux, 2003).

28. Particularly germane to the air war side of this tradition is the brilliant and eclectic work by Sven Lindqvist, *A History of Bombing*, trans. Linda Haverty Rugg (New York: New Press, 2001). See also I. F. Clarke, ed., *The Tale of the Next Great War, 1871–1914: Fictions of Future Warfare and of Battles Still-to-come* (Liverpool: Liverpool University Press, 1995).

29. For cultural histories of aviation, see Joseph J. Corn, *The Winged Gospel: America's Romance with Aviation, 1900–1950* (New York: Oxford University Press, 1983); Peter Fritzsche, *A Nation of Fliers: German Aviation and the Popular Imagination* (Cambridge, MA: Harvard University Press, 1992); Dominick A. Pisano, ed., *The Airplane in American Culture* (Ann Arbor: University of Michigan Press, 2003); and A. Bowdoin Van Riper, *Imagining Flight: Aviation and Popular Culture* (College Station: Texas A&M University Press, 2004). For a discussion of Amelia Earhart as a "queer modern," see Anne Hermann, *Queering the Moderns: Poses/Portraits/Performances* (New York: Palgrave, 2000), 14–35.

30. "On the Partiality of Total War" was delivered as a lecture at the City University of New York, March 2012, to be in the first chapter of a forthcoming book, tentatively titled *Archive, Bomb, Civilian: Modernism in the Shadow of Total War.*

31. For detailed discussion of a whole variety of works that represented the phenomenon of air-war panic, with a particular attention to fiction, see I. F. Clarke, *Voices Prophesying War 1763–1984* (London: Oxford University Press, 1966) and Ian Patterson, *Guernica and Total War* (Cambridge, MA: Harvard University Press, 2007). For the Blitz, see Marina MacKay, *Modernism and World War II* (Cambridge: Cambridge University Press, 2007) and Mark Rawlinson, *British Writing of the Second World War* (Oxford: Oxford University Press, 2000).

32. This was a theme Wells had pursued for years, including in his 1908 novel, *The War in the Air*, which features the destruction of world capitals by airship.

33. Quoted in Russell, *Power*, 30.

34. Bernd Hüppauf, "Modernism and the Photographic Representation of War and Destruction," in *Fields of Vision: Essays in Film Studies, Visual Anthropology, and Photography*, eds. Leslie Devereux and Roger Hillman (Berkeley: University of California Press, 1995), 104–5.

35. Paul Saint-Amour, "Air War Prophecy and Interwar Modernism," *Comparative Literature Studies*, 42:2 (2005): 156.

36. Hemingway's use of this term is frequently quoted. It first appeared in a letter of February 1937. See Ernest Hemingway, *Selected Letters, 1917–1961* (New York: Scribner, 1981), 458.

37. Ernest Hemingway, *For Whom the Bell Tolls* (New York: Scribner, 2003), 163.

38. The text of these dispatches is now available, thanks to the *Hemingway Review*, which has reproduced them in full. The Spanish Civil War issue also reproduces a propaganda article written for *Pravda* in 1938. See *The Hemingway Review* 7.2 (Spring 1988).

39. Earlier drafts of the novel had Robert Jordan espousing a clearer communist commitment, but Hemingway eviscerated his politics in the novel's final draft. In the published novel, the earliest and most drawn-out sequence of rampaging violence comprises a mass reprisal *against* fascists, though this is soon matched by a story of mass murder and rape at the hand of the Falangists. For discussion of Hemingway's ambivalent politics in the novel, see Michael K. Solow, "A Clash of Certainties, Old and New: *For Whom the Bell Tolls* and the Inner War of Ernest Hemingway," *The Hemingway Review* 29:1 (Fall 2009): 103–22, and

Ishiro Takayoshi, "The Wages of War: Liberal Gullibility, Soviet Intervention, and the End of the Popular Front," *Representations* 115:1 (Summer 2011): 102–29.

40. From a pamphlet published by the Socialist Alliance of Swiss Women, in Zurich. Quoted in *Voices Against Tyranny*, 63.

41. Quoted in Cunningham, ed., *Spanish Front: Writers on the Civil War*, 51.

42. Virginia Woolf, *The Moment and Other Essays*, 128–54.

43. Edward Mendelson notes that "Even in 1937, Auden grew more reticent about History after finishing *Spain*," and that his next prose work, an "Essay on Man," "adopt[ed] an almost entirely apolitical tone": Edward Mendelson, *Early Auden* (New York: Farrar, Straus and Giroux), 323.

44. See Stephen Spender, introduction to *Voices against Tyranny: Writing of the Spanish Civil War*, ed. John Miller (New York: Scribner, 1986), 12.

45. Patterson, *Guernica and Total War*, 19–20.

46. *The London Mercury*, August 1937, 334. The report was included, verbatim, in Steer's book *The Tree of Gernika*, published in 1938; see G. L. Steer, *The Tree of Gernika: A Field Study of Modern War* (London: Hodder and Stoughton, 1938).

47. For a thorough discussion of the many political controversies and complexities entwined with the Guernica attack, see Herbert Rutledge Southworth, *Guernica! Guernica!: A Study of Journalism, Diplomacy, Propaganda, and History* (Berkeley: University of California Press, 1977). We might note in this context, too, that Woolf included in full in her scrapbook a pamphlet by the French journalist L. Delaprée, which detailed the Madrid siege (*SB*, III: 20).

48. The show was given a mixed review in *The Times*, on October 5, 1938. For more extensive conversation, see *The Spectator* (October 8, 15, 22, 29, 1937); *Apollo*, 28 (November 1938), 266; and *London Studio*, 116 (December 1938), 310–12. I have not been able to ascertain for certain whether Woolf saw the show, but it seems unlikely.

49. The painting had its home in New York as of 1939, but continued to travel for nearly two decades after that, but not to Spain, Picasso having stipulated that the painting be barred from his native country until it was again a republic, and it accordingly was only moved to Madrid in 1981. Today it is seen in a beautiful dedicated gallery in the Museo Reina Sofía.

50. A third visual form of real import in the Spanish war was the poster art that proliferated on both sides. For discussion, see Raymond Conlon, "Loyalist Graphic Art," in *The Spanish Civil War and the Visual Arts*, ed. Kathleen Vernon (Ithaca: Cornell University, Center for International Studies, 1990), 104–25.

51. According to Patterson, initial reports from the scene, and the iconography that soon emerged in both visual and written representations, tended to stress a number of repeated features, including the town's historic tree and the presence of dead goats; one wonders whether Woolf's pig carcass obliquely gestures towards these goats?

52. I am grateful to Victoria Rosner for drawing my attention to these features of Sussex in the 1930s.

53. I have not filtered my discussion through the language of affect, though there certainly are overlaps here with the conversations emerging from affect theory. For the most influential account of affect in literary studies today, see Eve Kosofsky Sedgwick, *Touching Feeling: Affect, Pedagogy, Performativity* (Durham: Duke University Press, 2003).

54. For an excellent summary of these events in Spain, with reference to Woolf and *Three Guineas*, see Emily Dalgarno, *Virginia Woolf and the Visible World* (Cambridge: Cambridge University Press, 2001), 149–78.

55. See Arthur Koestler, *L'Espagne ensanglantée: Un livre noir sur l'Espagne* (Paris: Editions du Carrefour, 1937).

56. Koestler documented his time in Spain in a 1937 memoir, *Spanish Testament*, the second half of which was reprinted, and widely translated, as the highly readable prison memoir *Dialogue with Death* (1942).

57. Robert Stradling has argued that the bombings at Getafe never took place, and that the photographs were assembled and disseminated by the Republican government entirely as part of its propaganda effort. I have been unable to verify Stradling's claims, and most historians appear to believe in the verity of the Getafe narrative. What is certain is that the photographs, with their message of intense vulnerability on one side and ruthless cruelty on the other, circulated widely in the period. See Robert Stradling, *Your Children Will Be Next: Bombing and Propaganda in the Spanish Civil War, 1936–1939* (Cardiff: University of Wales Press, 2008).

58. Susan Sontag, *On Photography* (New York: Farrar Straus Giroud, 1977), 7.

59. The book, *Sombras de la Fotografía* (Shadows of Photography), by Jose Manuel Susperregui, is not currently available in English, but was widely discussed in newspapers and online in 2009, when it was published.

60. Eric J. Leed, *No Man's Land: Combat and Identity in World War I* (Cambridge: Cambridge University Press, 1979), 6.

61. Virginia Woolf, *The Waves* (San Diego: Harcourt, 1959), 142–43.

62. Filippo Marinetti, *Marinetti: Selected Writings*, trans. R. W. Flint and Arthur A. Coppotelli (New York: FSG, 1972), 41.

63. Martin Puchner, *Poetry of the Revolution: Marx, Manifestos, and the Avant-Gardes* (Princeton: Princeton University Press, 2006).

64. Benito Mussolini, *Fascism: Doctrine and Institutions* (New York: Howard Fertig, 1968), 10.

65. Mussolini, "The Political and Social Doctrine of Fascism," 8, 10, 11.

66. It was Jessica Berman's account of Woolf's politics that first drew my attention to the journal *Action*. See Berman, *Modernist Fiction, Cosmopolitanism, and the Politics of Community* (Cambridge: Cambridge University Press, 2001), 114–56.

67. Editorial, *Action* 1:1, October 8, 1931, 1.

68. See Peter Brock, *Pacifism in Europe to 1914* (Princeton: Princeton University Press, 1972).

69. The P.P.U. eventually came to enfold another large pacifist group, the War Resisters' International, a socialist organization.

70. The preeminent peace historian is Peter Brock. See, for instance, Brock, *Pacifism in Europe to 1914*; Brock, *Freedom from War: Nonsectarian Pacifism, 1814–1914* (Toronto: University of Toronto Press, 1991); and Brock and Nigel Young, *Pacifism in the Twentieth Century* (Syracuse: Syracuse University Press, 1999). See also Martin Ceadel, *Pacifism in Britain, 1914–1945: The Defining of a Faith* (Oxford: Oxford University Press, 1980). For discussion of feminism and pacifism in England, see Heloise Brown, *"The Truest Form of Patriotism": Pacifist Feminism in Britain, 1870–1902* (Manchester: Manchester University Press, 2003)

and Richard J. Evans, *Comrades and Sisters: Feminism, Socialism and Pacifism in Europe, 1870–1945* (Sussex: Wheatsheaf, 1987). For discussion of P.P.U. membership, see Ceadel, especially Appendix II, 321–22.

71. In addition to essays on such literary/cultural figures as Shaw, Wells, Freud, and D. H. Lawrence, Caudwell (pseudonym of Christopher St. John Sprigg) also wrote fiction and poetry.

72. For an appreciation of Caudwell, see E. P. Thompson, "Christopher Caudwell," *Critical Inquiry* 21.2 (Winter 1995): 305–53. Thompson's essay was originally published in *Socialist Register* in 1977.

73. Christopher Caudwell, *Studies and Further Studies in a Dying Culture* (New York: Monthly Review Press, 1971), 125.

74. Two other noteworthy titles from the 1930s pacifist canon are A. A. Milne, *Peace with Honour* (New York: Dutton, 1934) and Beverley Nichols, *Cry Havoc!* (Garden City: Doubleday, 1933). Milne revised his views over the course of the decade, publishing *War with Honour* in 1940.

75. C. E. M. Joad, *Why War?* (Harmondsworth: Penguin, 1939), 99, 102.

76. Indeed, Joad is a favorite target of both Woolfs; Leonard takes him to task in *Quack! Quack!*.

77. Virginia Woolf, *To the Lighthouse* (San Diego: Harcourt, 1981), 60. Cited hereafter in text as *TTL*. On the subject of animals in Woolf's writings, see Wendy B. Faris, "Bloomsbury's Beasts: The Presence of Animals in the Texts and Lives of Bloomsbury," *The Yearbook of English Studies*, 37:1 (2007): 107–25, and Vicki Tromanhauser, "Animal Life and Human Sacrifice in Virginia Woolf's *Between the Acts*," *Woolf Studies Annual*, 15 (2009): 67–90.

78. Virginia Woolf, *Moments of Being* (San Diego: Harcourt, 1985), 98. Cited in text hereafter as *MB*.

79. The literary legacies impacted in these moments and memories are rich, evoking not only contemporaries like Proust, but also nineteenth-century figures like Wordsworth and even Tennyson ("flower in the crannied nook . . .").

80. Virginia Woolf, *The Diary of Virginia Woolf, Volume Five, 1936–1941* (San Diego: Harcourt, 1977), 274, 351, 355.

81. Virginia Woolf, *The Death of the Moth and Other Essays* (San Diego: Harcourt, 1970), 243–48. The essay was originally given as a lecture in 1940, for an American group (*Death*, 243).

82. Virginia Woolf, "Anon," *Twentieth Century Literature*, 25: 3/4 (1979): 356. "Anon" is not included in any of Woolf's collected essay volumes.

83. Virginia Woolf, *The Voyage Out* (London: Penguin, 1992), 15–16. Cited in text hereafter as *VO*.

84. The earlier draft has been published under the title *Melymbrosia*. See Virginia Woolf, *Melymbrosia*, ed. Lousie De Salvo (San Francisco: Cleis Press, 2002), 19.

85. The attempt to look behind the scenes in modernism tends to operate as a psychic device; following the flaneur, the modernist voyeur finds his own repressed desires and fantasies—erotic, masochistic, sadistic, infantile—displayed in such working-class scenarios. Later in the twentieth century, by contrast, these become overtly politicized. Hence the commodity history or film, or works such as Jamaica Kincaid's *A Small Place*, emphasize that what hides behind the luxury hotel or the well-prepared chicken dinner or the imported wool coat is a whole history of exploitation, environmental degradation, and violence. See

Jamaica Kincaid, *A Small Place* (New York: FSG, 1988). For a discussion of the phenomenon of the commodity history, see Bruce Robbins, "Commodity Histories," *PMLA* 120:2 (March 2005): 454–63.

86. In my discussion, I will address *To the Lighthouse* and *Mrs. Dalloway* in reverse chronological order, for reasons of thematic continuity. With respect to violence, I am treating the two novels as a cluster, rather than as a progression. *The Waves*, written at the end of the decade, adds to Woolf's violence canon in creating a world of childhood imagination teeming with images and scenes of strange violence. Childhood consciousness in Woolf's novels is always fraught with violence and fear—her answer, at least in part, to Freud. In addition to the childhood dramas displayed in *The Waves*, we might think of the young Rose, at the outset of *The Years*, encountering a terrifying man who prepares to expose himself to her on the street, or James in *To the Lighthouse* fantasizing about demolishing his father. This stress on the half-conscious interiorization of violence in the young child in turn correlates with Woolf's personal history as she depicts it in *A Sketch of the Past*. For discussion of Woolf, childhood, and the psychoanalytic context of the period, see Elizabeth Abel, *Virginia Woolf and the Fictions of Psychoanalysis* (Chicago: University of Chicago Press, 1989).

87. Virginia Woolf, *Jacob's Room* (London: Penguin, 1992), 61, 96, 59, 49. Cited hereafter in text as *JR*.

88. For discussion of the fate of the bildungsroman in modernism, see Jed Esty, *Unseasonable Youth: Modernism, Colonialism, and the Fiction of Development* (New York: Oxford University Press, 2011).

89. Woolf stocks her novel with a medieval allegory's worth of descriptive names: Flanders; Captain Barfoot, with his lame walk; Jacob's closest friend Bonamy; and as for Florinda, the conceit becomes literalized (and also ironized): "her name had been bestowed upon her by a painter who had wished it to signify that the flower of her maidenhood was still unplucked" (*JR*, 65).

90. It is notable that in both of these scenarios, the character who most directly embodies such a trade-off (St. John Hirst, Bonamy) is modeled on Woolf's friend Lytton Strachey.

91. For a nice account of the brackets, see Roger Poole, "'We All Put Up with You, Virginia': Irreceivable Wisdom about War," in *Virginia Woolf and War*, 79–100.

92. For discussion of some of the large, formal constructs in the novel, see Thomas G. Matro, "Only Relations: Vision and Achievement in *To the Lighthouse*, *PMLA* 99:2 (March 1984): 212–24, and Alex Zwerdling, *Virginia Woolf and the Real World* (Berkeley: University of California Press, 1986), 180–209.

93. A suspicion about the value of this newfound interest in poetry was widespread among writers in the period.

94. For discussion of Scotland and Scottish themes in the novel, see Richard Zumkhawala-Cook, "Tae the Lighthoose," in *Virginia Woolf: Art, Education, and Internationalism*, eds, Diana Royer and Madelyn Detloff (Clemson, SC: Clemson University Digital, 2008), 57–63.

95. For a classic discussion, see Jane Marcus, *Virginia Woolf and the Languages of Patriarchy* (Bloomington: Indiana University Press, 1987), especially 136–62. See also Ellen Rosenman, "A Fish on the Line: Desire, Repression, and the Law of the Father in *A Room of One's Own*," in *Virginia Woolf: Emergent Perspectives*, ed. Mark Hussey and Vara Neverow (New York: Pace University Press, 1994), 272–77. Othere reflections on To the Lighthouse and violence include Sheldon Brivic, "Love as Destruction in Woolf's *To the Lighthouse*, *Mosaic* 27:3 (1994): 65–85;

Fuhito Endo, "Radical Violence Inside Out: Woolf, Klein, and Interwar Politics," *Twentieth-Century Literature*, 52:2 (Summer 2006): 175–98; Tracy Hargreaves, "The Grotesque and the Great War in *To the Lighthouse*," in *Women's Fiction and the Great War*, ed. Suzanne Raitt and Trudi Tate (Oxford: Clarendon, 1997), 132–50; and Jane Lilienfeld, "'Like a Lion Seeking Whom He Could Devour': Domestic Violence in *To the Lighthouse*," in *Virginia Woolf Miscellanies: Proceedings of the First Annual Conference on Virginia Woolf*, ed. Mark Hussey and Vara Neverow-Turk (New York: Pace University Press, 1992), 154–64.

96. Virginia Woolf, *Mrs. Dalloway* (San Diego: Harcourt, 1997). Cited hereafter in text as *MD*.

97. David Bradshaw, "'Vanished, Like Leaves': The Military, Elegy and Italy in *Mrs. Dalloway*," *Woolf Studies Annual* Vol. 8 (2002): 107.

98. October 14, 1922. See Virginia Woolf, *The Diary of Virginia Woolf, Volume Two, 1920–1924* (New York: Harcourt, 1978), 207.

99. In addition to Saint-Amour's spellbinding account of the airplane, several especially rich discussions are Gillian Beer, "The Island and the Aeroplane: the Case of Virginia Woolf," in Homi K. Bhabha, ed., *Nation and Narration* (London: Routledge, 1990), 265–90, and Vincent Sherry, *The Great War and the Language of Modernism* (Oxford: Oxford University Press, 2003), especially 264–66.

100. Jennifer Wicke, "Coterie Consumption: Bloomsbury, Keynes, and Modernism as Marketing," in *Marketing Modernisms: Self-Promotion, Canonization, Rereading*, eds. Kevin J. H. Dettmar and Stephen Watts (Ann Arbor: University of Michigan Press, 1996), 122. For a seminal discussion of modernism and advertising more generally, see Wicke, *Advertising Fictions: Literature, Advertisement, and Social Reading* (New York: Columbia University Press, 1988).

101. Michael North, *Reading 1922: A Return to the Scene of the Modern* (New York: Oxford University Press, 1999), 81–84.

102. The statement is cited in Siegfried Sassoon, *The Complete Memoirs of George Sherston* (London: Faber, 1952), 496.

103. Virginia Woolf, *The London Scene* (New York: Harper Collins, 1975), 10. For a lovely reflection on Woolf and objects, see Bill Brown, "The Secret Life of Things: Virginia Woolf and the Matter of Modernism," *Modernism/Modernity* 6:2 (1999): 1–28.

104. Virginia Woolf, *The Years* (San Diego: Harcourt, 1965), 292. Cited in text hereafter as *TY*.

105. Unlike *Orlando*, *The Years* does not name its "present," leaving the reader to calculate the year, based on the characters' ages, at around 1932. Perhaps Woolf simply could not bear to leave her characters in the actual present of 1936, when she finished the novel.

106. The full text of Wordsworth's sonnet "Composed upon Westminster Bridge, September 3, 1802" is as follows:

> Earth has not any thing to show more fair:
> Dull would he be of soul who could pass by
> A sight so touching in its majesty:
> This City now doth, like a garment, wear
> The beauty of the morning; silent, bare,
> Ships, towers, domes, theatres, and temples lie
> Open unto the fields, and to the sky;
> All bright and glittering in the smokeless air.
> Never did the sun more beautifully steep

In his first splendour, valley, rock, or hill;
Ne'er saw I, never felt, a calm so deep!
The river glideth at his own sweet will:
Dear God! the very houses seem asleep;
And all that mighty heart is lying still!

William Wordsworth, *Poems* (New York: Scribner, 1923), 190.

107. Virginia Woolf, *Three Guineas* (San Diego: Harcourt, 1966). Cited in text as *TG*.

108. For discussion of *Three Guineas* and the photographs, see Dalgarno, *Virginia Woolf and the Visible World*; Julia Duffy and Lloyd Davis, "Demythologizing Facts and Photographs in *Three Guineas*," in *Photo-Textualities: Reading Photographs and Literature*, ed. Marsha Bryant (Newark: University of Delaware Press, 1996), 128–40; Elena Gualtieri, "The Cut: Instantaneity and the Limits of Photography," *English Language Notes*, 44:2 (Fall-Winter 2006): 9–24; Jenny Hartley, "Clothes and Uniform in the Theatre of Fascism: Clemence Dane and Virginia Woolf," in *Gender and Warfare in the Twentieth Century: Textual Representations*, ed. Angela K. Smith (Manchester: University of Manchester Press, 2004), 96–110; Nancy Knowles, "A Community of Women Looking at Men: The Photographs in Virginia Woolf's *Three Guineas*," in *Virginia Woolf and Communities*, ed. Jeanne McVicker and Laura Davis (New York: Pace University Press, 1999), 91–96; and Merry Pawlowski, "Virginia Woolf's Veil: The Feminist Intellectual and the Organization of Public Space," *Modern Fiction Studies*, 53:4 (2007): 722–51.

109. For discussion of Woolf's relation to antifascism, see two comprehensive essays by David Bradshaw, "British Writers and Anti-Fascism in the 1930s, Part One: The Bray and Drone of Tortured Voices," *Woolf Studies Annual*, Volume 3 (1997): 3–27, and "British Writers and Anti-Fascism in the 1930s, Part Two: Under the Hawk's Wings," *Woolf Studies Annual*, Volume 4 (1998): 41–66. See also Pawlowski, ed., *Virginia Woolf and Fascism*, and Zwerdling, *Virginia Woolf and the Real World*, 271–301.

110. Two important discussions of Woolf, in the context of many of these topics, are Jessica Berman, *Modernist Fiction, Cosmopolitanism, and the Politics of Community* and Merry M. Pawlowski, ed., *Virginia Woolf and Fascism*.

111. Virginia Woolf, *The Common Reader* (San Diego: Harcourt, 1984), 150.

112. These tableaus recall the bonfire at the young Maggie's birthday party in *The Years*, which invites Eugénie's delighted and distinctly *Three Guineas*–like cry, "'Make it blaze! Make it blaze!'" (*TY*, 124).

113. Virginia Woolf, *Orlando: A Biography* (San Diego: Harcourt, 1956), 325.

114. I am thinking, here, of a lecture by Terry Castle, "Rococophilia: War, Beauty, and the Eighteenth Century in British Culture 1919–1933" delivered at Columbia University, November 11, 2010.

115. Nicholas Pronay, "British Newsreels in the 1930s: 1. Audience and Producers" (orig. 1971), in Luke McKernan, ed., *Yesterday's News: The British Cinema Newsreel Reader* (London: British Universities Film and Video Council, 2002), 141.

116. See Mary Favret, *War at a Distance*, for a wonderful rendering of time, "wartime," and the arrival of the news (via post boy) in the early nineteenth century—or perhaps in any time period.

117. For a historicized reading of the newspaper in the novel, see Karin E. Westman, "'For Her Generation the Newspaper Was a Book': Media, Mediation, and Oscillation in Virginia Woolf's *Between the Acts*," *Journal of Modern Literature* 29:2 (2006): 1–18.

118. For rich discussion of Woolf's writing in the context of the Blitz, see Marina MacKay, *Modernism and World War II*, 22–43; also MacKay, "Putting the House in Order: Virginia Woolf and Blitz Modernism," *Modern Language Quarterly* 66:2 (June 2005): 227–52. See also Gil Plain, *Women's Fiction of The Second World War: Gender, Power and Resistance* (New York: St. Martin's, 1996); Rawlinson, *British Writing of the Second World War*; and Karen Schneider, *Loving Arms: British Women Writing the Second World War* (Lexington: University Press of Kentucky, 1997). Another contribution to the discussion of Woolf and the 1930s is John Wittier-Ferguson, "Repetition, Remembering, Repetition: Virginia Woolf's Late Fiction and the Return of War," *Modern Fiction Studies*, 57:2 (Summer 2011): 230–53.

119. One might also consider *The Waves* in this regard, though in that novel Woolf's experiments with shared consciousness are generally less annihilative of the novel than experimentally expansive of its boundaries.

120. T. S. Eliot, *Selected Poems* (San Diego: Harcourt, 1964), 80.

121. Virginia Woolf, *The Captain's Death Bed and Other Essays* (London: Hogarth, 1950), 197.

122. This passage is not unique in formal terms; the creation of a communal voice or consciousness transpires in the novel in several registers, most obviously in the pageant, but also in narrational moments of ambiguity. For discussion of some of these formal features, see Galia Benziman, "'Dispersed Are We': Mirroring and National Identity in Virginia Woolf's *Between the Acts*," *JNT: Journal of Narrative Theory* 36:1 (Winter 2006): 53–71; Melba Cuddy-Keane, "The Politics of Comic Modes in Virginia Woolf's *Between the Acts*," *PMLA* 105:2 (March 1990): 273–85; Patricia Laurence, "The Facts and Fugue of War: From *Three Guineas* to *Between the Acts*," in *Virginia Woolf and War: Fiction, Reality, and Myth*, ed. Mark Hussey (Syracuse: Syracuse University Press, 1991), 225–45; James Naremore, *The World Without a Self: Virginia Woolf and the Novel* (New Haven: Yale University Press, 1973), 219–39; and Hana Wirth-Nesher, "Final Curtain on the War: Figure and Ground in Virginia Woolf's *Between the Acts*," *Style* 28:2 (Winter 1994): 183–200.

123. See, for instance, *The Times* on June 28, 29, 30, 1938. And the coverage did not stop with the trial of the troopers. The girl became pregnant and decided to have an abortion, which was, of course, illegal at the time; it was nevertheless provided, and the doctor who performed it was himself tried in July of 1938, to be found not guilty (see *The Times*, July 26, 1938). For a summary of these events, see Stuart N. Clarke, "The Horse with a Green Tail," *Virginia Woolf Miscellany* 34 (Spring 1990): 3–4.

124. Later, Miss La Trobe, in one of her agonized moments, will feel as if there were blood pouring from her shoes, a hyperbolic version of Giles's canvases (*BTA*, 180).

125. Edward Said, *On Late Style: Music and Literature against the Grain* (New York: Pantheon, 2006), 160.

Conclusion

1. For discussion of the invisibility of some of the most troubling photographs from the attacks, see Lauren Walsh, "Ten Years Later: Re-Viewing 9/11's Suppressed Images," http://www.nomadikon.net/ContentItem.aspx?ci=208.

2. Link to one such image: http://maasmedia.wordpress.com/2008/08/07/hiroshima-day/

A former student, Nicole Trifoletti, brought this photograph to my attention in the spring semester, 2011.

3. One enduring approach, following Maya Lin's Vietnam Veteran's Memorial, has been toward an aesthetic of simple, clean lines, abstraction, and reflectivity, and this, as Lin's critics at the time bemoaned, denotes modernism. For discussion of these debates, see Marita Sturken, *Tangled Memories: The Vietnam War, the AIDS Epidemic, and the Politics of Remembering* (Berkeley: University of California Press, 1997).

4. James Young, *The Texture of Memory: Holocaust Memorials and Meaning* (New Haven: Yale University Press, 1993).

5. Tim O'Brien, *The Things they Carried* (New York: Broadway Books, 1990), 84.

6. Kurt Vonnegut, *Slaughterhouse-Five* (New York: Dial Press, 2005), 227.

7. Brian Turner, *Here, Bullet* (Farmington, ME: Alice James Books, 2005), 13.

8. The subject of healing, touch, and care, in the context of war, is a rich one. Particularly germane to this discussion about the inversions between violence and healing is Santanu Das's *Touch and Intimacy in First World War Literature* (Cambridge: Cambridge University Press, 2005).

9. One could also point to *The Deer Hunter* as a canonical film of the same era that took an interest in forms of sacredness that might give meaning to an otherwise ghastly and insane rendering of war's violence.

10. For discussion of *Apocalypse Now* and modernism, see Margot Norris, *Writing War in the Twentieth Century* (Charlottesville: University of Virginia Press, 2000), 207–33.

11. See Eleanor Coppola, *Notes* (New York: Simon and Schuster, 1979).

12. Primo Levi, *Survival in Auschwitz*, trans. Stuart Woolf (New York: Simon and Schuster, 1996), 107–8.

13. Elaine Scarry, *The Body in Pain: The Making and Unmaking of the World* (New York: Oxford University Press, 1985).

14. Paul Virilio, *War and Cinema: The Logistics of Perception*, trans. Patrick Camiller (London: Verso, 1989), 7–8.

15. Bernd Hüppauf, "Modernism and the Photographic Representation of War and Destruction," in *Fields of Vision: Essays in Film Studies, Visual Anthropology, and Photography*, eds. Leslie Devereaux and Roger Hillman (Berkeley: University of California Press, 1995), 96–97.

16. Ron Kovic, *Born on the Fourth of July* (New York: Akashic Books, 2005), 214. Ellipses denote new paragraph.

17. For discussion of graphic novels, see Hillary Chute, *Graphic Women: Life Narrative and Contemporary Comics* (New York: Columbia University Press, 2010).

Works Cited

Abel, Elizabeth. *Virginia Woolf and the Fictions of Psychoanalysis*. Chicago: University of Chicago Press, 1989.

Abrams, M. H. *Natural Supernaturalism: Tradition and Revolution in Romantic Literature*. New York: Norton, 1971.

Aeschylus. *Aeschylus I: Oresteia*. Translated by Richmond Lattimore. Chicago: University of Chicago Press, 1953.

Agamben, Giorgio. *Remnants of Auschwitz: The Witness and the Archive*. Translated by Daniel Heller-Roazen. New York: Zone, 2002.

Alexiou, Margaret. *The Ritual Lament in Greek Tradition*. Cambridge: Cambridge University Press, 1974.

Allison, Jonathan. "Introduction: Fascism, Nationalism, Reception." In *Yeats's Political Identities: Selected Essays*. Ann Arbor: University of Michigan Press, 1996.

——. "The Rose, the Reader and Yeats's Intentions." *Yeats: An Annual of Critical and Textual Studies* 13 (1995): 3–10.

Apel, Dora. "Cultural Battlegrounds: Weimar Photographic Narratives of War." *New German Critique* 76 (Winter 1999): 49–84.

Arendt, Hannah. *On Violence*. San Diego: Harvest, 1970.

Armstrong, Nancy, and Leonard Tennenhouse, eds. *The Violence of Representation: Literature and the History of Violence*. New York: Routledge, 1989.

Armstrong, Nancy. *Desire and Domestic Fiction: A Political History of the Novel*. New York: Oxford University Press, 1987.

Arnold, Matthew. *Culture and Anarchy*. Cambridge: Cambridge University Press, 1990.

Avrich, Paul. *The Haymarket Tragedy*. Princeton: Princeton University Press, 1984.

——. *Anarchist Portraits*. Princeton: Princeton University Press, 1988.

Bakunin, Mikhail. *Bakunin on Anarchism*. Translated and edited by Sam Dolgoff. Montreal: Black Rose, 1980.

Barkan, Elazar, and Ronald Bush, eds. *Prehistories of the Future: The Primitivist Project and the Culture of Modernism*. Stanford, CA: Stanford University Press, 1995.

Bataille, Georges. *The Tears of Eros*. Translated by Peter Connor. San Francisco: City Lights, 1989.

——. *The Accursed Share: An Essay on General Economy, Volumes II & III*. Translated by Robert Hurley. New York: Zone, 1993.

Baucom, Ian. *Specters of the Atlantic: Finance Capital, Slavery, and the Philosophy of History*. Durham: Duke University Press, 2005.

Beer, Gillian. "The Island and the Aeroplane: the Case of Virginia Woolf," In *Nation and Narration*. Edited by Homi K. Bhabha. London: Routledge, 1990, 265–90.

Benjamin, Walter. *Illuminations*. Edited by Hannah Arendt. New York: Schocken, 1968.

Benziman, Galia. "'Dispersed Are We': Mirroring and National Identity in Virginia Woolf's *Between the Acts*." *JNT: Journal of Narrative Theory* 36, no. 1 (Winter 2006): 53–71.

Bergner, Gwen. "Who is That Masked Woman? or, the Role of Gender in Fanon's *Black Skin, White Masks*." *PMLA* 110, no. 1 (January 1995): 75–88.

Berkman, Alexander. *Prison Memoirs of an Anarchist*. New York: Schocken, 1970.

——. *What is Anarchism?* Edinburgh: AK, 2003.

Berman, Jessica. *Modernist Fiction, Cosmopolitanism, and the Politics of Community*. Cambridge: Cambridge University Press, 2001.

Berthoud, Jacques. "The Secret Agent." In *The Cambridge Companion to Joseph Conrad*. Edited by J. H. Stape. Cambridge: Cambridge University Press, 1996, 100–21.

Bhabha, Homi K. *The Location of Culture*. London: Routledge, 1994.

Bilgrami, Akeel. "Occidentalism, the Very Idea: An Essay on Enlightenment and Enchantment." *Critical Inquiry* 32 (Spring 2006): 381–411.

Booth, Allyson. *Postcards from the Trenches: Negotiating the Space between Modernism and the First World War*. New York: Oxford University Press, 1996.

Bowen, Elizabeth. *The Death of the Heart*. New York: Random House, 2000.

——. *The Mulberry Tree*. London: Virago, 1986.

——. *The Last September*. New York: Random House, 2000.

Bradley, Bruce. *James Joyce's Schooldays*. New York: St. Martin's 1982.

Bradshaw, David. "'Vanished, Like Leaves': The Military, Elegy and Italy in *Mrs. Dalloway*." *Woolf Studies Annual* 8 (2002): 107–25.

——. "British Writers and Anti-Fascism in the 1930s, Part One: The Bray and Drone of Tortured Voices." *Woolf Studies Annual* 3 (1997): 3–27.

——. "British Writers and Anti-Fascism in the 1930s, Part Two: Under the Hawk's Wings." *Woolf Studies Annual* 4 (1998): 41–66.

Brantlinger, Patrick. "What Is 'Sensational' about the 'Sensation Novel'?" *Nineteenth-Century Fiction* 37, no. 1 (June 1982): 1–28.

Brearton, Fran. *The Great War in Irish Poetry: W. B. Yeats to Michael Longley*. Oxford: Oxford University Press, 2000.

——. "Mapping the Trenches: Gyres, Switchbacks, and Zig-Zag Circles in W. B. Yeats and Ciaran Carson." *Irish Studies Review* 9, no. 3 (December 2001): 373–86.

Brivic, Sheldon. "Love as Destruction in Woolf's *To the Lighthouse*." *Mosaic* 27, no. 3 (1994): 65–85.

Brock, Peter, and Nigel Young. *Pacifism in the Twentieth Century*. Syracuse, NY: Syracuse University Press, 1999.

Brock, Peter. *Freedom from War: Nonsectarian Pacifism, 1814–1914*. Toronto: University of Toronto Press, 1991.

――. *Pacifism in Europe to 1914*. Princeton: Princeton University Press, 1972.

Brooke, Rupert. *The Poems of Rupert Brooke*. London: Black Swan 1989.

Brooker, Jewel Spears, and Joseph Bentley. *Reading The Waste Land Modernism and the Limits of Interpretation*. Amherst: University of Massachusetts Press, 1990.

Brooks, Peter. *The Melodramatic Imagination: Balzac, Henry James, Melodrama, and the Mode of Excess*. New York: Columbia University Press, 1985.

Brown, Bill. *The Material Unconscious: American Amusement, Stephen Crane, and the Economics of Play*. Cambridge, MA: Harvard University Press, 1996.

――. "The Secret Life of Things: Virginia Woolf and the Matter of Modernism." *Modernism/Modernity* 6, no. 2 (1999): 1–28.

Brown, Heloise. *"The Truest From of Patriotism": Pacifist Feminism in Britain, 1870–1902*. Manchester: Manchester University Press, 2003.

Bryant, Raymond L. *The Political Ecology of Forestry in Burma, 1824–1994*. Honolulu: University of Hawaii Press, 1997.

Buch, Robert. *The Pathos of the Real: On the Aesthetics of Violence in the Twentieth Century*. Baltimore: Johns Hopkins University Press, 2010.

Burke, Joanna. *Dismembering the Male: Men's Bodies, Britain, and the Great War*. Chicago: University of Chicago Press, 1996.

Butler, Judith. *Bodies That Matter*. New York: Routledge, 1993.

――. *Gender Trouble: Feminism and the Subversion of Identity*. New York: Routledge, 1990.

――. *Precarious Life: The Powers of Mourning and Violence*. London: Verso, 2004.

Caesar, Adrian. *Taking it Like a Man: Suffering, Sexuality and the War Poets: Brooke, Sassoon, Owen, Graves*. Manchester, UK: Manchester University Press, 1993.

Cahm, Caroline. *Kropotkin and the Rise of Revolutionary Anarchism 1872–1886*. Cambridge: Cambridge University Press, 1989.

Campbell, James. "Combat Gnosticism: The Ideology of First World War Poetry Criticism." *New Literary History* 30, no. 1 (1999): 203–15.

Carabine, Keith. *The Life and the Art: A Study of Conrad's "Under Western Eyes."* Amsterdam: Rodopi, 1996.

Carpentier, Martha C. *Ritual, Myth, and the Modernist Text: the Influence of Jane Ellen Harrison on Joyce, Eliot, and Woolf*. Amsterdam: Overseas Publishing Association, 1998.

Caruth, Cathy, ed. *Trauma: Explorations in Memory*. Baltimore: Johns Hopkins University Press, 1995.

――. *Unclaimed Experience: Trauma, Narrative, and History*. Baltimore: Johns Hopkins University Press, 1996.

Castle, Terry. "Courage, mon amie." *London Review of Books* 24, no. 7 (April, 2002): 3–12.

――. "Rococophilia: War, Beauty, and the Eighteenth Century in British Culture 1919–1933." Lecture at Columbia University. November 11, 2010.

Catullus et al. *Catullus, Tibullus and Pervigilium Veneris*. Edited by G. P. Gould. Cambridge, MA: Harvard University Press, 1976.

Caudwell, Christopher. *Studies and Further Studies in a Dying Culture*. New York: Monthly Review Press, 1971.

Ceadel, Martin. *Pacifism in Britain 1914–1945: The Defining of a Faith*. Oxford: Oxford University Press, 1980.

Chandos, John. *Boys Together: English Public Schools 1800–1864*. New Haven: Yale University Press, 1984.

Chapman, Wayne K. "Yeats and the Rose of Sharon." *English Language Notes* 29, no. 3 (March 1992): 51–53.

Cheng, Vincent J. *Joyce, Race, and Empire*. Cambridge: Cambridge University Press, 1995.

Chernyshevsky, N. G. *What is to Be Done?* Translated by Michael R. Katz. Ithaca: Cornell University Press, 1989.

Chesterton, G. K. *The Man Who was Thursday*. London: Penguin, 1986.

Chickering, Roger, and Stig Forster, eds. *Anticipating Total War: The German and American Experiences, 1871–1914*. Cambridge: Cambridge University Press and Washington, DC: German Historical Institute, 1999.

Christ, Carol. *Victorian and Modern Poetics*. Chicago: University of Chicago Press, 1984.

Chute, Hillary. *Graphic Women: Life Narrative and Contemporary Comics*. New York: Columbia University Press, 2010.

Clarke, I. F., ed. *The Tale of the Next Great War, 1871–1914: Fictions of Future Warfare and of Battles Still-to-Come*. Liverpool: Liverpool University Press, 1995.

Clarke, I. F. *Voices Prophesying War 1763–1984*. London: Oxford University Press, 1966.

Clarke, Stuart N. "The Horse with a Green Tail." *Virginia Woolf Miscellany* 34 (Spring 1990): 3–4.

Claybaugh, Amanda. *The Novel of Purpose: Literature and Social Reform in the Anglo-American World*. Ithaca: Cornell University Press, 2007.

Clymer, Jeffory A. *America's Culture of Terrorism: Violence, Capitalism, and the Written Word*. Chapel Hill: University of North Carolina Press, 2003.

Cohen, William A. *Sex Scandal: The Private Parts of Victorian Fiction*. Durham: Duke University Press, 1996.

Cole, Sarah. *Modernism, Male Friendship, and the First World War*. Cambridge: Cambridge University Press, 2003.

Conlon, Raymond. "Loyalist Graphic Art." In *The Spanish Civil War and the Visual Arts*. Edited by Kathleen Vernon. Ithaca: Cornell University, Center for International Studies, 1990: 104–25.

Connolly, James. *Collected Works, Volume Two*. Dublin: New Books, 1988.

Conrad, Joseph. *The Collected Stories of Joseph Conrad*. Hopewell, NJ: Ecco, 1991.

———. *Joseph Conrad's Letters to R. B. Cunninghame Graham*. Cambridge: Cambridge University Press, 1969.

———. *Lord Jim*. New York: New American Library, 1981.

———. *Nostromo*. New York: Penguin, 1960.

———. *Notes on Life and Letters*. London: Dent, 1934.

———. *The Secret Agent*. New York: Penguin, 1986.

———. *The Secret Agent: A Simple Tale*. Cambridge: Cambridge University Press, 1990.

Coppola, Eleanor. *Notes*. New York: Simon and Schuster, 1979.

Corille, Gary, and Patrick Luciano. *Jack the Ripper: His Life and Crimes in Popular Entertainment*. Jefferson, NC: McFarland, 1999.

Corn, Joseph. *The Winged Gospel: America's Romance with Aviation, 1900–1950*. New York: Oxford University Press, 1983.

Cowan, Bainard, "Walter Benjamin's Theory of Allegory." *New German Critique*, 22 (Winter 1981): 109–22.

Cuddy-Keane, Melba. "The Politics of Comic Modes in Virginia Woolf's *Between the Acts*." *PMLA* 105, no. 2 (March 1990): 273–85.

Cru, Jean Norton. *War Books: A Study in Historical Criticism*. San Diego: San Diego State University Press, 1976.

Cullingford, Elizabeth. *Gender and History in Yeats's Love Poetry*. Cambridge: Cambridge University Press, 1993.

———. *Yeats, Ireland and Fascism*. New York: New York University Press, 1981.

Cunningham, Valentine, ed. *Spanish Front: Writers on the Civil War*. Oxford: Oxford University Press, 1986.

Curtis, Perry. *Jack the Ripper and the London Press*. New Haven: Yale University Press, 2001.

Cvetkovich, Ann. *Mixed Feelings: Feminism, Mass Culture, and Victorian Sensationalism*. New Brunswick, NJ: Rutgers University Press, 1992.

Dalgarno, Emily. *Virginia Woolf and the Visible World*. Cambridge: Cambridge University Press, 2001.

Das, Santanu. *Touch and Intimacy in First World War Literature*. Cambridge: Cambridge University Press, 2005.

Daudet, Léon. *La Guerre totale*. Paris: Nouvelle Librairie Nationale, 1918.

Davidson, Harriet. "Improper Desire: Reading *The Waste Land*." In *Cambridge Companion to T. S. Eliot*. Edited by A. David Moody. Cambridge: Cambridge University Press, 1994: 121–31.

Davis, Thomas. *Essays and Poems*. Dublin: M. H. Gill, 1945.

Dawes, James. *The Language of War: Literature and Culture in the U.S. from the Civil War through World War II*. Cambridge, MA: Harvard University Press, 2002.

de Vere, Aubrey. *Poems from the Works of Aubrey de Vere*. London: Catholic Truth Society, 1904.

Deane, Seamus. *Celtic Revivals: Essays in Modern Irish Literature, 1880–1980*. London: Faber, 1985.

Derrida, Jacques. *The Animal That Therefore I Am*. New York: Fordham University Press, 2008.

Des Pres, Terrence. *The Survivor: An Anatomy of Life in the Death Camps*. Oxford: Oxford University Press, 1980.

Dietz, Mary G. *Between the Human and the Divine: The Political Thought of Simone Weil*. Totowa, NJ: Rowman and Littlefield, 1988.

Döblin, Alfred. *Berlin Alexanderplatz: The Story of Franz Biberkopf*. Translated by Eugene Jolas. London: Continuum, 2004.

Doggett, Rob. "Writing out (of) Chaos: Constructions of History in Yeats's 'Nineteen Hundred and Nineteen' and 'Meditations in Time of Civil War.'" *Twentieth Century Literature* 47, no. 2 (Summer 2001): 142–43.

Duffy, Enda. *The Speed Handbook: Velocity, Pleasure, Modernism*. Durham: Duke University Press, 2009.

———. *The Subaltern Ulysses*. Minneapolis: University of Minnesota Press, 1994.

Duffy, Julia, and Lloyd Davis. "Demythologizing Facts and Photographs in *Three Guineas*." In *Photo-Textualities: Reading Photographs and Literature*. Edited by Marsha Bryant. Newark: University of Delaware Press, 1996, 128–40.

Edelstein, Dan. "The Birth of Ideology from the Spirit of Myth: Georges Sorel among the *Idéologues*." In *The Re-enchantment of the World: Secular Magic in a Rational Age*. Edited by Joshua Landy and Michael Saler. Stanford: Stanford University Press, 2009, 201–24.

Eide, Marian. "Witnessing and Trophy Hunting: Writing Violence from the Great War Trenches." *Criticism* 49, no. 1 (Winter 2007): 85–104.

Einstein, Albert, and Sigmund Freud. *Why War?* Translated by Stuart Gilbert. Paris: International Institute of Intellectual Cooperation, 1933.

Eliot, T. S. *The Complete Poems and Plays, 1909–1950.* New York: Harcourt, 1967.

———. *Selected Essays.* New York: Harcourt, 1964, 281–85.

———. *The Waste Land: A Facsimile and Transcript of the Original Drafts.* San Diego: Harcourt, 1971.

———. *The Waste Land, A Norton Critical Edition.* New York: Norton, 2001.

Ellman, Richard. *James Joyce.* Oxford: Oxford University Press, 1983.

Eltis, Sos. *Revising Wilde: Society and Subversion in the Plays of Oscar Wilde.* Oxford: Clarendon, 1996.

Endo, Fuhito. "Radical Violence Inside Out: Woolf, Klein, and Interwar Politics." *Twentieth-Century Literature* 52, no. 2 (Summer 2006): 175–98.

English, James F. "Anarchy in the Flesh: Conrad's 'Counterrevolutionary' Modernism and the *Witz* of the Political Unconscious." *Modern Fiction Studies* 38, no. 3 (1992): 615–30.

Esty, Jed. *A Shrinking Island: Modernism and National Culture in England.* Princeton: Princeton University Press, 2004.

———. *Unseasonable Youth: Modernism, Colonialism, and the Fiction of Development.* New York: Oxford University Press, 2011.

———. "Virgins of Empire: *The Last September* and the Antidevelopmental Plot." *Modern Fiction Studies* 53, no. 2 (Summer 2007): 257–75.

Evans, Richard J. *Comrades and Sisters: Feminism, Socialism and Pacifism in Europe, 1870–1945.* Sussex: Wheatsheaf, 1987.

Fanon, Frantz. *Black Skin, White Masks.* New York: Grove, 1967.

———. *The Wretched of the Earth.* Translated by Richard Philcox. New York: Grove, 2004.

Faris, Wendy B. "Bloomsbury's Beasts: The Presence of Animals in the Texts and Lives of Bloomsbury." *The Yearbook of English Studies,* 37, no. 1 (2007): 107–25.

Faust, Drew Gilpin. *This Republic of Suffering: Death and the American Civil War.* New York: Knopf, 2008.

Favret, Mary A. *War at a Distance: Romanticism and the Making of Modern Wartime.* Princeton: Princeton University Press, 2010.

Fawcett, E. Douglas. *Hartmann the Anarchist: or the Doom of the Great City.* London: Edward Arnold, 1893.

Felman, Shoshanna, ed. *Literature and Psychoanalysis: The Question of Reading: Otherwise.* Baltimore: Hopkins University Press, 1982.

———. and Dori Laub, eds. *Testimony: Crises of Witnessing in Literature, Psychoanalysis, and History.* New York: Routledge, 1992.

Findley, Timothy. *The Wars.* Toronto: Penguin, 1977.

Fisher, Philip. *Hard Facts: Setting and Form in the American Novel.* Oxford: Oxford University Press, 1985.

Fleischman, Avrom. *Conrad's Politics: Community and Anarchy in the Fiction of Joseph Conrad.* Baltimore: Johns Hopkins University Press, 1967.

Foster, R. F. *W. B. Yeats: A Life.* 2 vols. Oxford: Oxford University Press, 1998 and 2003.

Frazer, Elizabeth, and Kimberly Hutchings. "Argument and Rhetoric in the Justification of Political Violence." *European Journal of Political Theory* 6, no. 2 (2007): 180–99.

Freud, Sigmund. *Civilization and its Discontents*. Translated by James Strachey. New York: Norton, 1989.

———. *Totem and Taboo: Some Points of Agreement between the Mental Lives of Savages and Neurotics*. Translated by James Strachey. New York: Norton, 1989.

Fried, Michael. "Almayer's Face: On 'Impressionism' in Conrad, Crane, and Norris." *Critical Inquiry* 17, no. 1 (Autumn 1990): 193–236.

Friedrich, Ernst. *War against War!* Seattle: Real Comet Press, 1987.

Fritzsche, Peter. *A Nation of Fliers: German Aviation and the Popular Imagination*. Cambridge, MA: Harvard University Press, 1992.

Frost, Christopher J. *Simone Weil: On Politics, Religion, and Society*. London: Sage, 1998.

Froula, Christine. "Eliot's Grail Quest, or, The Lover, the Police, and *The Waste Land*." *Yale Review* 78, no. 2 (Winter 1989): 235–53.

———. *Virginia Woolf and the Bloomsbury Avant-Garde: War, Civilization, Modernity*. New York: Columbia University Press, 2005.

Fry, Paul H. *The Poet's Calling and the English Ode*. New Haven: Yale University Press, 1980.

Fukuyama, Francis. "The End of History?" *The National Interest* (Summer 1989): 3–18.

Fussell, Paul. *The Great War and Modern Memory*. London: Oxford University Press, 1975.

Gane, Nicholas. *Max Weber and Postmodern Theory: Rationalization Versus Re-enchantment*. London: Palgrave, 2002.

Gilbert, Sandra M. "'Rats Alley': The Great War, Modernism, and the (Anti) Pastoral Elegy." *New Literary History* 30 (1999): 179–201.

Girard, René. *Violence and the Sacred*. Baltimore: Johns Hopkins University Press, 1979.

Goodway, David. *Anarchist Seeds beneath the Snow: Left-Libertarian Thought and British Writers from William Morris to Colin Ward*. Liverpool: Liverpool University Press, 2006.

Graf, Susan Johnston. "An Infant Avatar: The Mature Occultism of W. B. Yeats." *New Hibernia Review* 9, no. 4 (Winter 2005): 99–112.

Greenlaw, Duncan. *Borders of Mourning: Remembrance, Commitment, and the Contexts of Irish Identity*. Dublin: Maunsel, 2004.

Gregory, Adrian, and Senia Paseta, eds. *Ireland and the Great War: "A War to Unite Us All?"* Manchester: Manchester University Press, 2002.

Griffith, George. *The Angel of the Revolution: A Tale of the Coming Terror*. London: Routledge, 1995.

Gualtieri, Elena. "The Cut: Instantaneity and the Limits of Photography." *English Language Notes* 44, no. 2 (Fall–Winter 2006): 9–24.

Haaland, Bonnie. *Emma Goldman: Sexuality and the Impurity of the State*. Montreal: Black Rose Books, 1993.

Hadley, Elaine. *Melodramatic Tactics: Theatricalized Dissent in the English Marketplace, 1800–1885*. Stanford, CA: Stanford University Press, 1995.

Halliwell, Martin. *Images of Idiocy: The Idiot Figure in Modern Fiction and Film*. Aldershot: Ashgate, 2004.

Haraway, Donna. *Primate Visions: Gender, Race, and Nature in the World of Modern Science*. New York: Routledge, 1989.

———. *When Species Meet*. Minneapolis: University of Minnesota Press, 2008.

Hargreaves, Tracy. "The Grotesque and the Great War in *To the Lighthouse*." *Women's Fiction and the Great War*. Edited by Suzanne Raitt and Trudi Tate. Oxford: Clarendon, 1997: 132–50.

Harris, Frank. *The Bomb*. Portland, OR: Feral House, 1996.

Hart, W. C. *Confessions of an Anarchist*. London: G. Richards, 1911.

Hartley, Jenny. "Clothes and Uniform in the Theatre of Fascism: Clemence Dane and Virginia Woolf." In *Gender and Warfare in the Twentieth Century: Textual Representation*. Edited by Angela K. Smith. Manchester: University of Manchester Press, 2004: 96–110.

Hartman, Geoffrey, ed. *Holocaust Remembrance: The Shapes of Memory*. Cambridge: Blackwell, 1994.

Hartman, Saidiya. *Scenes of Subjection: Terror, Slavery, and Self-Making in Nineteenth-Century America*. Oxford: Oxford University Press, 1997.

Hegeman, Susan. *Patterns for America: Modernism and the Concept of Culture*. Princeton: Princeton University Press, 1999.

Hemingway, Ernest. *For Whom the Bell Tolls*. New York: Scribner, 2003.

——. *Selected Letters, 1917–1961*. New York: Scribner, 1981.

——. "War Dispatches to NANA (North-Atlantic Newspaper Alliance)." Edited by William Braasch Watson, *The Hemingway Review* 7, no. 2 (1988): 114–18.

Henn, T. R. *W. B. Yeats and the Poetry of War*. Oxford: Oxford University Press, 1967.

Hermann, Anne. *Queering the Moderns: Poses/Portraits/Performances*. New York: Palgrave, 2000.

Hirsch, Marianne. *Family Frames: Photography, Narrative, and Postmemory*. Cambridge, MA: Harvard University Press, 1997.

—— and Leo Spitzer, *Ghosts of Home: The Afterlife of Czernowitz in Jewish Memory*. Berkeley: University of California Press, 2010.

Holst-Warhaft, Gail. *Dangerous Voices: Women's Laments and Greek Literature*. London: Routledge, 1992.

Homer. *The Iliad*, Translated by Richmond Lattimore. Chicago: University of Chicago Press, 1951.

Houen, Alex. *Terrorism and Modern Literature: From Joseph Conrad to Ciaran Carson*. Oxford: Oxford University Press, 2002.

Howe, Irving. *Politics and the Novel*. London: Stevens, 1961.

Howes, Marjorie. *Yeats's Nations: Gender, Class, and Irishness*. Cambridge: Cambridge University Press, 1996.

Hunt, Lynn. *The Family Romance of the French Revolution*. Berkeley: University of California Press, 1992.

Hüppauf, Bernd. "Experiences of Modern Warfare and the Crisis of Representation." *New German Critique* 59 (Spring–Summer 1993): 41–76.

——. "Modernism and the Photographic Representation of War and Destruction." In *Fields of Vision: Essays in Film Studies, Visual Anthropology, and Photography*. Edited by Leslie Devereux and Roger Hillman. Berkeley: University of California Press, 1995, 94–126.

Hussey, Mark ed., *Virginia Woolf and War: Fiction, Reality, Myth*. Syracuse: Syracuse University Press, 1991.

Huxley, Aldous. *An Encyclopedia of Pacifism. The Handbook of Non-Violence*. Edited by Robert A. Seeley. Westport CT: Lawrence Hill, 1986.

Hyde, H. Montgomery. Introduction to *The Complete Plays of Oscar Wilde*. London: Methuen, 1988: 36–55.

Hynes, Samuel. *A War Imagined: The First World War and English Culture*. London: Bodley Head, 1990.

James, Henry. *The Princess Casamassima*. New York: Penguin, 1987.

James, William. *The Moral Equivalent of War*. New York: American Association of International Conciliation, 1910.

Jameson, Fredric. *The Political Unconscious: Narrative as a Socially Symbolic Act*. Ithaca: Cornell University Press, 1981.

———. *Postmodernism, or, the Cultural Logic of Late Capitalism*. Durham: Duke University Press, 1991.

Jeffery, Keith. *Ireland and the Great War*. Cambridge: Cambridge University Press, 2001.

Jenkyns, Richard. *Dignity and Decadence: Victorian Art and the Classical Inheritance*. Cambridge, MA: Harvard University Press, 1992.

———. *The Victorians and Ancient Greece*. Oxford: Blackwell, 1980.

Joad, C. E. M. *Why War?* Harmondsworth: Penguin, 1939.

Johnsen, William A. *Violence and Modernism: Ibsen, Joyce, and Woolf*. Gainesville: University Press of Florida, 2003.

Johnson, Nuala C. *Ireland, the Great War and the Geography of Remembrance*. Cambridge: Cambridge University Press, 2003.

Joplin, Patricia Klindienst. "The Voice of the Shuttle is Ours." In *Rape and Representation*. Edited by Lynn A. Higgins and Brenda R. Silver. New York: Columbia University Press, 1991: 35–64.

Joyce, James. *A Portrait of the Artist as a Young Man*. New York: Penguin, 1993.

———. *Ulysses*. New York: Vintage, 1986.

Kalisa, Chantal. "Black Women and Literature: Revisiting Frantz Fanon's Gender Politics." *Literary Griot: International Journal of Black Expressive Cultural Studies* 14, nos. 1–2 (Spring–Fall 2002): 1–22.

Kelley, Theresa M. *Reinventing Allegory*. Cambridge: Cambridge University Press, 1997.

Kiberd, Declan. *Inventing Ireland: The Literature of the Modern Nation*. Cambridge, MA: Harvard University Press, 1995.

———. *Synge and the Irish Language*. London: MacMillan, 1979.

Kincaid, Jamaica. *A Small Place*. New York: FSG, 1988.

Kirschner, Paul. "The French Face of Dostoevsky in Conrad's *Under Western Eyes*: Some Consequences for Criticism." *Conradiana* 30, no. 3 (Fall 1998): 163–82.

Knowles, Nancy. "A Community of Women Looking at Men: The Photographs in Virginia Woolf's *Three Guineas*." In *Virginia Woolf and Communities*. Edited by Jeanne McVicker and Laura Davis. New York: Pace University Press, 1999, 91–96.

Koestler, Arthur. *L'Espagne ensanglantée: Un livre noir sur l'Espagne*. Paris: Editions du Carrefour, 1937.

Kovic, Ron. *Born on the Fourth of July*. New York: Akashic Books, 2005.

Kreilkamp, Vera. *The Anglo-Irish Novel and the Big House*. Syracuse: Syracuse University Press, 1998.

Kropotkin, Peter. *The Conquest of Bread*. New York: Benjamin Blom, 1968. *Kropotkin's Revolutionary Pamphlets*. Edited by Roger N. Baldwin. New York: Benjamin Bloom, 1968.

———. *Mutual Aid: A Factor of Evolution*. Montreal: Black Rose Books, 1989.

LaCapra, Dominick. *History and its Limits: Human, Animal, Violence*. Ithaca: Cornell University Press, 2009.

Laity, Cassandra. "T. S. Eliot and A. C. Swinburne: Decadent Bodies, Modern Visualities, and Changing Modes of Perception." *Modernism/Modernity* 11, no. 3 (September 2004): 425–48.

Lamos, Colleen. *Deviant Modernism: Sexual and Textual Errancy in T. S. Eliot, James Joyce, and Marcel Proust*. Cambridge: Cambridge University Press, 1998.

Landy, Joshua, and Michael Saler, eds. *The Re-enchantment of the World: Secular Magic in a Rational Age*. Stanford: Stanford University Press, 2009.

Laurence, Patricia. "The Facts and Fugue of War: from *Three Guineas* to *Between the Acts*." In *Virginia Woolf and War: Fiction, Reality, and Myth*. Edited by Mark Hussey. Syracuse: Syracuse University Press, 1991: 225–45.

Lawrence, D. H. *Aaron's Rod*. New York: Penguin, 1976.

———. *Kangaroo*. New York: Penguin, 1980.

———. *Selected Literary Criticism*. New York: Viking, 1956.

Ledden, Patrick J. "Education and Social Class in Joyce's Dublin." *Journal of Modern Literature* 22, no. 2 (Winter 1998–1999): 329–47.

Lee, Hermione. *Virginia Woolf*. New York: Vintage, 1999.

Leed, Eric J. *No Man's Land: Combat and Identity in World War I*. Cambridge: Cambridge University Press, 1979.

Lehmann, John. *Rupert Brooke*. London: Weidenfeld and Nicolson, 1980.

Levenson, Michael. "Does *The Waste Land* Have a Politics?" *Modernism/Modernity* 6, no. 3 (1999): 1–13.

Levi, Primo. *The Drowned and the Saved*. Translated by Raymond Rosenthal. New York: Random House, 1989.

———. *Survival in Auschwitz*. Translated by Stuart Woolf. New York: Simon and Schuster, 1996.

Levinas, Emmanuel. *God, Death, and Time*. Translated by Bettina Bergo. Stanford: Stanford University Press, c. 2000.

Levine, George, ed. *The Joy of Secularism: 11 Essays on How We Live Now*. Princeton: Princeton University Press, 2011.

Lewis, Desiree. "Myths of Motherhood and Power: The Construction of 'Black Woman' in Literature." *English in Africa* 19, no. 1 (1992 May): 35–51.

Lewis, Wyndham, ed. *BLAST* (1914). Reprint, Santa Rosa, CA: Black Sparrow, 1997.

Leys, Ruth. *Trauma: A Genealogy*. Chicago: University of Chicago Press, 2000.

Lilienfeld, Jane. "'Like a Lion Seeking Whom He Could Devour': Domestic Violence in *To the Lighthouse*." In *Virginia Woolf Miscellanies: Proceedings of the First Annual Conference on Virginia Woolf*. Edited by Mark Hussey and Vara Neverow-Turk. New York: Pace University Press, 1992, 154–64.

Lindqvist, Sven. *A History of Bombing*. Translated by Linda Haverty Rugg. New York: The New Press, 2000.

Linse, Ulrich. "'Propaganda by Deed' and 'Direct Action': Two Concepts of Anarchist Violence." In *Social Protest, Violence, and Terror in Nineteenth-and Twentieth-Century Europe*. Edited by Wolfgang J. Mommsen and Gerhard Hirschefield. New York: St. Martin's, 1982, 201–29.

Lloyd, David. *Anomalous States: Irish Writing and the Post-Colonial Moment*. Dublin: Lilliput, 1993.

Loraux, Nicole. *Mothers in Mourning, with the Essay "Of Amnesty and Its Opposite."* Translated by Corinne Pache. Ithaca: Cornell University Press, 1998.

Lukács, Georg. *The Theory of the Novel: A Historico-Philosophical Essay on the Forms of Great Epic Literature*. Translated by Anna Bostock. Cambridge, MA: MIT Press, 1973.

MacDonagh, Thomas. *April and May, with Other Verse*. Dublin: Bryers and Walker, 1904.

McFarland, Dorothy Tuck. *Simone Weil*. New York: Frederick Ungar, 1983.

Mackay, John Henry. *The Anarchists: A Picture of Civilization at the Close of the Nineteenth Century*. Translated by George Schumm. Brooklyn, NY: Autonomedia, 1999.

MacKay, Marina. *Modernism and World War II*. Cambridge: Cambridge University Press, 2007.

———. "Putting the House in Order: Virginia Woolf and Blitz Modernism," *Modern Language Quarterly* 66:2 (June 2005): 227–52.

Mangan, J. A. *The Games Ethic and Imperialism: Aspects of the Diffusion of an Ideal*. New York: Viking, 1985.

———. and James Walvin eds. *Manliness and Morality: Middle-Class Masculinity in Britain and America: 1800–1940*. Manchester: Manchester University Press, 1984.

Mangan, James Clarence. *The Poems of James Clarence Mangan*. Dublin: O'Donaghue, 1903.

Manganaro, Marc. *Modernist Anthropology: From Fieldwork to Text*. Princeton: Princeton University Press, 1990.

———. "Modernist Studies and Anthropology: Reflections on the Past, Present, and Possible Futures." In *Disciplining Modernism*. Edited by Pamela L. Caughie. Houndsmills: Palgrave Macmillan, 2009, 210–20.

———. *Myth, Rhetoric, and the Voice of Authority: A Critique of Frazer, Eliot, Frye, and Campbell*. New Haven: Yale University Press, 1992.

Marchand, Ernest, and Stanley J. Pincetl Jr. Foreword to *War Books: A Study in Historical Criticism*, by Jean Norton Cru. San Diego: San Diego State University Press, 1976.

Marcus, Jane. *Virginia Woolf and the Languages of Patriarchy*. Bloomington: Indiana University Press, 1987.

Marinetti, Filippo. *Marinetti: Selected Writings*. Translated by R. W. Flint and Arthur A. Coppotelli. New York: FSG, 1972.

Marsh, Margaret S. *Anarchist Women, 1870–1920*. Philadelphia: Temple University Press, 1981.

Martin, Meredith. *The Rise and Fall of Meter: Poetry and English National Culture, 1860–1930*. Princeton: Princeton University Press, 2012.

———. "Therapeutic Measures: *The Hydra* and Wilfred Owen at Craiglockhart War Hospital." *Modernism/Modernity* 14, no. 1 (2007): 35–54.

Martin, Richard. *The Language of Heroes: Speech and Performance in the Iliad*. Ithaca: Cornell University Press, 1989.

Materer, Timothy. *Modernist Alchemy: Poetry and the Occult*. Ithaca: Cornell University Press, 1995.

Matro, Thomas G. "Only Relations: Vision and Achievement in *To the Lighthouse*." *PMLA* 99, no. 2 (March 1984): 212–24.

McLaughlin, Joseph. *Writing the Urban Jungle: Reading Empire in London from Doyle to Eliot*. Charlottesville: University Press of Virginia, 2000.

Meisel, Perry. *The Myth of the Modern: A Study in British Literature and Criticism after 1850.* New Haven: Yale University Press, 1987.

Melchiori, Barbara Arnett. *Terrorism in the Late Victorian Novel.* London: Croom Helm, 1985.

Mendelson, Edward. *Early Auden.* New York: FSG, 1981.

Mengham, Rod. "From Georges Sorel to *Blast.*" In *The Violent Muse: Violence and the Artistic Imagination in Europe, 1910–1939.* Edited by Jana Howlett and Rod Mengham. Manchester: Manchester University Press, 1994: 33–44.

Meredith, Isabel. *A Girl among the Anarchists.* Lincoln: University of Nebraska Press, 1992.

Mezey, Jason Howard. "Ireland, Europe, The World, The Universe: Political Geography in *A Portrait of the Artist as a Young Man.*" *Journal of Modern Literature* 22, no. 2 (1999): 337–48.

Michel, Andreas. "Differentiation vs. Disenchantment: The Persistence of Modernity from Max Weber to Jean-Francois Lyotard." *German Studies Review* 20, no. 3 (October 1997): 343–70.

Miller, D. A. *The Novel and the Police.* Berkeley: University of California Press, 1988.

Miller, David. *Anarchism.* London: J. M. Dent, 1984.

Miller, James E. *T. S. Eliot's Personal Waste Land: Exorcism of the Demons.* University Park: Pennsylvania State University Press, 1977.

Milne, A. A. *Peace with Honour.* New York: Dutton, 1934.

Mitchel, John. Introduction to *Poems of James Clarence Mangan.* Dublin: O'Donoghue, 1903.

———. *Jail Journal: 1876.* Washington, DC: Woodstock, 1996.

Moffat, Wendy. "Domestic Violence: The Simple Tale within *The Secret Agent.*" *English Literature in Transition* 37, no. 4 (1994): 465–89.

Montague, C. E. *Disenchantment.* New York: Brentano's, 1922.

Moore-Gilbert, Bart. "Frantz Fanon: En-Gendering Nationalist Discourse." *Women: A Cultural Review* 7, no. 2 (Autumn 1996): 125–35.

Morrison, Paul. *The Poetics of Fascism: Ezra Pound, T. S. Eliot, Paul de Man.* New York: Oxford University Press, 1996.

Mosse, George. *Fallen Soldiers: Reshaping the Memory of the World Wars.* New York: Oxford University Press, 1990.

———. *Nationalism and Sexuality: Respectability and Abnormal Sexuality in Modern Europe.* New York: Howard Fertig, 1985.

Muller, Jim. "John Henry Newman and the Education of Stephen Dedalus." *James Joyce Quarterly* 33, no. 4 (Summer 1996): 593–603.

Mulry, David. "Popular Accounts of the Greenwich Bombing and Conrad's *The Secret Agent.*" *Rocky Mountain Review* (Fall 2000): 43–64.

Mussolini, Benito. *Fascism: Doctrine and Institutions.* New York: Howard Fertig, 1968.

———. *The Political and Social Doctrine of Fascism.* Translated by Jane Soames. London: Hogarth, 1933.

Nagy, Gregory. *The Best of the Achaeans: Concepts of the Hero in Archaic Greek Poetry.* Baltimore: Johns Hopkins University Press, 1979.

Najder, Zdzislaw. "Joseph Conrad's *The Secret Agent*, or the Melodrama of Reality." *New York Literary Forum* 7 (1980): 159–66.

Naremore, James. *The World without a Self: Virginia Woolf and the Novel*. New Haven: Yale University Press, 1973.

Newsome, David. *Godliness and Good Learning: Four Studies on a Victorian Ideal*. London: Murray, 1961.

Nicholas, Beverly. *Cry Havoc!* Garden City: Doubleday, 1933.

Nietzsche, Friedrich. *On the Genealogy of Morals and Ecce Homo*. Translated by Walter Kaufmann. New York: Vintage, 1967.

Nixon, Rob. *Slow Violence and the Environmentalism of the Poor*. Cambridge, MA: Harvard University Press, 2011.

Nolan, Emer. *James Joyce and Nationalism*. New York: Routledge, 1995.

Norris, Margot. *Writing War in the Twentieth Century*. Charlottesville: University of Virginia Press, 2000.

North, Michael. *The Political Aesthetic of Yeats, Eliot, and Pound*. Cambridge: Cambridge University Press, 1991.

——. *Reading 1922: A Return to the Scene of the Modern*. New York: Oxford University Press, 1999.

O'Brien, Conor Cruise. *Passion and Cunning: Essays on Nationalism, Terrorism, and Revolution*. New York: Simon and Schuster, 1988.

O'Brien, Paul. *Shelley and Revolutionary Ireland*. London: Redwords, 2002.

O'Brien, Tim. *The Things They Carried*. New York: Broadway Books, 1990.

O'Casey, Sean. *Collected Plays, Volume One*. London: MacMillan, 1967.

——. *Collected Plays, Volume Two*. London: MacMillan, 1950.

O Cathasaigh, P. [Sean O'Casey]. *The Story of the Irish Citizen Army*. Dublin: Maunsel, 1919.

Ó Donghaile, Deaglán. *Blasted Literature: Victorian Political Fiction and the Shock of Modernism*. Edinburgh: Edinburgh University Press, 2011.

O'Grady, Standish. *History of Ireland, Volume I: The Heroic Period*. New York: Lemma, 1970.

Oliver, H. *The International Anarchist Movement in Late Victorian London*. London: Croom, 1983.

Orwell, George. *1984*. New York: Penguin, 1977.

——. *Burmese Days*. San Diego: Harvest, 1962.

Ovid. *Metamorphoses*. Translated by David Raeburn. New York: Penguin, 2004.

Owen, Alex. *The Place of Enchantment: British Occultism and the Culture of the Modern*. Chicago: University of Chicago Press, 2004.

Owen, Wilfred. *The Poems of Wilfred Owen*. London: Chatto, 1990.

Pantelia, Marcia C. "Helen and the Last Song for Hector." *Transactions of the American Philological Association* 132, nos. 1–2 (2002): 21–27.

Parker, Peter. *The Old Lie: the Great War and the Public-School Ethos*. London: Constable, 1987.

Patterson, Ian. *Guernica and Total War*. Cambridge, MA: Harvard University Press, 2007.

Pawlowski, Merry M. "Virginia Woolf's Veil: The Feminist Intellectual and the Organization of Public Space." *Modern Fiction Studies* 53, no. 4 (2007): 722–51.

——. ed. *Virginia Woolf and Fascism: Resisting the Dictator's Seduction*. New York: Palgrave, 2001.

Pearce, Donald R. "The Systematic Rose." *Yeats Annual* 4 (1986): 195–200.

Pearse, Padraic H. *Collected Works: Political Writings and Speeches*. Dublin: Maunsel and Roberts, 1922.

———. *Collected Works of Padraic H. Pearse: Plays, Stories, Poems*. New York: Stokes, 1917.

———. *Collected Works of Padraic H. Pearse: Songs of the Irish Rebels and Specimens from an Irish Anthology*. Dublin: Maunsel, 1918.

Perloff, Marjorie. *The Futurist Moment: Avant-Garde, Avant Guerre, and the Language of Rupture*. Chicago: University of Chicago Press, 1986.

Peter, John. "A New Interpretation of *The Waste Land* (1952)." *Essays in Criticism* 19, no. 2 (April 1969): 140–75.

Pétrement, Simone. *Simone Weil: A Life*. Translated by Raymond Rosenthal. New York: Pantheon, 1976.

Philips, David. *Crime and Authority in Victorian England: The Black Country, 1835–1860*. London: Croom Helm, 1977.

Picciotto, Joanna. *Labors of Innocence in Early Modern England*. Cambridge, MA: Harvard University Press, 2010.

Pick, Daniel. *War Machine: The Rationalization of Slaughter in the Modern Age*. New Haven: Yale University Press, 1993.

Pisano, Dominick A., ed. *The Airplane in American Culture*. Ann Arbor: University of Michigan Press, 2003.

Plain, Gil. *Women's Fiction of The Second World War: Gender, Power and Resistance*. New York: St. Martin's, 1996.

Plunkett, Joseph Mary. *The Poems of Joseph Mary Plunkett*. London: Unwin, 1916.

Poole, Roger. "We All Put Up with You, Virginia": Irreceivable Wisdom about War." In *Virginia Woolf and War: Fiction, Reality, and Myth*. Edited by Mark Hussey. Syracuse, NY: Syracuse University Press, 1991, 79–100.

Porter, Bernard. *The Origins of the Vigilant State: The London Metropolitan Police Special Branch before the First World War*. London: Weidenfeld, 1987.

Pronay, Nicholas. "British Newsreels in the 1930s: 1. Audience and Producers." In *Yesterday's News: The British Cinema Newsreel Reader*. Edited by Luke McKernan. London: British Universities Film and Video Council, 2002.

Puchner, Martin. *Poetry of the Revolution: Marx, Manifestos, and the Avant-Gardes*. Princeton: Princeton University Press, 2006.

———. *Stage Fright: Modernism, Anti-Theatricality, and Drama*. Baltimore: Johns Hopkins University Press, 2002.

Quail, John. *The Slow Burning Fuse: The Lost History of the British Anarchists*. London: Paladin, 1978.

Rae, Patricia. "Anthropology." In *A Companion to Modernist Literature and Culture*. Edited by David Bradshaw and Kevin J. H. Dettmar. Malden, MA: Blackwell, 2006.

Rawlinson, Mark. *British Writing of the Second World War*. Oxford: Oxford University Press, 2000.

Redding, Arthur F. *Raids on Human Consciousness: Writing, Anarchism, and Violence*. Columbia, SC: University of South Carolina Press, 1998.

Remarque, Erich Maria. *All Quiet on the Western Front*. Translated by A. H. Wheen. New York: Fawcett, 1996.

Reynolds, Paige. *Modernism, Drama, and the Audience for Irish Spectacle*. Cambridge: Cambridge University Press, 2007.

Rhys, Jean. *Wide Sargasso Sea*. New York: Norton, 1982.

Robbins, Bruce. "Commodity Histories." *PMLA* 120, No. 2 (March 2005): 454–63.

Roessel, David. "'Mr. Eugenides, the Smyrna Merchant,' and Post-War Politics in *The Waste Land*." *Journal of Modern Literature* 16, no. 1 (1989): 171–76.

Rosenberg, Isaac. *The Collected Poems of Isaac Rosenberg*. New York: Schocken, 1949.

Rosenman, Ellen. "A Fish on the Line: Desire, Repression, and the Law of the Father in *A Room of One's Own*." In *Virginia Woolf: Emergent Perspectives*. Edited by Mark Hussey and Vara Neverow. New York: Pace University Press, 1994, 272–77.

Roth, Jack J. *The Cult of Violence: Sorel and the Sorelians*. Berkeley: University of California Press, 1980.

Russell, Bertrand. *Power: A New Social Analysis*. New York: Norton, 1938.

Ryan, Mary. *Empire of the Mother: American Writing about Domesticity*. New York: Harrington Park Press, 1985.

Sacks, Peter. *The English Elegy: Studies in the Genre from Spenser to Yeats*. Baltimore: Johns Hopkins University Press, 1985.

Said, Edward. *On Late Style: Music and Literature Against the Grain*. New York: Pantheon, 2006.

———. "Yeats and Decolonization." In *Nationalism, Colonialism, and Literature*. Edited by Terry Eagleton, Fredric Jameson, and Edward Said. Minneapolis: University of Minnesota Press, 1990, 69–95.

Saint-Amour, Paul. "Air War Prophecy and Interwar Modernism." *Comparative Literature Studies* 42, no. 2 (2005): 130–61.

Salk, Candace Serena. *Love, Anarchy, and Emma Goldman*. New Brunswick: Rutgers University Press, 1990.

Sassoon, Siegfried. *The Complete Memoirs of George Sherston*. London: Faber, 1952.

———. *The War Poems*. London: Faber, 1983.

Scarry, Elaine. *The Body in Pain: The Making and Unmaking of the World*. Oxford: Oxford University Press, 1985.

Schneider, Karen. *Loving Arms: British Women Writing the Second World War*. Lexington: University Press of Kentucky, 1997.

Schrank, Bernice. "Sean O'Casey and the Dialectics of Violence." In *Shadows of the Gunmen: Violence and Culture in Modern Ireland*. eds. Danine Farquharson and Sean Farrell. Cork: Cork University Press, 2008, 38–62.

Schreiner, Olive. *The Story of an African Farm*. London: Penguin, 1995.

Sebald, W. G. *On the Natural History of Destruction*. Translated by Anthea Bell. New York: Modern Library, 2003.

Sedgwick, Eve Kosofsky. *Touching Feeling: Affect, Pedagogy, Performativity*. Durham: Duke University Press, 2003.

Shakespeare, William. *King Lear*. New York: Penguin, 1999.

———. *Richard III*. New York: Penguin, 2000.

Sharf, Frederic A., Anne Nishimura Morse, and Sebastian Dobson. *A Much Recorded War: The Russo-Japanese War in History and Imagery*. Boston: MFA Publications, 2005.

Shatz, Marshall S., ed. *The Essential Works of Anarchism*. New York: Quadrangle, 1972.

Shelley, Percy. *The Poetical Works of Shelley*. Boston: Houghton Mifflin, 1975.

Sherry, Norman. *Conrad's Western World*. Cambridge: Cambridge University Press, 1971.

Sherry, Vincent. *The Great War and the Language of Modernism*. New York: Oxford University Press, 2003.

Shpayer-Makov, Haia. "Anarchism in British Public Opinion 1880–1914." *Victorian Studies* (Summer 1988): 487–516.

Singer, Ben. *Melodrama and Modernity: Early Sensational Cinema and its Contexts.* New York: Columbia University Press, 2001.

Singer, Peter. *Animal Liberation.* New York: Avon, 1977.

Slotkin, Richard. *Regeneration through Violence: The Mythology of the American Frontier, 1600–1860.* Middletown, CT: Wesleyan University Press, 1973.

Smith, David R. "Conrad and Dostoevsky." *Conradian* 15, no. 2 (January 1991): 1–11.

Smith, Philip Thurmond. *Policing Victorian London: Political Policing, Public Order, and the London Metropolitan Police.* Westport, CT: Greenwood Press, 1985.

Snider, Denton J. *The Biographical Outline of Homer.* Saint Louis: William Harvey Miner, 1922.

Snyder, Cary J. *British Fiction and Cross-Cultural Encounters: Ethnographic Modernism from Wells to Woolf.* New York: Palgrave Macmillan, 2008.

Solow, Michael K. "A Clash of Certainties, Old and New: *For Whom the Bell Tolls* and the Inner War of Ernest Hemingway." *Hemingway Review* 29, no. 1 (2009): 103–22.

Sontag, Susan. *On Photography.* New York: Farrar Straus Giroux, 1977.

———. *Regarding the Pain of Others.* New York: Farrar Straus Giroux, 2003.

Sorel, Georges. *Reflections on Violence.* Translated by T. E. Hulme. New York: Huebsch, 1914.

Southam, B. C. *A Guide to The Selected Poems of T.S. Eliot.* San Diego: Harcourt, 1984.

Southworth, Herbert Rutledge. *Guernica! Guernica!: A Study of Journalism, Diplomacy, Propaganda, and History.* Berkeley: University of California Press, 1977.

Spender, Stephen. Introduction to *Voices Against Tyranny: Writing of the Spanish Civil War.* Edited by John Miller. New York: Scribner, 1986.

Spillers, Hortense J. *Black, White, and in Color.* Chicago: University of Chicago Press, 2003.

Spitzer, Leo. *Hotel Bolivia: The Culture of Memory in a Refuge from Nazism.* New York: Hill and Wang, 1998.

Steer, G. L. *The Tree of Gernika: A Field Study of Modern War.* London: Hodder and Stoughton, 1938.

Stepniak, S. *The Career of a Nihilist.* New York: Harper, 1889.

———. "The Dynamite Scare and Anarchy." *The New Review* 6 (May 1892): 529–41.

———. *Underground Russia: Revolutionary Profiles and Sketches from Life.* Westport: Hyperion Press, 1973.

Stradling, Robert. *Your Children Will Be Next: Bombing and Propaganda in the Spanish Civil War, 1936–1939.* Cardiff: University of Wales Press, 2008.

Sturken, Marita. *Tangled Memories: The Vietnam War, the AIDS Epidemic, and the Politics of Remembering.* Berkeley: University of California Press, 1997.

Surette, Leon, ed. *The Birth of Modernism: Ezra Pound, T. S. Eliot, W. B. Yeats, and the Occult.* Montreal: McGill-Queen's University Press, 1993.

———. *Literary Modernism and the Occult Tradition.* Orono, ME: National Poetry Foundation, 1996.

Swinburne, Algernon. *The Complete Works: Poetical Works, Vol. 1.* New York: Russell and Russell, 1968.

Sword, Helen. *Ghostwriting Modernism.* Ithaca, NY: Cornell University Press, 2002.

Synge, J. M. *The Aran Islands.* Evanston: Northwestern University Press, 1999.

——. *Collected Works, Volume III, Plays, Book I.* London: Oxford University Press, 1968.

——. *The Playboy of the Western World and Other Plays.* Oxford: Oxford University Press, 1998.

Sypher, Eileen. "Anarchism and Gender: James's *The Princess Casamassima* and Conrad's *The Secret Agent.*" *Conradiana* 9, no. 1 (Winter 1988): 1–16.

Takayoshi, Ichiro. "The Wages of War: Liberal Gullibility, Soviet Intervention, and the End of the Popular Front." *Representations* 115, No. 1 (Summer 2011): 102–29

Tal, Kali. *Worlds of Hurt: Reading the Literatures of Trauma.* Cambridge: Cambridge University Press, 1996.

Tate, Trudi. *Modernism, History, and the First World War.* Manchester, NY: Manchester University Press, 1998.

Taylor, Charles. *A Secular Age.* Cambridge, MA: Harvard University Press, 2007.

Taylor, Martin. Introduction to *Lads: Love Poetry of the Trenches.* London: Constable, 1989.

Teskey, Gordon. *Allegory and Violence.* Ithaca: Cornell University Press, 1996.

Thompson, E. P. "Christopher Caudwell." *Critical Inquiry* 21, no. 2 (Winter 1995): 305–53.

Tone, Theobald Wolfe. *The Autobiography of Theobald Wolfe Tone, 1763–1798, Volume 1.* Dublin: Maunsel, 1893.

Torgovnick, Marianna. *Gone Primitive: Savage Intellects, Modern Lives.* Chicago: University of Chicago Press, 1990.

Tratner, Michael. *Modernism and Mass Politics: Joyce, Woolf, Eliot, Yeats.* Stanford, CA: Stanford University Press, 1995.

Tromanhauser, Vicki. "Animal Life and Human Sacrifice in Virginia Woolf's *Between the Acts.*" *Woolf Studies Annual,* 15 (2009): 67–90.

Turner, Brian. *Here, Bullet.* Farmington, ME: Alice James Books, 2005.

Turner, Frank M. *Contesting Cultural Authority: Essays on Victorian Intellectual Life.* Cambridge: Cambridge University Press, 1993.

——. *The Greek Heritage in Victorian Britain.* New Haven: Yale University Press, 1981.

Van Riper, A. Bowdoin. *Imagining Flight: Aviation and Popular Culture.* College Station: Texas A&M University Press, 2004.

Vickery, John B. *The Literary Impact of the Golden Bough.* Princeton: Princeton University Press, 1973.

Virilio, Paul. *War and Cinema: The Logistics of Perception.* Translated by Patrick Camiller. London: Verso, 1992.

Vonnegut, Kurt. *Slaughterhouse-Five.* New York: Dial Press, 2005.

Walkowitz, Judith. *City of Dreadful Delight: Narratives of Sexual Danger in Late-Victorian London.* Chicago: University of Chicago Press, 1992.

Warner, Michael, Jonathan VanAntwerpen, and Craig Calhoun, eds. *Varieties of Secularism in a Secular Age.* Cambridge, MA: Harvard University Press, 2010.

Watt, Ian. *Essays on Conrad.* Cambridge: Cambridge University Press, 2000: 112–26.

Weber, Max. *From Max Weber: Essays in Sociology.* Translated by H. H. Gerth and C. Wright Mills. New York: Oxford University Press, 1958.

Weil, Simone. *The Iliad or the Poem of Force.* Translated by James P. Holoka. New York: Peter Lang, 2003.

——. *Selected Essays: 1934–1943.* Translated by Richard Rees. London: Oxford University Press, 1962.

Wenzel, Jennifer. "Past's Futures." Lecture at Columbia University. April 11, 2011.

Westman, Karin E. "'For Her Generation the Newspaper Was a Book': Media, Mediation, and Oscillation in Virginia Woolf's *Between the Acts*." *Journal of Modern Literature* 29, no. 2 (2006): 1–18.

White, Anna MacBride, and A. Norman Jeffares, eds. *The Gonne-Yeats Letters, 1893–1938*. London: Hutchinson, 1992.

Whitman, Jon, ed. *Interpretation and Allegory: Antiquity to the Modern Period*. Leiden: Brill, 2000.

Wicke, Jennifer. "Coterie Consumption: Bloomsbury, Keynes, and Modernism as Marketing." In *Marketing Modernisms: Self-Promotion, Canonization, Rereading*. Edited by Kevin J. H. Dettmar and Stephen Watts. Ann Arbor: University of Michigan Press, 1996.

———. *Advertising Fictions: Literature, Advertisement, and Social Reading*. New York: Columbia University Press, 1988.

Wilde, Oscar. *The Complete Plays of Oscar Wilde*. London: Methuen, 1988.

———. *The Letters of Oscar Wilde*. Edited by Rupert Hart-Davis. New York: Harcourt 1962.

Winkiel, Laura. *Modernism, Race, and Manifestos*. Cambridge: Cambridge University Press, 2008.

Winter, Jay. *Remembering War: The Great War between Memory and History in the Twentieth Century*. New Haven: Yale University Press, 2006.

———. *Sites of Memory, Sites of Mourning: The Great War in European Cultural History*. Cambridge: Cambridge University Press, 1995.

Wirth-Nesher, Hana. "Final Curtain on the War: Figure and Ground in Virginia Woolf's *Between the Acts*." *Style* 28, no. 2 (Winter 1994): 183–200.

Wittier-Ferguson, John. "Repetition, Remembering, Repetition: Virginia Woolf's Late Fiction and the Return of War." *Modern Fiction Studies* 57, no. 2 (Summer 2011): 230–53.

Wolfe, Cary. *Animal Rites: American Culture, the Discourse of Species, and Posthumanist Theory*. Chicago: University of Chicago Press, 2003.

———. "Human, All Too Human: 'Animal Studies' and the Humanities." *PMLA* 124, no. 2 (March 2009): 564–75.

Wollaeger, Mark A. *Modernism, Media, and Propaganda: British Narrative from 1900–1945*. Princeton: Princeton University Press, 2006.

Wood, Michael. *Yeats and Violence*. Oxford: Oxford University Press, 2010.

Woodcock, George. "Anarchism: A Historical Introduction." In *The Anarchist Reader*. Edited by George Woodcock. Hassocks: Harvester, 1977, 11–56.

Woolf, Leonard. *Barbarians Within and Without*. New York: Harcourt, 1939.

———. *Quack Quack!* London: Hogarth, 1935.

———. *The War for Peace*. London: Routledge, 1940.

Woolf, Virginia. "Anon." *Twentieth Century Literature* 25, nos. 3–4 (1979): 356–59.

———. *Between the Acts*. San Diego: Harcourt, 1969.

———. *The Captain's Death Bed and Other Essays*. London: Hogarth, 1950.

———. *The Common Reader*. San Diego: Harcourt, 1984.

———. *The Death of the Moth and Other Essays*. San Diego: Harcourt, 1970.

———. *The Diary of Virginia Woolf, Volume Five, 1936–1941*. San Diego: Harcourt, 1977.

———. *The Diary of Virginia Woolf, Volume Four, 1931–1935*. New York: Harcourt, 1982.

———. *The Diary of Virginia Woolf, Volume Two, 1920–1924*. New York: Harcourt, 1978.

———. *Jacob's Room*. London: Penguin, 1992.

———. *The London Scene*. New York: Harper Collins, 1975.

———. *Melymbrosia*. Edited by Louise De Salvo. San Francisco: Cleis Press, 2002.

———. *The Moment and Other Essays*. San Diego: Harcourt, 1976.

———. *Moments of Being*. San Diego: Harcourt, 1985.

———. *Mrs. Dalloway*. San Diego: Harcourt, 1997.

———. *Orlando: A Biography*. San Diego: Harcourt, 1956.

———. *Three Guineas*. San Diego: Harcourt, 1966.

———. *To the Lighthouse*. San Diego: Harcourt, 1981.

———. *The Voyage Out*. London: Penguin, 1992.

———. *The Waves*. San Diego: Harcourt, 1959.

———. *The Years*. San Diego: Harcourt, 1965.

Wordsworth, William. *Poems*. New York: Scribner, 1923.

Worth, Katharine. Introduction to *Where There Is Nothing and The Unicorn from the Stars*, by W. B. Yeats. Washington, DC: Catholic University of America Press, 1987.

Yeats, W. B. *The Autobiography of William Butler Yeats*. New York: MacMillan 1953.

———. *The Collected Plays of W. B. Yeats*. New York: Macmillan, 1952.

———. *Essays and Introductions*. York: Macmillan, 1961.

———. Introduction to *The Oxford Book of Modern Verse, 1892–1935*. Oxford: Oxford University Press, 1978.

———. *The Letters of W. B. Yeats*. London: Rupert Hart-Davis, 1954.

———. *Michael Robartes and the Dancer: Manuscript Materials*. Edited by Thomas Parkinson. Ithaca: Cornell University Press, 1994.

———. *On the Boiler*. Dublin: Cuala, 1971.

———. *The Variorum Edition of the Poems of W. B. Yeats*. New York: MacMillan, 1957.

Young, James. *The Texture of Memory: Holocaust Memorials and Meaning*. New Haven: Yale University Press, 1993.

Zimring, Rishona. "Conrad's Pornography Shop." *Modern Fiction Studies* 43, no. 2 (1997): 319–48.

Žižek, Slavoj. *Violence: Six Sideways Reflections*. London: Profile, 2008.

Zola, Émile. *Germinal*. Translated by Havelock Ellis. New York: Vintage, 1994.

Zumkhawala-Cook, Richard. "Tae the Lighthoose." In *Virginia Woolf: Art, Education, and Internationalism*. Edited by Diana Royer and Madelyn Detloff. Clemson, SC: Clemson University Digital, 2008.

Zwerdling, Alex. *Virginia Woolf and the Real World*. Berkeley: University of California Press, 1986.

Index